500 GREATEST-EVER PASTA RECIPES

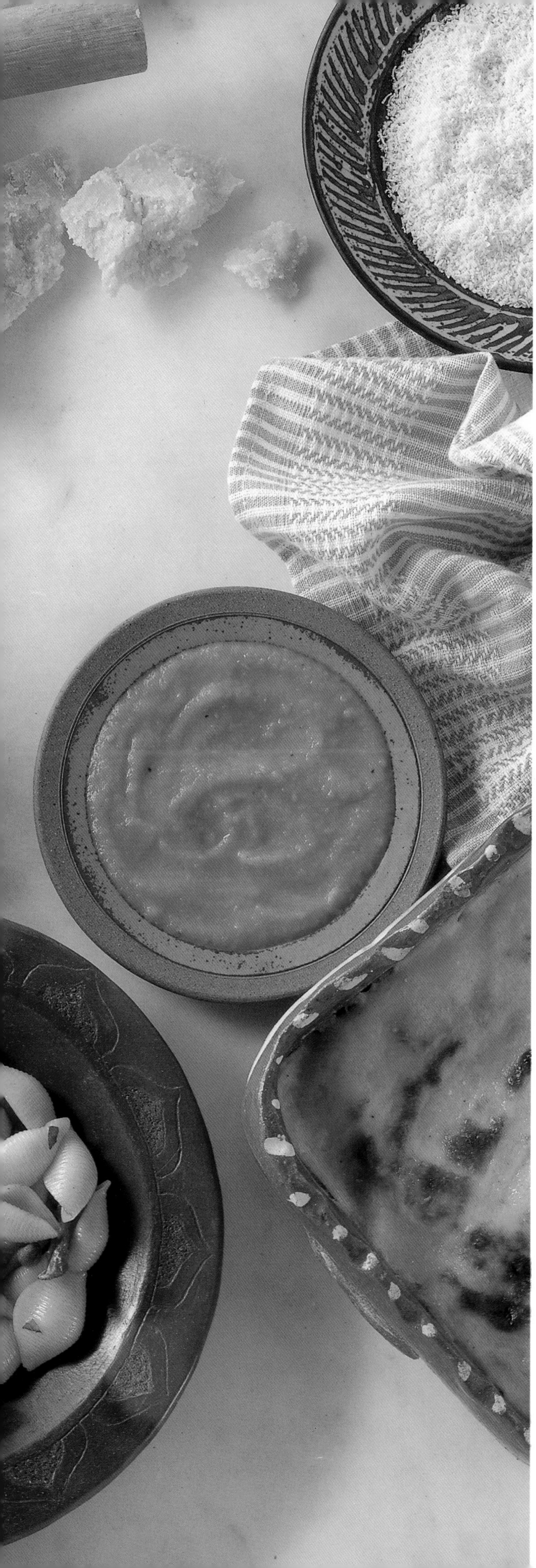

500 GREATEST-EVER PASTA RECIPES

A COOK'S GUIDE TO THE DELICIOUS WORLD OF PASTA AND NOODLES

EDITOR valerie ferguson

This edition is published by Hermes House, an imprint of Anness Publishing Ltd
Hermes House, 88–89 Blackfriars Road, London SE1 8HA
tel. 020 7401 2077; fax 020 7633 9499
www.hermeshouse.com; www.annesspublishing.com

If you like the images in this book and would like to investigate using them for publishing, promotions or advertising, please visit our website www.practicalpictures.com for more information.

Publisher: Joanna Lorenz
Editor: Valerie Ferguson
Designer: Carole Perks
Typesetter: Diane Pullen
Editorial Reader: Richard McGinlay
Production Controller: Stephen Lang
Recipes contributed by:
Catherine Atkinson, Alex Barker, Michelle Berriedale-Johnson, Angela Boggiano, Janet Brinkworth, Carla Capalbo, Kit Chan, Jacqueline Clark, Maxine Clarke, Frances Cleary, Trish Davies, Roz Denny, Patrizia Diemling, Matthew Drennan, Sarah Edmonds, Rafi Fernandez, Christine France, Sarah Gates, Shirley Gill, Nicola Graimes, Rosamund Grant, Rebekah Hassan, Deh-Ta Hsuing, Shehzad Husain, Christine Ingram, Judy Jackson, Masaki Ko, Lesley Mackley, Norma MacMillan, Sue Maggs, Kathy Man, Elizabeth Martin, Sallie Morris, Annie Nichols, Maggie Pannell, Katherine Richmond, Anne Sheasby, Jenny Stacey, Liz Trigg, Hilaire Walden, Laura Washburn, Steven Wheeler, Judy Williams, Jeni Wright

Photography:
William Adams-Lingwood, Karl Adamson, Edward Allwright, David Armstrong, Steve Baxter, Micki Dowie, James Duncan, John Freeman, Ian Garlick, Michelle Garrett, John Heseltine, Amanda Heywood, Janine Hosegood, David Jordan, Don Last, Patrick McLeavey, Thomas Odulate, Juliet Piddington, Peter Reilly

ETHICAL TRADING POLICY
Because of our ongoing ecological investment programme, you, as our customer, can have the pleasure and reassurance of knowing that a tree is being cultivated on your behalf to naturally replace the materials used to make the book you are holding. For further information about this scheme, go to www.annesspublishing.com/trees

A CIP catalogue record for this book is available from the British Library.

Previously published as *Pasta*

Notes

For all recipes, quantities are given in both metric and imperial measures and, where appropriate, measures are also given in standard cups and spoons. Follow one set, but not a mixture, because they are not interchangeable.

Standard spoon and cup measures are level.
1 tsp = 5ml, 1 tbsp = 15ml, 1 cup = 250ml/8fl oz

Australian standard tablespoons are 20ml. Australian readers should use 3 tsp in place of 1 tbsp for measuring small quantities of gelatine, cornflour, salt, etc.

Medium eggs are used unless otherwise stated.

Contents

Introduction

Many people are passionate about pasta, and it isn't difficult to see why. This fundamentally simple food – as basic as bread – comes in an enormous range of shapes, sizes and flavours, can be cooked in next to no time and is a wonderful vehicle for sauces and dressings.

Pasta is inexpensive, convenient and very easy to cook. It is a good source of protein, vitamins and minerals, is very low in fat and provides plenty of sustained energy so, as long as you are sensible about sauces, it has an important role to play in a healthy, balanced diet.

History is hazy when it comes to determining precisely where and when pasta was invented. There's a popular belief that Marco Polo introduced noodles to Italy when he returned from China towards the end of the 13th century. This doesn't really compute however, for an Italian cookery book that predates the explorer's return from the Orient has recipes for vermicelli and filled pasta. To muddy the waters still further, both Arabs and Indians had their own forms of pasta at this time. Perhaps pasta evolved simultaneously wherever a suitable grain could be found. Durum wheat was favoured, but Asian cooks also used rice, buckwheat and even starches derived from vegetables, such as mung beans. The grain was ground, mixed with water to make a dough, then rolled and cut into strips before being cooked in boiling water.

Cooks are nothing if not inventive. Soon doughs were being enriched with egg, and other flavourings followed. New shapes were devised, especially in Italy, and by the 19th century, factories were mass-producing dried pasta.

There is a lot of argument as to which is better – fresh pasta or dried. The simple answer is that both are excellent, but different, and only

you can decide which form you prefer. Dried pasta is a convenient store-cupboard staple; fresh pasta cooks even more quickly, and some swear it tastes better, although this is debatable.

Whichever sort of pasta you opt for – and you may choose to make your own, by hand or machine – what really matters is how you cook it. It is important to use plenty of lightly salted boiling water (4 litres/7 pints/4 quarts for every 450g/1lb/4 cups of pasta). A little oil is sometimes added to the water to stop the pasta from sticking together and the water from boiling over, but this is not essential. Tip the pasta into the water and let it return to a rolling boil. For advice on how long to cook the pasta, look at the instructions on the packet, but don't take that as gospel. The way to test pasta is to taste it. Bite a small piece; it should be *al dente*. This Italian term translates as "to the tooth" and means that the pasta should be just firm to the bite; neither too hard nor too soft. Fresh pasta cooks very quickly and is ready when it rises to the surface of the water. Some oriental noodles don't need to be cooked at all, especially if they have been soaked first, and are simply heated in freshly boiled water. Where necessary, detailed information on cooking times is given in recipes.

The more frequently you cook pasta, the easier you will find it to judge the precise moment when it is ready to serve, and with this sensational collection of recipes, you'll have more than 500 excuses to experiment. Soups, starters, salads and main courses are all included, with sauces based on fish, seafood, meat, poultry, all kinds of cheeses, fresh and canned vegetables, pulses or simply the very best olive oil and garlic. There's even a chapter devoted to delicious low-fat pasta recipes. Enjoy!

Types of Pasta

The first forms of pasta were thin strings or ribbons, but it wasn't long before people started experimenting with shapes. Soon there were hundreds of these, often starting out as regional specialities, but spreading to the wider world. Today the range is enormous, and continues to grow. Shapes range from the beautiful to the bizarre. This book introduces a wide selection, but there's no need to limit yourself to our suggestions. Feel free to make substitutions, but bear in mind that long strands work best with thinner sauces, while short shapes are good with chunky, meaty sauces. Choose tubes or shells if you want to trap the sauce inside. Remember, too, that pasta names often vary from region to region.

Long Pasta

Bucatini looks like chunky spaghetti, but is hollow. **Bucatoni** is a fatter version, while **perciatelli** is bucatini by another name.

Capelli or **capelli d'angelo** translates as angel hair pasta, which is a fanciful name for this superfine pasta. It is often packed in nests – **capelli d'angelo a nidi**. **Capellini** are similar strands.

Chitarra is a square-shaped form of spaghetti, so named because it is made on a frame that resembles a guitar.

Fusilli lunghi, also known as fusilli col buco, are long twisted strands or spirals.

Linguine are slim ribbons. The name means "little tongues". This popular form of pasta is very good for serving with creamy coating sauces.

Macaroni (maccheroni) was one of the first shapes to be made, and remains very popular. Two short forms, the curved elbow macaroni and short-cut macaroni, are particularly widely used. A thin form of the long strands is **maccheroncini**.

Pappardelle are broad ribbon noodles, with either plain or wavy edges. **Trenette** are similar.

Spaghetti needs no introduction, but do try the less familiar forms, such as the skinny **spaghettini** or the flavoured **spaghetti con spinaci** (with spinach) or **spaghetti integrali** (wholewheat).

Strangozzi is a thin noodle that is often sold as a loose plait. The basil flavour is delicious.

Tagliatelle is the most common form of ribbon noodle. It is sold in nests, which unravel on cooking. Several flavours – and therefore colours – are available, a popular mix being **paglia e fieno** (straw and hay) which consists of separate nests of egg noodles and spinach-flavoured noodles. The Roman version of tagliatelle is called **fettuccine**. **Tagliolini, tagliarini** and **fidelini** are thin ribbon noodles.

Vermicelli is very fine spaghetti.

Ziti is very long, thick and tubular, like macaroni, and is often broken into shorter lengths before being cooked.

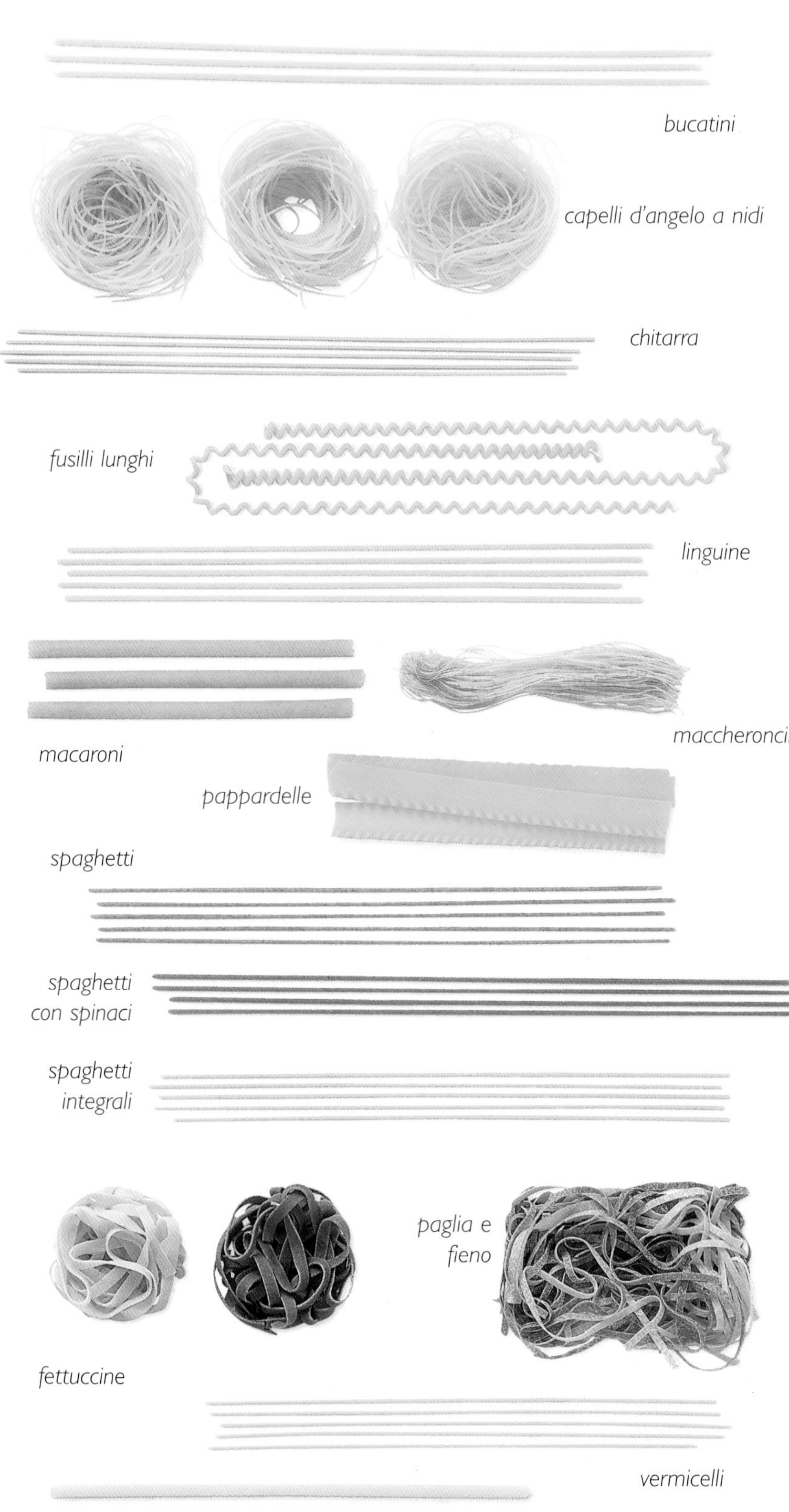

Short Pasta (Shapes)

Conchiglie are shells. Perfect for trapping sauces, they come in various sizes, from tiny **conchigliette** for soups to **conchiglione**, the jumbo shells which can be stuffed.

Eliche are among several spiral-shaped pastas, and resemble **fusilli** and **spirali** (which tend to be more open). They come in various thicknesses and flavours.

Farfalle are known in English as butterflies or bow-ties, which they resemble. They look very pretty on the plate, and are so popular that manufacturers produce several different varieties, including the ever-popular **farfalle tricolore**, which mixes plain or ridged red, green and yellow shapes.

Fiorelli These very pretty designer shapes look rather like oyster mushrooms, with frilly edges. They are not unlike the bell-shaped **campanelle**.

Fusilli are spirals, formed by winding fresh dough around a thin rod. They tend to relax and unwind a little when placed in boiling water.

Garganelli are a regional form of penne. Short and tubular, they look a little like scrolls, thanks to the special tool on which they are rolled. Called *il pettine*, this resembles a large comb.

Orecchiette are endearing small shapes, so named because they look like little ears. They are slightly chewy and are served with robust sauces.

Penne or quills are short lengths of tubular pasta which are cut on the slant so their ends are pointed. Sturdy and capable of holding sauces inside their hollow centres, they are deservedly popular. Both plain – **penne lisce** – and ridged versions – **penne rigate** – are available. **Rigatoni** are straight ridged tubes, somewhat fatter than penne.

Pipe are small pasta shapes. They don't look much like pipes, which is the translation of their Italian name, but rather resemble small shells. **Pipe rigate** is the ridged version. They are available plain and wholewheat.

Ruote or **Rotelle** are small wagon wheel shapes. They come in various flavours and colours, and are popular with children.

Strozzapretti sounds like such a pretty name. The word, however, means "priest stranglers", which is somewhat less attractive! Legend has it that the priest who originally tried them ate far too many and almost choked to death. Each shape consists of two slim strands of pasta that are twisted or "strangled" together.

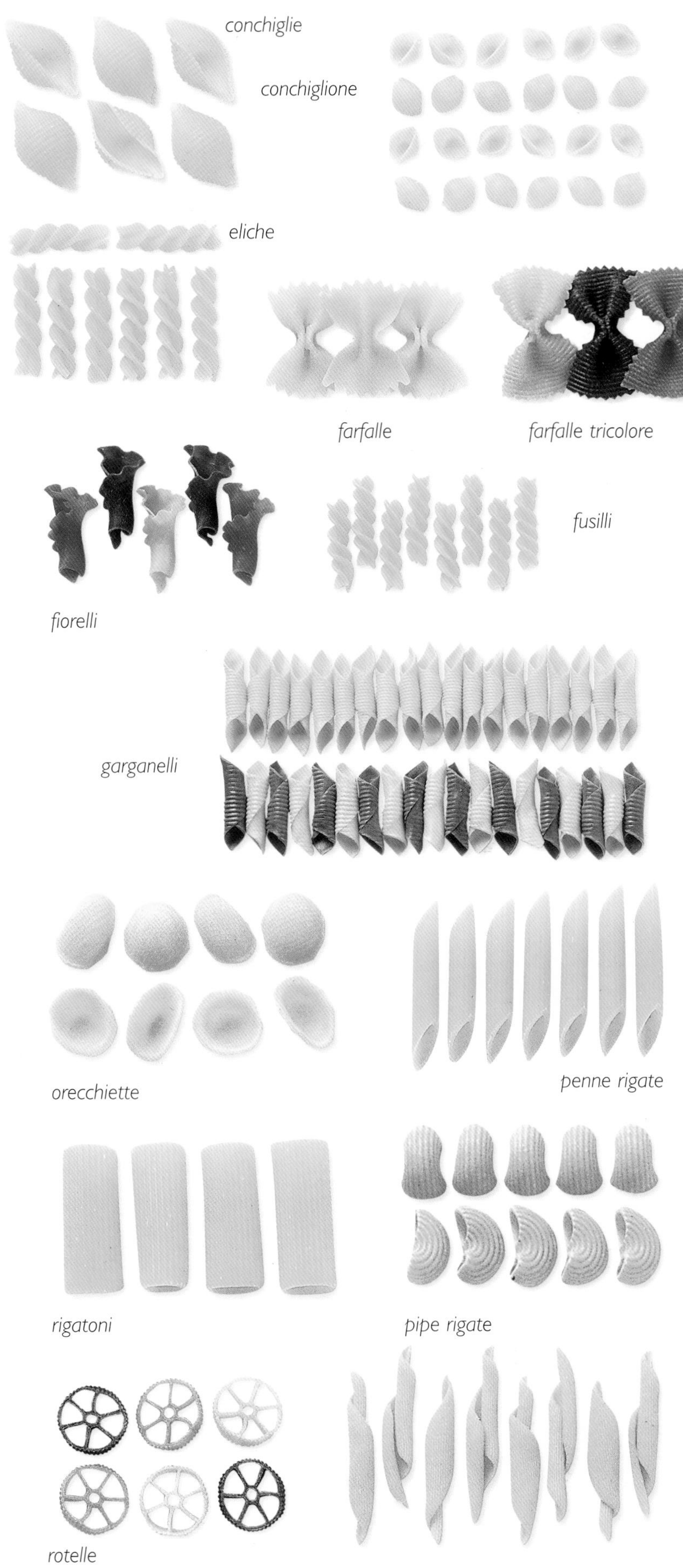

cannelloni

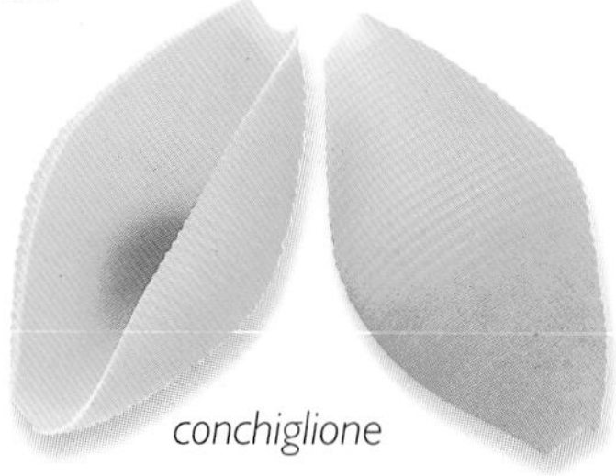

conchiglione

lasagne

lasagne verdi

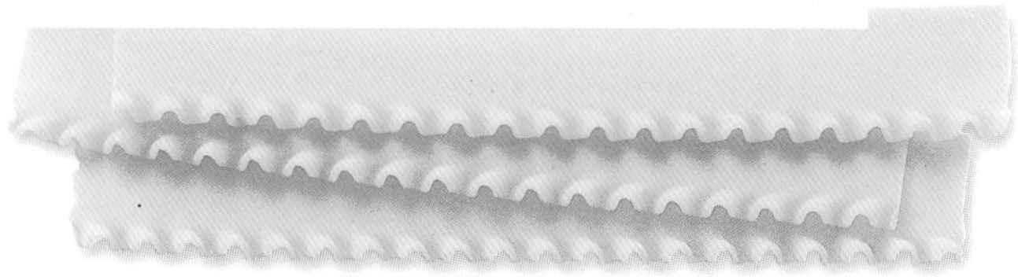

lasagnette

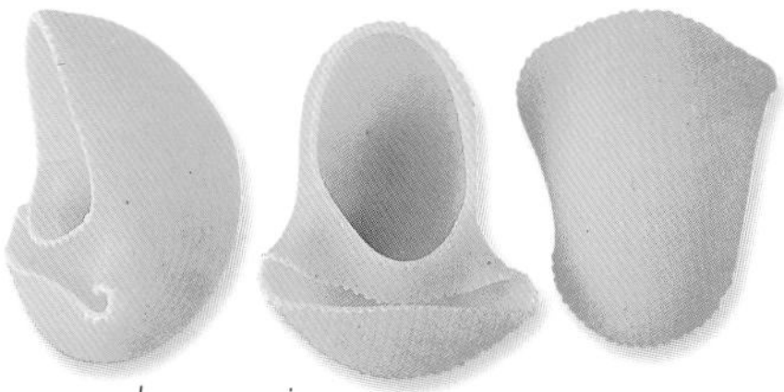

lumaconi

tortellini

ravioli

stellette

Pasta for Stuffing and Layering

Cannelloni About 10cm/4in in length, these large tubes are stuffed, coated in sauce and baked in the oven. In Italy, cannelloni are traditionally made by rolling fresh lasagne sheets around the filling, but the dried tubes are more convenient. Either pipe the filling in with a forcing bag, or use a teaspoon.

Conchiglione Jumbo pasta shells, these are wonderful for stuffing and look very pretty. They come in plain, spinach and tomato flavours, both smooth and ridged.

Lasagne This popular form of pasta comes in flat or wavy sheets, pre-cut for layering, and can be fresh or dried. There is also a no-precook version, which is very convenient, as it needs only to be layered with the sauce or sauces, and cooks as the dish bakes in the oven. There are some drawbacks with no-precook pasta – purists say it doesn't compare with other types in terms of taste, but as long as you buy a quality pasta, use more sauce than usual and cook the lasagne for at least 45 minutes, it gives a very good result. Sizes vary, so when you find one that fits your lasagne dish perfectly, it is well worth making a note of the manufacturer. You can snap sheets to fit, but they seldom break where you want them to. If you choose fresh or regular dried pasta, you will need to cook it before layering. Follow the instructions on the packet.

Flavoured lasagne Lasagne comes in several flavours, including green (spinach); brown (wholewheat) and two tones of yellow, one being the plain lasagne and the other being the version with added egg.

Lasagnette are long, narrow strips of flat pasta, which are crimped on one or two sides. They are used in the same way as lasagne sheets.

Lumaconi These look a bit like large snail shells, with an opening at either end. They are fiddly to stuff, but make an interesting change from more common shapes.

Filled Pasta

Fresh and dried filled pasta shapes are available. The range includes **ravioli** and **tortellini**, both of which can be served quite simply, with melted butter or a light sauce, and the lesser-known **agnolotti**, which look rather like round ravioli.

Pastina

These are miniature shapes, usually served in broth or soup. There are dozens of varieties, including **tubetti**, **stellette**, **risoni**, **peperini**, **ditalini** and **fregola**, which resembles couscous.

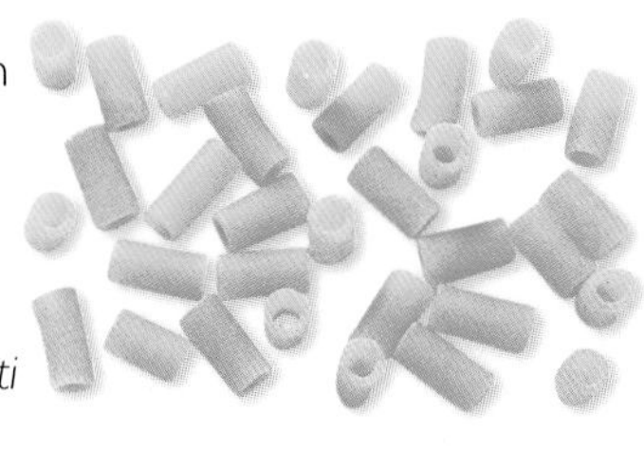

tubetti

Types of Noodle

Asian noodles are usually made from wheat, as is Italian pasta, but may also be made from rice, buckwheat, arrowroot or mung beans. The noodles are formed by various methods, the most dramatic of which is when the cook hurls pieces of dough into the air, twirling and twisting until they stretch and lengthen to form long, thin strands. In principle, the process is similar to that adopted by chefs when shaping pizza dough, but is even more impressive. There are many different types of noodle, some of which must be soaked in warm water before being cooked briefly – or just heated – in boiling water. Check the instructions on the packet, as timings can vary widely, but in general, the thinner the noodle, the less cooking it will need. In addition to being boiled, or heated in soups, noodles are an integral part of many vegetable dishes, and are often stir-fried or deep-fried. They may need to be boiled or soaked, then well drained, before frying.

Cellophane Noodles are made from ground mung beans, and are also known as bean thread, transparent or glass noodles. Although very thin, the strands are firm and resilient, and stay that way when cooked, never becoming soggy. Cellophane noodles are not served solo, but are added to soups or braised dishes.

Egg Noodles These can be fresh or dried, and come in various thicknesses, including fine, medium and broad. They are often packed in what look like skeins or coils, and the general rule is to use one of these per person. The Japanese equivalent are called **ramen**.

Rice Noodles come in several different forms and are usually sold in bundles. The very thin white ones are called **rice vermicelli**. These cook almost instantly when added to hot broth, provided they have first been soaked in warm water.

Soba Noodles Japanese buckwheat noodles, these often include wheat flour and/or yam flour. They are much darker in colour than regular wheat noodles and are sold in bundles.

Somen Noodles also come from Japan, and are made from wheat starch. Thin and delicate, they are sold in bundles tied with a paper band.

Udon Noodles are plain wheat noodles from Japan. They are available fresh, precooked or dried.

cellophane noodles

egg noodles

rice noodles

soba noodles

somen noodles

udon noodles

Noodle Know-how

- *Store dried noodles in airtight boxes, and store fresh noodles in the fridge, having checked the use-by date on the packaging.*
- *As a general rule, allow 75–115g/3–4oz noodles per person.*
- *Many recipes call for noodles to be soaked in warm water before being cooked; check the recipe, as you need to allow the requisite time.*
- *It is easy to overcook noodles. Remove them from the heat when they are barely tender and drain them in a colander. If you are not using them immediately, rinse them under the cold tap so they stop cooking, then drain them again.*
- *If you are going to fry the prepared noodles, it is a good idea to blot them dry with kitchen paper.*

Techniques

Basic Pasta Dough

Making pasta dough at home isn't difficult, especially if you use a food processor and a pasta machine. If you have neither, make the pasta by hand. It may not end up quite as thin as you would like, but it will still taste delicious. For enough pasta to serve 3–4 people, you will need 200g/7oz/1¾ cups plain white flour, a pinch of salt, 2 eggs and 15ml/1 tbsp olive oil. You can also use strong white flour. If you are going to make flavoured pasta (see below), the quantities may need to be slightly changed.

To make the dough by hand

1 To make the dough by hand, sift the flour and salt into a heap on a clean work surface and make a well in the centre with your fist.

2 Lightly beat the eggs with the oil and pour into the well. Gradually mix the egg mixture into the flour with the fingers of one hand until incorporated. Alternatively, add the eggs and oil to the well and beat lightly with a fork, gradually drawing in the flour.

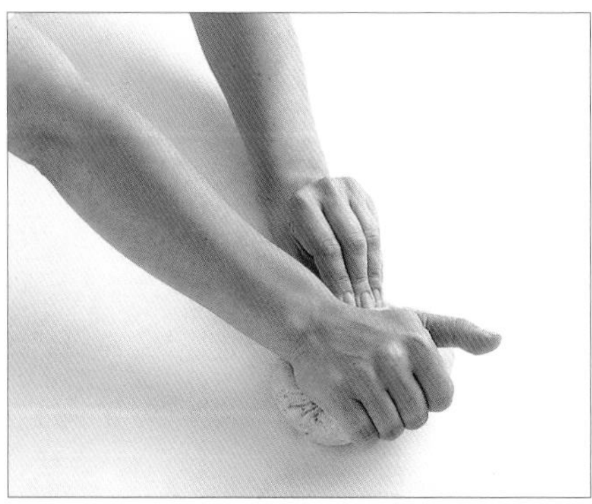

3 Knead the pasta until smooth, wrap it and set it aside to rest for at least 30 minutes before rolling it out. It will be much more elastic after resting.

To make the dough in a food processor

1 Sift the flour into the bowl of a food processor and add the salt.

2 Lightly beat the eggs with the oil and pour them in, together with any chosen flavouring. Process until the dough begins to come together, then tip it out and knead it until smooth. Wrap and rest for 40 minutes before shaping by hand or in a pasta machine.

Variations

Tomato Pasta *Add 30ml/2 tbsp tomato purée to the flour and use only 1½ eggs.*

Herb Pasta *Add 45ml/3 tbsp chopped fresh herbs to the flour.*

Wholemeal Pasta *Use 150g/5oz/1¼ cups wholemeal flour sifted with 25g/1oz/¼ cup plain white flour.*

Spinach Pasta *Cook 150g/5oz frozen leaf spinach, squeeze out the moisture, then blend with 2 eggs. Make as for Basic Pasta Dough, but use a little extra flour if the dough is sticky.*

To shape the dough in a pasta machine

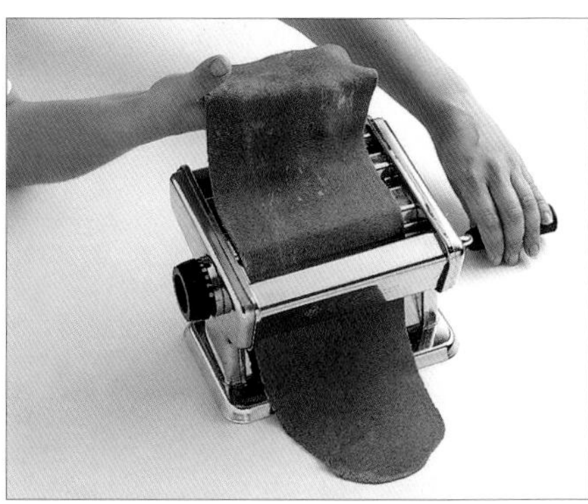

1 To shape the dough in a pasta machine, feed it several times through the machine, using the highest setting first, then reducing the setting until the required thickness is achieved.

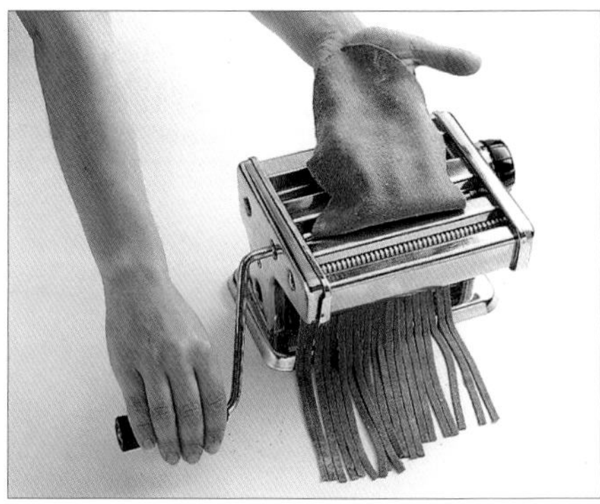

2 Fit the special cutter and turn the handle if you want to produce fettuccine or tagliatelle. A narrower cutter will produce spaghetti or tagliarini. Toss the pasta lightly in flour and spread it out on floured dish towels to dry.

Cook's Tip

The quantities given are guidelines, rather than hard-and-fast rules. Both the humidity on the day that you are making pasta and the type of flour you are using will affect the texture. The dough should not be too soft – it should be quite hard to knead – so extra flour may be required. However, too much extra will make the pasta tough and taste floury. With practice, you will get to know the "feel".

Shaping Pasta by Hand

Making your own noodles and pasta shapes is immensely satisfying, and not as difficult as you might expect. Who cares if the results are not perfectly uniform? Being able to shape your own tagliatelle, ravioli and tortellini is great fun. In the case of filled shapes, it means you can experiment with different fillings, and alter the size or shape. Guidance is given here for cutting or shaping three basic styles of pasta, and you will find more suggestions among the recipes in the book. Be bold – you'll be designing your own pasta in no time.

Ravioli

1 To make ravioli, use half the dough at a time, keeping the rest wrapped in clear film. On a lightly floured surface, roll out one piece of pasta thinly to a neat rectangle. Cover with a damp, clean dish towel and roll out an identical rectangle from the remaining pasta. Pipe or spoon small mounds of filling on to one sheet of pasta, spacing them at 4cm/1½in intervals. Brush the spaces between the fillings with beaten egg.

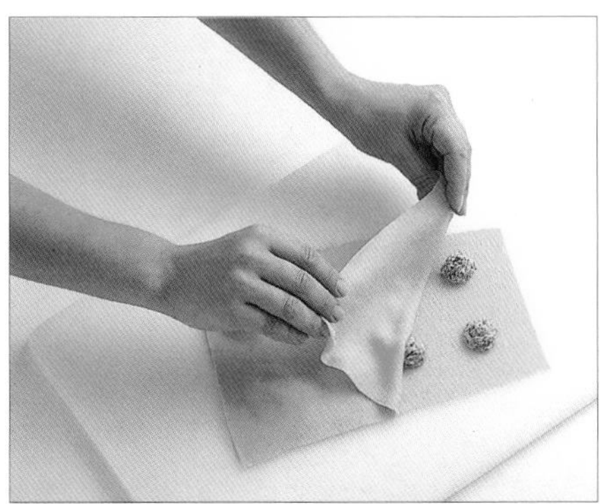

2 Gently lay the remaining pasta rectangle over the topped dough. Press down firmly between the pockets of filling, pushing out any air.

3 Cut the dough into squares, using a serrated ravioli cutter or a sharp knife. Spread out the ravioli on floured dish towels and leave to dry for 30 minutes before cooking.

Tortellini

1 To make tortellini, stamp out thin rounds of pasta, using a round ravioli or biscuit cutter. Pipe or spoon the filling into the middle of each round, then brush the edges with beaten egg.

2 Fold each round into a crescent, excluding all the air. Bend the two edges round to meet each other and press them together to seal. When all the tortellini have been shaped, spread them on floured dish towels and leave to dry for 30 minutes before cooking.

Tagliatelle

1 To make tagliatelle, lightly flour a thin sheet of pasta dough, then roll it up in the same way as a Swiss roll.

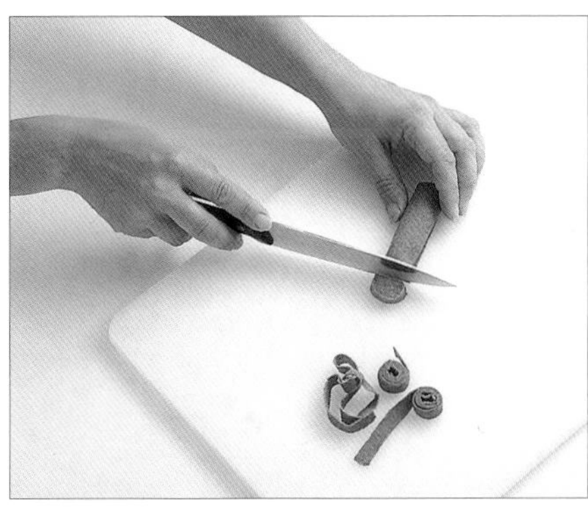

2 Cut the roll into thin slices, using a sharp knife. Immediately unravel the slices to uncurl the pasta ribbons, which should then be lightly tossed in flour and spread on floured dish towels to dry. (To make tagliarini, cut the rolled-up dough into slices 3mm/⅛in thick. To make pappardelle, simply roll out the dough and cut it into wide ribbons.)

Cooking Pasta

Allow 75–175g/3–6oz of pasta per person, depending on whether the pasta is for a starter or main course, and bearing in mind the type of sauce that is to be served.

Bring a large saucepan of lightly salted water to the boil. For long shapes such as spaghetti, hold all the pasta in one hand and gradually lower it into the water until it softens sufficiently to curl round into the pan and gradually becomes immersed completely.

If you are adding shapes, sprinkle them into the pan, trying not to let the water go off the boil.

Cooking times vary but, on average, fresh, unfilled pasta takes 2–3 minutes, although very fine pasta may cook almost instantly. Fresh filled pasta requires 8–10 minutes. Dried unfilled pasta needs to boil for 8–12 minutes and dried filled pasta requires about 15–20 minutes. Always test by tasting – the pasta should be *al dente*; tender but firm enough to retain a bit of "bite".

Consommé with Agnolotti

A clear winner, this delectable soup features round pasta shapes with a seafood filling.

Serves 4–6

75g/3oz cooked peeled prawns
75g/3oz canned crab meat, drained
5ml/1 tsp finely grated fresh root ginger
15ml/1 tbsp fresh white breadcrumbs
5ml/1 tsp light soy sauce
1 spring onion, finely chopped
1 garlic clove, crushed
1 quantity Basic Pasta Dough
1 egg white, beaten
400g/14oz can chicken consommé
30ml/2 tbsp sherry
salt and freshly ground black pepper
50g/2oz peeled cooked prawns and fresh coriander leaves, to garnish

1 Put the prawns, crab meat, ginger, breadcrumbs, soy sauce, onion and garlic into a food processor or blender. Season well, then process until smooth.

2 Roll the pasta into thin sheets. Stamp out 32 rounds, each 5cm/2in in diameter, with a fluted pastry cutter.

3 Place a small teaspoon of the filling in the centre of half the pasta rounds. Brush the edges of each round with egg white and sandwich with a second round on top. Pinch the edges together firmly to stop the filling from seeping out.

4 Cook the pasta in batches in a large pan of boiling, salted water until *al dente*. As each round cooks, lift it out and drop it into a bowl of cold water. Leave for 5 seconds before draining and placing on a tray.

5 Heat the consommé in a pan with the sherry. When piping hot, add the cooked pasta shapes and simmer for 1–2 minutes, until just heated through.

6 Serve the agnolotti in warmed, shallow soup bowls, covered with hot consommé. Garnish with extra peeled prawns and fresh coriander leaves.

Provençal Fish Soup with Pasta

This stunning soup has all the flavours of the Mediterranean. Serve it as a main course for a deliciously filling lunch.

Serves 4

30ml/2 tbsp olive oil
1 onion, sliced
1 garlic clove, crushed
1 leek, sliced
1 litre/1¾ pints/4 cups water
225g/8oz canned chopped tomatoes
5ml/1 tsp dried oregano
1.5ml/¼ tsp saffron strands (optional)
115g/4oz/1 cup small dried pasta shapes
450g/1lb skinned white fish fillets, cut into bite-size chunks
about 8 tightly closed live mussels, scrubbed and bearded
salt and freshly ground black pepper
sliced French bread, to serve

For the rouille

2 garlic cloves, crushed
1 drained canned pimiento, chopped
15ml/1 tbsp fresh white breadcrumbs
60ml/4 tbsp mayonnaise

1 First, make the rouille by pounding the garlic, canned pimiento and breadcrumbs together in mortar with a pestle (or in a food processor). Stir in the mayonnaise and season to taste with salt and pepper. Set aside.

2 Heat the olive oil in a large saucepan and add the onion, garlic and leek. Cover and cook gently, stirring occasionally, for 5 minutes, until soft.

3 Pour in the water, then add the chopped tomatoes, oregano and saffron strands, if using. Season with salt and pepper, and cook for 15–20 minutes.

4 Add the pasta shapes and cook for 5 minutes, then add the fish and place the mussels on top. Simmer with the lid on for 5–10 minutes, until the mussels open and the fish is just cooked. (If any mussels fail to open, discard them.)

5 Toast the French bread, spread it with the rouille and serve immediately with the soup.

Broccoli, Anchovy & Pasta Soup

In this tasty soup, broccoli and anchovies make excellent partners for pretty little orecchiette.

Serves 4

30ml/2 tbsp olive oil
1 small onion, finely chopped
1 garlic clove, finely chopped
1/4–1/3 fresh red chilli, seeded and finely chopped
2 drained canned anchovies
200ml/7fl oz/scant 1 cup passata
45ml/3 tbsp dry white wine
1.2 litres/2 pints/5 cups Vegetable Stock
300g/11oz/2 cups broccoli florets
200g/7oz/1 3/4 cups dried orecchiette
salt and freshly ground black pepper
freshly grated Pecorino cheese, to serve

1 Heat the olive oil in a large, heavy-based saucepan. Add the onion, garlic, chilli and anchovies and cook over a low heat, stirring constantly, for 5–6 minutes.

2 Add the passata and wine, and season with salt and pepper to taste. Bring to the boil, cover the pan, then cook over a low heat, stirring occasionally, for 12–15 minutes.

3 Pour in the stock. Bring to the boil, then add the broccoli florets and simmer for about 5 minutes. Add the pasta and bring back to the boil, stirring.

4 Lower the heat and simmer, stirring frequently, until the pasta is *al dente*. Taste for seasoning and adjust, if necessary. Serve the soup hot, in warmed bowls, and hand around the grated Pecorino cheese separately.

Cook's Tip

Salted dried anchovies have a better flavour and texture than canned anchovies, but are not so widely available. If using them, rinse thoroughly in cold water and pat dry on kitchen paper first. If they are still too salty, then soak them in milk for about 30 minutes, rinse in cold water and pat dry.

Clam & Pasta Soup

This soup is based on the classic pasta dish – spaghetti alle vongole – but uses store-cupboard ingredients. Serve it with hot focaccia or ciabatta for an informal supper with friends.

Serves 4

30ml/2 tbsp olive oil
1 large onion, finely chopped
2 garlic cloves, crushed
400g/14oz can chopped tomatoes
15ml/1 tbsp sun-dried tomato paste
5ml/1 tsp granulated sugar
5ml/1 tsp dried mixed herbs
about 750ml/1 1/4 pints/3 cups fish or Vegetable Stock
150ml/ 1/4 pint/ 2/3 cup red wine
50g/2oz/ 1/2 cup small dried pasta shapes
150g/5oz jar or can clams in natural juice
30ml/2 tbsp finely chopped fresh flat leaf parsley, plus a few whole leaves, to garnish
salt and freshly ground black pepper

1 Heat the oil in a large saucepan. Cook the onion gently, stirring frequently, for 5 minutes, until softened.

2 Add the garlic, tomatoes, sun-dried tomato paste, sugar, herbs, stock and wine, and season with salt and pepper to taste. Bring to the boil. Lower the heat, half cover the pan and simmer for 10 minutes, stirring occasionally.

3 Add the pasta and continue simmering, uncovered, until *al dente*. Stir occasionally, to prevent the pasta shapes from sticking together.

4 Add the clams and their juice to the soup and heat through for 3–4 minutes, adding more stock if required. Do not let the soup boil or the clams will be tough.

5 Remove from the heat, stir in the parsley and taste the soup for seasoning. Serve hot, sprinkled with coarsely ground black pepper and parsley leaves.

Courgette Soup with Pastina

Perfect for a summer lunch, this pretty green soup is light and fresh-tasting.

Serves 4–6

60ml/4 tbsp olive or sunflower oil
2 onions, finely chopped
1.5 litres/2½ pints/6 cups chicken stock
900g/2lb courgettes, grated
115g/4oz/1 cup pastina (small soup pasta shapes)
fresh lemon juice
30ml/2 tbsp chopped fresh chervil
salt and freshly ground black pepper
soured cream, to serve

1 Heat the oil in a large saucepan and add the onions. Cover and cook gently for about 20 minutes, until very soft but not coloured, stirring occasionally.

2 Add the stock. Bring to the boil, then stir in the grated courgettes and the pasta. Lower the heat and simmer until the pasta is *al dente.*

3 Season to taste with lemon juice, salt and pepper. Stir in the chervil. Serve the soup in warmed bowls, adding a swirl of soured cream to each.

Variations

Cucumber can be used instead of courgettes. If you don't have any fresh stock, use canned chicken or beef consommé.

Pumpkin & Spaghetti Soup

Creamy and rich, pumpkin soup is a wonderful way to celebrate the harvest of autumn, and tastes especially good when spaghetti and Parmesan are added.

Serves 4

50g/2oz/ ¼ cup butter
1 onion, finely chopped
450g/1lb piece of peeled pumpkin, cubed
750ml/1¼ pints/3 cups chicken or Vegetable Stock
475ml/16fl oz/2 cups milk
pinch of freshly grated nutmeg
40g/1½ oz dried spaghetti, broken into short lengths
90ml/6 tbsp freshly grated Parmesan cheese
salt and freshly ground black pepper

1 Heat the butter in a heavy-based saucepan and fry the onion over a low heat for 8 minutes. Stir in the pumpkin and cook for 2–3 minutes more.
2 Pour in the stock, bring to the boil, then lower the heat and cook for about 15 minutes, or until the pumpkin is soft.
3 Allow the mixture to cool slightly. Transfer it to a blender or food processor, process to a purée, then scrape it back into the pan. Stir in the milk and nutmeg, with salt and pepper to taste. Bring to the boil.
4 Add the spaghetti and cook until it is *al dente*. Stir in the Parmesan and serve at once.

Little Stuffed Hats in Broth

Cappelletti – little hats – are so delicious that you do not need an elaborate soup in which to serve them. Chicken stock, a splash of white wine and fresh herbs are all that are needed.

Serves 4

1.2 litres/2 pints/5 cups chicken stock
90–115g/3½–4oz/1 cup fresh or dried cappelletti
30ml/2 tbsp dry white wine
about 15ml/1 tbsp finely chopped fresh flat leaf parsley
salt and freshly ground black pepper
shredded flat leaf parsley, to garnish
about 30ml/2 tbsp freshly grated Parmesan cheese, to serve

1 Pour the chicken stock into a large saucepan and bring it to the boil. Season to taste, then add the pasta. When the stock boils, lower the heat and simmer, stirring frequently, until the pasta is *al dente*.

2 Swirl in the wine and chopped parsley, then taste for seasoning. Ladle into four warmed soup plates. Garnish with shredded flat leaf parsley, sprinkle with grated Parmesan cheese and serve immediately.

Cook's Tip

Cappelletti are very similar in shape to tortellini. You can buy them from delicatessens and supermarkets or make your own, and you can use either fresh or dried pasta.

Chicken Vermicelli Soup with Egg Shreds

This soup is quick and easy to make, and very versatile. Add extra ingredients if you like, such as spring onions, mushrooms, prawns or chopped salami.

Serves 4–6

3 large eggs
30ml/2 tbsp chopped fresh coriander or parsley
1.5 litres/2½ pints/6 cups chicken stock
115g/4oz/1 cup dried vermicelli or capelli d'angelo, broken into short lengths
115g/4oz cooked chicken breast, shredded
salt and freshly ground black pepper

1 First make the egg shreds. Whisk the eggs together in a small bowl and stir in the coriander or parsley.

2 Heat a small non-stick frying pan and pour in about 45ml/3 tbsp of the egg mixture, swirling to cover the base, and make a thin pancake. Cook until just set. Slide the pancake on to a plate and repeat until all the mixture is used up.

3 Roll each pancake up and, using a sharp knife, slice thinly crossways into shreds. Set aside.

4 Bring the stock to the boil and add the pasta. Cook until it is almost *al dente*, then add the chicken and season with salt and pepper to taste. Heat through for 2–3 minutes, then stir in the egg shreds. Serve immediately.

Variation
To make a Thai variation, use Chinese rice noodles instead of vermicelli. Stir 2.5ml/½ tsp dried lemon grass, 2 small whole fresh green chillies and 60ml/4 tbsp coconut milk into the chicken stock. Add 4 thinly sliced spring onions and plenty of chopped fresh coriander.

Chicken & Stellette Soup

Little pasta stars look very attractive in this tasty soup, which is sufficiently sophisticated to serve at a dinner party, yet has plenty of child appeal if you omit the wine.

Serves 4–6

900ml/1½ pints/3¾ cups chicken stock
1 bay leaf
4 spring onions, sliced
225g/8oz/3 cups button mushrooms, sliced
50g/2oz/½ cup stellette
115g/4oz cooked, skinless chicken breast, thinly sliced
150ml/¼ pint/⅔ cup dry white wine
15ml/1 tbsp chopped fresh parsley
salt and freshly ground black pepper

1 Put the stock and bay leaf into a pan and bring to the boil over a medium heat.

2 Add the spring onions, mushrooms and pasta. Lower the heat, cover and simmer for 7–8 minutes.

3 Just before serving, add the chicken, wine and parsley, and season to taste. Heat through for 2–3 minutes, then serve in warmed bowls.

Variations
Any small soup pasta can be substituted for stellette – old-fashioned alphabet shapes are very popular with young children and will amuse nostalgic adults. "Safari" pasta is also fun. Leave out the wine when making the soup for youngsters, and add a little extra stock instead.

Sweetcorn Chowder with Conchigliette

Chowders are always wonderfully satisfying, and this one is no exception. It is low in fat, but high on the flavour stakes.

Serves 6–8

1 small green pepper, diced
450g/1lb potatoes, peeled and diced
350g/12oz/2 cups drained canned or frozen sweetcorn
1 onion, chopped
1 celery stick, chopped
bouquet garni (bay leaf, parsley stalks and thyme)
600ml/1 pint/2½ cups chicken stock
300ml/ ½ pint/1¼ cups skimmed milk
50g/2oz/½ cup dried conchigliette
150g/5oz smoked turkey rashers, diced
salt and freshly ground black pepper
bread sticks, to serve

1 Put the diced green pepper in a bowl and pour over the boiling water to cover. Leave to stand for 2 minutes. Drain, rinse and drain again.

2 Put the green pepper into a large, heavy-based saucepan and add the potatoes, sweetcorn, onion, celery, bouquet garni and stock. Bring to the boil, lower the heat, cover and simmer for 20 minutes until tender.

3 Add the milk, then season with salt and pepper to taste. Process half of the soup in a food processor or blender and return it to the pan. Add the conchigliette and simmer over a low heat until the pasta is *al dente*.

4 Meanwhile, fry the diced turkey rashers quickly in a non-stick frying pan for 2–3 minutes. Stir them into the soup. Serve in warmed bowls, with bread sticks.

Pasta & Lentil Soup

Small brown lentils are partnered with pasta shapes in this wholesome soup, which is delicately flavoured with fresh herbs.

Serves 4–6

225g/8oz/1 cup brown lentils
30ml/2 tbsp olive oil
2 rindless lean back bacon rashers, diced
1 onion, finely chopped
1 celery stick, finely chopped
1 carrot, finely chopped
2 litres/3½ pints/8 cups chicken stock or water, or a combination
1 fresh sage leaf or a pinch of dried sage
1 fresh thyme sprig or 1.5ml/ ¼ tsp dried thyme
175g/6oz/1½ cups ditalini or other small soup pasta
salt and freshly ground black pepper
flat leaf parsley, to garnish

1 Pick over the lentils and remove any debris, such as small stones. Place the lentils in a bowl, pour over cold water to cover, and soak for 2–3 hours. Drain, rinse under cold running water and drain well again.

2 Heat the oil in a large saucepan and sauté the bacon for 2–3 minutes. Add the onion, and cook gently until it softens.

3 Stir in the celery and carrot, and cook for 5 minutes more, stirring frequently. Add the lentils, stirring well.

4 Pour in the stock or water and the herbs, then bring the soup to the boil. Cook over a medium heat for about 1 hour or until the lentils are tender. Add salt and pepper to taste.

5 Stir in the pasta, and cook until it is *al dente*. Allow the soup to stand for a few minutes before serving garnished with parsley.

Cook's Tip

If you use young organic vegetables, their flavour will probably be intense enough to make the addition of stock unnecessary. Just use water.

Chick-pea Soup with Ditalini

Chick-peas are often neglected when it comes to choosing ingredients for soup, but really prove their worth in this classic recipe from central Italy.

Serves 4–6

200g/7oz/1 cup dried chick-peas, soaked overnight in water to cover
3 garlic cloves, peeled but left whole
1 bay leaf
90ml/6 tbsp olive oil
50g/2oz/ ¼ cup diced salt pork, pancetta or bacon
1 fresh rosemary sprig, plus extra to garnish
600ml/1 pint/2½ cups water
150g/5oz dried ditalini or other short hollow pasta shapes
salt and freshly ground black pepper
freshly grated Parmesan cheese, to serve

1 Drain the chick-peas, rinse them under cold water and drain them again. Put them in a large saucepan with fresh water to cover. Boil for 15 minutes. Rinse and drain.

2 Return the chick-peas to the pan and again pour in water to cover. Add 1 garlic clove, the bay leaf and 45ml/3 tbsp of the oil and season with a pinch of pepper.

3 Bring to the boil, then lower the heat and simmer for about 2 hours, or until tender, adding more water as necessary. Remove the bay leaf. Lift out half the chick-peas with a slotted spoon and process them in a food processor with a few tablespoons of the cooking liquid. Return the purée to the pan.

4 In a frying pan, sauté the diced pork, pancetta or bacon gently in the remaining oil with the rosemary and remaining whole garlic cloves until just golden. Discard the rosemary and garlic.

5 Stir the pork with its oils into the chick-pea mixture, then add the water and bring to the boil.

6 Adjust the seasoning, if necessary. Stir in the pasta and cook until *al dente*. Serve in warmed bowls garnished with rosemary. Pass the grated Parmesan cheese separately.

Fresh Pea & Ham Soup

Frozen peas provide flavour, freshness and colour in this delicious winter soup, which is filling enough to make a light main course.

Serves 4

115g/4oz/1 cup small pasta shapes
30ml/2 tbsp vegetable oil
1 small bunch spring onions, chopped
350g/12oz/3 cups frozen peas
1.2 litres/2 pints/5 cups chicken stock
225g/8oz raw unsmoked ham or gammon
60ml/4 tbsp double cream
salt and freshly ground black pepper
warm crusty bread, to serve

1 Bring a large saucepan of salted water to the boil. Toss in the pasta and cook until it is *al dente*. Drain, cover with cold water and set aside until required.

2 Heat the vegetable oil in a large heavy-based saucepan, then add the spring onions and cook, stirring occasionally, until soft. Add the peas and chicken stock. Bring to the boil, then lower the heat and simmer for 10 minutes.

3 Allow the mixture to cool slightly. Process in a blender or food processor, then pour the purée back into the saucepan. Heat to simmering point.

4 Cut the ham or gammon into short fingers and add it to the saucepan. Drain and add the pasta. Simmer for 2–3 minutes, then season to taste. Stir in the cream and serve with the warm crusty bread.

Variation

Any pasta shapes can be used for this soup, although hoops or shells seem to work best of all. Whatever shape you choose, make sure that the pasta is not larger than the other ingredients in the soup.

Minestrone

This soup crops up on restaurant menus the world over, but seldom tastes as good as when made in a country kitchen, from freshly picked vegetables and home-made stock.

Serves 6–8
30ml/2 tbsp olive oil
50g/2oz rindless smoked streaky bacon rashers, diced
2 large onions, sliced
2 garlic cloves, crushed
2 carrots, diced
3 celery sticks, sliced
225g/8oz/generous 1 cup dried haricot beans, soaked overnight in water to cover
400g/14oz can chopped tomatoes
2.5 litres/4 pints/10 cups beef stock
3 potatoes, peeled and diced
175g/6oz/1½ cups small pasta shapes
225g/8oz green cabbage, thinly sliced
175g/6oz fine green beans, sliced
115g/4oz/1 cup frozen peas
45ml/3 tbsp chopped fresh parsley
salt and freshly ground black pepper
freshly grated Parmesan cheese, to serve

1 Heat the oil in a large saucepan and gently fry the bacon, onions and garlic, stirring occasionally, for 5 minutes, until soft.

2 Add the carrots and celery, and cook for 2–3 minutes, then drain the beans and add them to the pan with the tomatoes and stock. Bring to the boil, lower the heat, cover and simmer for 2 hours, or until the haricot beans are almost tender.

3 Add the potatoes and cook for 15 minutes more, then add the pasta, cabbage, green beans and peas. Cook for 15 minutes, until the vegetables are tender and the pasta is *al dente*. Season to taste, stir in the parsley and serve with Parmesan cheese.

Variation
For a delicious change, borrowed from Genoese cooks, stir in a little pesto just before serving.

Rich Minestrone

This is a special minestrone made with chicken. Served with crusty Italian bread, it makes a hearty meal.

Serves 4–6
15ml/1 tbsp olive oil
2 chicken thighs
3 rindless streaky bacon rashers, chopped
1 onion, finely chopped
a few fresh basil leaves, shredded
a few fresh rosemary leaves, finely chopped
15ml/1 tbsp chopped fresh flat leaf parsley
2 potatoes, peeled and cut into 1cm/½ in cubes
1 large carrot, cut into 1cm/½ in cubes
2 small courgettes, cut into 1cm/½ in cubes
1–2 celery sticks, cut into 1cm/½ in cubes
1 litre/1¾ pints/4 cups chicken stock
200g/7oz/1¾ cups frozen peas
90g/3½ oz/scant 1 cup dried stellette or other soup pasta
salt and freshly ground black pepper
fresh basil leaves, to garnish
coarsely shaved Parmesan cheese, to serve

1 Heat the oil in a large frying pan and fry the chicken thighs for about 5 minutes on each side. Remove with a slotted spoon and set aside.

2 Add the bacon, onion and herbs to the pan and cook gently, stirring constantly, for 5 minutes. Add the remaining vegetables, except the peas, and cook for 5–7 minutes, stirring frequently. Return the chicken thighs to the pan, add the stock and bring to the boil. Cover and cook over a low heat for 35–40 minutes, stirring occasionally.

3 Remove the chicken with a slotted spoon and place on a board. Stir the peas and pasta into the soup, bring back to the boil and simmer, stirring frequently until the pasta is *al dente*.

4 Remove the chicken skin, cut the meat from the bones into 1cm/½in pieces. Return the meat to the soup and heat. Taste for seasoning. Serve in warmed soup bowls. Garnish with one or two basil leaves and scatter over Parmesan shavings.

Minestrone with Pasta & Beans

This tasty soup is made using canned beans, so is ideal for a spur-of-the-moment lunch invitation. A small amount of pancetta gives depth to the flavour.

Serves 4

15ml/1 tbsp olive oil
50g/2oz pancetta, rind removed, roughly chopped
2–3 celery sticks, finely chopped
3 carrots, finely chopped
1 onion, finely chopped
1–2 garlic cloves, crushed
2 x 400g/14oz cans chopped tomatoes
about 1 litre/1¾ pints/4 cups chicken stock
400g/14oz can cannellini beans, drained and rinsed
50g/2oz/½ cup short-cut macaroni
30–60ml/2–4 tbsp chopped flat leaf parsley, to taste
salt and freshly ground black pepper
shaved Parmesan cheese, to serve

1 Heat the olive oil in a large, heavy-based saucepan. Add the pancetta, celery, carrots and onion, and cook over a low heat for 5 minutes, stirring constantly, until the vegetables have begun to soften.

2 Add the garlic and tomatoes, breaking the tomatoes up well with a wooden spoon. Pour in the chicken stock. Season with salt and pepper to taste and bring to the boil. Half cover the pan, lower the heat and simmer gently for about 20 minutes, until the vegetables are soft.

3 Add the cannellini beans to the pan, together with the macaroni. Bring to the boil again. Cover, lower the heat and continue to simmer for about 20 minutes more, until the pasta is *al dente*.

4 Check the consistency of the soup and add a little more stock, if necessary. Stir in the parsley. Taste and adjust the seasoning, if necessary.

5 Serve hot in warmed soup bowls, sprinkling each portion with a few shavings of Parmesan cheese.

Clear Vegetable Soup

The success of this clear soup depends on the quality of the stock, so it is best to use home-made vegetable stock, if possible, rather than stock cubes. Otherwise, you could use a good-quality canned bouillon.

Serves 4

1 small carrot
1 baby leek
1 celery stick
50g/2oz green cabbage
900ml/1½ pints/3¾ cups Vegetable Stock
1 bay leaf
115g/4oz/1 cup drained cooked cannellini beans
25g/1oz/¼ cup dried soup pasta, such as tiny shells, bows, stars or elbows
salt and freshly ground black pepper
snipped fresh chives, to garnish

1 Cut the carrot, leek and celery into 5cm/2in long strips. Slice the cabbage very finely.

2 Put the stock and bay leaf into a large, heavy-based saucepan and bring to the boil over a medium heat. Add the strips of carrot, leek and celery, lower the heat, cover the pan and simmer for 6 minutes.

3 Add the cabbage, cannellini beans and pasta shapes. Stir well to mix, then simmer, uncovered, for a further 4–5 minutes, or until all the vegetables are tender and the pasta is *al dente*.

4 Remove and discard the bay leaf, and season the soup to taste with salt and pepper. Ladle into four warmed soup bowls and garnish with the snipped chives. Serve immediately.

Variations

Use drained and rinsed canned cannellini beans to save time, if you like. Other beans that would also go well in this soup include flageolets, borlotti or haricots. You could also substitute a shallot for the leek, if liked.

Puglia-style Minestrone

Ricotta salata is the traditional garnish for this simple soup. You don't need to use much; even a small sprinkling boosts the flavour.

Serves 4

2 skinless, boneless chicken thighs
1 onion, quartered lengthways
1 carrot, roughly chopped
1 celery stick, roughly chopped
a few black peppercorns
1 small handful mixed fresh herbs, such as parsley and thyme
1 chicken stock cube
1.2 litres/2 pints/5 cups water
50g/2oz/ ½ cup dried tubetti
salt and freshly ground black pepper
50g/2oz ricotta salata, coarsely grated or crumbled and 30ml/2 tbsp fresh mint leaves, to serve

1 Put the chicken thighs in a large saucepan. Add the onion, carrot, celery, peppercorns and herbs, then crumble in the stock cube. Pour in the water and bring to the boil.

2 Lower the heat, half cover the pan and simmer gently for about 1 hour. Remove the pan from the heat. Leave the liquid to cool, then strain it into a clean large saucepan. Discard the flavouring ingredients. Blot the surface with kitchen paper to remove surface fat.

3 Cut the chicken into bite-size pieces and set aside.

4 Bring the stock in the pan to the boil, add the pasta and simmer, stirring until only just *al dente*.

5 Add the pieces of chicken and heat through for a few minutes. Taste for seasoning. Serve hot in warmed bowls, sprinkled with the ricotta salata and mint leaves.

Cook's Tip

Ricotta salata is a salted and dried version of ricotta, which can easily be crumbled. If it is not available, crumbled feta cheese can be used instead.

Pasta Soup with Chicken Livers

A soup that can be served as either a first or main course. The fried chicken livers are so delicious that even if you do not normally like them, you will relish them in this soup.

Serves 4–6

115g/4oz/ ⅔ cup chicken livers, thawed if frozen
3 sprigs each fresh parsley, marjoram and sage
leaves from 1 fresh thyme sprig
5–6 fresh basil leaves
15ml/1 tbsp olive oil
4 garlic cloves, crushed
15–30ml/1–2 tbsp dry white wine
2 x 300g/11oz cans condensed chicken consommé
225g/8oz/2 cups frozen peas
50g/2oz/ ½ cup dried farfalle
2–3 spring onions, sliced diagonally
salt and freshly ground black pepper

1 Cut the chicken livers into small pieces with scissors. Finely chop the herbs. Heat the olive oil in a frying pan, add the garlic and herbs, season with salt and pepper to taste, and fry gently for a few minutes.

2 Add the chicken livers, increase the heat to high and stir-fry for a few minutes, until they change colour and become dry. Pour over the wine, cook until it evaporates, then remove the livers from the heat and taste for seasoning.

3 Tip both cans of condensed chicken consommé into a large saucepan and add water to the condensed soup as directed on the labels. Add an extra can of water, then stir in a little salt and pepper to taste and bring to the boil.

4 Add the frozen peas to the pan and simmer for about 5 minutes, then add the pasta and bring the soup back to the boil, stirring. Allow to simmer, stirring frequently, until the pasta is only just *al dente*.

5 Add the fried chicken livers and spring onions, and heat through for 2–3 minutes. Taste for seasoning. Serve hot, in warmed bowls.

Tiny Pasta in Broth

Serve this quick and easy soup with warm bread rolls for an after-theatre supper, or as a light starter before a hearty main course.

Serves 4
1.2 litres/2 pints/5 cups beef stock
75g/3oz/ 3/4 cup dried funghetti or other tiny soup pasta
2 pieces drained bottled roasted red pepper
salt and freshly ground black pepper

To serve
coarsely shaved Parmesan cheese
warm bread rolls

1 Bring the beef stock to the boil in a large saucepan. Season with salt and pepper to taste, then drop in the dried pasta. Stir well and bring the stock back to the boil.

2 Lower the heat to a simmer and cook until the pasta is *al dente*. Stir frequently.

3 Finely dice the pieces of roasted pepper. Divide them equally among four warmed soup plates. Taste the soup for seasoning and adjust, if necessary. Ladle into the soup plates and serve immediately, with shavings of Parmesan handed separately and a basket of warm rolls.

Cook's Tip
Stock cubes are not really suitable for a recipe like this in which the flavour of the broth is crucially important. If you have insufficient time to make your own stock, use two 300g/11oz cans of good-quality condensed beef consommé, adding water as instructed on the labels.

Meatball & Pasta Soup

You can make a meal of this marvellous soup, and it is very popular with children.

Serves 4
2 x 300g/11oz cans condensed beef consommé
90g/3½ oz dried fidelini or spaghettini
fresh flat leaf parsley to garnish
freshly grated Parmesan cheese, to serve

For the meatballs
1 very thick slice of white bread, crusts removed
30ml/2 tbsp milk
225g/8oz minced beef
1 garlic clove, crushed
30ml/2 tbsp freshly grated Parmesan cheese
30–45ml/2–3 tbsp fresh flat leaf parsley leaves, coarsely chopped
1 egg
nutmeg
salt and freshly ground black pepper

1 First, make the meatballs. Break the bread into a small bowl, add the milk and set aside to soak. Meanwhile, put the minced beef, garlic, Parmesan, parsley and egg in another large bowl. Grate fresh nutmeg liberally over the top and add salt and pepper to taste.

2 Squeeze the bread with your hands to remove as much milk as possible, then add the bread to the meatball mixture and mix together well with your hands. Wash your hands, rinse them under cold water, then form the mixture into tiny balls about the size of small marbles.

3 Tip both cans of consommé into a large saucepan, add water as directed on the labels, then add an extra can of water. Stir in salt and pepper to taste and bring to the boil.

4 Drop in the meatballs, then break the pasta into small pieces and add it to the soup. Bring to the boil, stirring gently. Lower the heat and simmer, stirring frequently, until the pasta is *al dente*. Taste for seasoning and adjust, if necessary. Serve hot in warmed soup bowls, sprinkled with the parsley and freshly grated Parmesan cheese.

Classic Vegetarian Minestrone

You don't need meat to make a magnificent minestrone. This home-made version is a revelation based on pasta, beans and fresh vegetables.

Serves 4

45ml/3 tbsp olive oil
1 large leek, thinly sliced
2 carrots, chopped
1 courgette, thinly sliced
115g/4oz whole green beans, halved
2 celery sticks, thinly sliced
1.5 litres/2½ pints/6 cups Vegetable Stock or water
400g/14oz can chopped tomatoes
15ml/1 tbsp fresh basil, chopped
5ml/1 tsp fresh thyme leaves, chopped, or 2.5ml/ ½ tsp dried thyme
400g/14oz can cannellini or kidney beans
50g/2oz/ ½ cup small pasta shapes or macaroni
freshly grated Parmesan cheese and chopped fresh parsley, to garnish (optional)

1 Heat the oil in a large saucepan, add leek, carrots, courgette, green beans and celery, and mix well. Heat until sizzling, then cover, lower the heat and sweat the vegetables for 15 minutes, shaking the pan occasionally.

2 Add the stock or water, tomatoes and herbs, and season with salt and pepper to taste. Bring to the boil, replace the lid and simmer gently for about 30 minutes.

3 Add the beans, with the can juices, then tip in the pasta. Simmer until the pasta is *al dente*. Check the seasoning and adjust if necessary.

4. Serve in warmed bowls, sprinkled with the grated Parmesan cheese and parsley, if using.

Cook's Tip
The flavour of minestrone improves if it is made a day or two ahead and stored in the fridge. It can also be frozen and then gently reheated.

Genoese Minestrone

Packed with vegetables, this soup has a good strong flavour, making it an excellent vegetarian dish.

Serves 4–6

45ml/3 tbsp olive oil
1 onion, finely chopped
2 celery sticks, thinly sliced
1 large carrot, diced
150g/5oz French beans, cut into short lengths
1 courgette, thinly sliced
1 potato, cut into 1cm/ ½in cubes
¼ Savoy cabbage, shredded
1 small aubergine, cut into 1cm/ ½in cubes
200g/7oz can cannellini beans, drained and rinsed
2 Italian plum tomatoes, chopped
1.2 litres/2 pints/5 cups Vegetable Stock
90g/3½ oz dried spaghetti
salt and freshly ground black pepper

For the pesto
about 20 fresh basil leaves
1 garlic clove
10ml/2 tsp pine nuts
15ml/1 tbsp freshly grated Parmesan cheese
15ml/1 tbsp freshly grated Pecorino cheese
30ml/2 tbsp olive oil

1 Heat the oil in a large saucepan, add the onion, celery and carrot, and cook over a low heat, stirring frequently, for about 5–7 minutes, until the onion is soft and translucent.

2 Tip in the French beans, courgette, potato and cabbage. Stir-fry over a medium heat for about 3 minutes. Add the aubergine, cannellini beans and tomatoes, and stir-fry for 2–3 minutes more. Pour in the stock with salt and pepper to taste. Bring to the boil. Stir well, cover and lower the heat. Simmer for 40 minutes, stirring occasionally.

3 Meanwhile, make the pesto. Process all the ingredients in a food processor until the mixture forms a smooth sauce, adding 15–45ml/1–3 tbsp water through the feeder tube, if necessary.

4 Break the pasta into small pieces and add it to the soup. Simmer, stirring frequently, for 5 minutes. Genty stir in the pesto, then simmer until the pasta is *al dente*. Taste for seasoning. Serve hot, in warmed soup plates or bowls.

Cauliflower Soup with Farfalle

Serve this silky smooth, mildly cheesy soup with Melba toast for an elegant dinner-party starter.

Serves 6
1 large cauliflower
1.2 litres/2 pints/5 cups Vegetable Stock
175g/6oz/1½ cups dried farfalle
150ml/ ¼ pint/ ⅔ cup single cream or milk
freshly grated nutmeg
pinch of cayenne pepper
60ml/4 tbsp freshly grated Parmesan cheese
salt and freshly ground black pepper

1 Divide the cauliflower into florets. Bring the stock to the boil and add the florets. Simmer for 10 minutes, or until tender. Transfer the florets with a slotted spoon to a food processor.

2 Add the pasta to the pan and simmer until *al dente*. Drain, reserve the pasta, and pour the liquid into the food processor.

3 Add the cream or milk, nutmeg and cayenne, process until smooth, then press through a sieve into the clean pan. Stir in the cooked pasta. Reheat the soup and stir in the Parmesan. Taste and adjust the seasoning, then serve.

Melba Toast

Crisp Melba toast is wonderful with all types of soup.

3–4 thin slices day-old white bread
freshly grated Parmesan cheese, for sprinkling
1.5ml/ ¼ tsp paprika

1 Toast the bread on both sides. Cut off the crusts and split each slice in half horizontally. Scrape off any doughy bits and sprinkle with the grated Parmesan and paprika.

2 Place cut side up on a baking sheet under a medium grill until the toast is golden and has curled at the edges. Watch it closely as it will burn easily.

Beetroot & Ravioli Soup

Cook your own beetroot for this jewel-like soup.

Serves 4–6
1 quantity Basic Pasta Dough
egg white, beaten, for brushing
flour, for dusting
1 small onion, finely chopped
2 garlic cloves, crushed
5ml/1 tsp fennel seeds
600ml/1 pint/2½ cups Vegetable Stock
225g/8oz cooked beetroot
30ml/2 tbsp fresh orange juice
fennel or dill leaves, to garnish

For the filling
115g/4oz/1¾ cups mushrooms, finely chopped
1 small onion, finely chopped
1–2 garlic cloves, crushed
5ml/1 tsp chopped fresh thyme
15ml/1 tbsp chopped fresh parsley
90ml/6 tbsp fresh white breadcrumbs
salt and freshly ground black pepper
large pinch of freshly grated nutmeg

1 Process all the filling ingredients in a food processor or blender. Set aside.

2 Roll the pasta into thin sheets. Lay one piece over a ravioli tray and put a teaspoonful of the filling into each depression. Brush around the edges of each ravioli with egg white. Cover with another sheet of pasta and press the edges together. Cut into squares. Transfer to a floured dish towel and rest for 1 hour.

3 Cook the ravioli in batches in a pan of boiling, salted water for 2 minutes. Lift out on a slotted spoon and drop into a bowl of cold water. Leave for 5 seconds. Drain and place on a tray.

4 Put the onion, garlic and fennel seeds into a pan with 150ml/ ¼ pint/ ⅔ cup of the stock. Bring to the boil, lower the heat, cover and simmer for 5 minutes, until tender. Peel and finely dice the beetroot. Set aside 60ml/4 tbsp for the garnish. Add the rest to the soup with the remaining stock. Bring to the boil.

5 Add the orange juice and cooked ravioli, and simmer until *al dente*. Serve in shallow warmed soup bowls, garnished with the reserved diced beetroot and fennel or dill leaves.

Roasted Tomato & Pasta Soup

Roasting tomatoes really brings out their flavour, and the soup has a wonderful smoky taste.

Serves 4

450g/1lb ripe Italian plum tomatoes, halved lengthways
1 large red pepper, quartered lengthways and seeded
1 large red onion, quartered lengthways
2 whole garlic cloves, unpeeled
15ml/1 tbsp olive oil
1.2 litres/2 pints/5 cups Vegetable Stock or water
good pinch of granulated sugar
90g/3½oz/scant 1 cup dried tubetti or other small pasta shapes
salt and freshly ground black pepper
fresh basil leaves, to garnish

1 Preheat the oven to 190°C/375°F/Gas 5. Spread out the tomatoes, red pepper, onion and unpeeled garlic cloves in a roasting tin. Drizzle with the olive oil. Roast for 30–40 minutes, until the vegetables are soft and charred, stirring and turning them halfway through the cooking time.

2 Tip the vegetables into a food processor, add about 250ml/8fl oz/1 cup of the stock or water and process until puréed. Scrape into a sieve placed over a large saucepan and press the purée through into the pan.

3 Add the remaining stock or water, and the sugar, and season with salt and pepper to taste. Bring to the boil over a medium heat, stirring constantly.

4 Add the pasta and cook, stirring frequently, until it is *al dente*. Taste for seasoning. Serve hot in warmed bowls, garnished with the fresh basil leaves.

Cook's Tip
The soup can be frozen without the pasta. Thaw it thoroughly, pour it into a pan and bring it to the boil before adding the pasta.

Farmhouse Soup

Swedes and turnips are often forgotten by modern cooks, which is a shame, for they have excellent flavour. Try them in this chunky, rustic main-meal soup.

Serves 4

30ml/2 tbsp olive oil
1 onion, roughly chopped
3 carrots, cut into large chunks
1 turnip, about 200g/7oz, cut into large chunks
about 175g/6oz swede, cut into large chunks
400g/14oz can chopped Italian tomatoes
15ml/1 tbsp tomato purée
5ml/1 tsp dried mixed herbs
5ml/1 tsp dried oregano
50g/2oz/½ cup dried peppers, washed and thinly sliced (optional)
1.5 litres/2½ pints/6 cups Vegetable Stock or water
50g/2oz/½ cup dried conchiglie or other pasta shapes
400g/14oz can red kidney beans, rinsed and drained
30ml/2 tbsp chopped fresh flat leaf parsley
salt and freshly ground black pepper
freshly grated Parmesan cheese and crusty bread, to serve

1 Heat the olive oil in a large, heavy-based saucepan, add the onion and cook over a low heat, stirring occasionally, for about 5 minutes until softened.

2 Add the carrots, turnip, swede, canned tomatoes, tomato purée, dried mixed herbs, oregano and dried peppers, if using. Season with salt and pepper to taste. Pour in the stock or water and bring to the boil over a medium heat. Stir well, cover, lower the heat and simmer, stirring occasionally, for 30 minutes, until the vegetables are tender.

3 Add the pasta and bring to the boil, stirring constantly. Lower the heat and simmer until the pasta is only just *al dente*.

4 Stir in the kidney beans. Heat through for 2–3 minutes, then stir in the parsley. Serve hot in warmed soup bowls, with grated Parmesan handed separately and thick slices of crusty bread.

Cook's Tip
Packets of dried Italian peppers are sold in many supermarkets and in delicatessens. They are piquant and firm with a "meaty" bite to them, which makes them ideal for adding substance and concentrated flavour to soups.

Variation
Use two leeks instead of the onion and borlotti beans instead of the kidney beans. Virtually any small pasta shapes are suitable; chunky ones, such as pipe rigate or penne rigate work best.

Pasta Soup with Pulses

A simple, country-style soup. The shape of the pasta and the beans complement one another beautifully.

Serves 4–6

30ml/2 tbsp olive oil
1 onion, chopped
2 carrots, chopped
2 celery sticks, sliced
400g/14oz can chick-peas, rinsed and drained
200g/7oz can cannellini beans, rinsed and drained
150ml/ ¼ pint/ ⅔ cup passata
120ml/4fl oz/ ½ cup water
1.5 litres/2½ pints/6 cups Vegetable or light chicken stock
2 fresh rosemary sprigs
200g/7oz/scant 2 cups dried conchiglie
salt and freshly ground black pepper
freshly grated Parmesan cheese, to serve

1 Heat the oil in a large saucepan, add the fresh vegetables and cook over a low heat, stirring frequently, for 5–7 minutes.

2 Stir in the chick-peas and cannellini beans. Cook for about 5 minutes, then stir in the passata and water. Continue to cook, stirring constantly, for 2–3 minutes.

3 Add 475ml/16fl oz/2 cups of the stock, one of the rosemary sprigs and season with salt and pepper to taste. Bring to the boil, cover, then simmer gently, stirring occasionally, for 1 hour.

4 Pour in the remaining stock and bring to the boil. Add the pasta. Lower the heat and simmer, stirring frequently, until the pasta is *al dente*.

5 Taste for seasoning. Remove the rosemary sprig. Serve in warmed bowls, topped with Parmesan and rosemary leaves.

Variation
If you like, crush one to two garlic cloves and fry them with the vegetables in step 1.

Calabrian Pasta & Bean Soup

In Southern Italy, this soup is called *millecose*, meaning "a thousand things" as it is based on whatever ingredients are to hand.

Serves 4–6

75g/3oz/scant ½ cup brown lentils
475ml/16fl oz/2 cups cold water
15g/½ oz dried mushrooms
175ml/6fl oz/ ¾ cup warm water
30ml/2 tbsp olive oil
½ red pepper, cored, seeded and diced
1 carrot, diced
1 celery stick, diced
2 shallots, finely chopped
1 garlic clove, finely chopped
½ fresh red chilli, seeded and chopped
a little chopped fresh flat leaf parsley
1.5 litres/2½ pints/6 cups Vegetable Stock
150g/5oz/ ⅔ cup each drained canned red kidney beans, cannellini beans and chick-peas, rinsed
115g/4oz/1 cup dried penne
salt and freshly ground black pepper
chopped flat leaf parsley, to garnish
freshly grated Pecorino cheese, to serve

1 Put the lentils in a saucepan, pour in the cold water and bring to the boil. Lower the heat and simmer, stirring occasionally, for 15–20 minutes, until just tender. Meanwhile, soak the dried mushrooms in the measured warm water for 15–20 minutes.

2 Drain the lentils and rinse under cold water. Drain the soaked mushrooms through kitchen paper and reserve the soaking liquid. Finely chop the mushrooms and set them aside.

3 Heat the oil in a saucepan and fry the red pepper, carrot, celery, shallots, garlic and chilli over a low heat, stirring, for 5–7 minutes. Add the parsley and stock, then the mushrooms with their soaking liquid. Bring to the boil, add the beans and chick-peas, and season. Cover, and simmer for 20 minutes.

4 Add the pasta and lentils. Bring the soup back to the boil, stirring. Simmer, stirring frequently, until the pasta is *al dente*. Season, then serve in warmed soup bowls, garnished with chopped parsley and with grated Pecorino.

Haricot Bean Soup with Pasta Shells

Soup you can almost stand a spoon in – that's what you get when you make this wonderful winter warmer.

Serves 6

175g/6oz/1½ cups dried haricot beans, soaked overnight in cold water to cover
1.75 litres/3 pints/7 cups unsalted Vegetable Stock or water
115g/4oz/1 cup dried medium pasta shells
60ml/4 tbsp olive oil, plus extra to serve
2 garlic cloves, crushed
60ml/4 tbsp chopped fresh parsley
salt and freshly ground black pepper

1 Drain the beans and place them in a large saucepan. Add the stock or water. Bring to the boil, then lower the heat and simmer, half-covered, for 2–2½ hours, or until tender.

2 Scoop half the beans and a little of their cooking liquid into a blender or food processor. Process to a purée, then scrape this back into the pan. Stir well and add extra water or stock if the soup seems too thick.

3 Bring the soup back to the boil. Stir in the pasta, lower the heat and simmer gently until *al dente*.

4 Heat the olive oil in a small pan. Add the garlic and fry over a low heat until golden. Stir into the soup with the parsley, and season well with salt and pepper. Ladle into warmed bowls and drizzle each with a little extra olive oil. Serve immediately.

Cook's Tip
You can reduce the soaking time for the beans by putting them in a saucepan, covering with cold water and bringing very slowly to the boil over a very low heat. Then boil for 2 minutes, remove from the heat, cover and leave to soak for 1 hour.

Tomato, Borlotti & Pasta Soup

This peasant soup is very thick. It should always be made with dried or fresh beans, never canned ones.

Serves 4–6

300g/11oz/1½ cups dried borlotti or cannellini beans, soaked overnight in water to cover
400g/14oz can chopped tomatoes
3 garlic cloves, crushed
2 bay leaves
pinch of coarsely ground black pepper
90ml/6 tbsp olive oil
750ml/1¼ pints/3 cups water
10ml/2 tsp tomato purée
10ml/2 tsp salt
200g/7oz/1¾ cups dried ditalini or other small pasta shapes
45ml/3 tbsp chopped fresh parsley
freshly grated Parmesan cheese, to serve

1 Drain the beans, rinse under cold water, then place them in a large saucepan. Pour over fresh water to cover. Bring to the boil and boil hard for 10 minutes. Drain, rinse and drain again.

2 Return the beans to the pan. Add enough water to cover them by 2.5cm/1in. Stir in the tomatoes, garlic, bay leaves, black pepper and oil. Bring to the boil, then simmer for 1½–2 hours, or until the beans are tender. If necessary, add more water.

3 Remove and discard the bay leaves. Scoop out about half of the bean mixture and process to a purée in a food processor. Stir it back into the pan. Add the measured water and tomato purée, then bring the soup to the boil.

4 Add the salt and the pasta. Cook, stirring occasionally, until the pasta is *al dente*. Stir in the parsley. Allow to stand for at least 10 minutes before serving in warmed bowls. Serve with grated Parmesan passed separately.

Cook's Tip
Drizzle a little extra virgin olive oil into each portion when serving, or top with a dollop of sun-dried tomato pesto.

Thick Spinach & Pasta Soup

A complete meal in a bowl, this is a version of a classic Italian soup. Traditionally, the person who finds the bay leaf is honoured with a kiss from the cook.

Serves 4

75ml/5 tbsp olive oil
1 onion, chopped
½ celeriac root
2 carrots, chopped
1 bay leaf
175ml/6fl oz/¾ cup white wine
1.2 litres/2 pints/5 cups Vegetable Stock
3 tomatoes, peeled and chopped
400g/14oz can borlotti beans, rinsed and drained
175g/6oz/1½ cups dried farfalle
250g/9oz spinach, washed and thick stalks removed
salt and freshly ground black pepper
50g/2oz/⅔ cup freshly grated Parmesan cheese, to serve

1 Heat the olive oil in a large saucepan and fry the onion, celeriac and carrots. Cook over a medium heat, stirring occasionally, for 5 minutes, or until the vegetables are beginning to soften.

2 Add the bay leaf, wine, stock and tomatoes, and bring to the boil. Lower the heat and simmer for 10 minutes, until the vegetables are just tender.

3 Add the beans, bring the soup back to the boil, then stir in the pasta. Simmer, stirring occasionally, until the pasta is *al dente*.

4 Season with salt and pepper to taste, add the spinach and cook for 2 minutes more. Serve in warmed bowls, sprinkled with the Parmesan.

Cook's Tip

Avoid buying very large celeriac roots, as they tend to be woody. Peel carefully with a sharp knife to remove all traces of the brown, knobbly skin. Don't chop the flesh until you are ready to cook it, as it is apt to discolour. If necessary, place the chopped pieces in water acidulated with a little lemon juice.

Rustic Lentil & Pasta Soup

A thick wedge of wholemeal bread is all that's needed to turn this hearty soup into a warming meal.

Serves 4–6

175g/6oz/¾ cup brown lentils
3 garlic cloves
1 litre/1¾ pints/4 cups water
45ml/3 tbsp olive oil
25g/1oz/2 tbsp butter
1 onion, finely chopped
2 celery sticks, finely chopped
1.75 litres/3 pints/7 cups Vegetable Stock
pared rind and juice of 1 orange
a few fresh marjoram leaves
a few fresh basil leaves
leaves from 1 fresh thyme sprig
50g/2oz/½ cup dried tubetti
salt and freshly ground black pepper
tiny fresh herb leaves, to garnish

1 Put the lentils in a large saucepan. Smash 1 garlic clove (there's no need to peel it first) and add it to the lentils. Pour in the measured water and bring to the boil. Lower the heat to a gentle simmer and cook, stirring occasionally, for 20 minutes, or until the lentils are just tender.

2 Tip the lentils into a sieve, remove the garlic and set it aside. Rinse the lentils under cold water, then leave them to drain.

3 Heat 30ml/2 tbsp of the oil with half the butter in a large saucepan. Add the onion and celery, and cook over a low heat, stirring frequently, for 5–7 minutes, until softened.

4 Crush the remaining garlic, then peel and mash the reserved garlic. Add to the vegetables with the remaining oil and the lentils. Stir, then add the stock, orange juice, the fresh herbs and salt and pepper to taste. Bring to the boil, then simmer for 30 minutes, stirring occasionally.

5 Cut the orange rind into thin strips, taking care to avoid including any of the bitter white pith. Add the pasta and orange rind strips to the soup and bring back to the boil, stirring. Cook until the pasta is *al dente*. Stir in the remaining butter and taste for seasoning. Serve in warmed bowls, sprinkled with the herb leaves.

Snapper & Tamarind Noodle Soup

Tamarind gives this light, fragrant noodle soup a slightly sour taste. It is available from Asian food stores and there is really no substitute.

Serves 4

2 litres/3½ pints/8 cups water
1 whole red snapper or mullet, about 1kg/2¼ lb, cleaned
1 onion, sliced
50g/2oz tamarind pods
15ml/1 tbsp fish sauce
15ml/1 tbsp sugar
30ml/2 tbsp vegetable oil
2 garlic cloves, finely chopped
2 lemon grass stalks, very finely chopped
4 ripe tomatoes, roughly chopped
30ml/2 tbsp yellow bean paste
225g/8oz rice vermicelli, soaked in warm water until soft
115g/4oz/2 cups beansprouts
8–10 fresh basil or mint sprigs
30ml/2 tbsp roasted peanuts, finely chopped
salt and freshly ground black pepper

1 Bring the measured water to the boil in a large, heavy-based saucepan. Lower the heat and add the fish, with the onion slices and 2.5ml/ ½ tsp salt. Simmer over a low heat until the fish is cooked through.

2 Carefully remove the fish from the stock and set it aside. Add the tamarind, fish sauce and sugar to the stock. Cook for about 5 minutes, then strain the stock into a large jug or bowl. Carefully remove all the bones from the fish, keeping the flesh in big pieces.

3 Heat the oil in a large frying pan. Add the garlic and lemon grass and stir-fry for a few seconds. Stir in the tomatoes and bean paste. Cook gently for 5–7 minutes, until the tomatoes have softened. Add the stock, bring back to a simmer and adjust the seasoning, if necessary.

4 Drain the vermicelli. Plunge it into a saucepan of boiling water for a few minutes, drain and divide among four warmed soup bowls. Add the beansprouts, fish and basil or mint. Top up each bowl with the hot soup and sprinkle the peanuts on top. Serve immediately.

Seafood Soup Noodles

Described as a soup, but very substantial, this would be the ideal choice for a late night, after-theatre supper with friends.

Serves 6

175g/6oz tiger prawns, peeled and deveined
225g/8oz monkfish fillet, cut into chunks
225/8oz salmon fillet, cut into chunks
5ml/1 tsp vegetable oil
15ml/1 tbsp dry white wine
225g/8oz dried egg noodles
1.2 litres/2 pints/5 cups fish stock
1 carrot, thinly sliced
225g/8oz asparagus, cut into 5cm/2in lengths
30ml/2 tbsp dark soy sauce
5ml/1 tsp sesame oil
salt and freshly ground black pepper
2 spring onions, cut into thin rings, to garnish

1 Mix the prawns and fish in a bowl. Add the vegetable oil and wine with 1.5ml/ ¼ tsp salt and a little pepper. Mix lightly, cover and marinate in a cool place for 15 minutes.

2 Bring a large saucepan of water to the boil and cook the noodles for 4 minutes, until just tender, or according to the instructions on the packet. Drain the noodles thoroughly and divide among six serving bowls. Keep hot.

3 Bring the fish stock to the boil in a separate pan. Add the prawns and monkfish, cook for 1 minute, then add the salmon and cook for 2 minutes more.

4 Using a slotted spoon, carefully lift the fish and prawns out of the fish stock, add to the noodles in the bowls and continue to keep hot.

5 Strain the stock through a sieve lined with muslin or cheesecloth into a clean pan. Bring to the boil and cook the carrot and asparagus for 2 minutes, then stir in the soy sauce and sesame oil.

6 Pour the stock and vegetables over the noodles and seafood, garnish with the spring onions and serve immediately.

Crab & Egg Noodle Broth

This delicious broth takes only minutes to make and is both nutritious and filling.

Serves 4

75g/3oz fine egg noodles
25g/1oz/2 tbsp butter
1 small bunch spring onions, chopped
1 celery stick, sliced
1 carrot, cut into batons
1.2 litres/2 pints/5 cups chicken stock
60ml/4 tbsp dry sherry
115g/4oz fresh or thawed frozen white crab meat, flaked
pinch of celery salt
pinch of cayenne pepper
10ml/2 tsp lemon juice
1 small bunch fresh coriander or flat leaf parsley, to garnish

1 Bring a large saucepan of salted water to the boil. Toss in the egg noodles and cook according to the instructions on the packet. Drain, cool under cold running water and leave immersed in water until required.

2 Heat the butter in another large pan, add the spring onions, celery and carrot, cover and cook the vegetables over a gentle heat for 3–4 minutes, until softened.

3 Add the chicken stock and sherry, bring to the boil, then lower the heat and cook for 5 minutes more.

4 Drain the noodles and add to the broth, together with the crab meat. Season to taste with celery salt and cayenne pepper, and sharpen with the lemon juice. Return to a simmer.

5 Ladle the broth into warmed shallow soup plates, scatter with roughly chopped coriander or parsley and serve.

Cook's Tip

For the best flavour, buy a freshly cooked crab and remove the meat yourself. Frozen crab meat, available from supermarkets, is a good substitute, but avoid canned crab, as this tastes rather bland and has a slightly soggy texture.

Variation

You could use other vegetables in season for this soup. Julienne strips of celeriac, broccoli spears or cauliflower florets would also work well.

Spicy Prawn & Noodle Soup

Diners spoon noodles into their bowls, followed by the accompaniments before ladling in the broth.

Serves 4–6

150g/5oz rice vermicelli, soaked in warm water until soft
25g/1oz/ ¼ cup raw cashew nuts, chopped
3 shallots, sliced
5cm/2in piece of lemon grass, shredded
2 garlic cloves, crushed
30ml/2 tbsp vegetable oil
15ml/1 tbsp fish sauce
15ml/1 tbsp mild curry paste
400ml/14fl oz/1⅔ cups canned coconut milk
½ chicken stock cube
450g/1lb white fish fillet, cut into bite-size pieces
225g/8oz raw prawns, peeled and deveined
prawn crackers, to serve

For the vegetable platter

1 small cos lettuce, shredded
115g/4oz/2 cups beansprouts
3 spring onions, shredded
½ cucumber, cut in matchstick strips

1 Drain the noodles. Cook them in a pan of lightly salted boiling water according to the packet instructions. Cool under running water and leave immersed in water until required.

2 Put the nuts in a mortar and grind them with a pestle. Add the shallots, lemon grass and garlic, and grind the mixture to a paste. Heat the oil in a large wok or pan and fry the paste for 1–2 minutes, or until the nuts begin to brown.

3 Stir the fish sauce and curry paste into the fried paste, then add the coconut milk. Crumble in the stock cube, stir well, then bring to simmering point. Simmer for 10 minutes.

4 Add the fish and prawns. Cook for 3–4 minutes, until the prawns have turned pink and the fish is translucent. Remove the seafood with a slotted spoon and arrange it in separate piles on a large platter. Drain the noodles well and heap them on the platter, with the vegetables and prawn crackers in neat piles.

5 Pour the coconut stock into a tureen or earthenware pot and serve with the platter of seafood and vegetables.

Seafood Laksa

The red chillies in the paste make this a very spicy soup.

Serves 4

4 fresh red chillies, seeded and roughly chopped
1 onion, roughly chopped
1cm/ ½ in cube shrimp paste
1 lemon grass stalk, chopped
1 small piece of fresh root ginger, roughly chopped
6 macadamia nuts
60ml/4 tbsp vegetable oil
5ml/1 tsp paprika
5ml/1 tsp ground turmeric
475ml/16fl oz/2 cups fish stock or water
600ml/1 pint/2½ cups canned coconut milk
dash of fish sauce
12 raw king prawns, peeled and deveined
8 scallops, shelled
225g/8oz prepared squid, cut into rings
350g/12oz rice vermicelli, soaked in warm water until soft
salt and freshly ground black pepper
lime halves, to serve

For the garnish

¼ cucumber, cut into matchsticks
2 fresh red chillies, seeded and finely sliced
30ml/2 tbsp fresh mint leaves
30ml/2 tbsp fried shallots or onions

1 In a blender or food processor, process the chillies, onion, shrimp paste, lemon grass, ginger and nuts until smooth.

2 Heat 45ml/3 tbsp of the oil in a large saucepan. Add the chilli paste and fry for 6 minutes. Stir in the paprika and turmeric, and fry for 2 minutes more.

3 Pour in the stock or water and the coconut milk. Bring to the boil, lower the heat and simmer gently for 15–20 minutes. Season to taste with the fish sauce.

4 Season the seafood with salt and pepper. Heat the remaining oil in a frying pan and fry the seafood for 2–3 minutes.

5 Add the noodles to the soup and heat through. Divide among warmed serving bowls. Place the fried seafood on top, then garnish with the cucumber, chillies, mint and fried shallots or onions. Serve with the lime halves.

Chicken Soup with Noodles

Warm spices such as paprika and cinnamon give this chicken soup a superb flavour.

Serves 4–6

30ml/2 tbsp sunflower oil
15g/ ½ oz/1 tbsp butter
1 onion, chopped
2 chicken legs quartered
2 carrots, cut into 4cm/ 1½ in pieces
1 parsnip, cut into 4cm/ 1½ in pieces
1.5 litres/2½ pints/6 cups chicken stock
1 cinnamon stick
good pinch of paprika
2 egg yolks
juice of ½ lemon
30ml/2 tbsp chopped fresh coriander
30ml/2 tbsp chopped fresh parsley
pinch of saffron strands, soaked for 10 minutes in 30ml/2 tbsp boiling water
150g/5oz egg noodles
salt and freshly ground black pepper

1 Heat the oil and butter in a large saucepan and fry the onion until softened. Add the chicken pieces and fry them with the onion until brown on all sides.

2 Transfer the chicken to a plate, and add the carrot and parsnip pieces to the pan. Cook over a low heat, stirring frequently, for 3–4 minutes, then return the chicken to the pan. Stir in the stock, cinnamon stick and paprika. Season well. Bring to the boil, lower the heat, cover and simmer for 1 hour, until the vegetables are very tender.

3 Beat the egg yolks with the lemon juice in a bowl. Add the chopped coriander and parsley, then stir in the saffron water.

4 Lift the chicken pieces out of the soup and put them on a plate. Spoon off any fat from the soup, then increase the heat and stir in the noodles. Cook until the noodles are *al dente*.

5 Meanwhile, skin the chicken and chop the flesh into bite-size pieces. Add to the soup, with the egg mixture. Cook over a very low heat for 1–2 minutes, stirring all the time. Adjust the seasoning and serve.

Chicken Noodle Soup

Just like Grandma used to make, this is comfort food, pure and simple.

Serves 8

1 chicken, about 1.4kg/3lb, cut into pieces
2 onions, quartered
1 parsnip, quartered
2 carrots, quartered
2.5ml/ ½ tsp salt
1 bay leaf
2 allspice berries
4 black peppercorns
1.5 litres/2½ pints/6 cups water
115g/4oz very thin egg noodles
fresh dill sprigs, to garnish

1 Put the chicken pieces, onions, parsnip, carrots, salt, bay leaf, allspice berries and peppercorns in a large saucepan.

2 Add the measured water. Bring to the boil, skimming the surface frequently, then lower the heat and simmer for about 1½ hours, skimming occasionally.

3 Strain the stock into a large bowl. Discard the vegetables and flavourings in the strainer, but remove the chicken pieces and set them aside.

4 When the chicken pieces are cool enough to handle, skin them and chop the flesh into bite-size pieces. Put these in a bowl. When both the chicken and the stock are cold, cover both the bowls and put them in the fridge overnight.

5 Next day, remove the solidified fat from the surface of the chilled stock. Pour it into a saucepan and bring to the boil.

6 Add the chicken and noodles, and cook until the noodles are *al dente*. Serve in warmed bowls, garnished with dill sprigs.

Cook's Tip
If you haven't got time to chill the chicken stock in the fridge overnight, just blot the surface several times with kitchen paper to remove the excess fat.

Cock-a-Noodle Soup

Take a tasty trip to the Far East, with this quick and easy Chinese-style soup.

Serves 4–6

15ml/1 tbsp corn oil
4 spring onions, roughly chopped
225g/8oz skinless, boneless chicken breasts, cut into small cubes
1.2 litres/2 pints/5 cups chicken stock
15ml/1 tbsp soy sauce
115g/4oz/1 cup frozen sweetcorn niblets
115g/4oz medium egg noodles
salt and freshly ground black pepper
1 carrot, thinly sliced lengthways, to garnish

1 Heat the oil in a saucepan and fry the spring onions and chicken until the meat is evenly browned.

2 Add the stock and the soy sauce and bring to the boil, then stir in the sweetcorn.

3 Add the noodles, breaking them up roughly. Taste the soup and add salt and pepper if needed.

4 Use small cutters to stamp out shapes from the thin slices of carrot. Add them to the soup. Simmer for 5 minutes. Serve in warmed bowls.

Summer Minestrone

This brightly coloured, fresh-tasting soup makes the most of summer vegetables. Peperini are very tiny, but you could use larger pasta shapes if preferred.

Serves 4

15ml/1 tbsp olive oil
1 large onion, finely chopped
15ml/1 tbsp sun-dried tomato purée
450g/1lb ripe Italian plum tomatoes, peeled and finely chopped
225g/8oz green courgettes, trimmed and roughly chopped
225g/8oz yellow courgettes, trimmed and roughly chopped
3 waxy new potatoes, diced
2 garlic cloves, crushed
about 1.2 litres/2 pints/5 cups light chicken stock or water
25g/1oz/ ¼ cup peperini
60ml/4 tbsp shredded fresh basil
salt and freshly ground black pepper
grated Parmesan cheese, to serve (optional)

1 Heat the oil in a large saucepan. Add the onion and cook over a low heat, stirring constantly, for about 5 minutes, until softened. Stir in the sun-dried tomato purée, chopped tomatoes, courgettes, diced potatoes and garlic. Mix well and cook gently for 10 minutes, uncovered, shaking the pan frequently to stop the vegetables from sticking to the base.
2 Pour in the stock or water and bring to the boil. Add the peperini, lower the heat, half cover the pan and simmer gently for 10–15 minutes or until both the vegetables and the pasta are just tender. Add more stock if necessary.
3 Remove the pan from the heat and stir in the basil. Taste for seasoning and adjust, if necessary. Serve hot, sprinkled with a little Parmesan, if you like.

Noodles in Soup

Although this is known as *tang mein* – "noodles in soup" – in China, there is much less liquid than you would find in a conventional soup. The "dressing", which in this recipe comprises chicken or pork and vegetables, makes the dish quite substantial.

Serves 4

225g/8oz skinless, boneless chicken breasts or pork fillet
3–4 Chinese dried mushrooms, soaked in water for 30 minutes
115g/4oz/⅔ cup sliced bamboo shoots, drained
115g/4oz spinach leaves, lettuce hearts, or Chinese leaves
2 spring onions
350g/12oz dried egg noodles
600ml/1 pint/2½ cups chicken stock
30ml/2 tbsp vegetable oil
5ml/1 tsp salt
2.5ml/½ tsp light brown sugar
15ml/1 tbsp light soy sauce
10ml/2 tsp Chinese rice wine or dry sherry
a few drops of sesame oil

1 Shred the chicken or pork thinly. Drain the mushrooms, squeeze them dry and discard any hard stalks. Shred the mushrooms, bamboo shoots and spinach, lettuce or Chinese leaves and put them in a bowl. Shred the spring onions and put them in a separate bowl.

2 Cook the noodles in boiling water, following the instructions on the packet, then drain and rinse under cold water. Drain again and place in a serving bowl.

3 Bring the stock to the boil in a saucepan. Pour it over the noodles and keep them warm.

4 Heat the vegetable oil in a preheated wok, add about half the spring onions and all the meat, and stir-fry for about 1 minute. Add the mushroom mixture and stir-fry for 1 minute.

5 Stir in the salt, brown sugar, soy sauce, rice wine or sherry and sesame oil. Mix well, then pour the "dressing" over the noodles. Garnish with the remaining spring onions and serve in warmed shallow soup plates.

Thai Chicken Soup

Hot chilli, cool coconut and peanut butter are just some of the ingredients of this delicious and unusual soup.

Serves 4

15ml/1 tbsp vegetable oil
1 garlic clove, finely chopped
2 skinless, boneless chicken breasts, about 175g/6oz each, chopped
2.5ml/½ tsp ground turmeric
1.5ml/¼ tsp hot chilli powder
75g/3oz creamed coconut
900ml/1½ pints/3¾ cups hot chicken stock
30ml/2 tbsp freshly squeezed lemon or lime juice
30ml/2 tbsp crunchy peanut butter
50g/2oz dried egg thread noodles, broken into small pieces
15ml/1 tbsp finely chopped spring onion
15ml/1 tbsp chopped fresh coriander
salt and freshly ground black pepper
30ml/2 tbsp desiccated coconut and ½ fresh red chilli, seeded and finely chopped, to garnish

1 Heat the oil in a large, heavy-based saucepan. Add the garlic and fry for 1 minute, until lightly golden. Add the chicken, turmeric and chilli powder, and stir-fry for 3–4 minutes more, until the chicken is golden.

2 Crumble the creamed coconut into the hot chicken stock and stir until dissolved. Pour on to the chicken mixture and stir in the lemon or lime juice, peanut butter and egg noodles. Bring to the boil over a medium heat.

3 Lower the heat, cover the pan and simmer gently for about 15 minutes. Add the chopped spring onions and fresh coriander, and season well with salt and pepper. Stir well and cook for 5 minutes more.

4 Meanwhile, place the coconut and chilli for the garnish in a small frying pan. Heat for 2–3 minutes, stirring frequently, until the coconut is lightly browned.

5 Serve the soup in warmed bowls and sprinkle each portion with the fried coconut and chilli.

Chiang Mai Noodle Soup

A signature dish of the Thai city of Chiang Mai, this is a delicious soup.

Serves 4–6
600ml/1 pint/2½ cups canned coconut milk
30ml/2 tbsp bottled red curry paste
5ml/1 tsp ground turmeric
450g/1lb skinless, boneless chicken thighs, cut into bite-size chunks
600ml/1 pint/2½ cups chicken stock
60ml/4 tbsp fish sauce
15ml/1 tbsp dark soy sauce
juice of 1 lime
450g/1lb fresh egg noodles, blanched briefly in boiling water

For the garnish
3 spring onions, chopped
4 fresh red chillies, chopped
4 shallots, chopped
60ml/4 tbsp sliced pickled mustard leaves, rinsed
30ml/2 tbsp fried sliced garlic
fresh coriander leaves

1 Pour one-third of the coconut milk into a large saucepan. Bring to the boil, stirring with a wooden spoon, until it separates.

2 Stir in the curry paste and ground turmeric, and cook until fragrant, then add the chicken. Stir-fry for about 2 minutes, ensuring that all the chunks are coated with the paste.

3 Stir in the remaining coconut milk, the chicken stock, fish sauce and soy sauce. Bring to the boil, then simmer gently for 7–10 minutes. Remove from the heat and stir in the lime juice.

4 Reheat the noodles in boiling water, drain and divide among warmed individual bowls. Divide the soup among the bowls, making sure that the chicken pieces are evenly distributed. Top each serving with a little of each of the garnishes.

Cook's Tip
The quantity of fish sauce suggested here will give the soup quite a pronounced flavour. If you are not sure you will like it, start by using less.

Chicken & Buckwheat Noodle Soup

Buckwheat or soba noodles, served in hot, deliciously seasoned broth, are very popular in Japan.

Serves 4
225g/8oz skinless, boneless chicken breasts
120ml/4fl oz/½ cup soy sauce
15ml/1 tbsp saké
1 litres/1¾ pints/4 cups chicken stock
2 pieces of young leek, cut into 2.5cm/1in strips
175g/6oz spinach leaves, shredded
300g/11oz buckwheat or soba noodles
toasted sesame seeds, to garnish

1 Slice the chicken diagonally into bite-size pieces. Combine the soy sauce and saké in a saucepan. Bring to a simmer over a low heat. Add the chicken and cook gently for about 3 minutes, until it is tender. Keep hot.

2 Bring the stock to the boil in a separate saucepan. Add the leek strips and simmer for 3 minutes, then add the spinach. Remove from the heat but keep hot.

3 Cook the noodles in a large saucepan of boiling water, following the instructions on the packet, until *al dente*.

4 Drain the noodles and divide them among warmed shallow bowls. Ladle the hot soup into the bowls, then add a portion of chicken to each. Serve at once, sprinkled with sesame seeds.

Cook's Tips
- *If you make your own chicken stock for this recipe, flavour it with 2 slices of fresh root ginger, 2 garlic cloves, 4 spring onions, 2 celery sticks, a handful of coriander stalks and a few crushed black peppercorns.*
- *For an authentic flavour, use Japanese soy sauce, which is not as strong as Chinese. Known as shoyu, it is available from speciality stores and some supermarkets. Best for clear broths, usukuchi soy sauce is light coloured and quite salty.*

Pork & Noodle Broth with Prawns

The combination of pork and prawns works well in this tasty soup from Vietnam.

Serves 4–6

150g/5oz fine dried egg noodles
15ml/1 tbsp vegetable oil
10ml/2 tsp sesame oil
4 shallots, sliced
15ml/1 tbsp grated fresh root ginger
1 garlic clove, crushed
5ml/1 tsp granulated sugar
1.5 litres/2½ pints/6 cups chicken stock
2 lime leaves
45ml/3 tbsp fish sauce
juice of ½ lime
200g/7oz pork fillet, thinly sliced
225g/8oz raw tiger prawns, peeled and deveined
fresh coriander leaves and chopped spring onion green, to garnish

1 Bring a large saucepan of lightly salted water to the boil. Add the egg noodles and cook according to the instructions on the packet. Drain, refresh under cold running water and drain again. Set aside.

2 Heat the vegetable oil and sesame oil in a large saucepan, add the shallots and stir-fry for 3–4 minutes. Remove from the pan with a slotted spoon and set aside.

3 Add the ginger, garlic, sugar and chicken stock to the pan, together with the lime leaves. Heat until simmering, then stir in the fish sauce and lime juice. Add the pork and simmer for 15 minutes, until tender.

4 Add the prawns and noodles, and simmer for 3–4 minutes. Serve in warmed shallow soup bowls and garnish each portion with coriander, spring onion green and the browned shallots.

Cook's Tips

- *If you pop the pork fillet into the freezer for 30 minutes it will be much easier to slice thinly.*
- *You can also make this with 200g/7oz chicken breast fillet.*

Soupy Noodles, Malay-style

Savour this soup slowly – every mouthful is a medley of marvellous flavours.

Serves 4

15ml/1 tbsp vegetable oil
2 garlic cloves, crushed
2 shallots, chopped
900ml/1½ pints/3¾ cups chicken stock
225g/8oz lean beef or pork, thinly sliced
150g/5oz fish balls
4 raw king prawns, peeled and deveined
350g/12oz dried medium egg noodles
115g/4oz watercress
salt and freshly ground black pepper

For the garnish
115g/4oz/2 cups beansprouts
2 spring onions, sliced
15ml/1 tbsp coriander leaves
2 fresh red chillies, seeded and chopped
30ml/2 tbsp deep-fried onions

1 Heat the oil in a saucepan, fry the garlic and shallots for 1 minute, then stir in the stock. Bring to the boil, then lower the heat, add the beef or pork, fish balls and prawns, and simmer for about 2 minutes.

2 Meanwhile, bring a large saucepan of water to the boil, carefully add the noodles and cook until *al dente*. Drain them well and divide among warmed shallow serving bowls.

3 Season the soup with salt and pepper then add the watercress (the hot soup will cook it instantly).

4 Scoop out the beef or pork, fish balls, prawns and watercress from the soup and arrange over the noodles. Pour the hot soup on top. Serve at once, sprinkling each portion with a little of each of the garnishes.

Cook's Tip

Fish balls can be purchased from Chinese food markets. Look out for beef and squid balls, if you fancy a variation on this.

Noodle Soup with Pork & Pickle

A satisfying and warming soup from western China, a region famous for its delicious spicy pickles.

Serves 4

1 litre/1¾ pints/4 cups chicken stock
350g/12oz dried medium egg noodles
15ml/1 tbsp dried shrimp, soaked in water
30ml/2 tbsp vegetable oil
225g/8oz lean pork, finely shredded
15ml/1 tbsp yellow bean paste
15ml/1 tbsp soy sauce
115g/4oz Szechuan hot pickle, rinsed, drained and shredded
pinch of granulated sugar
salt and freshly ground black pepper
2 spring onions, finely sliced, to garnish

1 Bring the chicken stock to the boil in a large saucepan. Add the egg noodles and cook until almost tender. Drain the dried shrimp, rinse under cold running water, drain again and add to the stock. Lower the heat and simmer for 2 minutes. Season to taste. Keep hot.

2 Heat the oil in a frying pan or wok. Add the pork and stir-fry over a high heat for about 3 minutes.

3 Add the yellow bean paste and soy sauce to the pork and stir-fry for 1 minute, then add the hot pickle and sugar. Stir-fry for 1 minute more.

4 Divide the noodles and stock among warmed soup bowls. Spoon the pork mixture on top, then sprinkle with the spring onions and serve at once.

Cook's Tip

Available in cans from Chinese food stores, Szechuan hot pickle is based on kohlrabi. It has a very spicy and salty flavour. Other Chinese pickles that could be used include the milder winter pickle, made from salted cabbage or the sour snow pickle, made from salted mustard greens.

Hanoi Beef & Noodle Soup

Millions of Vietnamese enjoy this fragrant and sustaining soup for breakfast.

Serves 4–6

1 onion
1.5kg/3–3½lb beef shank with bones
1 bay leaf
2.5cm/1in piece of fresh root ginger
1 star anise
2 whole cloves
2.5ml/½ tsp fennel seeds
1 piece of cassia bark or cinnamon stick
3 litres/5 pints/12 cups water
dash of fish sauce
juice of 1 lime
150g/5oz fillet steak
450g/1lb fresh flat rice noodles
salt

For the garnish accompaniments

1 small red onion, sliced into rings
115g/4oz/2 cups beansprouts
2 fresh red chillies, seeded and sliced
2 spring onions, finely sliced
a handful of fresh coriander leaves
lime wedges

1 Cut the onion in half. Grill under a high heat, cut side up, until the exposed sides are caramelized, and deep brown. Set aside.

2 Cut the meat into large chunks and place with the bones in a large saucepan. Add the caramelized onion, bay leaf, ginger, star anise, cloves, fennel seeds and cassia bark or cinnamon.

3 Pour in the measured water, bring to the boil, then lower the heat and simmer for 2–3 hours, skimming occasionally.

4 Remove the meat from the stock. When cool enough to handle, cut it into small pieces, discarding the bones. Strain the stock and return to the pan with the meat. Bring back to the boil and season with the fish sauce and lime juice.

5 Slice the fillet steak very thinly. Place the garnishes in separate serving bowls. Cook the noodles in a large saucepan of lightly salted boiling water until *al dente*. Drain and divide among warmed bowls. Top with the steak, ladle hot stock over and serve, offering the accompaniments separately.

Star-gazer Vegetable Soup

If you have time, it is worth making your own vegetable stock for this soup.

Serves 4

1 yellow pepper
2 large courgettes
2 large carrots
1 kohlrabi
900ml/1½ pints/3¾ cups well-flavoured Vegetable Stock
50g/2oz rice vermicelli
salt and freshly ground black pepper

1 Cut the pepper into quarters, removing the seeds and core. Cut the courgettes and carrots lengthways into 5mm/ ¼in slices and slice the kohlrabi into 5mm/ ¼in rounds.

2 Using tiny confectionery cutters, stamp out decorative shapes from the vegetables. Place in a pan, add the stock and bring to the boil. Lower the heat and simmer for 10 minutes. Season.

3 Meanwhile, place the vermicelli in a heatproof bowl, cover with boiling water and set aside for 4 minutes. Drain, divide among four warmed soup bowls, ladle the hot soup over and serve.

Vegetable Stock

This is a delicately flavoured stock, suitable for many clear broths and soups.

Makes about 2.5 litres/ 4 pints/10 cups

2 onions, chopped
2 leeks, sliced
3 garlic cloves, crushed
2 carrots, chopped
4 celery sticks, sliced
a large strip of pared lemon rind
12 parsley stalks
a few fresh thyme sprigs
2 bay leaves
2.5 litres/4 pints/10 cups water

1 Put the ingredients in a large saucepan. Bring to the boil. Skim the surface, lower the heat and simmer for 30 minutes.

2 Strain the stock and leave to cool.

Cheat's Shark's Fin Soup

Shark's fin soup is a renowned delicacy. In this poor man's vegetarian version, cellophane noodles, cut into short lengths, mimic shark's fin needles.

Serves 4–6

4 dried Chinese mushrooms
25ml/1½ tbsp dried wood ears
115g/4oz cellophane noodles
30ml/2 tbsp vegetable oil
2 carrots, cut into fine strips
114g/4oz canned bamboo shoots, rinsed, drained and cut into fine strips
1 litre/1¾ pints/4 cups Vegetable Stock
15ml/1 tbsp soy sauce
15ml/1 tbsp arrowroot, mixed to a paste with 30ml/2 tbsp water
5ml/1 tsp sesame oil
salt and freshly ground black pepper
2 spring onions, finely chopped, to garnish

1 Soak the mushrooms and wood ears separately in warm water for 20 minutes. Drain well. Remove and discard the stems from the mushrooms and slice the caps thinly. Cut the wood ears into fine strips, discarding any hard bits. Soak the noodles in hot water until soft. Drain and cut into short lengths. Leave until required.

2 Heat the oil in a large, heavy-based saucepan. Add the mushrooms and stir-fry over a medium heat for 2 minutes. Add the wood ears and stir-fry for 2 minutes, then stir in the carrots, bamboo shoots and noodles.

3 Add the vegetable stock to the pan. Bring to the boil, lower the heat and simmer gently for 15–20 minutes. Season to taste with salt and pepper, and stir in the soy sauce.

4 Pour the arrowroot paste into the soup, stirring all the time to prevent the formation of lumps as the soup continues to simmer. Allow to thicken slightly.

5 Remove the pan from the heat. Stir in the sesame oil, then pour the soup into warmed individual soup bowls. Sprinkle each portion with chopped spring onions to garnish, and serve immediately.

Vegetable & Vermicelli Noodle Soup

With neatly shredded greens, thinly sliced mushrooms and fine noodles, this soup looks as good as it tastes.

Serves 4

1.2 litres/2 pints/5 cups Vegetable Stock
1 whole garlic clove, bruised
2.5cm/1in piece of fresh root ginger, cut into fine matchsticks
30ml/2 tbsp soy sauce
15ml/1 tbsp cider vinegar
75g/3oz/1 cup fresh shiitake or button mushrooms, stalks removed and thinly sliced
2 large spring onions, thinly sliced on the diagonal
40g/1½oz rice vermicelli or other fine noodles
175g/6oz Chinese leaves, finely shredded
a few fresh coriander leaves

1 Pour the stock into a saucepan. Add the garlic, ginger, soy sauce and vinegar. Bring to the boil, then cover the pan and reduce the heat to very low. Simmer gently for 10 minutes. Remove and discard the garlic clove.

2 Add the mushrooms and spring onions, and bring the soup back to the boil. Simmer for 5 minutes, stirring occasionally.

3 Add the noodles and shredded Chinese leaves. Simmer for 3–4 minutes, or until the noodles and vegetables are just tender. Stir in the coriander leaves. Simmer for 1 minute more, then serve in warmed soup bowls.

Cook's Tips

• *To bruise the peeled garlic clove, crush it lightly with the blade of a cook's knife.*

• *To shred the Chinese leaves, stack them 6–8 at a time and roll up tightly parallel with the central rib. If the leaves are very large, roll them individually. With a very sharp knife, slice across the roll of leaves into fine shreds, guiding the side of the knife with the knuckles of the hand holding the roll. Be sure to cut straight down through the roll to avoid unattractive bruising on the leaves.*

Japanese-style Noodle Soup

This delicate, fragrant soup is flavoured with the slightest hint of chilli.

Serves 4

1 litre/1¾ pints/4 cups water
45ml/3 tbsp mugi miso
200g/7oz udon noodles, soba noodles or Chinese egg noodles
30ml/2 tbsp saké or dry sherry
15ml/1 tbsp rice vinegar
45ml/3 tbsp Japanese soy sauce
115g/4oz asparagus tips or mangetouts, thinly sliced on the diagonal
50g/2oz/scant 1 cup shiitake mushrooms, stalks removed and thinly sliced
1 carrot, sliced into matchstick strips
3 spring onions, thinly sliced on the diagonal
salt and freshly ground black pepper
5ml/1 tsp dried chilli flakes, to serve

1 Bring the measured water to the boil in a saucepan. Put the miso in a heatproof bowl. Pour over 150ml/ ¼ pint/ ⅔ cup of the boiling water and stir until dissolved, then set aside.

2 Meanwhile, cook the noodles in a separate pan of boiling water until just tender. Drain, rinse under cold water, then drain again. Set aside.

3 Add the saké or sherry, vinegar and soy sauce to the pan of boiling water. Boil gently for 3 minutes, then lower the heat and stir in the miso mixture. Add the asparagus or mangetouts, mushrooms, carrot and spring onions. Simmer for 2 minutes or until the vegetables are just tender. Season to taste.

4 Divide the noodles among four warmed bowls and pour the soup over. Serve immediately, sprinkled with the chilli flakes.

Cook's Tip

Miso is made from fermented soya beans and is available as both a paste and a powder. There are several different varieties.

Sicilian Spaghetti with Sardines

Serving crisply fried sardines on a bed of spaghetti tossed with pine nuts and raisins is simply inspirational.

Serves 4

12 fresh sardines, cleaned and boned
50g/2oz/1 cup fresh white breadcrumbs
250ml/8fl oz/1 cup olive oil
1 onion, chopped
25g/1oz/¼ oz cup fresh dill sprigs
25g/1oz/3 tbsp raisins, soaked in water
50g/2oz/½ cup pine nuts
450g/1lb spaghetti
flour, for dusting
salt

1 Wash the sardines and pat them dry on kitchen paper. Open them out flat, then cut them in half lengthways. Set them aside. Spread out the breadcrumbs in a large ungreased frying pan and dry-fry them until golden.

2 Heat 30ml/2 tbsp of the oil in a saucepan and fry the onion for 4–5 minutes. Add the dill and cook over a low heat for 1 minute. Drain the raisins and add them to the pan, with the pine nuts. Season with salt and keep warm over a low heat.

3 Bring a large saucepan of lightly salted water to the boil. Add the spaghetti and cook until *al dente*.

4 Meanwhile, heat the remaining oil in a large frying pan. Dust the sardines with flour and fry them in the hot oil for 2–3 minutes. Drain on kitchen paper.

5 Drain the spaghetti and return it to the clean pan. Add the onion mixture and toss well. Spread out the spaghetti mixture on a large serving platter and arrange the fried sardines on top. Sprinkle with the toasted breadcrumbs and serve immediately.

Cook's Tip

To scale the fish, hold it under cold running water by the tail and gently run your finger and thumb along the body.

Noodles with Tomatoes, Sardines & Mustard

Every cook needs some simple recipes made with store-cupboard ingredients. This one is a real winner.

Serves 4

350g/12oz tagliatelle or broad egg noodles
225g/8oz ripe tomatoes, roughly chopped
1 small red onion, finely chopped
1 green pepper, seeded and finely diced
60ml/4 tbsp chopped fresh parsley
225g/8oz drained canned sardines
salt and freshly ground black pepper
croûtons, to serve (optional)

For the dressing
60ml/4 tbsp olive oil
30ml/2 tbsp lemon juice
15ml/1 tbsp wholegrain mustard
1 garlic clove, finely chopped

1 Bring a large saucepan of lightly salted water to the boil. Add the noodles and cook until *al dente*.

2 Meanwhile, make the dressing. Whisk together the oil, lemon juice, mustard and garlic in a small bowl, then season with salt and pepper to taste.

3 Drain the noodles, tip them into a large bowl and toss with the dressing. Add the tomatoes, onion, pepper, parsley and sardines, and toss lightly again. Season to taste and serve immediately, with crisp croûtons, if using.

Cook's Tip

To make croûtons, cut the crusts off 50g/2oz day-old bread (about 2 thick slices). Cut the bread into 5mm/¼in squares or stamp into an attractive shape with a cutter. Heat 30 ml/2 tbsp olive oil in a frying pan, add the bread and sauté, stirring and tossing constantly, until golden all over. Drain on kitchen paper. For garlic-flavoured croûtons, stir a large clove of garlic in the oil until golden, then remove before adding the bread.

Farfalle with Tuna

A quick and simple dish that makes a good weekday supper if you have canned tomatoes and tuna in the store cupboard.

Serves 4

30ml/2 tbsp olive oil
1 small onion, finely chopped
1 garlic clove, finely chopped
400g/14oz can chopped tomatoes
45ml/3 tbsp dry white wine
8–10 stoned black olives, cut into rings
10ml/2 tsp chopped fresh oregano or 5ml/1 tsp dried, plus extra fresh oregano to garnish
400g/14oz/3½ cups dried farfalle
175g/6oz can tuna in olive oil, drained and flaked
salt and freshly ground black pepper

1 Heat the olive oil in a large, heavy-based saucepan. Add the onion and garlic and fry gently for 2–3 minutes, until the onion is soft and golden.

2 Stir in the tomatoes. Bring to the boil, then add the white wine and simmer for 1–2 minutes. Stir in the olives and oregano, and season with salt and pepper to taste. Cover and cook for 20–25 minutes, stirring from time to time.

3 Meanwhile, cook the pasta in a large saucepan of lightly salted boiling water until *al dente*.

4 Add the tuna to the sauce with about 60ml/4 tbsp of the water used for cooking the pasta. Taste and adjust the seasoning, if necessary.

5 Drain the cooked pasta well and tip it into a warmed large serving bowl. Pour the tuna sauce over the top and toss to mix. Serve immediately, garnished with oregano sprigs.

Spaghetti with Tuna & Anchovies

This simple pasta dish is fresh, light and full of flavour. Serve it as soon as it is cooked to enjoy it at its very best.

Serves 4

300g/11oz dried spaghetti
30ml/2 tbsp olive oil
6 ripe Italian plum tomatoes, chopped
5ml/1 tsp granulated sugar
50g/2oz jar anchovies in olive oil, drained
about 60ml/4 tbsp dry white wine
200g/7oz can tuna in olive oil, drained
50g/2oz/½ cup stoned black olives, quartered lengthways
125g/4½ oz packet mozzarella cheese, drained and diced
salt and freshly ground black pepper
fresh basil leaves, to garnish

1 Bring a large pan of lightly salted water to the boil, add the pasta and cook until it is *al dente*.

2 Meanwhile, heat the oil in a medium saucepan. Add the tomatoes and sugar, and season with pepper to taste. Toss over a medium heat for a few minutes, until the tomatoes have softened and the juices run.

3 Using kitchen scissors, snip a few anchovies at a time into the pan of tomatoes. Add the wine, tuna and olives, and stir once or twice until they are evenly mixed into the sauce.

4 Add the mozzarella and heat through without stirring. Taste and add salt, if necessary.

5 Drain the pasta and tip it into a warmed bowl. Pour the sauce over, toss gently and sprinkle with the basil leaves to garnish. Serve immediately.

Cook's Tip

Plum tomatoes have firmer flesh and are less watery than many other varieties. Look for sun-ripened specimens, which will be sweeter and have more flavour than glasshouse tomatoes.

Rigatoni with Tomato & Tuna Sauce

Ridged pasta tubes are perfect for this dish as they trap the delectable sauce.

Serves 4

30ml/2 tbsp olive oil
1 onion, chopped
2 garlic cloves, chopped
400g/14oz can chopped tomatoes
60ml/4 tbsp tomato purée
350g/12oz dried rigatoni
50g/2oz/ ½ cup stoned black olives, quartered
5ml/1 tsp dried fresh oregano
225g/8oz can tuna in oil, drained and flaked
2.5ml/ ½ tsp anchovy purée
15ml/1 tbsp bottled capers, rinsed and drained
115g/4oz/1 cup grated Cheddar cheese
45ml/3 tbsp fresh white breadcrumbs
salt and freshly ground black pepper
fresh flat leaf parsley sprigs, to garnish

1 Heat the oil in a frying pan and fry the onion and garlic for about 10 minutes, until softened. Stir in the tomatoes and tomato purée, with salt and pepper to taste. Bring to the boil, then simmer gently for 10–15 minutes, stirring occasionally.

2 Meanwhile, bring a large saucepan of lightly salted water to the boil. Add the pasta and cook until *al dente.*

3 Stir the olives, oregano, tuna, anchovy purée and capers into the tomato sauce. Heat through for 2 minutes, then spoon the mixture into a bowl. Drain the pasta, toss it with the sauce, then divide it among four heatproof serving bowls.

4 Combine the cheese and breadcrumbs, and sprinkle a quarter of the mixture over each portion. Place under a hot grill until the cheese has melted. Serve immediately, garnished with the flat leaf parsley.

Cook's Tip
This speedy sauce is perfect for impromptu suppers, because most of the ingredients are standard store-cupboard items.

Tagliatelle with Avocado & Haddock Sauce

Start making this dish the day before you plan to serve it, as the haddock needs to marinate overnight.

Serves 4

2.5ml/ ½ tsp each ground cumin, ground coriander and ground turmeric
150ml/ ¼ pint/ ⅔ cup fromage frais
150ml/ ¼ pint/ ⅔ cup double cream
15ml/1 tbsp lemon juice
350g/12oz fresh haddock fillets, skinned and cut into bite-size chunks
25g/1oz/2 tbsp butter
1 onion, chopped
15ml/1 tbsp plain flour
150ml/ ¼ pint/ ⅔ cup fish stock
350g/12oz fresh tagliatelle
1 avocado, peeled, stoned and sliced
2 tomatoes, seeded and chopped
salt and freshly ground black pepper
fresh rosemary sprigs, to garnish

1 Mix the cumin, coriander, turmeric, fromage frais, cream and lemon juice in a bowl. Add a little salt and pepper, then stir in the haddock until all the chunks are coated. Cover and marinate in the fridge overnight.

2 Heat the butter in a frying pan and fry the onion over a low heat for about 10 minutes, until softened. Stir in the flour, then blend in the stock until smooth.

3 Carefully stir in the haddock mixture. Cook over a medium heat, stirring frequently, until the haddock is cooked.

4 Meanwhile, bring a pan of lightly salted water to the boil, add the pasta and cook until it is *al dente.*

5 Gently stir the avocado slices and chopped tomatoes into the haddock mixture.

6 Drain the pasta and return it to the pan. Pour over the sauce and toss gently to mix. Divide among four serving plates, garnish with the fresh rosemary and serve.

Fish with Fregola

This is a cross between a soup and a stew. Serve it with crusty Italian bread.

Serves 4–6

75ml/5 tbsp olive oil
4 garlic cloves, finely chopped
½ small fresh red chilli, seeded and finely chopped
1 large handful fresh flat leaf parsley, roughly chopped
1 red snapper, about 450g/1lb, cleaned, with head and tail removed
1 red or grey mullet, about 500g/1¼lb, cleaned, with head and tail removed
350–450g/12oz–1lb thick cod fillet
400g/14oz can chopped tomatoes
175g/6oz/1½ cups dried fregola or any other very tiny pasta shapes, such as corallini
250ml/8fl oz/1 cup water
salt and freshly ground black pepper
ciabatta, to serve

1 Heat 30ml/2 tbsp of the olive oil in a large flameproof casserole. Add the chopped garlic and chilli, with about half the chopped fresh parsley. Fry over a medium heat, stirring occasionally, for about 5 minutes.

2 Cut all of the fish into large chunks – including the skin and the bones in the case of the snapper and mullet – adding the pieces to the casserole as you cut them. Sprinkle the fish with a further 30ml/2 tbsp of the olive oil and fry for a few minutes.

3 Add the tomatoes, then fill the empty can with water and pour this into the pan. Bring to the boil. Season with salt and pepper to taste, stir well, lower the heat and cook, stirring occasionally for 10 minutes.

4 Add the fregola or other pasta shapes and simmer for 5 minutes, then add the measured water and the remaining olive oil. Simmer until the pasta is *al dente*.

5 If the sauce becomes too thick, add more water, then taste for seasoning and adjust, if necessary. Serve hot in warmed bowls sprinkled with the remaining parsley and accompanied by fresh ciabatta.

Spaghetti with Bottarga

This unusual recipe, featuring salted and dried fish roe, comes from Sardinia. It is simplicity itself to make and tastes very, very good.

Serves 4

350g/12oz fresh or dried spaghetti
about 60ml/4 tbsp olive oil
2–3 whole garlic cloves, peeled
60–90ml/4–6 tbsp grated bottarga, to taste
salt and freshly ground black pepper

1 Bring a large saucepan of lightly salted water to the boil and cook the spaghetti until it is *al dente*.

2 Meanwhile, heat half the olive oil in a separate saucepan. Add the garlic and cook gently, stirring, for a few minutes. Remove the pan from the heat, scoop out the garlic with a slotted spoon and discard it.

3 Drain the pasta very well. Return the pan of garlic-flavoured oil to the heat and add the pasta. Toss well, season with pepper and moisten with the remaining oil.

4 Divide the pasta among four warmed bowls, sprinkle the grated bottarga over the top and serve immediately.

Cook's Tip
You can buy bottarga, made from mullet or tuna roe, in Italian delicatessens. Small jars of ready-grated bottarga are convenient, but the best flavour comes from vacuum-packed slices of mullet bottarga. These are very easy to grate on a box grater. Keep any leftover bottarga tightly wrapped in the fridge, so that it does not taint other foods.

Spaghetti with Hot-&-Sour Fish

Hoi-sin sauce is the secret ingredient that makes this taste so good.

Serves 4

15ml/1 tbsp olive oil
1 large onion, chopped
5ml/1 tsp ground turmeric
1 fresh green chilli, cored, seeded and finely chopped
225g/8oz courgettes, thinly sliced
115g/4oz/1 cup shelled peas, thawed if frozen
350g/12oz dried spaghetti
450g/1lb monkfish tail, skinned and cut into bite-size pieces
10ml/2 tsp lemon juice
75ml/5 tbsp hoi-sin sauce
150ml/ ¼ pint/ ⅔ cup water
salt and freshly ground black pepper
a sprig of fresh dill, to garnish

1 Heat the oil in a large frying pan and fry the onion for 5 minutes, until softened. Stir in the turmeric and cook for 1 minute more.

2 Add the chilli, courgettes and peas, and fry over a low heat until the vegetables have softened.

3 Meanwhile, bring a large saucepan of lightly salted water to the boil, add the spaghetti and cook until it is *al dente*.

4 Stir the fish, lemon juice, hoi-sin sauce and water into the vegetable mixture. Bring to the boil, then lower the heat and simmer for 5 minutes, or until the fish is tender. Season to taste with salt and pepper.

5 Drain the spaghetti thoroughly and tip it into a serving bowl. Add the sauce and toss to coat. Serve immediately, garnished with a sprig of fresh dill.

Cook's Tip
Monkfish tail is quite often skinned before the shop displays it for sale. Nevertheless, it is still essential to strip off the transparent membrane surrounding the flesh, as this will become tough on cooking.

Tagliatelle with Cucumber & Smoked Salmon

The light texture of the cucumber complements the fish perfectly in this summery dish.

Serves 4

½ cucumber
350g/12oz dried tagliatelle
75g/3oz/6 tbsp butter
grated rind of 1 orange
30ml/2 tbsp chopped fresh dill
300ml/ ½ pint/1 ¼ cups single cream
15ml/1 tbsp freshly squeezed orange juice
115g/4oz smoked salmon, skinned and cut into thin strips
salt and freshly ground black pepper

1 Cut the cucumber in half lengthways, then, using a small spoon, scoop out and discard the seeds from the centre. Slice the cucumber thinly.

2 Bring a large pan of lightly salted water to the boil, add the tagliatelle and cook until *al dente*.

3 Melt the butter in a heavy-based saucepan and stir in the orange rind and dill. Add the cucumber and cook over a low heat, stirring occasionally, for about 2 minutes.

4 Pour in the cream and orange juice, season with salt and pepper to taste and simmer for 1 minute, then stir in the salmon and heat through.

5 Drain the pasta, return it to the pan and add the sauce. Toss lightly to coat. Serve immediately.

Cook's Tip
An economical way to make this sauce is to use smoked salmon offcuts, available from most supermarkets and delicatessens, as they are much cheaper than slices. Smoked trout is also a less expensive alternative.

Spaghetti with Salmon & Prawns

Light and fresh-tasting, this is perfect for an *al fresco* meal in summer. Serve with warm ciabatta.

Serves 4

300g/11oz salmon fillet
200ml/7fl oz/scant 1 cup dry white wine
a few fresh basil sprigs, plus extra basil leaves, to garnish
6 ripe Italian plum tomatoes, peeled and finely chopped
150ml/ ¼ pint/ ⅔ cup very low-fat fromage frais
350g/12oz fresh or dried spaghetti
115g/4oz cooked peeled prawns, thawed if frozen
salt and freshly ground black pepper

1 Put the salmon skin side up in a wide shallow pan. Pour over the wine, then add the basil sprigs. Sprinkle the fish with salt and pepper. Bring to the boil, cover and simmer gently for no more than 5 minutes. Using a fish slice, lift the fish out of the pan and set it aside to cool a little.

2 Stir the tomatoes and fromage frais into the liquid remaining in the pan and heat gently, without letting the sauce approach boiling point. Meanwhile, bring a large pan of lightly salted water to the boil. Add the pasta and cook until *al dente*.

3 Flake the fish into large chunks, discarding the skin and any bones. Add the fish to the sauce with the prawns, shaking the pan until they are well coated. Taste for seasoning.

4 Drain the pasta and tip it into a warmed bowl. Pour the sauce over the pasta and toss to combine. Serve immediately, garnished with the fresh basil leaves.

Cook's Tip
Check the salmon fillet carefully for small bones when you are flaking the flesh. Although the salmon is already filleted, you will always find a few stray "pin" bones. Pick them out carefully, using tweezers or your fingertips.

Linguine with Smoked Salmon & Mushrooms

Proof positive that pasta dishes need not be high in fat, even when their sauces seem very creamy.

Serves 6

30ml/2 tbsp olive oil
115g/4oz/1¼ cups button mushrooms, thinly sliced
250ml/8fl oz/1 cup dry white wine
7.5ml/1½ tsp fresh dill or 5ml/1 tsp dried dill weed
handful of fresh chives, snipped
300ml/ ½ pint/1¼ cups very low-fat fromage frais
225g/8oz smoked salmon, cut into thin strips
lemon juice
350g/12oz fresh linguine or spaghetti
salt and freshly ground black pepper
whole fresh chives, to garnish

1 Heat the oil in a wide, shallow saucepan. Add the mushrooms and fry over a gentle heat for 4–5 minutes, until they have softened but not coloured.

2 Pour the white wine into the pan. Increase the heat and boil rapidly for about 5 minutes, until the wine has reduced.

3 Stir in the herbs and fromage frais. Fold in the salmon and reheat gently. Stir in pepper and lemon juice to taste. Cover the pan and keep the sauce warm.

4 Bring a large saucepan of lightly salted water to the boil, add the pasta and cook until it is *al dente*. Drain, rinse thoroughly in boiling water and drain again. Turn into a warmed serving dish. Toss gently with the salmon sauce. Serve in warmed bowls, garnished with chives.

Cook's Tip
After you have added the fromage frais to the sauce, do not allow it to boil or it will curdle.

Orecchiette with Anchovies & Broccoli

Puglia, in southern Italy, specializes in imaginative pasta and vegetable combinations. Cooking the pasta in the water used for boiling the broccoli, then using some of it in the sauce, intensifies the flavour.

Serves 6

800g/1¾ lb broccoli
450g/1lb dried orecchiette or penne
90ml/6 tbsp olive oil
3 garlic cloves, finely chopped
6 drained canned anchovy fillets in oil
salt and freshly ground black pepper

1 Cut off the broccoli florets and divide them into sprigs. Peel the stems, then cut them into 5cm/2in lengths, discarding the woody parts.

2 Bring a large pan of water to the boil. Drop in the broccoli stems, bring back to the boil and cook for 3 minutes, then add the florets and boil for a further 3 minutes. Lift out all the broccoli with a slotted spoon and transfer it to a serving bowl. Do not discard the cooking water.

3 Add a little salt to the water used for cooking the broccoli. Bring it back to the boil. Drop in the pasta, stir well, and cook until it is *al dente*.

4 While the pasta is boiling, heat the oil in a small frying pan. Add the garlic and cook over a low heat for 2–3 minutes. Add the anchovy fillets. Using a fork, mash the anchovies and garlic to a paste. Cook for 3–4 minutes more.

5 Before draining the pasta, ladle about 175ml/6fl oz/ ¾ cup of the cooking water over the broccoli. Drain the pasta and add it to the bowl, with the hot anchovy and garlic mixture. Mix well, season with pepper if necessary and serve.

Pasta with Spinach & Anchovy Sauce

Deliciously earthy, this quick and easy dish would make a good starter or light supper.

Serves 4

900g/2lb fresh spinach or 500g/1¼lb frozen leaf spinach, thawed
450g/1lb capelli d'angelo
60ml/4 tbsp olive oil
45ml/3 tbsp pine nuts
2 garlic cloves, crushed
6 drained canned anchovy fillets or whole salted anchovies, chopped
butter, for tossing the pasta
salt

1 Remove the tough stalks from the spinach, wash the leaves thoroughly in a colander and place them in a large saucepan with only the water that still clings to them. Cover with a lid and cook over a high heat, shaking the pan occasionally, until the spinach has just wilted and is bright green. Drain well and set aside until required.

2 Bring a pan of lightly salted water to the boil. Add the pasta and cook until it is *al dente*.

3 Meanwhile, heat the oil in a saucepan, add the pine nuts and fry until golden. Remove with a slotted spoon and set aside. Add the garlic to the oil in the pan and fry until golden. Add the anchovies to the pan.

4 Stir in the spinach and cook for 2–3 minutes, or until it is hot. Stir in the pine nuts. Drain the pasta, toss it in a little butter and turn it into a warmed serving bowl. Top with the sauce, fork it through roughly and serve.

Variation
Add some sultanas, if you like. Their sweetness will counteract the salty flavour of the anchovies.

Chilli, Anchovy & Tomato Pasta

The sauce for this tasty pasta dish packs a punch, thanks to the robust flavours of red chillies, anchovies and capers.

Serves 4

45ml/3 tbsp olive oil
2 garlic cloves, crushed
2 fresh red chillies, seeded and chopped
6 drained canned anchovy fillets
675g/1½lb ripe tomatoes, peeled, seeded and chopped
30ml/2 tbsp sun-dried tomato purée
30ml/2 tbsp drained capers
115g/4oz/1 cup stoned black olives, roughly chopped
350g/12oz/3 cups dried penne
salt and freshly ground black pepper
chopped fresh basil, to garnish

1 Heat the oil in a saucepan, and fry the garlic and chilli over a low heat for 2–3 minutes.

2 Add the anchovies, mashing them with a fork, then stir in the tomatoes, sun-dried tomato purée, capers and olives. Add salt and pepper to taste. Simmer gently, uncovered, for 20 minutes, stirring occasionally.

3 Meanwhile, bring a large pan of lightly salted water to the boil and add the penne. Cook until *al dente*.

4 Drain the pasta, return it to the clean pan and add the sauce. Mix thoroughly, tip into a heated serving dish, garnish with the basil and serve at once.

Cook's Tip

If ripe well-flavoured tomatoes are not available, use two 400g/14oz cans chopped tomatoes. If the chillies are a very hot variety, use only one.

Macaroni with Anchovies & Mixed Vegetables

This southern Italian dish is colourful and full of flavour.

Serves 4

175g/6oz cauliflower florets, cut into small sprigs
175g/6oz broccoli florets, cut into small sprigs
350g/12oz/3 cups short-cut macaroni
45ml/3 tbsp extra virgin olive oil
1 onion, finely chopped
45ml/3 tbsp pine nuts
1 sachet of saffron powder, dissolved in 15ml/1 tbsp warm water
15–30ml/1–2 tbsp raisins
30ml/2 tbsp sun-dried tomato purée
4 drained canned anchovies in olive oil, chopped, plus extra anchovies, to serve (optional)
salt and freshly ground black pepper
freshly grated Pecorino cheese, to serve

1 Bring a large pan of lightly salted water to the boil and cook the cauliflower sprigs for 3 minutes. Add the broccoli and boil for 2 minutes more. Remove the vegetables from the pan with a large slotted spoon and set them aside.

2 Reboil the water, add the pasta and cook until it is *al dente*.

3 Meanwhile, heat the olive oil in a large, shallow pan, and fry the onion over a low heat, for 2–3 minutes, or until golden. Add the pine nuts, broccoli, cauliflower, and saffron water.

4 Stir in the raisins, sun-dried tomato purée and a couple of ladlefuls of the pasta cooking water until the vegetable mixture has the consistency of a sauce. Finally, add plenty of pepper.

5 Stir well, cook for 1–2 minutes, then add the chopped anchovies. Drain the pasta and tip it into the vegetable mixture. Toss well, then taste for seasoning and add salt if necessary.

6 Serve the pasta in four warmed bowls, sprinkling each portion liberally with freshly grated Pecorino. If you like the flavour of anchovies, add 1–2 whole anchovies to each serving.

Spaghetti with Anchovies & Aubergine

Sun-ripened vegetables such as red peppers, aubergines and vine tomatoes are partnered with olives and anchovies in this Mediterranean dish.

Serves 4

45ml/3 tbsp olive oil
1 large red pepper, seeded and chopped
1 small aubergine, finely chopped
1 onion, finely chopped
6 ripe vine tomatoes, peeled, seeded and finely chopped
2 garlic cloves, finely chopped
120ml/4fl oz/ ½ cup dry red wine
120ml/4fl oz/ ½ cup water
1 handful fresh herbs, such as basil, flat leaf parsley and rosemary
300g/11oz dried spaghetti
50g/2oz drained canned anchovies, roughly chopped, plus extra whole anchovies to garnish
12 stoned black olives
15–30ml/1–2 tbsp drained capers, to taste
salt and freshly ground black pepper

1 Heat the olive oil in a large, heavy-based saucepan and add the red pepper, aubergine, onion, tomatoes and garlic. Cook over a low heat, stirring frequently, for 10–15 minutes, until all the vegetables are soft.

2 Pour in the wine and measured water, add the fresh herbs and bring to the boil. Lower the heat and simmer, stirring occasionally, for 10–15 minutes.

3 Meanwhile, bring a large saucepan of lightly salted water to the boil. Add the pasta and cook until it is *al dente*.

4 Add the chopped anchovies, olives and capers to the sauce and heat through for a few minutes. Taste for seasoning.

5 Drain the pasta and tip it into a warmed bowl. Pour the sauce over, toss well and serve immediately, garnished with whole anchovies.

Trout & Ricotta Ravioli

Making ravioli is easier than it looks, and the results are well worth the effort.

Serves 4

75g/3oz fresh spinach, tough stalks removed and leaves torn
275g/10oz/2½ cups strong white flour
3 eggs, beaten
15ml/1 tbsp oil
salt and freshly ground black pepper
fresh coriander sprigs, to garnish

For the filling

115g/4oz trout fillet, poached and drained, skin and bones removed
50g/2oz/ ⅓ cup ricotta cheese
grated rind of 1 lemon
30ml/2 tbsp chopped fresh coriander

For the sauce

300ml/ ½ pint/1¼ cups double cream
15ml/1 tbsp chopped fresh coriander
30ml/2 tbsp freshly grated Parmesan cheese, plus extra to serve

1 Put the spinach in a large saucepan with only the water that clings to the leaves. Cover and cook over a high heat, shaking the pan, until the spinach wilts. Drain and squeeze dry. Put the spinach, flour, eggs and oil into a food processor. Season and process to a dough. Transfer to a floured surface and knead until smooth. Wrap in clear film and rest for 30 minutes.

2 Roll out the dough on a floured surface to a 50 x 46cm/ 20 x 18in rectangle. Leave to dry for 15 minutes. Trim the edges then cut the dough in half, lengthways.

3 Make the filling. Combine the trout, ricotta, lemon rind and coriander, and season. Put spoonfuls of the filling in rows on one sheet of pasta. Lay the second sheet on top. Press the dough together and cut out the ravioli. Cook in lightly salted boiling water until *al dente*. Drain and return to the pan.

4 Make the sauce by heating all the ingredients in a small saucepan, without boiling. Pour over the ravioli and stir to coat. Serve, sprinkled with Parmesan and garnished with coriander.

Cannelloni Sorrentina-style

Anchovies add zing to the filling in these pasta rolls.

Serves 4–6

60ml/4 tbsp olive oil
1 small onion, finely chopped
900g/2lb ripe tomatoes, peeled and finely chopped
2 garlic cloves, crushed
1 large handful fresh basil leaves, shredded, plus extra basil leaves, to garnish
250ml/8fl oz/1 cup Vegetable Stock
250ml/8fl oz/1 cup dry white wine
30ml/2 tbsp sun-dried tomato purée
2.5ml/ ½ tsp granulated sugar
16–18 fresh or dried lasagne sheets
250g/9oz/1 ⅓ cups ricotta cheese
130g/4½ oz packet mozzarella cheese, drained and diced small
8–9 drained canned anchovy fillets in olive oil, halved lengthways
50g/2oz/ ⅔ cup freshly grated Parmesan cheese
salt and freshly ground black pepper

1 Heat the oil in a pan and fry the onion gently, until softened. Stir in the tomatoes, garlic and half the basil. Season, then toss over a medium heat for 5 minutes.

2 Scoop half the mixture into a bowl and set aside to cool. Stir the stock, wine, tomato purée and sugar into the remaining mixture and simmer for about 20 minutes, stirring occasionally.

3 Meanwhile, cook the lasagne sheets according to the instructions on the packet. Drain and lay flat on a clean towel.

4 Preheat the oven to 190°C/375°F/Gas 5. Add the ricotta and mozzarella to the mixture in the bowl. Stir in the remaining basil and season. Spread a little of the mixture over each lasagne sheet. Top with anchovy, then roll up like a Swiss roll.

5 Purée the tomato sauce in a food processor. Spread one-third over the base of an ovenproof dish. Arrange the cannelloni seam side down and spoon the remaining sauce over them. Sprinkle the Parmesan over the top and bake for 20 minutes. Serve hot, garnished with the extra basil leaves.

Cannelloni with Tuna

Everyone loves this pasta dish and it's a particular favourite with children. Italian Fontina cheese has a sweet, nutty flavour and melts beautifully.

Serves 4–6

50g/2oz/ ¼ cup butter
50g/2oz/ ½ cup plain flour
about 900ml/1 ½ pints/3¾ cups hot milk
2 x 200g/7oz cans tuna, drained
115g/4oz/1 cup grated Fontina cheese
1.5 ml/ ¼ tsp freshly grated nutmeg
12 no-precook cannelloni tubes
50g2oz/ ⅔ cup freshly grated Parmesan cheese
salt and freshly ground black pepper
fresh herbs, to garnish

1 Melt the butter in a heavy-based saucepan, add the flour and cook over a low heat, stirring constantly, for 1–2 minutes. Gradually add 350ml/12fl oz/1 ½ cups of the milk, stirring constantly until the sauce boils and thickens. Remove the white sauce from the heat.

2 Transfer 120ml/4fl oz/ ½ cup of the warm white sauce to a bowl. Flake the tuna and stir it into the sauce in the bowl. Season with salt and pepper to taste. Preheat the oven to 180°C/350°F/Gas 4.

3 Return the pan containing the rest of the sauce to the heat, gradually whisk in the remaining milk, then add the grated Fontina and nutmeg, and season with salt and pepper to taste. Simmer over a low heat, stirring constantly, for a few minutes, until the cheese has melted and the sauce is smooth.

4 Pour about one-third of the sauce into an ovenproof dish and spread to the corners.

5 Fill the cannelloni tubes with the tuna mixture. Place them in a single layer in the dish. Pour over the remaining cheese sauce and sprinkle with grated Parmesan. Bake for 30 minutes, or until the top is golden and bubbling. Serve immediately, garnished with the fresh herbs.

Cannelloni with Smoked Salmon

Smoked salmon used to be a luxury buy, and still is, if you choose the finest quality. That type of salmon begs to be served very simply, with a squeeze of lemon or lime and a grinding of black pepper. Offcuts or cheaper packs of smoked salmon are ideal for using in bakes like this one, and the fish tastes wonderful with the combination of ricotta and blue cheese.

Serves 4

25g/1oz/2 tbsp butter
4 spring onions, finely chopped
1 small celery stick, finely chopped
175g/6oz/¾ cup ricotta cheese
75g/3oz Stilton or other crumbly blue cheese
5ml/1 tsp grated lemon rind
25g/1oz/½ cup fresh white breadcrumbs
115g/4oz smoked salmon, preferably offcuts, chopped
16 no-precook cannelloni tubes
salt and freshly ground black pepper

For the sauce

40g/1½oz/3 tbsp butter
40g/1½oz/6 tbsp plain flour
600ml/1 pint/2½ cups milk
nutmeg

1 Melt the butter in a pan and add the spring onions and celery. Fry for about 5 minutes over a low heat, until the spring onions have softened but not browned. Leave to cool slightly.

2 Put the ricotta in a bowl and beat it until it softens. Crumble in the blue cheese and mix well, then beat in the spring onions and celery. Stir in the grated lemon rind and breadcrumbs, then add the salmon and mix well. Taste the mixture and add a little seasoning if necessary. Preheat the oven to 190°C/375°F/Gas 5.

3 Make the sauce. Melt the butter in a pan, add the flour and cook, stirring, for 1–2 minutes. Gradually add the milk, stirring until the sauce boils and thickens. Grate in fresh nutmeg to taste, then season with salt and pepper. Whisk well. Remove the pan from the heat.

4 Spoon a little of the white sauce into a baking dish which will hold the cannelloni tubes in a single layer. Fill the cannelloni tubes with the salmon mixture and place them in the dish. Pour the remaining white sauce over.

5 Bake for 35–40 minutes, or until the pasta feels tender when pierced with a skewer. Allow to stand for 10 minutes before serving.

Cook's Tip

If you would like to serve this as a starter, make it in individual oval gratin dishes. It may be necessary to increase the amount of white sauce.

Tuna Lasagne

Simple and very satisfying, this pasta bake is ideal for a midweek meal.

Serves 6

15g/½oz/1 tbsp butter
1 small onion, finely chopped
1 garlic clove, finely chopped
115g/4oz mushrooms, thinly sliced
150ml/¼ pint/⅔ cup whipping cream
45ml/3 tbsp chopped fresh parsley
350g/12oz no-precook lasagne sheets
2 x 200g/7oz cans tuna, drained and flaked
2 drained canned pimientos, cut into strips
75g/3oz/¾ cup frozen peas, thawed
115g/4oz mozzarella cheese, grated
25g/1oz/⅓ cup freshly grated Parmesan cheese
salt and freshly ground black pepper
red pepper strips and fresh parsley, to garnish

For the white sauce

50g/2oz/¼ cup butter
50g/2oz/½ cup plain flour
600ml/1 pint/2½ cups milk

1 Preheat the oven to 180°C/350°F/Gas 4. Melt the butter in a saucepan. Add the onion, cook for 4–5 minutes, then stir in the garlic and mushrooms, and cook until soft, stirring occasionally.

2 Make the white sauce. Melt the butter in a saucepan, stir in the flour and cook for 1 minute, stirring. Gradually add the milk, whisking until the sauce boils and thickens. Stir in the mushroom mixture, cream and parsley. Season to taste.

3 Spoon a thin layer of sauce over the base of a 30 x 23cm/12 x 9in ovenproof dish. Cover with a layer of lasagne sheets. Strew half of the tuna, pimiento strips, peas and mozzarella over the lasagne. Spoon one-third of the remaining sauce evenly over the top and cover with another layer of lasagne.

4 Repeat the layers, ending with lasagne and sauce. Sprinkle with the Parmesan. Bake for 30–40 minutes, or until bubbling hot and the top is lightly browned. Cut into squares and serve from the dish garnished with the pepper strips and parsley.

Farfalle with Prawns

Cream sauces are not always the best way to serve fish with pasta. This simple fresh prawn sauce allows the distinctive flavour of the seafood to shine.

Serves 4

225g/8oz/2 cups dried farfalle
115g/4oz/ ½ cup butter
2 garlic cloves, crushed
45ml/3 tbsp chopped fresh parsley, plus extra, to garnish
350g/12oz cooked peeled prawns
salt and freshly ground black pepper

1 Bring a large pan of lightly salted water to the boil. Add the pasta and cook until *al dente*.

2 Meanwhile, melt the butter in a large, heavy-based saucepan. Add the garlic and fresh parsley, and cook over a low heat, stirring occasionally, for 2 minutes. Toss in the prawns and sauté, stirring occasionally, for 4 minutes.

3 Drain the pasta and return it to the clean pan. Stir in the prawn mixture. Season to taste with salt and pepper. Serve immediately in warmed shallow bowls. Garnish with the extra chopped parsley.

Variation

For extra colour, fry 1 diced red pepper with the garlic and parsley. Add some chopped red onion too, if you like, but avoid adding too much, as it might overwhelm the delicate flavour of the prawns. A splash of dry white vermouth, added with the prawns, would work well.

Cook's Tip

For the best flavour and texture, buy prawns with their shells on and peel them yourself. Ready-peeled and frozen prawns tend to become rather mushy.

Pasta with Prawns & Petits Pois

A small amount of saffron in the sauce gives this dish a lovely golden colour.

Serves 4

400g/14oz dried farfalle or fusilli
45ml/3 tbsp olive oil
25g/1oz/2 tbsp butter
2 spring onions, chopped
225g/8oz/2 cups frozen petits pois, thawed
250ml/8fl oz/1 cup dry white wine
a few saffron strands
350g/12oz cooked peeled prawns
salt
30ml/2 tbsp chopped fresh dill, to serve

1 Bring a large saucepan of lightly salted water to the boil. Add the pasta and cook until *al dente*.

2 Meanwhile, heat the oil and butter in a large, heavy-based frying pan and sauté the spring onions until soft and translucent. Add the peas and cook for 2–3 minutes.

3 Stir the white wine and saffron into the spring onion mixture. Increase the heat and cook until the wine has reduced to about half. Gently stir in the prawns, cover the pan and reduce the heat to low.

4 Drain the pasta and return it to the clean pan. Add the prawn sauce. Stir over a high heat for 2–3 minutes, coating the pasta with the sauce. Sprinkle with the dill and serve.

Cook's Tip

Prawns vary in size and colour, offering a wide variety of choice. Mediterranean prawns – the most authentic for this dish – grow to 20–23cm/8–9in, are brown before cooking and bright red afterwards. Pale brown, deep-water prawns, found in both the Mediterranean and the Atlantic, and blue-brown Pacific prawns are much larger. Both turn bright pink when cooked. Greenland prawns are relatively small and pink.

Prawn & Pasta Packets

A quick and impressive dish, which can be prepared in advance and cooked at the last minute, this is ideal for midweek entertaining.

Serves 4

450g/1lb dried tagliatelle
150ml/¼ pint/⅔ cup pesto
1 garlic clove, crushed
20ml/4 tsp olive oil
750g/1½lb medium raw prawns, peeled and deveined
120ml/4fl oz/½ cup dry white wine
salt and freshly ground black pepper

1 Preheat the oven to 200°C/400°F/Gas 6. Cut out four 30cm/12in squares of non-stick baking paper.

2 Bring a large pan of lightly salted water to the boil. Add the tagliatelle and cook for 2 minutes only, then drain and tip into a bowl. Mix with half the pesto. Put the rest of the pesto in a small bowl and stir the garlic into it.

3 Place 5ml/1 tsp olive oil in the centre of each paper square. Pile equal amounts of pasta in the middle of each square.

4 Top with equal amounts of prawns and spoon the garlic-flavoured pesto over. Season with pepper and sprinkle each serving with 30ml/2 tbsp wine.

5 Brush the edges of the paper lightly with water and bring them loosely up around the filling, twisting tightly to enclose. (The parcels should look like money bags.)

6 Place the parcels on a baking sheet. Bake for 10–15 minutes. Transfer the parcels to four serving plates. Serve immediately, allowing each person to open his or her own packet.

Cook's Tip
You can use greaseproof paper instead of baking paper.

Pink & Green Farfalle

In this modern recipe, pink prawns and green courgettes combine prettily with cream and pasta bows to make a delicious and substantial main course.

Serves 4

50g/2oz/¼ cup butter
2–3 spring onions, very thinly sliced on the diagonal
350g/12oz courgettes, thinly sliced on the diagonal
60ml/4 tbsp dry white wine
300g/11oz/2¾ cups dried farfalle
75ml/5 tbsp crème fraîche
225g/8oz/1⅓ cups cooked peeled prawns
15ml/1 tbsp finely chopped fresh marjoram
salt and freshly ground black pepper

1 Melt the butter in a large, heavy-based saucepan, add the spring onions and cook over a low heat, stirring frequently, for about 5 minutes, until softened.

2 Add the courgettes, season with salt and pepper to taste and stir-fry over a medium heat for 5 minutes. Pour over the wine and let it bubble, then cover and simmer for 10 minutes.

3 Bring a large pan of lightly salted water to the boil. Add the pasta and cook until it is *al dente*.

4 Meanwhile, add the crème fraîche to the courgette mixture and simmer for about 10 minutes, until well reduced.

5 Add the prawns to the courgette mixture, heat through gently and taste for seasoning. Drain the pasta and tip it into a warmed bowl. Add the sauce and chopped marjoram, and toss well. Serve immediately.

Cook's Tip
Marjoram has a special affinity with fish and seafood. If you dislike its pungency, use flat leaf parsley instead.

Penne with Prawns & Artichokes

This is a good dish for late spring or early summer, when baby artichokes appear in shops and on market stalls.

Serves 4

juice of ½ lemon
4 baby globe artichokes
90ml/6 tbsp olive oil
2 garlic cloves, crushed
30ml/2 tbsp chopped fresh mint
30ml/2 tbsp chopped fresh flat leaf parsley
350g/12oz/3 cups dried penne
8–12 cooked king or tiger prawns, peeled, deveined and each cut into 2–3 pieces
25g/1oz/2 tbsp butter
salt and freshly ground black pepper

1 Fill a medium bowl with cold water and add the lemon juice to acidulate it. (This is to prevent the cut surfaces of the artichokes from discolouring.)

2 Prepare the artichokes one at a time. Cut off the stalks, if present, and cut across the tops of the leaves. Peel off and discard any tough outer leaves. Cut the artichokes lengthways into quarters and remove the hairy chokes. Then cut the pieces of artichoke lengthways into 5mm/ ¼in slices and put these in the bowl of acidulated water as you prepare them.

3 Drain the artichoke slices and pat them dry with kitchen paper. Heat the olive oil in a frying pan and add the artichokes, garlic and half the mint and parsley. Season with salt and pepper to taste and cook over a low heat, stirring, until the artichokes feel tender when pierced with a sharp knife.

4 Meanwhile, bring a large pan of lightly salted water to the boil and cook the pasta until *al dente*. Add the prawns to the artichokes, stir thoroughly to mix, then heat through gently for 1–2 minutes.

5 Drain the pasta and tip it into a warmed bowl. Add the butter and toss until it has melted. Add the artichoke mixture and toss to combine. Serve immediately, sprinkled with the remaining herbs.

Paglia e Fieno with Prawns & Vodka

The combination of prawns, vodka and pasta may seem unusual, but it has become something of a modern classic in Italy.

Serves 4

30ml/2 tbsp olive oil
¼ large onion, finely chopped
1 garlic clove, crushed
15–30ml/1–2 tbsp sun-dried tomato purée
200ml/7fl oz/scant 1 cup panna da cucina or double cream
350g/12oz fresh or dried paglia e fieno
12 raw tiger prawns, peeled, deveined and chopped
30ml/2 tbsp vodka
salt and freshly ground black pepper

1 Heat the oil in a medium saucepan, add the onion and garlic, and cook gently, stirring frequently, for 5 minutes, until softened.

2 Add the tomato purée and stir for 1–2 minutes, then add the cream and bring to the boil, stirring. Season with salt and pepper to taste and let the sauce bubble until it starts to thicken slightly. Remove from the heat.

3 Bring a large saucepan of lightly salted water to the boil and cook the pasta until it is *al dente*. When it is almost ready, add the prawns and vodka to the sauce; toss quickly over a medium heat for 2–3 minutes, until the prawns turn pink.

4 Drain the pasta and tip it into a warmed bowl. Pour the sauce over and toss well. Divide among four warmed bowls and serve immediately.

Cook's Tip
Make sure that the pasta has only a minute or two of cooking time left before adding the prawns to the sauce. Otherwise the prawns will overcook and become tough.

Spaghetti with Mussels

Mussels are delicious with pasta. The combination of the black shells and creamy spaghetti strands looks stylish too.

Serves 4

900g/2lb live mussels, scrubbed and bearded
250ml/8fl oz/1 cup water
400g/14oz dried spaghetti
75ml/5 tbsp olive oil
3 garlic cloves, finely chopped
60ml/4 tbsp chopped fresh parsley
60ml/4 tbsp white wine
salt and freshly ground black pepper

1 Check the mussels, discarding any which are not tightly closed or which fail to close when tapped on the work surface. Put them in a large heavy-based pan. Pour in the measured water and place the pan over a moderate heat. As soon as the mussels open, lift them out one by one.

2 When all the mussels have opened (discard any that do not), pour the liquid in the pan through a strainer lined with kitchen paper and reserve until needed.

3 Bring a large pan of lightly salted water to the boil and cook the spaghetti until it is *al dente*.

4 Meanwhile, heat the oil in a large frying pan. Add the garlic and parsley, and cook for 2–3 minutes. Add the mussels, their strained juices and the wine, with plenty of pepper. Heat the mixture gently, but do not let the mussels toughen.

5 Drain the pasta and return it to the clean pan. Add the sauce, and toss to coat. Serve at once.

Cook's Tip
To clean mussels, scrub off any sand or mud under cold running water and knock off any barnacles with a knife. Pull away the beard – the tuft that protrudes from the hinge of the shell – with your fingers.

Spaghetti with Creamy Mussel & Saffron Sauce

In this recipe the pasta is tossed with a delicious pale yellow mussel sauce, streaked with yellow strands of saffron.

Serves 4

900g/2lb live mussels, scrubbed and bearded
150ml/ ¼ pint/ ⅔ cup dry white wine
2 shallots, finely chopped
450g/1lb dried spaghetti
25g/1oz/2 tbsp butter
2 garlic cloves, crushed
10ml/2 tsp cornflour
300ml/ ½ pint/1 ¼ cups double cream
pinch of saffron strands
juice of ½ lemon
1 egg yolk
salt and freshly ground black pepper
chopped fresh parsley, to garnish

1 Check the mussels, discarding any which are not tightly closed, or which fail to close when tapped on the work surface. Put them in a large, heavy-based pan. Add the wine and shallots, cover and cook over a high heat, shaking the pan frequently, for 5–10 minutes, until the mussels have opened. Discard any that remain shut.

2 Remove the mussels with a slotted spoon and pour the cooking liquid through a strainer lined with kitchen paper. Return it to the pan and boil until reduced by half. Meanwhile, reserve a few mussels and remove the rest from their shells.

3 Bring a large saucepan of lightly salted water to the boil, add the pasta and cook until *al dente*. Meanwhile, melt the butter in a saucepan, add the garlic and cook until golden. Stir in the cornflour and gradually stir in the mussel liquid and the cream. Add the saffron to the sauce, with salt and pepper to taste. Simmer until slightly thickened. Stir in lemon juice to taste, then the egg yolk and shelled mussels. Keep warm, but do not boil.

4 Drain the pasta and return it to the clean pan. Add the mussel sauce and toss. Serve in warmed bowls, garnished with the reserved mussels in their shells and the parsley.

Spaghetti with Clams

Clams, especially the hard-shell varieties and ocean quahogs, are particularly popular on the Atlantic seaboard of America, which is where this version of the well-known dish originated.

Serves 4

24 live clams, in their shells, scrubbed
250ml/8fl oz/1 cup water
120ml/4fl oz/ ½ cup dry white wine
450g/1lb dried spaghetti
30ml/2 tbsp olive oil
2 garlic cloves, finely chopped
45ml/3 tbsp finely chopped fresh parsley
salt and freshly ground black pepper

1 Rinse the clams well in cold water and drain. Discard any that are open and do not shut when sharply tapped on a work surface. Place the clams in a large pan with the measured water and wine. Bring to the boil, cover and steam, shaking the pan frequently, for 6–8 minutes, or until the shells open.

2 Discard any clams that have not opened. Remove the rest from their shells. Cut off and discard the siphon from any large clams and roughly chop the flesh.

3 Pour the cooking liquid through a strainer lined with kitchen paper. Place in a small saucepan and boil rapidly until it has reduced by about half. Set aside.

4 Bring a large pan of lightly salted water to the boil. Add the spaghetti and cook until it is *al dente*.

5 Meanwhile, heat the olive oil in a large frying pan. Add the garlic and cook for 2–3 minutes, but do not let it brown. Add the reduced clam liquid and the parsley. Leave it to cook over low heat until the spaghetti is ready.

6 Drain the spaghetti. Add it to the frying pan, raise the heat to medium, and add the clams. Cook for 3–4 minutes, tossing the pasta with the sauce. Season to taste with salt and pepper, and serve immediately.

Linguine with Clam & Tomato Sauce

Simple and supremely satisfying, this classic Italian dish is low in fat, so will suit those who are watching their diet.

Serves 4

900g/2lb live clams in their shells, scrubbed
250ml/8fl oz/1 cup water
350g/12oz dried linguine
30ml/2 tbsp olive oil
1 garlic clove, crushed
400g/14oz tomatoes, fresh or canned, very finely chopped
60ml/4 tbsp chopped fresh parsley
salt and freshly ground black pepper

1 Rinse the clams well in cold water and drain. Discard any that are open and do not shut when sharply tapped on a work surface. Place them in a large saucepan with the measured water. Bring to the boil, cover and steam, for 6–8 minutes, until the shells open. Lift out the clams with a slotted spoon, discarding any that remain shut.

2 Remove the clams from their shells, adding any juices to the liquid in the pan. Cut off and discard the siphon from any large clams and chop the flesh into two or three pieces. Strain the cooking juices through a sieve lined with kitchen paper.

3 Bring a large pan of lightly salted water to the boil and cook the pasta until it is *al dente*. Meanwhile, heat the olive oil in a separate pan. Add the garlic and cook over a medium heat until the garlic is golden, then discard it.

4 Add the chopped tomatoes to the oil, and pour in the clam cooking liquid. Mix well and cook until the sauce begins to dry out and thicken slightly.

5 Stir the parsley and clams into the tomato sauce and increase the heat. Season to taste with pepper. Drain the pasta and tip it into a warmed serving bowl. Pour on the hot sauce and mix well before serving.

Tagliolini with Clam, Leek & Tomato Sauce

Canned or bottled clams make this a speedy sauce for cooks in a hurry.

Serves 4

350g/12oz dried tagliolini
25g/1oz/2 tbsp butter
2 leeks, thinly sliced
150ml/ 1/4 pint/ 2/3 cup dry white wine
4 tomatoes, peeled, seeded and chopped
250g/9oz can or jar clams in brine, drained
30ml/2 tbsp chopped fresh basil
60ml/4 tbsp crème fraîche
salt and freshly ground black pepper

1 Bring a large pan of lightly salted water to the boil and cook the pasta until it is *al dente*.

2 Meanwhile, melt the butter in a small saucepan and fry the leeks for about 5 minutes, until softened. Add the wine and tomatoes. Cook over a high heat until reduced by half.

3 Lower the heat, stir in the clams, basil and creme fraîche, and season with salt and pepper to taste. Heat through gently without boiling.

4 Drain the pasta, return it to the clean pan and add the sauce. Toss well to mix. Serve immediately.

Variations

Try salmon-flavoured tagliolini for an attractive presentation. It looks good with the tomato-based clam sauce and intensifies the seafood flavour. Alternatively, for a very dramatic presentation, use a mixture of plain pasta and black tagliolini flavoured with squid or cuttlefish ink.

Spaghetti with Red Wine Clam Sauce

Small sweet clams make this a delicately succulent spaghetti sauce, while fresh chilli gives it a kick.

Serves 4

90ml/6 tbsp olive oil
1 onion, finely chopped
1/2 fresh red chilli, seeded and finely chopped
2 garlic cloves, crushed
2 x 400g/14oz cans chopped tomatoes
120ml/4fl oz/ 1/2 cup red wine
2 x 400g/14oz cans clams in brine, drained
45ml/3 tbsp chopped fresh parsley
450g/1lb dried spaghetti
salt and freshly ground black pepper

1 Heat the olive oil in a heavy-based saucepan and add the onion, chilli and garlic. Cook over a low to medium heat, stirring occasionally, for about 5 minutes, until the onion is soft and translucent.

2 Add the tomatoes and red wine, and bring to the boil. Lower the heat and cook for 10 minutes, until the sauce is thick and flavoursome. Stir in the canned clams and half the parsley. Season to taste with salt and pepper, and heat through.

3 Meanwhile, bring a large pan of lightly salted water to the boil and cook the pasta until *al dente*.

4 Drain the pasta and turn it into a warmed serving dish. Pour over the sauce, sprinkle with the remaining chopped parsley and serve immediately.

Cook's Tip

Use more chilli if you like. Clams have a much more robust flavour than mussels and other shellfish, so they can take quite a hot sauce. For those who like their food fiery, use chilli-flavoured pasta instead of plain.

Fettuccine with Scallops in Tomato Sauce

Scallops have a rich yet delicate flavour and so are best combined with ingredients that will not overpower it.

Serves 4

450g/1lb dried fettuccine
30ml/2 tbsp olive oil
2 garlic cloves, finely chopped
450g/1lb shelled scallops, sliced in half horizontally
30ml/2 tbsp chopped fresh basil
salt and freshly ground black pepper
fresh basil sprigs, to garnish

For the sauce

30ml/2 tbsp olive oil
½ onion, finely chopped
1 garlic clove, finely chopped
2 x 400g/14oz cans peeled tomatoes

1 Make the sauce. Heat the oil in a large, shallow saucepan. Add the onion and garlic, and cook for about 5 minutes, until just softened, stirring occasionally.

2 Add the tomatoes, with their can juice, and crush roughly with a fork. Bring to the boil, then reduce the heat and simmer gently for 15 minutes, until thickened. Remove the pan from the heat and set aside.

3 Bring a large pan of lightly salted water to the boil. Add the pasta and cook until *al dente*.

4 Meanwhile, heat the oil in a frying pan, add the garlic and cook for about 30 seconds, until just sizzling. Add the scallops, with 2.5ml/ ½ tsp salt. Cook over a high heat for about 3 minutes, tossing the scallops until they are cooked through.

5 Reheat the tomato sauce, stir in the scallops and keep warm.

6 Drain the fettuccine, return it to the clean pan and add the scallops and tomato sauce and the chopped basil. Toss thoroughly to mix. Transfer to four warmed plates, garnish with the basil sprigs and serve immediately.

Rigatoni with Scallops & Pernod

Scallops have the sweetest flavour and need very little cooking, which makes them perfect partners for pasta.

Serves 4

350g/12oz scallops
45ml/3 tbsp olive oil
1 garlic clove, chopped
1 onion, chopped
2 carrots, cut into matchsticks
350g/12oz dried rigatoni
30ml/2 tbsp chopped fresh parsley
30ml/2 tbsp dry white wine
30ml/2 tbsp Pernod
150ml/ ¼ pint/ ⅔ cup double cream
salt and freshly ground black pepper

1 Trim the scallops, cut off the corals, then cut the scallops in half lengthways.

2 Heat the oil in a frying pan and fry the garlic, onion and carrots over a low heat for about 10 minutes, until the carrots are softened.

3 Meanwhile, bring a large pan of lightly salted water to the boil. Add the pasta and cook until *al dente*.

4 Stir the scallops, parsley, wine and Pernod into the vegetable mixture and bring to the boil. Cover, lower the heat and simmer for 1 minute. Using a slotted spoon, transfer the scallops and vegetables to a plate and keep them warm.

5 Bring the pan juices back to the boil and boil rapidly until reduced by half. Stir in the cream and heat the sauce through.

6 Stir the scallops and vegetables into the creamy sauce in the pan and heat through. Season to taste. Drain the pasta and toss it with the sauce. Serve immediately.

Cook's Tip

The key to this sauce is not to overcook the scallops, or they will become tough and rubbery.

Tagliatelle with Brandied Scallops

Scallops and brandy make this a relatively expensive dish, but it is so delicious that you will find it well worth the cost.

Serves 4

200g/7oz shelled scallops, sliced
30ml/2 tbsp plain flour
40g/1½oz/3 tbsp butter
2 spring onions, thinly sliced
½–1 small fresh red chilli, seeded and very finely chopped
30ml/2 tbsp finely chopped fresh flat leaf parsley
60ml/4 tbsp brandy
105ml/7 tbsp fish stock
275g/10oz fresh spinach-flavoured tagliatelle
salt and freshly ground black pepper

1 Toss the scallops in the flour, then shake off the excess. Bring a saucepan of lightly salted water to the boil, ready for cooking the pasta.

2 Meanwhile, melt the butter in a large shallow pan. Add the spring onions, chilli and half the parsley. Fry over a medium heat, stirring frequently, for 1–2 minutes. Add the scallops and toss over the heat for 1–2 minutes.

3 Pour the brandy over the scallops, then set it alight with a match or taper. As soon as the flames have died down, stir in the fish stock and season with salt and pepper to taste. Mix well. Simmer for 2–3 minutes, then cover the pan and remove it from the heat.

4 Add the pasta to the boiling water and cook it until it is *al dente*. Drain, add to the sauce and toss over a medium heat until mixed. Serve at once, in warmed bowls. Sprinkle the remaining parsley over each portion.

Cook's Tip

Buy fresh scallops, with their corals if possible. Fresh scallops have a better texture and flavour than frozen scallops, which tend to be watery.

Squid Ink Pasta with Ricotta

Black pasta looks very dramatic and is the perfect vehicle for the creamy sauce. This dish would make a perfect first course for a dinner party, in which case, it would serve six.

Serves 4

300g/11oz dried squid ink spaghetti
60ml/4 tbsp ricotta cheese
60ml/4 tbsp extra virgin olive oil
1 small fresh red chilli, seeded and finely chopped
1 small handful fresh basil leaves
salt and freshly ground black pepper

1 Bring a pan of lightly salted water to the boil and cook the pasta until it is *al dente*.

2 Meanwhile, put the ricotta in a bowl, add salt and pepper to taste and use a little of the hot water from the pasta pan to mix it to a smooth, creamy consistency.

3 Drain the pasta. Heat the olive oil gently in the clean pan and return the pasta to it with the chilli. Season with salt and pepper to taste. Toss quickly over a high heat to combine.

4 Divide the pasta equally among four warmed bowls, then top with the ricotta. Sprinkle with the basil leaves and serve immediately. Each diner then tosses his or her own portion of pasta and cheese.

Cook's Tips

- *If you are not keen on the flavour of squid ink, use another coloured pasta, such as green (spinach-flavoured) pasta, red (tomato-flavoured) pasta, brown (mushroom- or porcini-flavoured) pasta or simple multi-coloured pasta instead.*
- *Do make sure that you use extra virgin olive oil, as this has the best flavour and the lowest acidity. The olive oil forms an integral part of the dish, and poorer quality oils would be likely to spoil the delicate and subtle flavour.*

Black Pasta with Squid Sauce

Tagliatelle flavoured with squid ink looks amazing and tastes deliciously of the sea. Marrying it with rings of fresh squid doubles the impact on the eyes and on the taste buds.

Serves 4

105ml/7 tbsp olive oil
2 shallots, chopped
3 garlic cloves, crushed
45ml/3 tbsp chopped fresh parsley
675g/1 ½lb prepared squid, cut into rings and rinsed
150ml/ ¼ pint/ ⅔ cup dry white wine
400g/14oz can chopped tomatoes
2.5ml/½ tsp dried chilli flakes
450g/1lb dried squid ink tagliatelle
salt and freshly ground black pepper

1 Heat the oil in a saucepan and add the shallots. Cook over a low heat, stirring occasionally, until pale golden, then add the garlic. When the garlic has begun to colour a little, stir in 30ml/2 tbsp of the parsley, then add the squid and stir again. Cook for 3–4 minutes.

2 Add the white wine, simmer for a few seconds, then stir in the tomatoes and chilli flakes, and season with salt and pepper to taste. Cover and simmer gently for about 1 hour, until the squid is tender. Thin the sauce with a little water if necessary.

3 Bring a large pan of lightly salted water to the boil, add the pasta and cook until it is *al dente*.

4 Drain the tagliatelle and return it to the pan. Add the squid sauce and mix well. Serve in warmed bowls, sprinkled with the remaining chopped parsley.

Cook's Tip
Squid is available all year round, both fresh and frozen. It is one of the few types of seafood that freezes well.

Spaghetti with Squid & Peas

In Italy, squid is often cooked with peas in a tomato sauce. This recipe is a variation on the theme.

Serves 4

450g/1lb prepared squid
30ml/2 tbsp olive oil
1 small onion, finely chopped
1 garlic clove, finely chopped
400g/14oz can chopped tomatoes
15ml/1 tbsp red wine vinegar
5ml/1 tsp sugar
10ml/2 tsp finely chopped fresh rosemary
115g/4oz/1 cup frozen peas
350g/12oz fresh or dried spaghetti
15ml/1 tbsp chopped fresh flat leaf parsley
salt and freshly ground black pepper

1 Cut the squid into strips about 5mm/¼in wide. Finely chop the tentacles.

2 Heat the oil in a large shallow pan, add the onion and garlic, and cook gently, stirring, for about 5 minutes until softened. Add the squid, tomatoes, red wine vinegar and sugar. Stir in the rosemary, with salt and pepper to taste. Bring to the boil, stirring, then cover and simmer gently for 20 minutes.

3 Uncover the pan, add the peas and cook for 10 minutes. Meanwhile, bring a large pan of lightly salted water to the boil, add the pasta and cook until it is *al dente*.

4 Drain the pasta and tip it into a warmed serving bowl. Pour the sauce over the pasta, add the parsley, toss well and serve.

Cook's Tip
A good fishmonger will prepare squid for you, but if you do need to prepare it yourself, here's how. Holding the body in one hand, gently pull away the head and tentacles. Discard the head; chop and reserve the tentacles. Remove the transparent "quill" from inside the body. Peel off the brown skin, rub a little salt into the squid and wash under cold running water.

Linguine with Crab

This makes a rich and tasty first course, or can be served for a lunch or supper with crusty Italian bread.

Serves 4

about 250g/9oz crab meat
45ml/3 tbsp olive oil
1 small handful fresh flat leaf parsley, roughly chopped, plus extra, to garnish
1 garlic clove, crushed
350g/12oz ripe plum tomatoes, peeled and chopped
60–90ml/4–6 tbsp dry white wine
350g/12oz fresh or dried linguine
salt and freshly ground black pepper

1 Put the crab meat in a mortar and pound it to a rough pulp with a pestle or use a sturdy bowl and a rolling pin. Set aside.

2 Heat 30ml/2 tbsp of the oil in a saucepan. Add the parsley and garlic, fry briefly, then stir in the tomatoes, crab meat and wine. Cover and simmer for 15 minutes, stirring occasionally.

3 Meanwhile, bring a large pan of lightly salted water to the boil and cook the pasta until it is *al dente*.

4 Drain the pasta, reserving a little of the cooking water, and return to the clean pan. Add the remaining oil and toss quickly over a medium heat until the oil coats the strands.

5 Add the tomato and crab mixture to the pasta and toss again, adding a little of the reserved cooking water if the sauce seems too thick. Season to taste with salt and pepper. Serve hot, in warmed bowls, sprinkled with parsley.

Cook's Tip

The best way to obtain crab meat is to ask a fishmonger to remove it from the shell for you, or to buy dressed crab from the supermarket. For this recipe you will need one large crab, and you should use both the white and dark meat.

Crab Ravioli

This recipe for a dinner party starter uses chilli-flavoured pasta, which looks and tastes good with crab, but you can use plain pasta.

Serves 4

3-egg quantity Basic Pasta Dough, flavoured with 5–10ml/1–2 tsp crushed, dried red chillies
flour, for dusting
75g/3oz/6 tbsp butter
juice of 1 lemon

For the filling

175g/6oz/¾ cup mascarpone cheese
175g/6oz/¾ cup crab meat
30ml/2 tbsp finely chopped fresh flat leaf parsley, plus extra to garnish
finely grated rind of 1 lemon
pinch of crushed dried chillies
salt and freshly ground black pepper

1 Make the filling. Put the mascarpone in a bowl and mash it with a fork. Stir in all the remaining ingredients.

2 Using a pasta machine, roll out one-quarter of the pasta into a 90–100cm/36–39in strip. Cut the strip with a sharp knife into two 45–50cm/18–20in lengths (you can do this during rolling if the strip gets too long to manage). With a 6cm/2½in fluted biscuit cutter, cut out 8 squares from each pasta strip.

3 Using a teaspoon, put a mound of filling in the centre of half the squares. Brush a little water around the edge of the filled squares, then top with the plain squares and press the edges to seal. Press the edges with the tines of a fork to decorate.

4 Put the ravioli on floured dish towels, sprinkle lightly with flour and leave to dry while repeating the process with the remaining dough to make 32 ravioli altogether.

5 Cook the ravioli in a large saucepan of salted boiling water for 4–5 minutes. Meanwhile, heat the butter and lemon juice in a small saucepan until sizzling.

6 Drain the ravioli and divide among four warmed bowls. Drizzle the lemon butter over the ravioli and serve with parsley.

Spaghettini with Vodka & Caviar

This is an elegant yet easy way to serve spaghettini. Serve it for a sophisticated after-theatre supper.

Serves 4

60ml/4 tbsp olive oil
3 spring onions, thinly sliced
1 garlic clove, finely chopped
400g/14oz dried spaghettini
120ml/4fl oz/ ½ cup vodka
150ml/ ¼ pint/ ⅔ cup double cream
75g/3oz/ ½ cup caviar
salt and freshly ground black pepper

1 Heat the oil in a small pan. Add the spring onions and garlic, and cook gently for 4–5 minutes.

2 Bring a large saucepan of lightly salted water to the boil. Add the pasta and cook until *al dente*.

3 Pour the vodka and cream into the spring onion mixture and cook over a low heat for 5–8 minutes.

4 Remove the vodka sauce from the heat and stir in half the caviar. Season with salt and pepper to taste.

5 Drain the pasta, return it to the clean pan and toss immediately with the sauce. Serve in warmed plates, with a little of the reserved caviar in the centre of each portion.

Cook's Tip

True caviar is salted sturgeon roe, and ranges in colour from greenish grey through brown and golden to very dark grey. Red "caviar" is salmon or salmon trout roe, or red-dyed lumpfish roe. This may also be dyed black. Look-alike caviars are generally saltier than the real thing.

Pasta with Prawns & Feta

This dish combines the richness of fresh prawns with the tart saltiness of feta cheese.

Serves 4

450g/1lb/4 cups dried penne, garganelli or rigatoni
50g/2oz/ ¼ cup butter
450g/1lb raw prawns, peeled and deveined
6 spring onions, chopped
225g/8oz feta cheese, cubed
small bunch fresh chives, snipped
salt and freshly ground black pepper

1 Bring a large pan of lightly salted water to the boil. Add the pasta and cook until *al dente*.
2 Melt the butter in a frying pan and stir in the prawns. When they turn pink, add the spring onions and cook, stirring occasionally, for 1 minute. Stir in the feta and half the chives. Season to taste with pepper.
3 Drain the pasta, pile it on a warmed serving dish and top with the sauce. Scatter with the remaining chives and serve.

Capelli d'Angelo with Lobster

This is a sophisticated, stylish dish for an extra-special occasion.

Serves 4

meat from the body, tail and claws of 1 cooked lobster
juice of ½ lemon
40g/1½ oz/3 tbsp butter
4 fresh tarragon sprigs, leaves stripped and chopped
60ml/4 tbsp double cream
90ml/6 tbsp sparkling dry white wine
60ml/4 tbsp fish stock
300g/11oz fresh capelli d'angelo
salt and freshly ground black pepper
about 10ml/2 tsp lumpfish roe, to garnish (optional)

1 Cut the lobster meat into small pieces and put it in a bowl. Sprinkle with the lemon juice.

2 Melt the butter in a large saucepan, add the lobster meat and tarragon, and stir over the heat for a few seconds.

3 Pour in the cream and stir for a further few seconds, then add the sparkling wine and stock, and season with salt and pepper to taste. Simmer for 2 minutes, then remove from the heat and cover.

4 Bring a large pan of lightly salted water to the boil and cook the pasta until it is *al dente*. It will require only a few minutes. Drain well, reserving a few spoonfuls of the cooking water.

5 Place the pan of lobster sauce over a medium to high heat, add the pasta and toss for just long enough to combine and heat through, moistening with a little of the reserved water from the pasta. Serve immediately in warmed bowls and sprinkle each portion with lumpfish roe if you like.

Variation

Make the sauce with Champagne rather than sparkling white wine, if you are planning to serve Champagne with the meal.

Spaghetti Marinara

Shrimps, prawns and clams combine to make a superb seafood sauce which can be used with any type of pasta.

Serves 4

45ml/3 tbsp olive oil
1 medium onion, chopped
1 garlic clove, finely chopped
225g/8oz dried spaghetti
600ml/1 pint/2½ cups passata
15ml/1 tbsp tomato purée
5ml/1 tsp dried oregano
1 bay leaf
5ml/1 tsp sugar
115g/4oz/1 cup cooked peeled shrimps
115g/4oz/1 cup cooked peeled prawns
175g/6oz/1½ cups cooked clams or cockles, rinsed well if canned or bottled
15ml/1 tbsp lemon juice
45ml/3 tbsp chopped fresh parsley
25g/1oz/2 tbsp butter
salt and freshly ground black pepper

1 Heat the oil in a large saucepan and add the onion and garlic. Fry over a medium heat, stirring occasionally, for 6–7 minutes, until the onion has softened.

2 Bring a large saucepan of lightly salted water to the boil and cook the spaghetti until *al dente*.

3 Meanwhile, stir the passata, tomato purée, oregano, bay leaf and sugar into the onions, and season to taste with salt and pepper. Bring to the boil, then lower the heat and simmer for 2–3 minutes.

4 Add the shrimps, prawns, clams or cockles, lemon juice and 30ml/2 tbsp of the parsley to the passata mixture. Stir well, then cover and cook for 6–7 minutes.

5 Drain the spaghetti. Melt the butter in the clean pan. Return the drained pasta to the pan and toss with the butter. Season to taste with salt and pepper.

6 Divide the spaghetti among four warmed plates and top with the seafood sauce. Sprinkle with the remaining parsley and serve immediately.

Baked Seafood Spaghetti

Good things come in small packages, and in this case parchment parcels are opened at the table to reveal a tasty seafood and pasta filling.

Serves 4

450g/1lb live mussels, scrubbed and bearded
120ml/4fl oz/½ cup dry white wine
60ml/4 tbsp olive oil
2 garlic cloves, finely chopped
450g/1lb tomatoes, peeled and finely chopped
400g/14oz dried spaghetti or other long pasta
225g/8oz cooked peeled prawns
30ml/2 tbsp chopped fresh parsley
salt and freshly ground black pepper

1 Check the mussels, discarding any which are not tightly closed, or which fail to close when tapped on the work surface. Put them in a large pan with the wine. Cover the pan and place it over a moderate heat. As soon as the mussels open, lift them out with a slotted spoon. Discard any that remain closed.

2 Pour the cooking liquid through a strainer lined with kitchen paper, and reserve. Preheat the oven to 150°C/300°F/Gas 2.

3 Heat the oil in a medium saucepan and cook the garlic for 1–2 minutes. Add the tomatoes and cook until they soften. Stir in 175ml/6fl oz/ ¾ cup of the cooking liquid from the mussels.

4 Bring a large pan of lightly salted water to the boil. Add the spaghetti and cook until it is *al dente*.

5 When the pasta is almost cooked, add the prawns and parsley to the tomato sauce. Season and remove from the heat. Drain the pasta and mix it with the sauce and mussels.

6 Cut out four 45 x 30cm/18 x 12in pieces of non-stick baking paper. Divide the pasta and seafood mixture among them and twist the paper ends together to make a sealed packet. Arrange in a roasting tin and bake for 8–10 minutes. Place one unopened packet on each plate and serve.

Trenette with Shellfish

Colourful and delicious, this is ideal for a dinner party.

Serves 4

45ml/3 tbsp olive oil
1 small onion, finely chopped
1 garlic clove, crushed
½ fresh red chilli, seeded and chopped
200g/7oz can chopped tomatoes
30ml/2 tbsp chopped fresh parsley
400g/14oz live clams, scrubbed
400g/14oz live mussels, scrubbed and bearded
60ml/4 tbsp dry white wine
400g/14oz/3½ cups dried trenette
a few fresh basil leaves
90g/3½oz cooked peeled prawns
salt and freshly ground black pepper
chopped fresh herbs, to garnish

1 Heat 30ml/2 tbsp of the oil in a saucepan and cook the onion, garlic and chilli for 1–2 minutes. Stir in the tomatoes, half the parsley and pepper to taste. Bring to the boil, lower the heat, cover and simmer for 15 minutes.

2 Discard any shellfish that are open or that do not close when sharply tapped against the work surface. Heat the remaining oil in a large saucepan. Add the clams and mussels, with the rest of the parsley and toss over a high heat for a few seconds.

3 Pour in the wine, then cover tightly. Cook for 5 minutes, shaking the pan frequently, until the clams and mussels have opened. Using a slotted spoon, transfer them to a bowl, discarding any shellfish that have failed to open.

4 Strain the cooking liquid and set aside. Reserve some clams and mussels, then shell the rest. Bring a large pan of lightly salted water to the boil and cook the pasta until it is *al dente*.

5 Meanwhile, add 120ml/4fl oz/ ½ cup of the reserved seafood liquid to the tomato sauce. Bring to the boil, lower the heat, tear in the basil leaves and stir in the prawns and shellfish.

6 Drain the pasta and tip it into a warmed bowl. Add the seafood sauce and toss well. Serve in warmed bowls. Sprinkle each portion with herbs and garnish with the reserved shellfish.

Tagliolini with Mussels & Clams

This makes a stunning starter for a dinner party.

Serves 4

450g/1b fresh clams, scrubbed
450g/1lb fresh mussels, scrubbed and bearded
60ml/4 tbsp olive oil
1 small onion, finely chopped
2 garlic cloves, finely chopped
1 large handful fresh flat leaf parsley, plus extra chopped parsley to garnish
175ml/6fl oz/¾ cup dry white wine
250ml/8fl oz/1 cup fish stock
1 small fresh red chilli, seeded and chopped
350g/12oz dried squid ink tagliolini
salt and freshly ground black pepper

1 Check the clams and mussels, and discard any that are open, or which fail to close when tapped on the work surface.

2 Heat half the oil in a saucepan and cook the onion until soft. Add the garlic, half the parsley and seasoning. Add the clams, mussels and wine, cover and bring to the boil. Cook for 5 minutes, shaking the pan frequently, until the shellfish have opened.

3 Drain the shellfish in a fine sieve set over a bowl. Discard the aromatics, with any shellfish that have failed to open. Return the strained liquid to the clean pan and add the stock. Chop the remaining parsley finely; add it to the pan with the chilli. Bring to the boil, then simmer, until slightly reduced. Turn off the heat.

4 Remove and discard the top shells from about half the clams and mussels. Put all the clams and mussels in the pan of liquid and seasonings, then cover the pan tightly and set aside.

5 Bring a large pan of lightly salted water to the boil and cook the pasta until *al dente*. Drain it, return it to the clean pan and toss with the remaining olive oil. Put the pan of shellfish over a high heat and toss to heat through. Divide the pasta among four warmed plates, spoon the shellfish mixture over, sprinkle with the extra parsley and serve.

Seafood Conchiglione with Spinach

Conchiglione are very large pasta shells, measuring about 4cm/1½in; don't try stuffing smaller shells – they're much too fiddly!

Serves 4

32 conchiglione
25g/1oz/2 tbsp butter, plus extra for greasing
8 spring onions, finely sliced
6 tomatoes, peeled and chopped
225g/8oz/1 cup low-fat soft cheese
90ml/6 tbsp milk
pinch of freshly grated nutmeg
225g/8oz cooked peeled prawns
175g/6oz can white crab meat, drained and flaked
115g/4oz frozen chopped spinach, thawed and drained
salt and freshly ground black pepper

1 Preheat the oven to 150°C/300°F/Gas 2. Bring a large pan of lightly salted water to the boil and cook the conchiglione for 10 minutes. Drain, rinse with boiling water, then drain again.

2 Melt the butter in a small saucepan. Add the spring onions and cook over a low heat, stirring occasionally, for 3–4 minutes, or until softened. Stir in the tomatoes and cook for a further 4–5 minutes.

3 Put the soft cheese and milk in a saucepan and heat gently, stirring until blended. Season to taste with salt, pepper and a pinch of nutmeg. Spoon 30ml/2 tbsp of the cheese sauce into a bowl and set the remainder aside.

4 Add the spring onion and tomato mixture to the sauce in the bowl, together with the prawns and flaked crab meat. Mix thoroughly.

5 Spoon the seafood filling into the pasta shells and place in a single layer in a lightly greased shallow ovenproof dish. Cover with foil and bake for 10 minutes.

6 Stir the spinach into the remaining cheese sauce. Bring to the boil, then simmer gently for 1 minute, stirring all the time. Drizzle over the filled conchiglione and serve hot.

Baked Seafood Pasta

So simple to make it's bound to become a family favourite, this is a wonderful way of serving pasta.

Serves 6

65g/2½ oz/5 tbsp butter, plus extra for greasing
225g/8oz dried fettuccine
25g/1oz/¼ cup plain flour
475ml/16fl oz/2 cups milk
2.5ml/½ tsp dried mustard
5ml/1 tsp lemon juice
15ml/1 tbsp tomato purée
½ onion, finely chopped
2 celery sticks, diced
115g/4oz/1¼ cups small mushrooms, sliced
225g/8oz cooked peeled shrimp
225g/8oz crab meat
15ml/1 tbsp chopped fresh dill
salt and freshly ground black pepper
fresh dill sprigs, to garnish

1 Preheat the oven to 180°C/350°F/Gas 4. Generously grease a large ovenproof dish with butter.

2 Bring a large pan of lightly salted water to the boil and cook the pasta until it is *al dente*.

3 Meanwhile, melt 40g/1½oz/3 tbsp of the butter in a saucepan. Stir in the flour and cook for 1 minute, stirring constantly, then gradually add the milk, stirring until the sauce boils and thickens.

4 Add the mustard, lemon juice and tomato purée to the sauce, and mix well. Season to taste with salt and pepper.

5 Melt the remaining butter in a frying pan. Add the onion, celery and mushrooms. Cook over a medium heat, stirring occasionally, for about 5 minutes, until softened.

6 Drain the pasta and tip it into a large mixing bowl. Add the sauce, vegetable mixture, shrimp, crab meat and chopped dill. Stir thoroughly.

7 Pour the mixture evenly into the prepared dish. Bake for 30–40 minutes, until the top is lightly browned. Garnish with the dill sprigs and serve immediately.

Monkfish & Prawn Lasagne

Rich and creamy, this flavoursome lasagne makes a good supper-party dish.

Serves 6

65g/2½oz/5 tbsp butter
450g/1lb monkfish fillets, skinned and diced
225g/8oz raw prawns, peeled and deveined
225g/8oz/3 cups button mushrooms, chopped
40g/1½oz/⅓ cup plain flour
600ml/1 pint/2½ cups hot milk
300ml/½ pint/1¼ cups double cream
400g/14oz can chopped tomatoes
30ml/2 tbsp shredded fresh basil
8 sheets no-precook lasagne
75g/3oz/1 cup freshly grated Parmesan cheese
salt and freshly ground black pepper
fresh herbs, to garnish

1 Melt 15g/½oz/1 tbsp of the butter in a large saucepan, add the monkfish and prawns, and sauté for 2–3 minutes. When the prawns turn pink, transfer the fish and prawns to a bowl.

2 Add the mushrooms to the pan and sauté for 5 minutes. Remove with a slotted spoon and add to the fish in the bowl.

3 Melt the remaining butter in the pan, add the flour and cook for 1 minute. Gradually add the milk, stirring until the sauce boils and thickens. Whisk in the cream and cook over a low heat for 2 minutes more.

4 Remove the sauce from the heat and stir in the fish and mushroom mixture with all the juices that have collected in the bowl. Season to taste. Preheat the oven to 190°C/375°F/Gas 5.

5 Spread half the chopped tomatoes over the base of an ovenproof dish. Sprinkle with half the basil and season to taste. Ladle one-third of the seafood sauce over the tomatoes. Cover with four lasagne sheets. Spread the remaining tomatoes over and sprinkle with the rest of the basil. Ladle another third of the sauce over. Top with lasagne, spread the remaining sauce over and cover with the cheese. Bake for 30–40 minutes, until golden and bubbling. Serve hot, garnished with fresh herbs.

Shellfish Lasagne

This is a luxury lasagne suitable for a special occasion meal.

Serves 4–6

4–6 scallops, with corals
450g/1lb raw tiger prawns, peeled and deveined
1 garlic clove, crushed
75g/3oz/6 tbsp butter
50g/2oz/½ cup plain flour
600ml/1 pint/2½ cups hot milk
100ml/3½ fl oz/scant ½ cup double cream
100ml/3½ fl oz/7 tbsp dry white wine
2 sachets of saffron powder
good pinch of cayenne pepper
130g/4½ oz Fontina cheese, thinly sliced
75g/3oz/1 cup freshly grated Parmesan cheese
6–8 sheets fresh egg lasagne
salt and freshly ground black pepper

1 Preheat the oven to 190°C/375°F/Gas 5. Cut the scallops, corals and prawns into bite-size pieces and spread them in a dish. Sprinkle with the garlic and season to taste. Melt about one-third of the butter in a saucepan and toss the seafood over a medium heat for 1–2 minutes, or until the prawns turn pink. Remove with a slotted spoon and set aside.

2 Melt the remaining butter in the pan. Add the flour and cook for 1 minute. Gradually add the hot milk, stirring constantly until the sauce boils and becomes very thick and smooth.

3 Whisk in the cream, wine, saffron powder, cayenne, and salt and pepper to taste, then remove the sauce from the heat.

4 Spread one-third of the sauce over the base of an ovenproof dish. Arrange half the Fontina slices over and sprinkle with one-third of the grated Parmesan. Scatter half the seafood evenly on top, then cover with half the lasagne sheets. Repeat the layers, then cover with the remaining sauce and Parmesan.

5 Bake the lasagne for 30–40 minutes, or until the topping is golden brown and bubbling. Allow to stand for 10 minutes before serving.

Soba Noodles with Nori

Tender noodles, crisp toasted seaweed and a savoury dipping sauce make for a simple, but delicious light meal.

Serves 4
350g/12oz dried soba noodles
1 sheet nori seaweed

For the dipping sauce
300ml/ ½ pint/1 ¼ cups bonito stock
120ml/4fl oz/ ½ cup dark soy sauce
60ml/4 tbsp mirin
5ml/1 tsp sugar
10g/ ¼ oz loose bonito flakes

For the flavourings
4 spring onions, finely chopped
30ml/2 tbsp grated mooli (daikon)
wasabi paste

1 Make the dipping sauce. Combine the stock, soy sauce, mirin and sugar in a saucepan. Bring rapidly to the boil, add the bonito flakes, then remove from the heat. When cool, strain the sauce into a bowl and cover.

2 Bring a pan of lightly salted water to the boil and cook the soba noodles for 6–7 minutes or until just tender, following the manufacturer's directions on the packet.

3 Drain the noodles and then rinse them under cold running water, agitating them gently to remove the excess starch. Drain well again.

4 Toast the nori over a high gas flame or under a preheated grill, then crumble into thin strips. Divide the noodles among four serving dishes and top with the nori. Serve each portion with an individual bowl of dipping sauce and offer the flavourings separately.

Cook's Tip
The dipping sauce can be made up to a week before it is needed. Cover it and keep it in the fridge.

Egg Noodles with Tuna & Tomato Sauce

Raid the store cupboard, add a few fresh ingredients and you can produce a scrumptious main meal in a matter of moments.

Serves 4
15ml/1 tbsp olive oil
2 garlic cloves, finely chopped
2 dried red chillies, seeded and chopped
1 large red onion, thinly sliced
175g/6oz can tuna in brine, drained
6–8 stoned black olives
400g/14oz can chopped tomatoes
30ml/2 tbsp chopped fresh parsley
350g/12oz medium-thick dried egg noodles
salt and freshly ground black pepper

1 Heat the oil in a large frying pan. Add the garlic and dried chillies, and fry for a few seconds, then add the sliced onion. Cook over a medium heat, stirring occasionally, for about 5 minutes, until the onion softens.

2 Add the tuna and olives to the pan, and stir until well mixed. Stir in the tomatoes, with any juices. Bring to the boil, season well, stir in the parsley, then lower the heat and simmer gently.

3 Meanwhile, bring a large pan of lightly salted water to the boil. Add the noodles and cook them until just tender, following the directions on the packet.

4 Drain the noodles well and return them to the clean pan. Add the sauce, toss to mix and serve immediately.

Cook's Tip
Depending on the contents of your store cupboard, you could substitute other canned fish for the tuna. Try mackerel, sardines or salmon, for example. You could also add bottled clams or canned anchovies.

Stir-fried Noodles with Sweet Soy Salmon

Teriyaki sauce forms the marinade for the salmon, which is served with soft-fried noodles.

Serves 4

350g/12oz salmon fillet
30ml/2 tbsp Japanese soy sauce (shoyu)
30ml/2 tbsp saké
60ml/4 tbsp mirin or sweet sherry
5ml/1 tsp soft light brown sugar
10ml/2 tsp grated fresh root ginger
3 garlic cloves, 1 crushed, and 2 sliced into rounds
30ml/2 tbsp groundnut oil
225g/8oz dried egg noodles, cooked and drained
50g/2oz/1 cup alfalfa sprouts
30ml/2 tbsp sesame seeds, lightly toasted

1 Slice the salmon into thin strips and place these in a shallow dish. Mix the soy sauce, saké mirin or sherry, sugar, ginger and crushed garlic in a jug. Pour the mixture over the salmon, cover and leave for 30 minutes.

2 Preheat the grill. Drain the salmon, scraping off and reserving the marinade. Place the salmon in a single layer on a baking sheet. Cook under the grill for 2–3 minutes without turning.

3 Meanwhile, heat a wok until hot, add the oil and swirl it around. Add the garlic rounds and cook until golden brown, but not burnt. Add the cooked noodles and reserved marinade to the wok, and stir-fry for 3–4 minutes, until the marinade has reduced slightly to a syrupy glaze that coats the noodles.

4 Toss in the alfalfa sprouts, then remove from the heat. Transfer to warmed serving plates and top with the salmon. Sprinkle over the toasted sesame seeds. Serve at once.

Cook's Tip
It is important to scrape the marinade off the fish, as any pieces of ginger or garlic would burn during grilling.

Noodles with Prawns, Chicken & Ham

A delectable stir-fry, this contrasts crunchy vegetables with tender noodles, and introduces prawns, chicken and ham in key roles.

Serves 4–6

300g/10oz dried egg noodles
15ml/1 tbsp vegetable oil
1 medium onion, chopped
1 garlic clove, crushed
2.5cm/1in piece of fresh root ginger, peeled and chopped
50g/2oz/ ½ cup drained canned water chestnuts, chopped
15ml/1 tbsp soy sauce
30ml/2 tbsp fish sauce
225g/8oz cooked peeled prawns
175g/6oz cooked chicken breast, sliced
150g/5oz thickly sliced cooked ham, cut into short fingers
115g/4oz/2 cups beansprouts
200g/7oz/generous 1 cup drained canned baby corn cobs
lime wedges and shredded fresh coriander, to garnish

1 Bring a large saucepan of lightly salted water to the boil and cook the noodles until they are just tender, following the instructions on the packet.

2 Meanwhile, heat a wok. Add the oil, dribbling it around the rim so that it runs down to coat the surface. When the oil is hot, stir-fry the onion, garlic and ginger for 2–3 minutes. Add the water chestnuts, soy sauce, fish sauce, prawns, chicken and ham. Toss over the heat for 2 minutes.

3 Drain the noodles very well, then add them to the wok, with the beansprouts and corn cobs. Toss over the heat for 6–8 minutes, until all the ingredients are hot. Tip on to a large platter, garnish with the lime and coriander, and serve at once.

Cook's Tip
If you preheat the wok as described in the recipe, you can get away with using only a small amount of oil.

Seafood & Vermicelli Stir-fry

Seafood is the perfect choice for stir-fries, as it requires the fastest of cooking and combines superbly with noodles.

Serves 4

450g/1lb rice vermicelli, soaked in warm water until soft
15ml/1 tbsp vegetable oil
50g/2oz/ ½ cup drained sun-dried tomatoes, reconstituted in water then drained and sliced
3 spring onions, sliced on the diagonal
2 large carrots, cut into batons
1 courgette, cut into batons
225g/8oz raw prawns, peeled and deveined
225g/8oz shelled scallops
2.5cm/1in piece of fresh root ginger, finely grated
45ml/3 tbsp lemon juice
45ml/3 tbsp chopped fresh basil
salt and freshly ground black pepper

1 Bring a large pan of lightly salted water to the boil. Add the rice vermicelli and cook until tender, following the instructions on the packet. Drain, rinse with boiling water, and drain again thoroughly. Keep warm.

2 Heat a wok, add the oil, then stir-fry the sun-dried tomatoes, spring onions and carrots over a high heat for 5 minutes.

3 Add the courgette, prawns, scallops and ginger. Stir-fry for 3 minutes.

4 Pour in the lemon juice. Add the basil, with salt and pepper to taste, and stir well. Stir-fry for 2 minutes more. Divide the rice vermicelli among individual plates and spoon the stir-fried mixture on top. Serve immediately.

Cook's Tip

The easiest way to prepare the carrots and courgette is to slice them lengthways, then cut them across in thin sticks. Don't make them matchstick-thin or they will overcook.

Buckwheat Noodles with Smoked Trout

The light, crisp texture of the pak choi balances the tender shiitake mushrooms and noodles and perfectly complements the delicate flesh of smoked trout.

Serves 4

350g/12oz buckwheat or soba noodles
15ml/1 tbsp vegetable oil
115g/4oz fresh shiitake mushrooms, quartered
2 garlic cloves, finely chopped
15ml/1 tbsp grated fresh root ginger
225g/8oz pak choi, trimmed and separated into leaves
1 spring onion, finely sliced on the diagonal
5ml/1 tsp dark sesame oil
30ml/2 tbsp mirin or dry sherry
30ml/2 tbsp soy sauce
2 smoked trout, skinned and boned
salt
30ml/2 tbsp coriander leaves and 10ml/2 tsp toasted sesame seeds, to garnish

1 Bring a large pan of lightly salted water to the boil and cook the buckwheat or soba noodles until just tender, following the instructions on the packet.

2 Meanwhile, heat a wok until hot, add the oil and swirl it around. Add the shiitake mushrooms and stir-fry over a medium heat for 3 minutes.

3 Add the garlic, ginger and pak choi and toss over the heat for a further 2 minutes.

4 Drain the noodles very well and add them to the mushroom mixture, together with the spring onion, sesame oil, mirin or sherry and soy sauce. Stir briefly until heated through.

5 Break the smoked trout into bite-size pieces. Arrange the noodle mixture on individual serving plates. Place the smoked trout on top, garnish with coriander leaves and sesame seeds, and serve immediately.

Fried Cellophane Noodles & Prawns

Cellophane noodles look like delicate strands of blown glass, and make an attractive and tasty contribution to this stir-fry.

Serves 4

175g/6oz dried cellophane noodles
45ml/3 tbsp vegetable oil
3 garlic cloves, finely chopped
115g/4oz cooked peeled prawns
2 lap cheong, rinsed, drained and finely diced
2 eggs
2 celery sticks, including leaves, diced
115g/4oz/2 cups beansprouts
115g/4oz spinach, cut into large pieces
2 spring onions, chopped
15–30ml/1–2 tbsp fish sauce
5ml/1 tsp sesame oil
15ml/1 tbsp toasted sesame seeds, to garnish

1 Soak the cellophane noodles in a bowl of hot water for about 10 minutes, or until soft. Drain the noodles and cut them into 10cm/4in lengths.

2 Heat a wok until hot, add the oil and swirl it around. Stir-fry the garlic until golden brown. Add the prawns and lap cheong and stir-fry for 2–3 minutes. Stir in the noodles and stir-fry for 2 minutes more.

3 Make a well in the centre of the prawn mixture, break in the eggs and slowly stir them until they are creamy and just set.

4 Stir in the celery, beansprouts, spinach and spring onions. Season with fish sauce and stir in the sesame oil. Continue to stir-fry until all the ingredients are cooked, mixing well. Transfer to a serving dish. Garnish with the sesame seeds and serve.

Cook's Tip
Lap cheong are Chinese wind-dried sausages. Sold in pairs, tied together with string, they are available from Chinese and Asian supermarkets.

Thai Fried Noodles

This tasty dish, made with rice noodles, is one of the national dishes of Thailand.

Serves 4–6

45ml/3 tbsp vegetable oil
15ml/1 tbsp chopped garlic
16 raw king prawns, peeled, tails left intact and deveined
2 eggs, lightly beaten
15ml/1 tbsp dried shrimp, rinsed
30ml/2 tbsp pickled white radish
50g/2oz fried beancurd (tofu), cut into small slivers
2.5ml/½ tsp dried chilli flakes
350g/12oz rice noodles, soaked in warm water until soft
115g/4oz garlic chives, snipped
225g/8oz/4 cups beansprouts
50g/2oz/½ cup roasted peanuts, coarsely ground
5ml/1 tsp sugar
15ml/1 tbsp dark soy sauce
30ml/2 tbsp fish sauce
30ml/2 tbsp tamarind juice
fresh coriander leaves and kaffir lime wedges, to garnish

1 Heat a wok until hot, add 15ml/1 tbsp of the oil and swirl it around. Sir-fry the garlic until golden. Stir in the prawns and cook for 1–2 minutes until pink, tossing from time to time. Remove and set aside.

2 Heat another 15ml/1 tbsp of oil in the wok. Add the eggs and scramble them lightly. Remove from the wok and set aside with the prawns.

3 Heat the remaining oil in the wok. Add the dried shrimp, pickled radish, beancurd (tofu) and dried chilli flakes. Stir-fry briefly. Drain the rice noodles thoroughly, add them to the wok and stir-fry for 5 minutes.

4 Add the garlic chives with half the beansprouts and half the peanuts. Season with the sugar, soy sauce, fish sauce and tamarind juice. Mix well and cook, stirring frequently, until the noodles are heated through.

5 Return the prawn and egg mixture to the wok and mix with the noodles, tossing the mixture together. Garnish with the rest of the beansprouts and peanuts, the coriander leaves and the lime wedges. Serve immediately.

Lemon Grass Prawns on Crisp Noodle Cakes

This looks spectacular and has a wonderful flavour.

Serves 4

300g/11oz thin dried egg noodles
60ml/4 tbsp vegetable oil
500g/1¼lb raw king prawns, peeled and deveined
2.5ml/½ tsp ground coriander
15ml/1 tbsp ground turmeric
2 garlic cloves, finely chopped
2 slices fresh root ginger, finely chopped
2 lemon grass stalks, finely chopped
2 shallots, finely chopped
15ml/1 tbsp tomato purée
250ml/8fl oz/1 cup coconut cream
15–30ml/1–2 tbsp freshly squeezed lime juice
15–30ml/1–2 tbsp fish sauce
1 cucumber, peeled, seeded and cut into 5cm/2in batons
1 tomato, seeded and cut into strips
2 fresh red chillies, seeded and finely sliced
salt and freshly ground black pepper
sliced spring onions and fresh coriander sprigs, to garnish

1 Bring a large pan of lightly salted water to the boil and cook the egg noodles until just tender. Drain, rinse under cold running water and drain again.

2 Heat 10ml/2 tsp of the oil in a small crêpe pan. Add a quarter of the noodles, spread them to make a small cake and fry for 4–5 minutes, until crisp and golden. Turn the noodle cake over and fry the other side. Remove from the pan. Make three more cakes in the same way. Keep hot.

3 In a bowl, toss the prawns with the ground coriander, turmeric, garlic, ginger and lemon grass. Season with salt and pepper to taste.

4 Heat the remaining oil in a large frying pan. Add the shallots and fry for 1 minute, then add the prawns and fry for a further 2 minutes. Remove the prawns with a slotted spoon.

5 Stir the tomato purée and coconut cream into the mixture remaining in the pan, with lime juice and fish sauce to taste. Return the prawns to the sauce and add the cucumber. Simmer gently until the prawns are cooked and the sauce has reduced to a coating consistency.

6 Stir in the tomato and red chillies, let them warm through, then ladle a quarter of the mixture on to each noodle cake. Garnish with the spring onions and coriander, and serve.

Cook's Tip
Lemon grass features widely in the cuisines of South-east Asia, especially in Vietnam and Thailand. The stems of fresh lemon grass must be chopped very finely or used whole and removed before serving, as they have a woody texture. The bulb may be crushed, sliced or chopped. Dried, powdered and bottled lemon grass are increasingly available, but grated lemon rind may be used as a substitute.

Noodles with Sun-dried Tomatoes & Prawns

East meets West in this modern marriage of Japanese somen noodles and sun-dried tomatoes.

Serves 4

350g/12oz dried somen noodles
45ml/3 tbsp olive oil
20 raw king prawns, peeled and deveined
2 garlic cloves, finely chopped
45–60ml/3–4 tbsp sun-dried tomato purée
salt and freshly ground black pepper

For the garnish
handful of fresh basil leaves
30ml/2 tbsp drained sun-dried tomatoes in oil, cut into strips

1 Bring a large pan of lightly salted water to the boil and cook the noodles until tender.

2 Meanwhile, heat half the oil in a large frying pan, and fry the prawns and garlic for 3–5 minutes, until the prawns turn pink and are firm to the touch.

3 Stir in 15ml/1 tbsp of the sun-dried tomato purée. Using a slotted spoon, transfer the prawns to a bowl and keep hot.

4 Add the remaining oil to the pan and stir in the remaining sun-dried tomato purée. You may need to add a spoonful of water if the mixture is very thick. Heat the mixture until it sizzles, then toss in the noodles. Return the prawns to the pan and toss to combine. Season and serve, garnished with the basil and strips of sun-dried tomatoes.

Cook's Tip
Ready-made sun-dried tomato purée is readily available – however, you can make your own simply by processing bottled sun-dried tomatoes with their oil. You could also add a couple of anchovy fillets and some capers if you like.

Straw Noodle Prawns

We have Japan to thank for this beautiful dish, which tastes as good as it looks.

Serves 4–6

75g/3oz dried somen noodles, soaked in warm water until soft
2 sheets nori seaweed
12 large fresh prawns, peeled and deveined
vegetable oil, for deep-frying

For the dipping sauce

90ml/6 tbsp soy sauce
30ml/2 tbsp sugar
2cm/¾ in piece of fresh root ginger, grated

1 Make the dipping sauce. Put the soy sauce, sugar and ginger into a small pan and mix well. Bring to the boil, then lower the heat and simmer for 2–3 minutes. Strain into a small dish and leave to cool.

2 Drain the noodles, dry them on kitchen paper, then cut them into 7.5cm/3in lengths. Cut the nori into 1cm/ ½ in strips, 5cm/ 2in long and set aside.

3 Line up the noodles on a board. Straighten each prawn by pushing a bamboo skewer through its length. Roll the prawns in the noodles so that they adhere in neat horizontal strands. Moisten one end of each nori strip and fix it around the wide end of each noodle-coated prawn, like a collar.

4 In a wok, heat the vegetable oil for deep-frying to 180°C/ 350°F, or until a cube of day-old bread browns in about 30 seconds. Add the prawns, two at a time, and fry for about 30 seconds, until the noodle coating on each is crisp and golden, using chopsticks or tongs to handle them. Drain thoroughly on kitchen paper.

5 To neaten the prawns, cut through the bottom of each nori collar with a sharp knife. Remove the skewers.

6 Serve the straw noodle prawns with the dipping sauce.

Singapore Noodles

Dried mushrooms add an intense flavour to this lightly curried dish. Use Chinese mushrooms if possible.

Serves 4

20g/ ¾oz/ ⅓ cup dried Chinese mushrooms
225g/8oz fine dried egg noodles
10ml/2 tsp sesame oil
45ml/3 tbsp groundnut oil
2 garlic cloves, crushed
1 small onion, chopped
1 fresh green chilli, seeded and thinly sliced
10ml/2 tsp curry powder
115g/4oz green beans, topped, tailed and halved
115g/4oz Chinese leaves, thinly shredded
4 spring onions, sliced
30ml/2 tbsp soy sauce
115g/4oz cooked peeled prawns, deveined
salt

1 Put the mushrooms in a bowl. Cover with warm water and soak for 30 minutes. Drain, reserving 30ml/2 tbsp of the soaking water, then slice lengthways.

2 Bring a pan of lightly salted water to the boil and cook the noodles until just tender. Drain, tip into a bowl and toss with the sesame oil.

3 Heat a wok and add the groundnut oil. When it is hot, stir-fry the garlic, onion and chilli for 3 minutes. Stir in the curry powder and cook, stirring, for 1 minute. Add the mushrooms, green beans, Chinese leaves and spring onions. Stir-fry for 3–4 minutes, until the vegetables are crisp-tender.

4 Add the noodles, soy sauce, reserved mushroom soaking water and prawns. Toss over the heat for 2–3 minutes, until the noodles and prawns are heated through. Serve immediately.

Variations

Ring the changes with the vegetables used in this dish. Try mangetouts, broccoli, peppers or baby sweetcorn. The prawns can be left out or you could use ham or chicken instead.

Noodles with Prawns in Lemon Sauce

In this Chinese dish, it is the noodles that are the prime ingredient, with seafood playing a minor, but still important, role in terms of flavour and colour.

Serves 4

2 packets dried egg noodles
15ml/1 tbsp sunflower oil
2 celery sticks, cut into matchsticks
2 garlic cloves, crushed
4 spring onions, sliced
2 carrots, cut into matchsticks
7.5cm/3in piece of cucumber, cut into matchsticks
115g/4oz raw prawns, in their shells
pared rind and juice of 1 lemon
5ml/1 tsp cornflour
60–75ml/4–5 tbsp fish stock
115g/4oz/1 cup cooked peeled prawns
salt and freshly ground black pepper
fresh dill sprigs, to garnish

1 Bring a large pan of lightly salted water to the boil and cook the noodles until tender.

2 Meanwhile, heat the oil in a pan and stir-fry the celery, garlic, spring onions and carrots for 2–3 minutes. Add the cucumber and shell-on prawns, and cook for 2–3 minutes. Blanch the pared lemon rind in boiling water for 1 minute.

3 Mix the lemon juice with the cornflour and stock, and add to the pan. Bring gently to the boil, stirring, and cook for 1 minute.

4 Drain the lemon rind and add it to the pan, with the peeled prawns. Season to taste. Drain the noodles and serve with the prawn sauce. Garnish each portion with dill.

Cook's Tip

Dried egg noodles need very little cooking. In some cases you just immerse them in boiling water for a few minutes. Always check the instructions on the packet.

Chilli Squid & Noodles

In China, this popular noodle dish is traditionally cooked in a clay pot.

Serves 4

675g/1½ lb prepared squid
15ml/1 tbsp vegetable oil
3 slices of fresh root ginger, finely shredded
2 garlic cloves, finely chopped
1 red onion, thinly sliced
1 carrot, thinly sliced
1 celery stick, sliced
50g/2oz/⅓ cup sugar snap peas, topped and tailed
5ml/1 tsp sugar
15ml/1 tbsp chilli bean paste
2.5ml/½ tsp chilli powder
75g/3oz cellophane noodles, soaked in warm water until soft
120ml/4fl oz/½ cup light chicken stock
15ml/1 tbsp soy sauce
15ml/1 tbsp oyster sauce
5ml/1 tsp sesame oil
salt
fresh coriander leaves, to garnish

1 Cut the body of the squid into rings or split it open lengthways, score criss-cross patterns on the inside of the body and cut it into 5 x 4cm/2 x 1½in pieces.

2 Heat the oil in a flameproof casserole. Add the ginger, garlic and onion, and fry, stirring occasionally, for 1–2 minutes.

3 Add the squid, carrot, celery and sugar snap peas. Fry until the squid curls up. Season with salt to taste and stir in the sugar, chilli bean paste and chilli powder. Transfer the mixture to a bowl and set aside.

4 Drain the soaked noodles and add them to the casserole. Stir in the stock and sauces. Cover and cook for 10 minutes, or until the noodles are tender.

5 Return the squid and vegetables to the casserole. Cover and cook for about 5–6 minutes more, until all the flavours are combined. Serve in warmed bowls.

6 Drizzle each portion with sesame oil and sprinkle with the coriander leaves.

Tossed Noodles with Seafood

Surprisingly substantial, this is a very good way of serving seafood.

Serves 4–6

350g/12oz thick dried egg noodles
225g/8oz mussels, scrubbed and bearded
60ml/4 tbsp vegetable oil
3 slices of fresh root ginger, grated
2 garlic cloves, finely chopped
225g/8oz raw prawns, peeled and deveined
225g/8oz prepared squid, cut into rings
115g/4oz oriental fried fish cake, sliced
1 red pepper, seeded and cut into rings
50g/2oz/ ⅓ cup sugar snap peas, topped and tailed
30ml/2 tbsp soy sauce
2.5ml/ ½ tsp sugar
120ml/4fl oz/ ½ cup fish stock
15ml/1 tbsp cornflour
5–10ml/1–2 tsp sesame oil
salt and freshly ground black pepper
chopped spring onions and fresh red chillies, to garnish

1 Bring a large pan of lightly salted water to the boil and cook the noodles until just tender. Drain and set aside.

2 Check the mussels and discard any that are not tightly closed, or which fail to shut when tapped on the work surface.

3 Heat a wok until hot, add the oil and swirl it around. Stir-fry the ginger and garlic for 30 seconds. Add the mussels, prawns and squid, put a lid on the wok and steam the seafood for about 4–5 minutes, until the prawns have changed colour and the mussel shells have opened. Discard any that remain shut. Add the fish cake slices, red pepper rings and sugar snap peas, and stir well.

4 In a bowl, mix the soy sauce, sugar, stock and cornflour. Stir into the seafood and bring to the boil. Add the noodles and cook until they are heated through.

5 Add the sesame oil to the noodle mixture, and season with salt and pepper to taste. Serve at once, garnished with the spring onions and red chillies.

Seafood Chow Mein

Chow Mein originated in North America and is based on a traditional Chinese dish. It tastes delicious.

Serves 4

75g/3oz prepared squid
75g/3oz raw prawns, peeled and deveined
3–4 shelled fresh scallops
½ egg white
15ml/1 tbsp cornflour mixed to a paste with 30ml/2 tbsp water
250g/9oz dried egg noodles
75–90ml/5–6 tbsp vegetable oil
50g/2oz/ ⅓ cup mangetouts
2.5ml/ ½ tsp salt
2.5ml/ ½ tsp soft light brown sugar
15ml/1 tbsp Chinese rice wine or dry sherry
30ml/2 tbsp light soy sauce
2 spring onions, finely shredded, and a few drops of sesame oil, to garnish

1 Open up the squid and, using a sharp knife, score the inside in a criss-cross pattern. Cut the squid into pieces, each about the size of a postage stamp. Soak these in a bowl of boiling water until all the pieces curl up. Drain, rinse in cold water and drain again.

2 Cut each prawn in half lengthways and cut each scallop into 3–4 slices. Whisk the egg white and cornflour paste in a bowl, add the scallops and prawns, and toss them in the mixture.

3 Bring a large pan of lightly salted water to the boil and cook the noodles until tender. Drain, rinse under cold water and drain again. Put into a bowl and mix with about 15ml/1 tbsp of the vegetable oil.

4 Heat a wok and add 30–45ml/2–3 tbsp of the oil. When it is hot, stir-fry the mangetouts and seafood for 2 minutes. Add the salt, sugar, wine or sherry and half of the soy sauce, and toss over the heat for 1 minute, then remove and keep warm.

5 Heat the remaining oil in the wok and stir-fry the noodles for 2–3 minutes with the remaining soy sauce. Place in a large serving dish, pour the seafood mixture on top, garnish with the spring onions and sprinkle with the sesame oil.

Conchiglie with Chicken Livers & Herbs

Fresh herbs and chicken livers are a good combination. Tossed with pasta shells, they make a very tasty supper dish.

Serves 4

50g/2oz/ ¼ cup butter
115g/4oz pancetta or rindless streaky bacon, diced
250g/9oz frozen chicken livers, thawed, drained and diced
2 garlic cloves, crushed
10ml/2 tsp chopped fresh sage
300g/11oz/2¾ cups dried conchiglie
150ml/ ¼ pint/ ⅔ cup dry white wine
4 ripe tomatoes, peeled and diced
15ml/1 tbsp chopped fresh parsley
salt and freshly ground black pepper

1 Melt half the butter in a saucepan, add the pancetta or bacon and fry over a medium heat for a few minutes until it is lightly coloured but not crisp.

2 Add the diced chicken livers, garlic and half the sage, and season with plenty of pepper. Increase the heat and toss the livers for about 5 minutes, until they change colour all over.

3 Meanwhile, bring a large pan of lightly salted water to the boil and cook the pasta until it is *al dente*.

4 Pour the white wine over the chicken livers in the pan and let it sizzle for a few moments, then lower the heat and simmer gently for 5 minutes.

5 Add the remaining butter to the pan. As soon as it has melted, add the diced tomatoes, toss to mix, then add the remaining sage and the parsley. Stir thoroughly. Taste and add salt if needed.

6 Drain the pasta and tip it into a warmed serving bowl. Pour the chicken liver and herb sauce over and toss well to mix. Serve immediately.

Tagliatelle with Aubergines & Chicken Livers

Aubergines in a rich tomato sauce go very well with chicken livers. If cooking for vegetarian guests, use black olives instead.

Serves 4

675g/1½ lb dried tagliatelle
275g/10oz frozen chicken livers, thawed and drained
chopped flat leaf parsley, to garnish

For the sauce

2 large aubergines, about 350g/12oz each
2 garlic cloves
1 large onion
90–120ml/6–8 tbsp oil
500ml/17fl oz/1¾ cups passata
250ml/8fl oz/1 cup boiling water
salt and freshly ground black pepper

1 To make the tomato sauce, peel the aubergines and dice the flesh. Place in a colander. Sprinkle with salt and leave to drain in the sink for 30 minutes. Rinse thoroughly under cold running water and squeeze dry. Crush the garlic and chop the onion.

2 Heat half the oil in a frying pan and sauté the onion for about 1 minute. Add the garlic and cook until the onion starts to brown. Using a slotted spoon, transfer the onion mixture to a plate. Brown the aubergine in the remaining oil.

3 Return the onion mixture to the pan and add the passata, boiling water and seasoning. Simmer for 30 minutes.

4 Preheat the grill. Bring a large pan of lightly salted water to the boil and cook the tagliatelle until it is *al dente*.

5 Meanwhile, place the chicken livers on oiled foil and grill for 3–4 minutes on each side. Snip into strips.

6 Drain the tagliatelle and place on warmed individual plates. Top each portion with the aubergine sauce and chicken livers. Garnish with the chopped flat leaf parsley.

Orecchiette with Bacon & Chicken Livers

Sherry balances the saltiness of the bacon in this superbly rich sauce.

Serves 4

350g/12oz/3 cups dried orecchiette
225g/8oz frozen chicken livers, thawed and drained
15ml/1 tbsp olive oil
175g/6oz rindless smoked back bacon, roughly chopped
2 garlic cloves, crushed
400g/14oz can chopped tomatoes
150ml/ ¼ pint/ ⅔ cup chicken stock
15ml/1 tbsp tomato purée
15ml/1 tbsp dry sherry
30ml/2 tbsp chopped fresh mixed herbs
salt and freshly ground black pepper
freshly grated Parmesan cheese, to serve

1 Bring a large pan of lightly salted water to the boil and cook the pasta until it is *al dente*.

2 Meanwhile, trim the chicken livers and cut them into bite-size pieces. Heat the olive oil in a sauté pan, add the bacon and fry for 3–4 minutes.

3 Add the garlic and chicken livers to the pan and fry for a further 2–3 minutes. Stir in the tomatoes, chicken stock, tomato purée, sherry and herbs, and season with salt and pepper.

4 Bring to the boil, then lower the heat and simmer gently, uncovered, for about 5 minutes, until the sauce has thickened.

5 Drain the pasta, return it to the clean pan and toss it with the sauce. Serve hot, sprinkled with Parmesan cheese.

Variation
You could substitute smoked or unsmoked pancetta for the back bacon, if you prefer.

Tagliatelle with Chicken & Vermouth

Vermouth gives this chicken sauce a delicious flavour, with the fromage frais taking the edge off the acidity.

Serves 4

15ml/1 tbsp olive oil
1 red onion, cut into wedges
350g/12oz dried tagliatelle
1 garlic clove, chopped
350g/12oz skinless, boneless chicken breasts, diced
300ml/ ½ pint/1 ¼ cups dry vermouth
45ml/3 tbsp chopped fresh mixed herbs
150ml/ ¼ pint/ ⅔ cup very-low-fat fromage frais
salt and freshly ground black pepper
shredded fresh mint, to garnish

1 Heat the oil in a large heavy-based frying pan. Add the onion and fry for about 10 minutes, until it starts to soften and the layers separate.

2 Bring a large pan of lightly salted water to the boil and cook the pasta until it is *al dente*.

3 Meanwhile, add the garlic and chicken to the onion and fry, stirring occasionally, for 10 minutes, until the chicken has browned all over and is cooked through.

4 Pour in the vermouth, bring to the boil and boil rapidly until reduced by about half. Stir in the herbs and fromage frais, and season with salt and pepper to taste. Heat through gently, but do not let the sauce boil.

5 Drain the pasta, return it to the clean pan and toss it with the sauce to coat. Serve in warmed bowls, garnished with the shredded mint.

Variation
If you don't want to use vermouth, use dry white wine instead. Orvieto or Frascati would be ideal.

Farfalle with Chicken & Cherry Tomatoes

Quick to prepare and easy to cook, this colourful dish is full of flavour.

Serves 4

350g/12oz skinless, boneless chicken breasts, cut into bite-size pieces
60ml/4 tbsp dry vermouth
10ml/2 tsp chopped fresh rosemary
15ml/1 tbsp olive oil
1 onion, finely chopped
90g/3½ oz piece Italian salami, diced
275g/10oz/2½ cups dried farfalle
15ml/1 tbsp balsamic vinegar
400g/14oz can Italian cherry tomatoes
good pinch of crushed dried red chillies
salt and freshly ground black pepper
4 fresh rosemary sprigs, to garnish

1 Put the chicken in a bowl, pour in the vermouth and sprinkle with half the rosemary. Season to taste, stir well and set aside.

2 Heat the oil in a saucepan and fry the onion and salami for 5 minutes, stirring frequently. Bring a large pan of lightly salted water to the boil and cook the pasta until it is *al dente*.

3 Add the chicken and vermouth to the onion and salami, increase the heat to high and fry for 3 minutes, or until the chicken is white all over. Sprinkle the vinegar over the chicken. Add the cherry tomatoes and dried chillies. Stir well and simmer for a few minutes more. Taste the sauce for seasoning.

4 Drain the pasta and return it to the clean pan. Add the sauce and remaining chopped rosemary, and toss well. Serve in warmed bowls, garnished with the rosemary sprigs.

Cook's Tip
If you prefer, you can crush the tomatoes with the back of a wooden spoon while they are simmering in the pan.

Pappardelle with Chicken & Mushrooms

Rich and creamy, this is a good supper party dish.

Serves 4

15g/½ oz/¼ cup dried porcini mushrooms
175ml/6fl oz/¾ cup warm water
25g/1oz/2 tbsp butter
1 garlic clove, crushed
1 small handful fresh parsley, roughly chopped
1 small leek, chopped
120ml/4fl oz/½ cup dry white wine
250ml/8fl oz/1 cup chicken stock
400g/14oz fresh or dried pappardelle
2 skinless, boneless chicken breasts, cut into thin strips
105ml/7 tbsp mascarpone cheese
salt and freshly ground black pepper
fresh basil leaves, shredded, to garnish

1 Put the mushrooms in a bowl. Pour over the warm water. Leave to soak for 15–20 minutes, then tip into a fine sieve set over a large pan and squeeze the mushrooms with your hands to release as much liquid as possible. Chop the mushrooms finely and set them aside. Reserve the strained soaking liquid.

2 Melt the butter in a wide, shallow pan, and add the mushrooms, garlic, parsley and leek, with salt and pepper to taste. Cook over a low heat, stirring frequently, for 5 minutes, then pour in the wine and stock, and bring to the boil. Lower the heat and simmer for about 5 minutes, or until the liquid has reduced and is thickened.

3 Add plenty of lightly salted water to the strained soaking liquid, bring to the boil and cook the pasta until *al dente*.

4 Add the chicken to the sauce and simmer for 5 minutes, or until just tender. Add the mascarpone, a spoonful at a time, stirring well after each addition, then add 1–2 spoonfuls of the water used for cooking the pasta. Taste for seasoning.

5 Drain the pasta and tip it into a large bowl. Add the chicken and sauce, and toss well. Serve, topped with the shredded basil.

Fusilli with Chicken & Tomato Sauce

For a speedy supper, serve this dish with a salad of dressed leaves.

Serves 4

15ml/1 tbsp olive oil
1 onion, chopped
1 carrot, chopped
1 garlic clove, chopped
400g/14oz can chopped tomatoes
15ml/1 tbsp tomato purée
150ml/ ¼ pint/ ⅔ cup chicken stock
350g/12oz/3 cups dried fusilli
50g/2oz/ ½ cup drained sun-dried tomatoes in olive oil, chopped
225g/8oz skinless, boneless chicken breasts, diagonally sliced
salt
fresh mint sprigs, to garnish

1 Heat the oil in a large frying pan, and fry the onion and carrot for 5 minutes, stirring occasionally.

2 Stir in the garlic, canned tomatoes, tomato purée and stock. Bring to the boil, then lower the heat and simmer for about 10 minutes, stirring occasionally.

3 Meanwhile, bring a large pan of lightly salted water to the boil and cook the pasta until *al dente*.

4 Pour the sauce into a blender or food processor and process until smooth. Return it to the pan and stir in the sun-dried tomatoes and chicken. Bring to the boil, then simmer for 10 minutes, until the chicken is cooked.

5 Drain the pasta and return it to the clean pan. Toss it with the sauce. Serve in heated bowls, garnished with the mint.

Cook's Tip

If you have a hand-held food processor, simply purée the sauce in the pan.

Chicken & Pasta Balti

Of course, this is not a traditional Balti dish, as pasta is seldom served in India or Pakistan, but nonetheless it is delicious.

Serves 4–6

75g/3oz/ ¾ cup dried conchiglie
60ml/4 tbsp corn oil
4 curry leaves
4 whole dried red chillies
1 large onion, sliced
1–2 garlic cloves, crushed
5ml/1 tsp chilli powder
2.5cm/1in piece of fresh root ginger, grated
5ml/1 tsp crushed pomegranate seeds
5ml/1 tsp salt
2 tomatoes, chopped
175g/6oz skinless, boneless chicken, cubed
275g/10oz can chick-peas, drained
115g/4oz/ ⅔ cup drained canned sweetcorn
50g/2oz/ ⅓ cup mangetouts, diagonally sliced

1 Bring a large pan of lightly salted water to the boil. Cook the pasta until it is *al dente*, then drain it, rinse it under hot water and drain it again.

2 Heat the oil in a deep frying pan and fry the curry leaves, whole dried chillies and onion for 5 minutes. Add the garlic, chilli powder, ginger, pomegranate seeds, salt and tomatoes. Stir-fry for 3 minutes.

3 Add the chicken, chick-peas, sweetcorn and mangetouts to the onion mixture. Cook over a medium heat, stirring constantly, for 5 minutes.

4 Tip in the pasta and stir well. Cook for 7–10 minutes more, or until the chicken is cooked through. Transfer to warmed individual bowls and serve immediately.

Cook's Tip

Using coloured pasta shells makes this dish look especially attractive and appetizing.

Penne with Chicken & Broccoli

The combination of crisp broccoli, garlic and creamy Gorgonzola cheese is very good, and goes especially well with chicken.

Serves 4

115g/4oz/scant 1 cup broccoli florets, divided into tiny sprigs
400g/14oz/3½ cups dried penne
50g/2oz/ ¼ cup butter
2 skinless, boneless chicken breasts, cut into thin strips
2 garlic cloves, crushed
120ml/4fl oz/ ½ cup dry white wine
250ml/8fl oz/1 cup double cream
90g/3½oz Gorgonzola cheese, rind removed and finely diced
salt and freshly ground black pepper
freshly grated Parmesan cheese, to serve

1 Bring a large pan of lightly salted water to the boil. Add the broccoli and boil for 2 minutes, then lift out the sprigs with a slotted spoon, put them in a colander and refresh them under cold running water. Drain well. Add the pasta to the boiling water and cook it until it is *al dente*.

2 Meanwhile, melt the butter in a deep frying pan. Add the chicken and garlic, and stir-fry over a medium heat, stirring frequently, for 3 minutes, or until the chicken is white all over.

3 Pour in the wine and cream, stir to mix, then simmer, stirring occasionally, for 5 minutes, or until the sauce has reduced and thickened. Add the broccoli, increase the heat and toss to heat it through. Season with salt and pepper.

4 Drain the pasta and return it to the clean pan. Add the sauce and Gorgonzola, and toss well. Serve immediately in warmed bowls, with the grated Parmesan.

Variation
Use leeks instead of broccoli if you prefer. Fry them at the same time as the chicken.

Chicken Lasagne

This is an easy and excellent dish for entertaining guests of all ages.

Serves 8

30ml/2 tbsp olive oil
900g/2lb minced chicken
225g/8oz rindless streaky bacon rashers, chopped
2 garlic cloves, crushed
450g/1lb leeks, sliced
225g/8oz carrots, diced
30ml/2 tbsp tomato purée
450ml/ ¾ pint/scant 2 cups chicken stock
12 sheets no-precook lasagne verde
salt and freshly ground black pepper
salad leaves, to serve

For the cheese sauce

50g/2oz/ ¼ cup butter
50g/2oz/ ½ cup plain flour
600ml/1 pint/2½ cups milk
115g/4oz/1 cup grated mature Cheddar cheese
1.5ml/ ¼ tsp dry English mustard

1 Heat the oil in a large pan and brown the minced chicken and bacon over a high heat, stirring constantly. Add the garlic, leeks and carrots, and cook for 5 minutes, until softened. Stir in the tomato purée, stock and seasoning. Bring to the boil, cover and simmer for 30 minutes.

2 Make the sauce. Melt the butter in a saucepan over a low heat, stir in the flour and cook for 1 minute, stirring constantly. Gradually add the milk, stirring constantly until the mixture boils and thickens. Stir in three-quarters of the grated cheese until it melts, then add the mustard, and season to taste.

3 Preheat the oven to 190°C/375°F/Gas 5. Make layers of the chicken mixture, lasagne and half the cheese sauce in a 2.5 litre/ 4 pint/10 cup ovenproof dish, starting and finishing with a layer of the chicken mixture.

4 Pour the remaining cheese sauce evenly over the top, ensuring that the last layer is completely covered. Sprinkle with the remaining grated cheese and bake for 1 hour, or until bubbling and lightly browned on top. Leave to stand for about 5 minutes before serving with salad leaves.

Broccoli & Chicken Lasagne

A great example of how vegetables can add flavour and texture to a favourite dish, and make it possible to use less meat.

Serves 6

25g/1oz/2 tbsp butter, plus extra for greasing
450g/1lb broccoli, broken into florets
15ml/1 tbsp sunflower oil
450g/1lb skinless, boneless chicken breasts, cut into thin strips
1 onion, finely chopped
1 garlic clove, chopped
600ml/1 pint/2½ cups passata
2.5ml/½ tsp dried thyme
2.5ml/½ tsp dried oregano
12 sheets no-precook lasagne
275g/10oz/1¼ cups fromage frais
75g/3oz/1 cup freshly grated Parmesan cheese, plus extra for sprinkling
225g/8oz mozzarella cheese, thinly sliced
salt and freshly ground black pepper

1 Preheat the oven to 180°C/350°F/Gas 4 and grease a large shallow ovenproof dish with butter. Steam or boil the broccoli until nearly tender. Strain and set aside.

2 Heat the oil and butter in a frying pan and fry the chicken until lightly browned. Using a slotted spoon, transfer to a plate and set aside.

3 Add the onion and garlic to the pan and fry for 3–4 minutes. Stir in the passata and herbs, and season with salt and pepper to taste. Cook, stirring frequently, for about 3–4 minutes, until the sauce has thickened slightly.

4 Spoon half the tomato sauce into the prepared dish. Add a layer of four lasagne sheets and then half the chicken and half the broccoli. Dot with half the fromage frais and layer with half the Parmesan cheese. Repeat the layers, then top with the remaining lasagne.

5 Arrange the mozzarella cheese slices on top and sprinkle with the extra Parmesan. Bake for 30–35 minutes, until the top is golden. Leave to stand for 5 minutes before serving.

Farfalle with Chicken & Sausage

Just the thing for a mid-week supper, this has a tasty, piquant flavour, thanks largely to the Italian sausage and sun-dried tomatoes.

Serves 4

45ml/3 tbsp olive oil
450g/1lb skinless, boneless chicken breasts, cubed
3 Italian sausages, cut diagonally in 5mm/¼in slices
6 spring onions, sliced
10 drained sun-dried tomatoes in oil, chopped
250ml/8fl oz/1 cup passata
350g/12oz/3 cups dried farfalle
1 courgette, cut diagonally in 5mm/¼in slices
salt and freshly ground black pepper

1 Heat the olive oil in a large, heavy-based frying pan. Add the chicken and sausage slices, with a little salt and pepper, and cook for about 10 minutes, until browned. With a slotted spoon, remove the chicken and sausage pieces from the pan, and drain on kitchen paper.

2 Add the spring onions and sun-dried tomato pieces to the pan, and cook for 5 minutes, then stir in the passata. Cook the sauce for about 10 minutes, stirring occasionally, until it is thick and flavoursome.

3 Meanwhile, bring a large pan of lightly salted water to the boil and cook the pasta until it is *al dente*.

4 Add the courgette to the tomato sauce, with the chicken and sausage slices. Cook for 5 minutes.

5 Drain the pasta, return it to the clean pan and toss with the sauce. Serve immediately in heated bowls.

Cook's Tip
A wide variety of Italian cooking sausages – salsiccia *– is available from good delicatessens.*

Penne with Chicken & Ham Sauce

A meal in itself, this colourful pasta dish is perfect for lunch or dinner.

Serves 4

350g/12oz/3 cups dried penne
25g/1oz/2 tbsp butter
1 onion, chopped
1 garlic clove, chopped
1 bay leaf
450ml/ ¾ pint/1¾ cups dry white wine
150ml/ ¼ pint/ ⅔ cup crème fraîche
225g/8oz cooked chicken, skinned, boned and diced
115g/4oz cooked lean ham, diced
115g/4oz/1 cup grated Gouda cheese
15ml/1 tbsp chopped fresh mint, plus extra to garnish
salt and freshly ground black pepper

1 Bring a pan of lightly salted water to the boil and cook the pasta until it is *al dente*.

2 Meanwhile, melt the butter in a large frying pan. Add the onion and fry over a medium heat, stirring occasionally, for 5 minutes, until softened. Add the garlic, bay leaf and wine and bring to the boil. Boil rapidly until reduced by half.

3 Remove and discard the bay leaf, then stir in the crème fraîche, chicken, ham and grated cheese. Lower the heat and simmer for 5 minutes, stirring occasionally, until heated through. Do not let the sauce boil. Stir in the chopped mint and season to taste with salt and pepper.

4 Drain the pasta and return it to the clean pan. Add the chicken and ham sauce, and toss well. Serve immediately in warmed bowls, garnished with the extra chopped mint.

Variations

- *Soured cream can be used instead of crème fraîche, or use 75g/3oz/6 tbsp cream cheese, thinned with a little milk.*
- *Cooked turkey can be used instead of the chicken and Parma ham instead of cooked ham.*

Fusilli with Turkey & Roasted Tomatoes

Roasting tomatoes gives them a depth of flavour that is delicious with the pasta and broccoli.

Serves 4–6

675g/1½lb ripe but firm plum tomatoes, quartered
45ml/3 tbsp olive oil
5ml/1 tsp dried oregano
350g/12oz broccoli florets
450g/1lb/4 cups dried fusilli
1 small onion, sliced
5ml/1 tsp dried thyme
450g/1lb skinless, boneless turkey breast, cubed
3 garlic cloves, crushed
15ml/1 tbsp lemon juice
salt and freshly ground black pepper

1 Preheat the oven to 200°C/400°F/Gas 6. Place the tomato quarters in a single layer in an ovenproof dish. Add 15ml/1 tbsp of the olive oil, the oregano and 2.5ml/½ tsp salt, and stir to mix. Roast, without stirring, for 30–40 minutes, until the tomatoes are just browned.

2 Meanwhile, bring a large pan of lightly salted water to the boil. Add the broccoli and cook for 5 minutes until just tender. Using a slotted spoon, transfer the broccoli to a colander, refresh it under cold water and leave it to drain. Reserve the pan of water.

3 Bring the reserved water back to the boil, add the pasta and cook it until it is *al dente*.

4 Meanwhile, heat the remaining oil in a large frying pan. Add the onion, thyme and turkey. Cook over a high heat, stirring often, for 5–7 minutes, until the meat is cooked.

5 Add the garlic and cook for 1 further minute, stirring frequently, then stir in the lemon juice and broccoli. Season with pepper and keep hot.

6 Drain the pasta, return it to the clean pan and toss it with the sauce. Serve at once in warmed bowls.

Turkey, Mushroom & Pasta Bake

This is an excellent recipe for using up leftover roast turkey. Baking the pasta gives you time to make an accompanying salad.

Serves 4

65g/2½oz/5 tbsp butter, plus extra for greasing
225g/8oz/3 cups mushrooms, thinly sliced
25g/1oz/¼ cup plain flour
400ml/14fl oz/1⅔ cups milk
450ml/¾ pint/1¾ cups chicken stock
60ml/4 tbsp dry white wine
275g/10oz dried spaghetti
350g/12oz cooked turkey, chopped
115g/4oz/1 cup frozen peas, thawed
75g/3oz/1 cup freshly grated Parmesan cheese
25g/1oz/½ cup fresh white breadcrumbs
salt and freshly ground black pepper
green salad, to serve

1 Preheat the oven to 190°C/375°F/Gas 5. Grease a 3 litre/5 pint/6 cup ovenproof dish.

2 Melt 50g/2oz/4 tbsp of the butter in a saucepan. Add the mushrooms and cook for 5 minutes, stirring frequently. Stir in the flour and cook for 3 minutes, stirring constantly. Gradually add the milk, stock and white wine, stirring constantly until the sauce boils and thickens. Lower the heat and simmer gently for 5 minutes.

3 Meanwhile, bring a large pan of lightly salted water to the boil and cook the pasta until it is *al dente*. Drain the pasta and put it in a mixing bowl.

4 Pour in the mushroom sauce and mix well. Stir in the turkey, peas and half the Parmesan, and season with salt and pepper to taste. Transfer the mixture to the prepared dish.

5 In a small bowl, combine the remaining Parmesan with the breadcrumbs. Sprinkle evenly over the turkey mixture. Dot with the remaining butter, cut into pieces. Bake for 30–40 minutes, until bubbling and golden. Serve with a green salad.

Spaghetti Tetrazzini

This American-Italian recipe makes a rich and filling family meal.

Serves 4–6

75g/3oz/6 tbsp butter
350g/12oz turkey breast fillet, cut into thin strips
2 pieces drained bottled roasted pepper, rinsed, dried and cut into thin strips
175g/6oz dried spaghetti
50g/2oz/½ cup plain flour
900ml/1½ pints/3¾ cups hot milk
115g/4oz/1⅓ cups freshly grated Parmesan cheese
1.5–2.5ml/¼–½ tsp dried English mustard
salt and freshly ground black pepper
salad leaves, to garnish

1 Melt about one-third of the butter in a saucepan, add the turkey, and sprinkle with a little salt and plenty of pepper. Toss the turkey over a medium heat for about 5 minutes, until the meat turns white, then add the roasted pepper strips and toss to mix. Remove with a slotted spoon and set aside.

2 Preheat the oven to 180°C/350°F/Gas 4. Bring a large saucepan of lightly salted water to the boil and cook the spaghetti until it is *al dente*.

3 Meanwhile, melt the remaining butter in the pan in which the turkey was cooked. Add the flour and cook, stirring constantly, for 1 minute. Gradually add the hot milk, stirring constantly until the sauce boils and thickens.

4 Add two-thirds of the grated Parmesan to the white sauce, then whisk in mustard, with salt and pepper to taste. Remove the sauce from the heat.

5 Drain the pasta and return it to the clean pan. Mix in half the cheese sauce, then spoon the mixture around the edge of an ovenproof dish. Stir the turkey mixture into the remaining cheese sauce and spoon into the centre of the dish.

6 Sprinkle the remaining Parmesan over the top and bake for 15–20 minutes until the topping is crisp. Serve with salad leaves.

Mixed Meat Cannelloni

Using three types of meat in a rich sauce makes this an exceptionally good cannelloni.

Serves 4

60ml/4 tbsp olive oil
1 onion, finely chopped
1 carrot, finely chopped
2 garlic cloves, crushed
2 ripe tomatoes, peeled and finely chopped
115g/4oz minced beef
150g/5oz minced pork
250g/9oz minced chicken
30ml/2 tbsp brandy
25g/1oz/2 tbsp butter
90ml/6 tbsp double cream
16 no-precook dried cannelloni tubes
75g/3oz/1 cup freshly grated Parmesan cheese
salad leaves, to garnish

For the white sauce

50g/2oz/ ¼ cup butter
50g/2oz/ ½ cup plain flour
900ml/1 ½ pints/3¾ cups milk
pinch of grated nutmeg
salt and freshly ground black pepper

1 Heat the oil in a frying pan and fry the onion, carrot and garlic for 5 minutes. Stir in the tomatoes and cook over a low heat for about 10 minutes.

2 Add all the minced meats to the pan and cook gently for about 10 minutes, stirring frequently to break up any lumps. Add the brandy, increase the heat and stir until it has reduced, then add the butter and cream, and cook gently, stirring occasionally, for 10 minutes more. Allow to cool.

3 Preheat the oven to 190°C/375°F/Gas 5. Make the white sauce. Melt the butter in a saucepan, add the flour and cook, stirring, for 1–2 minutes. Gradually add the milk, stirring until the sauce boils and thickens. Season with nutmeg, salt and pepper to taste, and whisk well. Remove the pan from the heat.

4 Spoon a little of the white sauce into an ovenproof dish. Fill the cannelloni tubes with the meat mixture and place in a single layer in the dish. Pour the remaining white sauce over them, then sprinkle with the Parmesan. Bake for 35–40 minutes, or until the pasta feels tender when pierced with a skewer. Allow to stand for 10 minutes before serving with salad leaves.

Spaghetti alla Carbonara

This justifiably famous pasta dish has a light and creamy sauce flavoured with bacon and lightly cooked eggs.

Serves 4

350g/12oz dried spaghetti
15ml/1 tbsp olive oil
1 onion, chopped
115g/4oz pancetta or rindless streaky bacon, diced
1 garlic clove, chopped
3 medium eggs
300ml/ ½ pint/1 ¼ cups double cream
50g/2oz/ ⅔ cup freshly grated Parmesan cheese
salt and freshly ground black pepper
chopped fresh basil, to garnish

1 Bring a large pan of lightly salted water to the boil and cook the spaghetti until it is *al dente*.

2 Meanwhile, heat the olive oil in a heavy-based frying pan and fry the onion and pancetta or bacon over a fairly low heat, stirring occasionally, for 10 minutes. Stir in the garlic and fry, stirring occasionally, for 2 minutes.

3 Beat the eggs in a bowl, then stir in the cream and Parmesan, and season with salt and pepper to taste.

4 When the pasta is almost ready, stir the cream mixture into the onion and pancetta or bacon, and cook over a low heat for a few minutes, stirring constantly until heated through. Do not allow the eggs to scramble.

5 Drain the pasta and turn it into a large warmed serving bowl. Pour over the sauce and toss to coat. Serve immediately, garnished with chopped fresh basil.

Cook's Tip

Use pancetta if possible, as it has a much greater depth of flavour than bacon and will make this dish taste really authentic. It is on sale in most supermarkets and delicatessens.

Spaghetti with Bacon & Onion

This easy dish can be made quickly from ingredients that are almost always to hand.

Serves 6

30ml/2 tbsp olive oil
115g/4oz rindless unsmoked streaky bacon rashers, cut into matchsticks
1 small onion, finely chopped
120ml/4fl oz/ ½ cup dry white wine
450g/1lb tomatoes, chopped
1.5ml/ ¼ tsp thyme leaves
500g/1¼lb dried spaghetti
salt and freshly ground black pepper
freshly grated Parmesan cheese, to serve

1 Heat the oil in a heavy-based frying pan. Add the bacon and onion, and cook over a medium heat, stirring occasionally, for 8–10 minutes, until the onion is golden and the bacon has rendered its fat and is beginning to brown.

2 Add the wine to the bacon mixture, raise the heat and cook rapidly until the liquid has evaporated. Stir in the tomatoes and thyme, and season with salt and pepper to taste. Cover, and cook over a moderate heat for 10–15 minutes.

3 Meanwhile, bring a large pan of lightly salted water to the boil and cook the pasta until it is *al dente*. Drain, return to the clean pan and toss with the sauce. Serve with the grated Parmesan.

Variations

This recipe is easily adapted to use whatever ingredients you have in your store cupboard and fridge. For example, you could add 1 finely chopped carrot or celery stick with the onion in step 1. For a spicy flavour, add a pinch of chilli powder or cayenne pepper instead of black pepper in step 2.

Pasta with Fresh Tomato & Smoky Bacon Sauce

This is a wonderful pasta sauce to prepare in mid-summer when the tomatoes are ripe and sweet.

Serves 4

900g/2lb ripe tomatoes
50g/2oz/ ¼ cup butter
6 rindless smoked streaky bacon rashers, chopped
1 medium onion, chopped
15ml/1 tbsp chopped fresh oregano
450g/1lb/4 cups dried pasta shapes
salt and freshly ground black pepper
fresh marjoram sprigs, to garnish
freshly grated Parmesan cheese, to serve

1 Cut a cross in the blossom end of each tomato. Plunge them into boiling water for 1 minute, then into cold water. Slip off the skins, peeling them back from the crosses. Cut the tomatoes in half, remove the seeds and cores, and roughly chop the flesh.

2 Melt the butter in a saucepan. Add the bacon and fry until lightly browned. Add the onion and cook gently for 5 minutes until softened.

3 Add the tomatoes and oregano, and season with salt and pepper to taste. Simmer gently for 10 minutes.

4 Bring a large pan of lightly salted water to the boil and cook the pasta until *al dente*. Drain, return to the clean pan and toss with the sauce. Ladle into warmed bowls. Garnish with marjoram sprigs and serve with grated Parmesan cheese.

Stir-fried Bacon & Pak Choi with Pasta

Quick, easy and tasty, this is an ideal dish for those hectic nights when everyone is in a hurry.

Serves 4

350g/12oz/3 cups dried spaghettini
15ml/1 tbsp vegetable oil
4 rindless streaky bacon rashers, cut in thin strips
2 leeks, sliced
1 celeriac, peeled and diced
1 head pak choi, stems and leaves chopped separately
soy sauce, to season
salt

1 Bring a large pan of lightly salted water to the boil and cook the pasta until *al dente*.
2 Meanwhile, preheat a wok. Add the oil and stir-fry the bacon with the leeks until the bacon is beginning to become crisp.
3 Add the celeriac and pak choi stems, and toss over the heat for 3–4 minutes.
4 Stir in the pak choi leaves, add a generous drizzle of soy sauce, cover the wok with a tight-fitting lid and steam the leaves for 2–3 minutes.
5 Drain the pasta, add it to the stir-fried ingredients and toss lightly. Serve immediately, with extra soy sauce if needed.

Spätzle

This simple pasta dish comes from Germany, where it is served with many savoury dishes. It goes particularly well with poached celery hearts.

Serves 4
350g/12oz/3 cups plain flour
2 eggs, beaten
about 200ml/7fl oz/scant 1 cup milk and water combined
15ml/1 tbsp sunflower oil
25g/1oz/2 tbsp butter
4 rindless streaky bacon rashers, diced
salt and freshly ground black pepper

1 Sift the flour and 2.5ml/½ tsp salt into a bowl, and make a well in the centre. Add the eggs and enough of the milk and water to make a very soft dough. Beat the dough until it develops bubbles, then stir in the oil and beat again. Bring a large pan of lightly salted water to the boil.

2 Dampen a chopping board with water and place the dough on it. Using the broad side of a knife, shave off strips of the dough, then gently push them off the board so that they fall into the boiling water. Do not overcrowd the pan.

3 Cook the spätzle for 3 minutes, then lift them out with a slotted spoon and put them in a colander. Rinse quickly under hot water, put in a warmed serving bowl and cover to keep warm. Repeat until all the dough has been used up.

4 Melt the butter in a frying pan and fry the bacon until crisp. Pour the contents of the pan over the spätzle and season with black pepper. Serve immediately.

Cook's Tip
When shaving the dough, occasionally rinse the knife with water, so that the dough does not stick to it. The faster you work at this stage, the lighter the texture of the spätzle will be.

Spaghetti with Pancetta & Two-way Tomatoes

Sun-dried tomatoes add an extra dimension to a fresh tomato sauce in this simple spaghetti dish.

Serves 4
115g/4oz diced pancetta
15ml/1 tbsp olive oil
1 large onion, finely chopped
4 drained sun-dried tomatoes in oil, diced
2 beefsteak tomatoes, peeled and diced
350g/12oz dried spaghetti
leaves from 2–3 fresh marjoram sprigs
salt and freshly ground black pepper
thin shavings of Pecorino cheese, to serve

1 Put the pancetta in a heavy-based saucepan. Stir over a low heat until the fat runs. Add the oil. When it is hot, add the onion and sun-dried tomatoes, and cook gently, stirring constantly, for about 10 minutes.

2 Stir in the fresh tomatoes and season with salt and pepper to taste. Cook for about 10 minutes, stirring occasionally.

3 Meanwhile, bring a large pan of lightly salted water to the boil. Add the pasta and cook until it is *al dente*. Drain and return to the clean pan.

4 Stir the marjoram into the sauce, then add it to the pasta and toss well. Serve immediately in warmed bowls, topped with the shavings of Pecorino.

Cook's Tips
- *Look for diced pancetta in packets in the chiller cabinet of your local supermarket. Some delicatessens sell it in slices cut from a roll, which you can dice yourself.*
- *For an even stronger tomato flavour, substitute the oil from the sun-dried tomatoes for the olive oil.*

Macaroni with Ham & Prawns

A distant relation of Surf 'n' Turf, this supper dish tastes truly delicious.

Serves 4

350g/12oz/3 cups short-cut macaroni
45ml/3 tbsp olive oil
175g/6oz smoked ham, diced
12 raw king prawns, peeled and deveined
1 garlic clove, chopped
150ml/ ¼ pint/ ⅔ cup red wine
½ small head of radicchio, shredded
2 egg yolks, beaten
30ml/2 tbsp chopped fresh flat leaf parsley
150ml/ ¼ pint/ ⅔ cup double cream
salt and freshly ground black pepper
shredded fresh basil, to garnish

1 Bring a large pan of salted water to the boil and cook the pasta until it is *al dente*.

2 Meanwhile, heat the oil in a frying pan and cook the ham, prawns and garlic for about 5 minutes, stirring occasionally until the prawns have turned pink. Remove the prawns with a slotted spoon.

3 Add the wine and radicchio to the ham mixture, bring to the boil and boil rapidly until the juices are reduced by half.

4 Stir in the egg yolks, parsley and cream, and simmer until the sauce thickens slightly. Return the prawns to the sauce and season to taste.

5 Drain the pasta and return it to the clean pan. Add the sauce and toss to coat. Serve, garnished with shredded fresh basil.

Cook's Tip
Flat leaf parsley is a pretty herb with more flavour than the curly variety. If you buy a large bunch, finely chop the leftover parsley and freeze it in a small plastic bag. It will then be ready to sprinkle on to bubbling soups or casseroles as a garnish.

Pasta with Spinach, Bacon & Mushrooms

Spinach and bacon are often teamed together. Mushrooms complete the trio in this American recipe.

Serves 4

6 rindless streaky bacon rashers, cut in small pieces
1 shallot, finely chopped
225g/8oz/3 cups small mushrooms, quartered
450g/1lb fresh spinach leaves, coarse stems removed
1.5ml/ ¼ tsp freshly grated nutmeg
350g/12oz/3 cups dried conchiglie
salt and freshly ground black pepper
freshly grated Parmesan cheese, to serve

1 Heat the bacon gently in a frying pan until the fat runs, then raise the heat and cook the bacon until it is crisp. Drain it on kitchen paper, then put it in a bowl.

2 Add the shallot to the bacon fat in the pan and cook for about 5 minutes, until softened.

3 Add the mushrooms and cook until lightly browned, stirring frequently. With a slotted spoon, add the shallot and mushrooms to the bacon.

4 Pour off most of the bacon fat from the pan, add the spinach and cook over a medium heat until wilted, stirring constantly. Sprinkle with the nutmeg, then cook over a high heat until the excess liquid from the spinach has evaporated.

5 Transfer the spinach to a board and chop it coarsely. Return it to the pan. Add the bacon mixture and stir well. Season with salt and pepper and keep warm.

6 Bring a large pan of lightly salted water to the boil and cook the pasta until it is *al dente*. Drain it well and return it to the clean pan. Add the spinach mixture and toss well. Serve in warmed bowls, sprinkled with Parmesan.

Tagliatelle with Bacon & Radicchio

This modern recipe is deliciously rich, and makes a good dinner-party first course or, served with salad, an excellent lunch dish.

Serves 4

225g/8oz dried tagliatelle
75–90g/3–3½oz pancetta or rindless streaky bacon, diced
25g/1oz/2 tbsp butter
1 onion, finely chopped
1 garlic clove, crushed
1 head of radicchio, about 115–175g/4–6oz finely shredded
150ml/¼ pint/⅔ cup double cream
50g/2oz/⅔ cup freshly grated Parmesan cheese
salt and freshly ground black pepper

1 Bring a large pan of lightly salted water to the boil and cook the tagliatelle until it is *al dente*.

2 Meanwhile, put the pancetta or bacon in a medium saucepan and heat gently until the fat runs. Increase the heat slightly and stir-fry the pancetta or bacon for 5 minutes.

3 Add the butter to the pan. When it melts, add the onion and garlic, and stir-fry for 5 minutes. Add the radicchio and toss for 1–2 minutes until wilted.

4 Pour in the cream, add the grated Parmesan and season with salt and pepper to taste. Stir for 1–2 minutes, until the cream is bubbling and the ingredients are evenly mixed. Taste the sauce for seasoning.

5 Drain the pasta and tip it into a warmed bowl. Pour the sauce over and toss well. Serve immediately.

Cook's Tip
Italian cooks use radicchio di Treviso, which has long, pointed leaves that are dramatically striped in dark red and white, but other varieties, such as Castelfranco, may also be used. Sadly, they all lose their lovely red colouring when cooked.

Penne with Pancetta & Cream

This makes a gloriously rich supper dish. The egg yolks are lightly cooked on contact with the hot pasta.

Serves 3–4

300g/11oz/2¾ cups dried penne
30ml/2 tbsp olive oil
1 small onion, finely chopped
175g/6oz dried pancetta
1–2 garlic cloves, crushed
5 egg yolks
175ml/6fl oz/¾ cup double cream
115g/4oz/1⅓ cups grated Parmesan cheese, plus extra to serve
salt and freshly ground black pepper

1 Bring a large pan of lightly salted water to the boil and cook the penne until *al dente*.

2 Meanwhile, heat the oil in a separate large pan and cook the onion over a low heat, stirring frequently, for about 5 minutes, until soft and translucent.

3 Add the pancetta and garlic. Cook over a medium heat until the pancetta is cooked but not crisp.

4 Put the egg yolks in a jug and add the cream and Parmesan. Grind in plenty of pepper and beat well to mix.

5 Drain the penne thoroughly, tip into the pan containing the pancetta mixture and toss over a high heat to mix. Remove the pan from the heat and immediately pour in the egg yolk mixture, tossing well to combine. Spoon into a large, shallow serving dish, grind a little extra black pepper over and sprinkle with some of the extra Parmesan. Serve at once, with the rest of the Parmesan.

Cook's Tip
Use free-range eggs from a reputable source. Having added the egg yolks, don't return the pan to the heat or the egg yolks will scramble and spoil the appearance of the dish.

Piquant Penne with Bacon & Chillies

This can be mildly spicy or fiercely fiery, depending on how much chilli you use.

Serves 4

25g/1oz/scant ½ cup dried porcini mushrooms
90g/3½ oz/7 tbsp butter
150g/5oz rindless smoked streaky bacon, diced
1–2 dried red chillies, or to taste
2 garlic cloves, crushed
8 ripe plum tomatoes, peeled and chopped
a few fresh basil leaves, torn, plus extra to garnish
350g/12oz/3 cups fresh or dried penne
50g/2oz/ ⅔ cup freshly grated Parmesan cheese
25g/1oz/ ⅓ cup freshly grated Pecorino cheese
salt

1 Soak the dried mushrooms in warm water to cover for 15–20 minutes. Drain, then squeeze dry with your hands. Finely chop the mushrooms.

2 Melt 50g/2oz/4 tbsp of the butter in a pan and fry the bacon until slightly crisp. Remove it with a slotted spoon and set it aside. Add the chopped mushrooms to the pan, fry for about 2 minutes, then add to the bacon. Crumble 1 chilli into the fat remaining in the pan, and cook the garlic until it is golden.

3 Add the tomatoes and basil, and season with salt. Cook gently, stirring occasionally, for 10–15 minutes. Meanwhile, bring a large pan of lightly salted water to the boil and cook the penne until *al dente*.

4 Add the bacon and mushrooms to the tomato sauce. Taste and add more chillies if you prefer a hotter flavour. If the sauce is too dry, stir in a little of the pasta water.

5 Drain the pasta and tip it into a warmed bowl. Dice the remaining butter, add it to the pasta with the cheeses, then toss until coated. Pour the tomato sauce over the pasta, toss well and serve immediately, with a few basil leaves sprinkled on top.

Pumpkin, Bacon & Parmesan Pasta

The sweetness of pumpkin is nicely balanced by the mature flavour of the Parmesan incorporated in the sauce.

Serves 4

800g/1¾ b fresh pumpkin flesh, cut into small cubes
300g/11oz dried tagliatelle
25g/1oz/2 tbsp butter
115g/4oz rindless smoked back bacon, diced
1 onion, sliced
150ml/ ¼ pint/ ⅔ cup single cream
50g/2oz/ ⅔ cup freshly grated Parmesan cheese
freshly grated nutmeg
30ml/2 tbsp chopped fresh parsley
15ml/1 tbsp snipped fresh chives
salt and freshly ground black pepper
sprigs of flat leaf parsley, to garnish
Garlic Breadcrumbs, to serve

1 Bring a large saucepan of lightly salted water to the boil. Tip in the pumpkin cubes. Cook over a medium heat for about 10 minutes, until just tender.

2 Using a slotted spoon, remove the pumpkin cubes from the water, put them in a bowl and keep them warm. Add the pasta to the boiling water in the pan and cook until *al dente*. Drain and set aside.

3 Heat the butter in the clean pasta pan and fry the bacon and onion for 5 minutes. Stir in the cream and bring to just below boiling point. Add the pasta and toss in the sauce until hot.

4 Stir in the pumpkin, Parmesan, nutmeg, chopped parsley and chives, and season with salt and pepper to taste. Serve at once, garnished with flat leaf parsley sprigs and sprinkled with the garlic breadcrumbs.

Cook's Tip

Pumpkins can grow to an enormous size – the record is about 180kg/400lb – and even more reasonable specimens, at about 3kg/6½lb, are still often too large for a single meal. Consequently, many supermarkets now sell pumpkin already cut into pieces. If buying this way, make sure that the flesh is firm, but not dried out or fibrous.

Garlic Breadcrumbs

These are beautifully crunchy and can be used to top any pasta dish.

Makes 75g/3oz/1½ cups

40g/1½ oz/3 tbsp butter
15ml/1 tbsp olive oil
2 garlic cloves, crushed
75g/3oz/1½ cups fresh white breadcrumbs

Melt the butter and oil in a frying pan. Add the garlic and breadcrumbs. Fry gently until the crumbs are golden brown and crisp. Drain on kitchen paper.

Pasta-stuffed Peppers

Stuffed peppers always look so inviting, with their bright colours and tempting aroma.

Serves 4

30ml/2 tbsp olive oil, plus extra for brushing
6 rindless streaky bacon rashers, chopped
1 small onion, chopped
350ml/12fl oz/1 ½ cups passata
a generous pinch of crushed dried red chillies
50g/2oz/ ½ cup dried short-cut macaroni
175g/6oz mozzarella cheese, diced
12 stoned black olives, thinly sliced
2 large red peppers
2 large yellow peppers
salt and freshly ground black pepper
fresh parsley, to garnish

1 Preheat the oven to 180°C/350°F/Gas 4. Brush a 20cm/8in ovenproof dish with oil. Heat the bacon gently in a frying pan until the fat runs, then raise the heat and cook it until it is crisp. Drain the bacon on kitchen paper.

2 Add the onion to the bacon fat in the pan and cook for 5 minutes, until softened, then stir in the passata and dried chillies. Cook over a high heat for 10 minutes, until thickened.

3 Meanwhile, bring a large pan of lightly salted water to the boil and cook the pasta until *al dente*. Drain it well and put it in a mixing bowl. Add the bacon, tomato sauce, mozzarella cheese and olives, and toss well to mix. Season to taste.

4 Cut the stem end off each pepper and reserve these "lids". Remove the seeds and ribs from inside the peppers, then fill them with the pasta mixture.

5 Stand the filled peppers in the prepared dish, put on the "lids", then brush the peppers all over with the olive oil.

6 Cover the dish with foil and bake for 30 minutes. Remove the foil and bake for 25–30 minutes more, or until the peppers are tender. Serve immediately garnished with parsley.

Fettuccine with Ham & Cream

Prosciutto is perfect for this rich and delicious dish, which can be served either as a starter or as a light main course.

Serves 4

115g/4oz prosciutto crudo *or other unsmoked ham (raw or cooked)*
50g/2oz/ ¼ cup butter
2 shallots, very finely chopped
150ml/ ¼ pint/ ⅔ cup double cream
350g/12oz fresh fettuccine
50g/2oz/ ⅔ cup freshly grated Parmesan cheese
salt and freshly ground black pepper
fresh parsley sprigs, to garnish

1 Cut the fat from the ham and chop both lean and fat parts separately into small squares.

2 Melt the butter in a medium frying pan and add the shallots and the squares of ham fat. Cook until golden. Add the lean ham, and cook for 2 minutes more. Season to taste with black pepper. Stir in the cream and keep warm over low heat while the pasta is cooking.

3 Bring a large pan of lightly salted water to the boil and cook the fettuccine until it is *al dente*. Drain well and return to the clean pan. Add the sauce, toss to mix, then stir in the cheese. Serve at once, garnished with parsley.

Cook's Tip

Prosciutto crudo *is salted and air-dried ham. The most famous is Parma ham, which comes from the area between the Taro and Baganza rivers. The pigs are fed on the whey produced as a by-product of cheese-making. This makes the ham very mild and sweet. As the pigs are kept in rearing sheds and not allowed to roam freely,* prosciutto di Parma *tends to be rather fatty. Similar hams are produced in Veneto, Tuscany, Friuli and Emilia-Romagna. Many people consider* prosciutto di San Daniele *the equal of Parma ham. It is also less fatty.*

Tagliatelle with Leeks & Parma Ham

The mild, slightly sweet flavour of leeks makes them the perfect partner for Parma ham and pasta in this prettily coloured dish. For the best effect, use a mixture of green and white tagliatelle if possible.

Serves 4

40g/1½ oz/3 tbsp butter
5 leeks, sliced
225g/8oz fresh or dried tagliatelle, preferably green and white
20ml/4 tsp dry sherry
30ml/2 tbsp lemon juice
10ml/2 tsp chopped fresh basil
115–150g/4–5oz Parma ham or other prosciutto crudo, *torn into strips*
175g/6oz/¾ cup fromage frais
salt and freshly ground black pepper
fresh basil leaves and thin shavings of Parmesan cheese, to garnish

1 Melt the butter in a large, heavy-based saucepan, add the leeks and fry over a gentle heat for 3–4 minutes, until tender but not too soft.

2 Meanwhile, bring a large saucepan of lightly salted water to the boil and cook the tagliatelle until it is *al dente*.

3 Stir the sherry, lemon juice and chopped basil into the leek mixture. Season with salt and pepper to taste, and cook for 1–2 minutes so that the flavours blend.

4 Add the strips of Parma ham or other *prosciutto crudo* and the fromage frais, stir and cook over a low heat for about 1–2 minutes, until heated through.

5 Drain the pasta and return it to the clean pan. Pour the leek and Parma ham mixture on top and mix lightly together. Spoon into warmed individual bowls and garnish each serving with fresh basil leaves. Top with shavings of Parmesan cheese and serve immediately.

Tagliatelle with Prosciutto & Parmesan

A really simple dish, prepared in minutes from the best ingredients.

Serves 4

115g/4oz prosciutto crudo
450g/1lb dried tagliatelle
75g/3oz/6 tbsp butter
50g/2oz/⅔ cup freshly grated Parmesan cheese
salt and freshly ground black pepper
a few fresh sage leaves, to garnish

1 Cut the prosciutto into strips, making them the same width as the tagliatelle. Bring a large pan of lightly salted water to the boil and cook the pasta until it is *al dente*.

2 Meanwhile, melt the butter in a saucepan, stir in the prosciutto strips and heat them through, but do not fry.

3 Drain the pasta and pile it into a warm serving dish. Sprinkle with the Parmesan and pour over the buttery prosciutto. Season with pepper, garnish with the sage leaves and serve.

Variation

This dish also works well with thin strips of peeled red peppers. Grill the peppers under a medium heat until they are blistered. Place in a bowl and cover with clear film until cool enough to handle. Peel off the skins, discard the seeds and cut the flesh into strips the same width as the tagliatelle. Warm them in the butter with the prosciutto.

Linguine with Smoked Ham & Artichokes

Canned artichoke hearts are a wonderful store-cupboard ingredient and taste superb in this simple sauce. Use bacon if you haven't got any smoked ham.

Serves 4

350g/12oz dried linguine
45ml/3 tbsp olive oil
1 onion, chopped
2 garlic cloves, chopped
400g/14oz can artichoke hearts, drained and sliced
225g/8oz smoked ham, diced
30ml/2 tbsp chopped fresh basil
15ml/1 tbsp herb vinegar
150ml/ 1/4 pint/ 2/3 cup soured cream
salt and freshly ground black pepper
fresh mint sprigs, to garnish

1 Bring a large pan of lightly salted water to the boil and cook the pasta until *al dente*.

2 Meanwhile, heat the oil in a heavy-based frying pan. Add the onion and garlic, and fry over a medium heat, stirring occasionally, for 5 minutes until the onion has softened.

3 Add the artichoke hearts and toss gently over the heat for 2 minutes. Try not to break them up.

4 Add the ham and basil, and fry, stirring constantly, for about 2 minutes. Pour in the herb vinegar, season with salt and pepper to taste and heat through. Stir in the soured cream and heat through again, stirring constantly.

5 Drain the pasta and return it to the clean pan. Add the sauce and toss to coat. Spoon into a warmed bowl, garnish with the mint sprigs and serve immediately.

Variation
Smoked chicken, poussin or turkey also work well in this delicious recipe.

Parma Pasta with Asparagus

Make this dish with young asparagus, when it first comes into the shops in the late spring. You can also use sprue, the first thinnings of asparagus, which are very thin and often cheaper.

Serves 4

350g/12oz dried tagliatelle
25g/1oz/2 tbsp butter
15ml/1 tbsp olive oil
225g/8oz fresh asparagus tips
1 garlic clove, chopped
115g/4oz Parma ham or other prosciutto crudo, cut into strips
30ml/2 tbsp chopped fresh sage
150ml/ 1/4 pint/ 2/3 cup single cream
115g/4oz double Gloucester or Cheddar cheese, grated
115g/4oz Gruyère cheese, grated
salt and freshly ground black pepper
fresh sage sprigs, to garnish

1 Bring a large pan of lightly salted water to the boil and cook the pasta until it is *al dente*.

2 Melt the butter in the oil in a heavy-based frying pan. Add the asparagus tips and fry gently over a low heat, stirring occasionally, for about 5 minutes, until almost tender.

3 Stir in the garlic and ham, and fry for 1 minute, then add the chopped sage leaves and fry for 1 minute more.

4 Pour in the cream, bring to the boil, then lower the heat and stir in the double Gloucester or Cheddar and the Gruyère. Simmer gently, stirring occasionally, until the cheeses have melted. Season with salt and pepper to taste.

5 Drain the pasta and return it to the clean pan. Add the sauce and toss to coat. Serve immediately in warmed bowls, garnished with the fresh sage.

Spaghetti with Ham & Saffron

A quick and easy dish that makes a delicious midweek supper. The ingredients are all staples that you are likely to have to hand.

Serves 4
350g/12oz dried spaghetti
a few saffron strands
30ml/2 tbsp water
150g/5oz cooked ham, cut into matchsticks
200ml/7fl oz/scant 1 cup double cream
50g/2oz/⅔ cup freshly grated Parmesan cheese, plus extra to serve
2 egg yolks
salt and freshly ground black pepper

1 Bring a pan of lightly salted water to the boil and cook the pasta until it is *al dente*.

2 Meanwhile, put the saffron strands in a medium saucepan, add the water and bring to the boil immediately. Remove the pan from the heat and leave to stand for 5 minutes.

3 Add the ham to the pan containing the saffron. Stir in the cream and Parmesan, with a little salt and pepper. Heat gently, stirring constantly. When the cream starts to bubble around the edges, remove the pan from the heat and beat in the egg yolks.

4 Drain the pasta and return it to the clean pan. Immediately pour the sauce over and toss well. Serve in warmed bowls, with extra grated Parmesan handed separately.

Cook's Tip
Use a heavy-based pan for heating the cream so that it does not catch on the base. Make sure you beat the sauce immediately the eggs are added.

Tortellini with Ham

This is a very easy recipe; ideal for busy people as an after-work supper.

Serves 4
250g/9oz dried tortellini alla carne (meat-filled tortellini)
30ml/2 tbsp olive oil
1 shallot, finely chopped
115g/4oz cooked ham, diced
150ml/¼ pint/⅔ cup passata
150ml/¼ pint/⅔ cup water
120ml/4fl oz/½ cup double cream
about 90g/3½ oz/generous 1 cup freshly grated Parmesan cheese
salt and freshly ground black pepper

1 Bring a pan of lightly salted water to the boil and cook the pasta until *al dente*.

2 Meanwhile, heat the oil in a large heavy-based saucepan, add the shallot and cook over a low heat, stirring frequently, for about 5 minutes, until softened. Add the ham and cook, stirring occasionally, until it darkens.

3 Add the passata and water. Stir well, then season with salt and pepper to taste. Bring to the boil, lower the heat and simmer the sauce until it has reduced slightly. Stir in the cream.

4 Drain the pasta well and add it to the sauce. Add a handful of grated Parmesan to the pan. Stir, toss well and taste for seasoning. Serve immediately in warmed bowls, topped with the remaining Parmesan.

Cook's Tip
Tortellini come with all sorts of fillings, and most would be suitable for this recipe. Meat-filled pasta includes mortadella sausage and pork, and chicken or turkey stuffings. A common vegetarian filling is spinach or chard, mixed with ricotta and Parmesan or Pecorino, sometimes with a flavouring of garlic and nutmeg. Four-cheese tortellini are also popular. A more unusual, but quite delicious, filling is a mixture of pumpkin, cheese, almonds, fruit and nutmeg.

Baked Fusilli with Ham & Cheese

With its crispy crust and moist and creamy centre, this quick, easy and inexpensive pasta bake is both filling and nutritious.

Serves 4

butter, for greasing
300g/11oz/2¾ cups dried fusilli
3 eggs
200ml/7fl oz/scant 1 cup milk
150ml/¼ pint/⅔ cup single cream
150g/5oz Gruyère cheese, grated
nutmeg
115g/4oz cooked ham, cut into strips
30ml/2 tbsp freshly grated Parmesan cheese
salt and freshly ground black pepper

1 Preheat the oven to 190°C/375°F/Gas 5. Grease a baking sheet with butter.

2 Bring a large saucepan of lightly salted water to the boil. Add the pasta and cook for 5 minutes.

3 Meanwhile, beat the eggs in a jug with the milk, cream and half the grated Gruyère. Grate in a little fresh nutmeg and season to taste with salt and pepper.

4 Drain the pasta and tip half of it into the prepared dish. Arrange half the strips of ham on top, then follow with the remaining pasta and ham.

5 Pour the egg and cream mixture into the dish, stir to mix a little, then sprinkle the remaining Gruyère and the Parmesan over the top.

6 Bake for 30 minutes, or until golden brown and bubbling. Serve immediately.

Cook's Tip
You can use any dried pasta shapes for this dish. Eliche and farfalle both work well.

Linguine with Ham & Mascarpone

Mascarpone cheese masquerades as cream in this recipe. Its rich, thick consistency makes it perfect for sauces.

Serves 6

25g/1oz/2 tbsp butter
150g/5oz/⅔ cup mascarpone cheese
90g/3½oz cooked ham, cut into thin strips
30ml/2 tbsp milk
45ml/3 tbsp freshly grated Parmesan cheese, plus extra to serve
500g/1¼lb fresh linguine
salt and freshly ground black pepper

1 Melt the butter in a medium saucepan, add the mascarpone, strips of ham and milk, and stir well over a low heat until the mascarpone has melted completely. Add 15ml/1 tbsp of the grated Parmesan and plenty of freshly ground black pepper and stir well.

2 Bring a large pan of lightly salted water to the boil and cook the pasta until *al dente*.

3 Drain the cooked pasta well and tip it into a warmed bowl. Pour the sauce over the pasta, add the remaining measured Parmesan and toss well.

4 Taste for seasoning and transfer the pasta to warmed serving plates. Serve immediately, with more ground black pepper and extra grated Parmesan handed separately.

Cook's Tip
Gruyère, a Swiss cheese, is pale yellow with a firm texture and a scattering of small holes. It is made from unpasteurized cow's milk and has a sweet, almost nutty flavour. Check its authenticity by looking for "Switzerland" stamped on the rind. It melts well, without becoming rubbery, so it is a good choice for cooking. When buying, avoid cheeses with too many holes or that show signs of cracking or drying out.

Pipe Rigate with Peas & Ham

Prettily flecked with pink and green, this is a lovely dish for an informal spring or summer supper party.

Serves 4

350g/12oz/3 cups dried pipe rigate or other pasta shapes
25g/1oz/2 tbsp butter
15ml/1 tbsp olive oil
150–175g/5–6oz/1¼–1½ cups frozen peas, thawed
1 garlic clove, crushed
150ml/¼ pint/⅔ cup chicken stock
30ml/2 tbsp chopped fresh flat leaf parsley
175ml/6fl oz/¾ cup double cream
115g/4oz prosciutto crudo, shredded
salt and freshly ground black pepper
chopped fresh herbs, such as flat leaf parsley, basil and marjoram, to garnish

1 Bring a large pan of lightly salted water to the boil and cook the pasta until it is *al dente*.

2 Meanwhile, melt half the butter with the olive oil in a separate pan. Add the peas, garlic and stock. Sprinkle in the chopped parsley and season with salt and pepper to taste. Cook over a medium heat, stirring frequently, for 5–8 minutes, or until most of the liquid has been absorbed.

3 Add about half the cream, increase the heat to high and let the cream bubble, stirring constantly, until it thickens and coats all the peas. Remove from the heat, stir in the prosciutto and taste for seasoning.

4 Tip the cooked pasta into a colander and drain it well. Immediately add the remaining butter to the pasta pan. When it has melted, add the remaining double cream and heat until it is just bubbling.

5 Add the pasta and toss over a medium heat until it is evenly coated. Pour in the pea and ham sauce, toss lightly and heat through. Spoon into warmed bowls and serve immediately, sprinkled with fresh herbs.

Ham & Spinach Cannelloni

Keep dried cannelloni tubes in the store cupboard, and tasty bakes like this one will be easy to make.

Serves 4

25g/1oz/2 tbsp butter
½ onion, very finely chopped
175g/6oz/1½ cups frozen chopped spinach, thawed and drained
75g/3oz cooked ham, minced or very finely diced
25g/1oz/½ cup fresh white breadcrumbs
115g/4oz/½ cup ricotta cheese
75g/3oz/1 cup freshly grated Parmesan cheese
16 dried no-precook cannelloni tubes
salt and freshly ground black pepper

For the white sauce

50g/2oz/¼ cup butter
50g/2oz/¼ cup plain flour
900ml/1½ pints/3¾ cups milk
nutmeg

1 Melt the butter in a frying pan. Add the onion and fry over a medium heat, stirring occasionally, for 5 minutes, until softened but not browned.

2 Add the spinach and cook for 3 minutes, then tip the mixture into a strainer set over a bowl and press the spinach with the back of a wooden spoon to remove as much liquid as possible. Discard the liquid.

3 Put the spinach mixture into a separate bowl and stir in the ham, breadcrumbs, ricotta and one-third of the grated Parmesan. Season with salt and pepper to taste. Preheat the oven to 190°C/375°F/Gas 5.

4 Make the white sauce. Melt the butter in a saucepan, add the flour and cook, stirring constantly, for 1–2 minutes. Gradually add the milk, stirring until the sauce boils and thickens. Grate in fresh nutmeg to taste, then season with salt and pepper. Whisk well. Remove the pan from the heat.

5 Spoon a little of the white sauce into an ovenproof dish large enough to hold the cannelloni tubes in a single layer. Fill the cannelloni tubes with the ham and spinach mixture, and place them in the dish. Pour the remaining white sauce over, then sprinkle with the remaining Parmesan.

6 Bake for 35–40 minutes, or until the pasta feels tender when pierced with a skewer. Remove from the oven and allow to stand for 10 minutes before serving.

Variations

- *Use 500g/1¼lb fresh spinach instead of frozen. Discard any stalks and wash the leaves well in cold water. Transfer to a saucepan with just the water clinging to the leaves. Cook over a medium heat for 2–3 minutes, until wilted. Turn into a colander and press out as much liquid as possible. Chop finely and add to the onions.*
- *You can also use fresh Swiss chard, which has a similar flavour and can be prepared in exactly the same way.*

Golden-Topped Pasta

This simple dish is a good choice for when the children bring friends home, and is always popular. It can easily be stretched if you end up with more guests than you bargained for.

Serves 4–6
225g/8oz/2 cups dried conchiglie or fusilli
5ml/1 tsp vegetable oil
115g/4oz chopped cooked ham or turkey
350g/12oz par-cooked mixed chopped vegetables, such as carrots, cauliflower, beans and sweetcorn
salt and freshly ground black pepper

For the cheese sauce
25g/1oz/2 tbsp butter
25g/1oz/ ¼ cup plain flour
300ml/ ½ pint/1 ¼ cups milk
175g/6oz/1 ½ cups grated Cheddar cheese
5–10ml/1–2 tsp mustard

1 Bring a large pan of lightly salted water to the boil and cook the pasta until it is *al dente*.

2 Make the cheese sauce. Melt the butter in a saucepan, stir in the flour and cook over a low heat, stirring constantly, for 1 minute. Gradually stir in the milk, until the sauce boils and thickens. Stir in half the grated cheese and the mustard, and season with salt and pepper to taste.

3 Drain the pasta well and place in a large ovenproof dish. Stir in the vegetable oil, then the chopped meat and vegetables. Spoon the cheese sauce evenly over the top.

4 Preheat the grill. Sprinkle the rest of the cheese over the sauce-topped pasta and grill quickly until golden and bubbling. Serve immediately.

Cook's Tip
For extra colour, arrange thin slices of tomato in an overlapping line over the cheese topping and dot with a little butter before grilling the dish.

Rotolo di Pasta

This impressive-looking dish consists of a giant spinach-filled Swiss roll of pasta, which is poached, sliced and baked with white sauce.

Serves 6
50g/2oz/ ¼ cup butter
1 medium onion, chopped
115g/4oz ham, diced
700g/1 ½lb frozen chopped spinach, thawed and drained
225g/8oz/1 cup full-fat soft cheese
1 egg, lightly beaten
freshly grated nutmeg
1 quantity Basic Pasta Dough
50g/2oz/ ⅔ cup freshly grated Parmesan cheese
salt and freshly ground black pepper

For the white sauce
50g/2oz/ ¼ cup butter
50g/2oz/ ½ cup plain flour
900ml/1 ½ pints/3¾ cups milk

1 Melt the butter in a saucepan and fry the onion until golden. Add the ham and spinach. Cook for 2 minutes, then beat in the soft cheese and egg. Season well with salt, pepper and nutmeg.

2 Roll out the pasta to a rectangle measuring 40 x 30cm/ 16 x 12in. Spread the spinach filling all over, leaving a 1cm/ ½in border all around the edge. Roll up the topped pasta from a short side and wrap in muslin, tying the ends with string. Poach in a very large pan of simmering water for 20 minutes, or until firm. Carefully remove, drain and unwrap. Leave to cool.

3 Make the sauce. Melt the butter in a pan, stir in the flour and cook, stirring constantly, for 1–2 minutes. Gradually add the milk, stirring until the sauce boils and thickens. Season to taste.

4 Preheat the oven to 200°C/400°F/Gas 6. Cut the pasta roll into 2.5cm/1in slices. Spoon a little of the sauce over the base of a shallow ovenproof dish and arrange the slices on top, so that they are slightly overlapping.

5 Spoon over the remaining sauce, sprinkle with the Parmesan and bake for 15–20 minutes, or until browned and bubbling. Allow to stand for a few minutes before serving.

Pepperoni Pasta

Add extra zip to pasta dishes, which can sometimes seem a little bland, with spicy pepperoni sausage.

Serves 4

275g/10oz/2½ cups dried penne
175g/6oz pepperoni sausage, sliced
1 small or ½ large red onion, sliced
45ml/3 tbsp bottled pesto
150ml/ ¼ pint/ ⅔ cup double cream
225g/8oz cherry tomatoes, halved
15g/½ oz fresh chives
salt
breadsticks, to serve

1 Bring a large pan of lightly salted water to the boil and cook the pasta until it is *al dente*.

2 Meanwhile, heat the pepperoni sausage slices in a heavy-based frying pan over a medium-low heat until the fat runs. Add the sliced onion and cook, stirring occasionally, until it is soft and translucent.

3 Mix the pesto sauce and cream together in a small bowl. Add this mixture to the frying pan and stir over a low heat until the sauce is smooth.

4 Add the cherry tomatoes to the pepperoni mixture and snip the chives over the top with scissors. Stir again.

5 Drain the pasta and return it to the clean pan. Pour the sauce over and toss thoroughly, making sure all the pasta is coated. Serve immediately with breadsticks.

Cook's Tips
• *Use a mixture of red and yellow cherry tomatoes for a really colourful meal.*
• *You can use any fairly firm spicy cooking sausage for this recipe. Try mild or hot chorizo, or even black pudding.*

Rigatoni with Spicy Sausage & Tomato Sauce

This is really a cheat's version of Bolognese sauce, using the wonderful fresh spicy sausages sold in every Italian delicatessen.

Serves 4

450g/1lb fresh spicy Italian cooking sausage
30ml/2 tbsp olive oil
1 medium onion, chopped
450ml/ ¾ pint/1¾ cups passata
150ml/ ¼ pint/ ⅔ cup dry red wine
6 sun-dried tomatoes in oil, drained and sliced
450g/1lb/4 cups dried rigatoni
salt and freshly ground black pepper
chopped mixed fresh herbs, to garnish
freshly grated Parmesan cheese, to serve

1 Squeeze the sausages out of their skins. Put them in a bowl and break up the meat.

2 Heat the oil in a heavy-based saucepan. Add the onion and fry over a medium heat, stirring occasionally, for 5 minutes, until soft and golden. Stir in the sausagemeat and cook, browning it all over and breaking up the lumps with a wooden spoon.

3 Pour in the passata and the wine, and bring to the boil. Add the sun-dried tomatoes and season with salt and pepper to taste. Lower the heat and simmer for 10–12 minutes, or for as long as it takes to cook the pasta.

4 Bring a saucepan of lightly salted water to the boil and cook the pasta until *al dente*. Drain well and divide among warmed bowls. Top with the sauce. Garnish with fresh herbs and serve with grated Parmesan.

Cook's Tip
Passata, available in jars and cartons, is a concentrate of crushed, strained tomatoes, which has a deep, rich flavour.

Penne with Salame Napoletano

Spicy sausage tossed in cheesy tomato sauce is delicious with pasta.

Serves 4

350g/12oz/3 cups dried penne
30ml/2 tbsp olive oil
225g/8oz salame napoletano or chorizo sausage, diagonally sliced
450g/1lb ripe tomatoes, peeled and chopped
1 garlic clove, chopped
30ml/2 tbsp chopped fresh flat leaf parsley, plus extra to garnish
grated rind of 1 lemon
50g/2oz/⅔ cup freshly grated Parmesan cheese
salt and freshly ground black pepper

1 Bring a large pan of lightly salted water to the boil and cook the pasta until *al dente*.

2 Meanwhile, heat the oil in a heavy-based frying pan. Add the salame or chorizo and fry over a medium heat, stirring occasionally, for 5 minutes, until browned.

3 Add the tomatoes, garlic, parsley and grated lemon rind. Heat through, stirring constantly, for 1 minute, then stir in the Parmesan and season with salt and pepper to taste.

4 Drain the pasta thoroughly and return it to the clean pan. Add the sauce and toss to coat. Serve in warmed bowls, garnished with the extra parsley.

Cook's Tip

Salame napoletano is a spicy Italian sausage, made with a mixture of pork and beef and flavoured with red and black pepper. It is quite fiery, so if you prefer a milder flavour, try salame fiorentino – a pure pork sausage – or genovese – a mixture of pork and veal. Look for salame at Italian delicatessens. If you are unable to locate it, use mild or hot Spanish chorizo sausage instead.

Spirali with Wild Mushrooms & Chorizo Sauce

The delicious combination of wild mushrooms and spicy sausage make this a tempting supper dish.

Serves 4

350g/12oz/3 cups dried spirali
60ml/4 tbsp olive oil
1 garlic clove, chopped
1 celery stick, chopped
225g/8oz chorizo sausage, sliced
225g/8oz/3 cups mixed wild mushrooms, such as oyster, brown cap, shiitake
15ml/1 tbsp lemon juice
30ml/2 tbsp chopped fresh oregano
salt and freshly ground black pepper
finely chopped fresh parsley, to garnish

1 Bring a large pan of lightly salted water to the boil and cook the pasta until it is *al dente*.

2 Meanwhile, heat the oil in a heavy-based frying pan. Add the garlic and celery, and fry over a medium heat, stirring occasionally, for 5 minutes, until the celery has softened.

3 Add the chorizo and cook, stirring occasionally, for 5 minutes, until browned, then stir in the wild mushrooms. Cook for 4 minutes, stirring occasionally until slightly softened.

4 Stir in the lemon juice and oregano. Season with salt and pepper to taste, and heat through.

5 Drain the pasta thoroughly and turn it into a warmed serving bowl. Toss with the sauce to coat. Serve immediately, garnished with fresh parsley.

Cook's Tip

Use any combination of wild mushrooms for this flavoursome sauce or even a mixture of wild and cultivated. Season the dish sparingly, as chorizo is quite peppery.

Pasta with Sausage, Corn & Red Peppers

This Italian-American recipe cleverly combines reduced fat with all the flavour of traditional ingredients in this quick and easy supper dish.

Serves 4

350g/12oz/3 cups dried fusilli or eliche
15ml/1 tbsp olive oil
1 onion, chopped
1 garlic clove, finely chopped
2 red peppers, seeded and sliced
250g/9oz/1½ cups frozen sweetcorn kernels, thawed
1 reduced-fat U-shaped smoked pork sausage
15ml/1 tbsp chopped fresh basil
salt and freshly ground black pepper
fresh basil sprigs, to garnish

1 Bring a large pan of lightly salted water to the boil and cook the pasta until it is *al dente*.

2 Meanwhile, heat the oil in a frying pan. Add the onion, garlic and red peppers, and cook over a medium heat, stirring frequently, for 5 minutes, until the onion is softened.

3 Stir in the sweetcorn kernels and heat through gently, stirring occasionally, for about 5 minutes. Season with salt and pepper to taste.

4 Heat the U-shaped sausage in a pan of simmering water, following the instructions on the packet. Do not allow the water to boil, as this will cause the skin to split. Alternatively, heat the sausage in the microwave, following the instructions on the packet.

5 Drain the sausage if necessary, remove the outer covering and slice the meat thinly. Stir the slices into the onion and pepper mixture.

6 Drain the pasta and return it to the clean pan. Add the sauce and chopped basil. Toss well. Serve in a warmed bowl, garnished with the basil sprigs.

Fusilli Lunghi with Sausage & Tomato Sauce

A warming supper dish, perfect for cold winter nights. Save time by using smoked sausages that only need to be reheated. They are sold, singly, in packets in the chiller compartments of supermarkets.

Serves 4

15ml/1 tbsp olive oil
1 medium onion, finely chopped
1 red pepper, seeded and diced
1 green pepper, seeded and diced
2 x 400g/14oz cans chopped tomatoes
30ml/2 tbsp tomato purée
10ml/2 tsp mild paprika
450g/1lb/4 cups fusilli lunghi
1 reduced-fat U-shaped smoked pork sausage
45ml/3 tbsp chopped fresh parsley
salt and freshly ground black pepper

1 Heat the oil in a medium saucepan. Add the onion and fry over a medium heat, stirring occasionally, for 5 minutes, until it is beginning to colour.

2 Stir in the peppers, tomatoes, tomato purée and paprika. Bring to the boil, lower the heat and simmer, uncovered, for 15–20 minutes, until the sauce has reduced and thickened.

3 Meanwhile, bring a large pan of water to the boil, add the pasta and cook until it is *al dente*.

4 Heat the U-shaped sausage in a pan of simmering water, following the instructions on the packet. Do not allow the water to boil, as this will cause the skin to split. Alternatively, heat the sausage in the microwave, following the instructions on the packet.

5 Drain the pasta and divide it among four warmed bowls. Drain the sausage, if necessary, remove the outer covering and slice the meat thinly. Add the slices to the sauce, with the parsley, season with salt and pepper to taste and mix well. Top each portion of pasta with sauce and serve immediately.

Fusilli with Spicy Pork Sausage

Spicy hot sausage and tomato sauce combine with spirals of pasta to make this really tasty dish from southern Italy.

Serves 4

400g/14oz spicy pork sausages
30ml/2 tbsp olive oil
1 small onion, finely chopped
2 garlic cloves, crushed
1 large yellow pepper, seeded and cut into strips
5ml/1 tsp paprika
5ml/1 tsp dried mixed herbs
5–10ml/1–2 tsp chilli sauce
400g/14oz can chopped tomatoes
250–300ml/8–10fl oz/1–1¼ cups Vegetable Stock
300g/11oz/2¾ cups fresh or dried fusilli
salt and freshly ground black pepper
freshly grated Pecorino cheese, to serve

1 Grill the sausages for 10–12 minutes, until they are browned on all sides, then drain them on kitchen paper.

2 Heat the oil in a large saucepan, add the onion and garlic, and cook over a low heat, stirring frequently, for 5–7 minutes, until the onions are soft.

3 Add the yellow pepper, paprika, herbs and chilli sauce to taste. Cook gently for 5–7 minutes, stirring occasionally.

4 Tip in the canned tomatoes, then season to taste and stir well. Cook over a medium heat for 10–12 minutes, adding the vegetable stock gradually as the sauce reduces.

5 While the tomato sauce is cooking, cut the grilled sausages diagonally into 1cm/½in pieces. Add them to the sauce, reduce the heat to low and cook for 10–12 minutes.

6 Meanwhile, bring a large pan of lightly salted water to the boil and cook the pasta until it is *al dente*.

7 Taste the sauce for seasoning. Drain the pasta and add it to the pan of sauce. Toss well, then divide among four warmed bowls. Sprinkle with Pecorino and serve.

Eliche with Sausage & Radicchio

Sausage and radicchio may seem unlikely companions, but the powerful flavours of these ingredients are really delicious together. This robust and filling dish makes a good midweek supper.

Serves 4

30ml/2 tbsp olive oil
1 onion, finely chopped
200g/7oz Italian pure pork sausage
175ml/6fl oz/¾ cup passata
90ml/6 tbsp dry white wine
300g/11oz/2¾ cups dried eliche
50g/2oz radicchio leaves, finely shredded
salt and freshly ground black pepper

1 Heat the olive oil in a large frying pan. Add the onion and cook over a medium heat, stirring occasionally, for 5 minutes, until softened. Snip the end off the sausage skin and squeeze the sausagemeat into the pan. Stir to break it up and mix it with the onion.

2 Fry the mixture, until the sausagemeat is brown all over and looks crumbly. Stir in the passata and wine, and season with salt and pepper to taste. Lower the heat and simmer, stirring occasionally, for 10–12 minutes.

3 Meanwhile, bring a large pan of lightly salted water to the boil and cook the pasta until it is *al dente*. Just before draining the pasta, add a ladleful or two of the cooking water to the sausage sauce and stir it in well. Taste the sauce to check the seasoning.

4 Drain the cooked pasta and tip it into the pan of sausage sauce. Add the shredded radicchio and toss well to combine. Transfer to warmed bowls and serve immediately.

Cook's Tip

The best sausage to use is salsiccia puro suino, *which is made from 100 per cent pure pork, plus garlic and other flavourings and seasonings.*

Sardinian Sausage & Pasta

In Sardinia they call this dish "malloreddus", which is the local name for the type of pasta used to make it.

Serves 4–6

30ml/2 tbsp olive oil
6 garlic cloves
200g/7oz Italian pure pork sausage, diced small
2 small handfuls of fresh basil leaves
400g/14oz can chopped Italian plum tomatoes
a good pinch of saffron strands
15ml/1 tbsp granulated sugar
350g/12oz/3 cups dried malloreddus (gnocchi sardi) or other pasta shapes
75g/3oz/1 cup freshly grated Pecorino cheese
salt and freshly ground black pepper

1 Heat the oil in a saucepan and fry the garlic, sausage and half the basil leaves until the sausage is browned all over. Remove and discard the garlic.

2 Add the tomatoes. Fill the empty can with water; pour it into the pan, then stir in the saffron, sugar, 5ml/1 tsp salt and pepper to taste. Bring to the boil, lower the heat and simmer, stirring occasionally, for 20–30 minutes.

3 Meanwhile, bring a pan of lightly salted water to the boil and cook the pasta until it is *al dente*.

4 Drain the pasta and tip it into a warmed bowl. Pour the sauce over the pasta and toss well. Add about one-third of the Pecorino and the remaining basil, and toss again. Serve immediately, with the remaining Pecorino sprinkled on top.

Cook's Tip

In Sardinia, a special type of sausage is used for malloreddus. *It is flavoured with aniseed and black pepper, and is called* sartizzu sardo. *A good alternative would be the piquant* salsiccia piccante. *If, however, you prefer a slightly milder flavour, try* luganega, *which is much more widely available.*

Tortiglioni with Salami

This heady pasta dish is not for the faint-hearted. Serve it with a robust red wine.

Serves 4

30ml/2 tbsp olive oil
1 onion, finely chopped
1 celery stick, finely chopped
2 large garlic cloves, crushed
1 fresh red chilli, seeded and chopped
450g/1lb ripe plum tomatoes, peeled and finely chopped
30ml/2 tbsp tomato purée
150ml/¼ pint/⅔ cup red wine
5ml/1 tsp granulated sugar
300g/11oz/2¾ cups dried tortiglioni
175g/6oz spicy salami, rind removed, chopped into large chunks
salt and freshly ground black pepper
30ml/2 tbsp chopped fresh parsley, to garnish
freshly grated Parmesan cheese, to serve

1 Heat the oil in a large pan. Add the onion, celery, garlic and chilli and cook over a low heat, stirring frequently, for about 10 minutes, until softened.

2 Add the tomatoes, tomato purée, wine and sugar, and season with salt and pepper to taste. Bring to the boil, stirring constantly. Lower the heat, cover and simmer gently, stirring occasionally, for about 20 minutes. Add a few spoonfuls of water from time to time if the sauce becomes too thick.

3 Meanwhile, bring a large pan of lightly salted water to the boil and cook the pasta until it is *al dente*. Add the salami to the sauce and stir until heated through.

4 Drain the pasta, tip it into a large bowl, then pour the sauce over and toss to mix. Scatter over the parsley and serve with the grated Parmesan.

Cook's Tip

Buy the salami for this dish in one piece so that you can chop it into large chunks.

Bucatini with Sausage & Pancetta

This is a rich and satisfying main course dish, which needs no accompaniment.

Serves 4
115g/4oz pork sausagemeat
400g/14oz can Italian plum tomatoes
15ml/1 tbsp olive oil
1 garlic clove, bruised
115g/4oz pancetta or rindless streaky bacon, roughly chopped
30ml/2 tbsp chopped fresh flat leaf parsley
400g/14oz dried bucatini
60–75ml/4–5 tbsp double cream
2 egg yolks
salt and freshly ground black pepper

1 Remove any skin from the sausagemeat and break the meat up roughly with a knife. Put the tomatoes in a food processor or blender and process to a purée.

2 Heat the oil in a pan and fry the garlic over a low heat for 1–2 minutes. Remove it with a slotted spoon and discard. Add the pork sausagemeat and pancetta or bacon and stir-fry over a medium heat for 3–4 minutes, until the sausagemeat breaks up and looks brown and crumbly.

3 Stir in the puréed tomatoes with half the parsley. Season to taste. Bring to the boil, scraping the base of the pan, to loosen any sausagemeat that has stuck. Lower the heat, cover and simmer for 30 minutes, stirring from time to time.

4 Meanwhile, bring a large pan of lightly salted water to the boil and cook the pasta until it is *al dente*.

5 Put the cream and egg yolks in a warmed large bowl and mix with a fork. Drain the pasta well and add it to the bowl. Toss to coat, then pour the sausagemeat sauce over the pasta and toss again. Serve immediately, sprinkled with the remaining parsley.

Cook's Tip
To save time puréeing the tomatoes, use passata.

Orecchiette with Pork in Mustard Sauce

The combination of slices of lean pork and spicy wholegrain mustard gives this filling pasta dish a real country taste.

Serves 4
350g/12oz/3 cups dried orecchiette
30ml/2 tbsp olive oil
2 garlic cloves, chopped
350g/12oz pork fillet, thinly sliced
50g/2oz/ ¼ cup butter
175g/6oz/2½ cups flat mushrooms, sliced
15ml/1 tbsp wholegrain mustard
45ml/3 tbsp snipped fresh chives, plus extra, to garnish
salt and freshly ground black pepper

1 Bring a large pan of lightly salted water to the boil and cook the pasta until it is *al dente*.

2 Meanwhile, heat the olive oil in a large, deep frying pan. Add the garlic and pork, and fry over a medium heat, stirring occasionally, for about 10 minutes, until the pork is tender and well browned all over.

3 Add the butter, mushrooms and mustard to the pan and cook for 2 minutes, stirring occasionally. Add the chives and season with salt and pepper to taste.

4 Drain the pasta thoroughly. Stir it into the pork mixture and cook for 1 minute until heated through. Pile into a warmed bowl and serve immediately, garnished with the extra chives.

Variations
• *Stir 150ml/ ¼ pint/ ⅔ cup double cream into the pork mixture with the chives for a rich sauce.*
• *For a hot, spicy flavour, substitute chilli mustard for the wholegrain mustard.*
• *Add 15g/½oz dried porcini mushrooms, reconstituted in hot water, with the flat mushrooms.*

Rigatoni with Pork

This is an excellent meat sauce using minced pork rather than the more usual minced beef.

Serves 4
25g/1oz/2 tbsp butter
30ml/2 tbsp olive oil
1 small onion, finely chopped
½ carrot, finely chopped
½ celery stick, finely chopped
2 garlic cloves, crushed
150g/5oz minced pork
60ml/4 tbsp dry white wine
400g/14oz can chopped Italian plum tomatoes
a few fresh basil leaves, plus extra, to garnish
400g/14oz/3½ cups dried rigatoni
salt and freshly ground black pepper
freshly shaved Parmesan cheese, to serve

1 Heat the butter and oil in a large pan until just sizzling, add the chopped vegetables and garlic, and cook over a medium heat, stirring frequently, for 3–4 minutes.

2 Add the minced pork and cook gently for 2–3 minutes, breaking up any lumps in the meat with a wooden spoon. Fry for 2–3 minutes more.

3 Stir in the wine, tomatoes, basil leaves, salt to taste and plenty of pepper. Bring to the boil, then lower the heat, cover and simmer for 40 minutes, stirring from time to time.

4 Bring a large pan of lightly salted water to the boil and cook the pasta until it is *al dente*. Just before draining it, add 1–2 ladles of the cooking water to the sauce. Stir well.

5 Drain the pasta, add it to the pan of sauce and toss well. Serve, sprinkled with the basil and shaved Parmesan.

Variation
To give the sauce a more intense flavour, soak 15g/½oz dried porcini mushrooms in 175ml/6fl oz/¾ cup warm water for 15–20 minutes, then drain, chop and add with the meat.

Pork Meatballs with Pasta

Serve these tasty meatballs on a bed of spaghetti.

Serves 6
450g/1lb lean minced pork
1 leek, finely chopped
115g/4oz/3 cups mushrooms, finely chopped
15ml/1 tbsp chopped fresh thyme
15ml/1 tbsp tomato purée
1 egg, beaten
30ml/2 tbsp flour
oil, for frying the meatballs
500g/1¼lb dried spaghetti
salt and freshly ground black pepper
fresh thyme sprigs, to garnish

For the tomato sauce
15ml/1 tbsp olive oil
1 onion, finely chopped
1 carrot, finely chopped
1 celery stick, finely chopped
1 garlic clove, crushed
675g/1½ lb ripe tomatoes, peeled, seeded and chopped
150ml/¼ pint/⅔ cup dry white wine
150ml/¼ pint/⅔ cup well-flavoured Vegetable Stock
15ml/1 tbsp tomato purée
15ml/1 tbsp chopped fresh basil

1 Preheat the oven to 180°C/350°F/Gas 4. Put the pork, leek, mushrooms, chopped thyme, tomato purée, egg and flour in a bowl and stir together until thoroughly mixed. Shape into small balls, place on a plate, cover and chill.

2 Make the tomato sauce. Heat the olive oil in a frying pan and fry the onion and carrot until softened. Add all the remaining sauce ingredients, season to taste, then bring to the boil. Boil, uncovered, for 10 minutes, until thickened.

3 Heat the oil in a frying pan, add the meatballs in batches and cook until lightly browned. Using a slotted spoon, place them in a shallow, ovenproof dish and pour the tomato sauce over. Cover and bake for about 1 hour, until cooked through.

4 Shortly before the meatballs are ready, bring a pan of lightly salted water to the boil and cook the pasta until it is *al dente*.

5 Drain the pasta well, divide it among warmed bowls, spoon in the meatballs and sauce, and serve garnished with thyme sprigs.

Sicilian Lasagne

In Sicily their lasagne is traditionally made with pork rather than beef.

Serves 6

45ml/3 tbsp olive oil
1 small onion, finely chopped
½ carrot, finely chopped
½ celery stick, finely chopped
250g/9oz boneless pork
60ml/4 tbsp dry white wine
400ml/14fl oz/1⅔ cups passata
200ml/7fl oz/scant 1 cup chicken stock
15ml/1 tbsp tomato purée
2 bay leaves, torn
15ml/1 tbsp chopped fresh flat leaf parsley
250g/9oz fresh lasagne sheets
2 hard-boiled eggs, sliced
125g/4½ oz packet mozzarella cheese, drained and sliced
60ml/4 tbsp freshly grated Pecorino cheese
salt and freshly ground black pepper

1 Heat 30ml/2 tbsp of the oil in a large pan and cook the chopped vegetables over a medium heat, stirring frequently, for about 10 minutes.

2 Add the pork and fry until well browned all over. Pour in the wine and let it bubble and reduce for a few minutes, then add the passata, stock, tomato purée and bay leaves, with the parsley and salt and pepper to taste. Mix well, cover and cook, stirring occasionally, for 30–40 minutes, until the pork is tender.

3 Using a slotted spoon, remove the bay leaves and meat. Discard the bay leaves. Chop the meat and return it to the pan.

4 Preheat the oven to 190°C/375°F/Gas 5. Bring a saucepan of lightly salted water to the boil. Cut the lasagne sheets into 2.5cm/1in strips and add to the water. Cook for 3–4 minutes until just *al dente*. Drain well, then stir the strips into the sauce.

5 Spoon half the pasta and sauce mixture into a shallow ovenproof dish. Cover with half the egg and mozzarella slices and half the Pecorino. Repeat the layers, drizzle the remaining oil over the top and bake for 30–35 minutes, until golden and bubbling. Allow to stand for about 10 minutes before serving.

Lamb & Sweet Pepper Sauce

Not a speedy pasta dish – the sauce needs to be cooked for about an hour – but well worth waiting for.

Serves 4–6

60ml/4 tbsp olive oil
250g/9oz boneless lamb neck fillet, diced quite small
2 garlic cloves, finely chopped
2 bay leaves, torn
250ml/8fl oz/1 cup dry white wine
4 ripe plum tomatoes, peeled and chopped
2 large red peppers, seeded and diced
350–425g/12–15oz dried maccheroni alla chitarra or any long macaroni
salt and freshly ground black pepper

1 Heat half the olive oil in a flameproof casserole, add the lamb and sprinkle with a little salt and pepper. Cook the meat over a medium to high heat, stirring frequently, for about 10 minutes, until the pieces of meat are browned on all sides.

2 Sprinkle in the garlic and add the bay leaves, then pour in the wine and let it bubble until reduced.

3 Stir in the remaining olive oil, with the tomatoes and the red peppers. Cover and simmer over a low heat, stirring occasionally, for 45–55 minutes, or until the lamb is very tender.

4 Bring a large pan of lightly salted water to the boil and cook the pasta until it is *al dente*.

5 Drain the pasta well and return it to the clean pan. Remove the bay leaves from the sauce, then add the sauce to the pasta, toss well and serve immediately.

Cook's Tips

- *The peppers don't have to be red. Use yellow, orange or green if you prefer; either one colour or a mixture.*
- *If you need to add water to the sauce towards the end of cooking, take it from the pan used for cooking the pasta.*

Pasta with Devilled Kidneys

The spicy, savoury flavour of the kidneys goes particularly well with tender tagliatelle.

Serves 4

8–10 lamb's kidneys
15ml/1 tbsp sunflower oil
25g/1oz/2 tbsp butter
10ml/2 tsp paprika
5–10ml/1–2 tsp mild wholegrain mustard
350g/12oz fresh tagliatelle
salt
chopped fresh parsley, to garnish

1 Bring a large pan of lightly salted water to the boil. Cut the kidneys in half and neatly cut out the white cores with scissors.

2 Heat the oil and butter together in a frying pan. Add the kidneys and cook, turning frequently, for about 2 minutes.

3 In a cup, mix the paprika and mustard with a little salt. Stir the mixture into the pan and continue to cook the kidneys, basting them frequently, for 3–4 minutes.

4 Meanwhile, bring a large pan of lightly salted water to the boil and cook the pasta until *al dente*, then drain thoroughly and divide among warmed bowls. Top with the kidneys, garnish with the parsley and serve.

Pasta with Devilled Liver

Cook as for Pasta with Devilled Kidneys, but use 450g/1lb lamb's liver.

1 Trim the liver, removing any skin, and slice it into strips. Toss these in flour, seasoned with plenty of salt and pepper.

2 Use twice as much oil and butter as for the kidneys. Fry the floured liver strips, then stir in the paprika and mustard. Add a generous dash of Tabasco sauce, if you like. Cook for 3–4 minutes, basting the liver frequently.

3 Serve with the fresh tagliatelle, garnished with chopped parsley.

Spaghetti with Meatballs

Meatballs are fun to make and delicious to eat. This is real hands-on cooking!

Serves 4

350g/12oz dried spaghetti
4 fresh rosemary sprigs, to garnish
freshly grated Parmesan cheese, to serve

For the meatballs

1 onion, chopped
1 garlic clove, chopped
350g/12oz minced lamb
1 egg yolk
15ml/1 tbsp dried mixed herbs
salt and freshly ground black pepper
30ml/2 tbsp olive oil

For the sauce

300ml/ ½ pint/1 ¼ cups passata
30ml/2 tbsp chopped fresh basil
1 garlic clove, chopped

1 Start by making the meatballs. Put the onion, garlic, minced lamb, egg yolk and mixed herbs in a bowl and season to taste with salt and pepper. Mix together thoroughly, using a spoon at first, then your hands.

2 Divide the mixture into 20 equal-size pieces and mould into balls. Place on a baking sheet, cover with clear film and chill for about 30 minutes.

3 Heat the oil in a large, heavy-based frying pan. Add the meatballs and fry over a medium heat, turning occasionally, for about 10 minutes, until browned all over.

4 Add all the sauce ingredients and bring to the boil. Cover, lower the heat and simmer for about 20 minutes, until the meatballs are tender.

5 Bring a large pan of lightly salted water to the boil and cook the pasta until it is *al dente*.

6 Drain the pasta thoroughly and divide it among four warmed serving plates. Spoon over the meatballs and some of the sauce. Garnish each portion with a fresh rosemary sprig and serve immediately with plenty of Parmesan.

Greek Pasta & Lamb Bake

Economical and filling, this makes an excellent main course for a family supper.

Serves 4

15ml/1 tbsp oil
450g/1lb minced lamb
1 onion, chopped
2 garlic cloves, crushed
30ml/2 tbsp tomato purée
30ml/2 tbsp plain flour
300ml/ ½ pint/1 ¼ cups lamb stock
115g/4oz/1 cup dried short-cut macaroni or small pasta shapes
2 large tomatoes, sliced
500ml/17fl oz/generous 2 cups Greek yogurt
2 eggs, beaten
salt and freshly ground black pepper
mixed salad, to serve

1 Heat the oil in a large pan. Add the lamb and cook over a moderate heat, stirring frequently, for 5 minutes. Add the onion and garlic, and fry for 5 minutes more.

2 Stir in the tomato purée and flour. Cook, stirring constantly, for 1 minute, then stir in the stock and season with salt and pepper to taste. Bring to the boil, lower the heat and simmer for 20 minutes, stirring occasionally. Preheat the oven to 190°C/375°F/Gas 5.

3 Meanwhile, bring a large pan of lightly salted water to the boil. Add the macaroni and cook until *al dente*.

4 Spread out the meat mixture in an ovenproof dish and arrange the tomatoes on top.

5 Drain the pasta well and tip it into a bowl. Stir in the yogurt and eggs. Spoon the mixture on top of the tomatoes, smooth the surface and bake for 1 hour. Remove from the oven and leave to stand for 5–10 minutes before serving with salad.

Variation
This pasta bake is also delicious made with minced beef or minced chicken.

Lasagne with Lamb

It may be unusual to make lasagne with lamb, but the flavour is excellent.

Serves 4–6

15ml/1 tbsp olive oil
1 small onion, finely chopped
450g/1lb minced lamb
1 garlic clove, crushed
45ml/3 tbsp dry white wine
5ml/1 tsp dried mixed herbs
5ml/1 tsp dried oregano
450ml/ ¾ pint/1 ¾ cups passata
12–16 fresh lasagne sheets, precooked if necessary
30ml/2 tbsp freshly grated Parmesan cheese
salt and freshly ground black pepper
salad leaves, to serve

For the white sauce
50g/2oz/ ¼ cup butter
50g/2oz/ ½ cup plain flour
900ml/1 ½ pints/3¾ cups hot milk
30ml/2 tbsp freshly grated Parmesan cheese
pinch of grated nutmeg

1 Heat the oil in a saucepan and cook the onion over a low heat, stirring frequently, for about 5 minutes, until softened. Add the lamb and garlic, and cook for 10 minutes, stirring frequently.

2 Season to taste, then add the wine and cook rapidly for about 2 minutes, stirring constantly. Stir in the herbs and passata. Simmer for 45 minutes–1 hour, stirring occasionally.

3 Preheat the oven to 190°C/375°F/Gas 5. Make the white sauce. Melt the butter in a saucepan, add the flour and cook, stirring, for 1–2 minutes. Gradually add the milk, stirring constantly, until the sauce boils and thickens. Add the Parmesan and nutmeg, season and whisk well. Remove from the heat.

4 Spread a few spoons of meat sauce over the base of an ovenproof dish and cover with 3–4 sheets of lasagne. Spread about a quarter of the remaining meat sauce over the lasagne, then a quarter of the white sauce. Repeat the layers three times.

5 Sprinkle the Parmesan over the surface and bake for 30–40 minutes, or until the topping is brown and bubbling. Allow to stand for 10 minutes before serving with salad.

Tagliatelle with Bolognese Sauce

Many people serve Bolognese sauce with spaghetti. To be absolutely correct, it should be served with tagliatelle.

Serves 4

30ml/2 tbsp olive oil
1 onion, finely chopped
1 carrot, finely chopped
1 celery stick, finely chopped
1 garlic clove, crushed
350g/12oz minced beef
150ml/ 1/4 pint/ 2/3 cup red wine
250ml/8fl oz/1 cup milk
400g/14oz can chopped tomatoes
15ml/1 tbsp sun-dried tomato purée
350g/12oz fresh or dried tagliatelle
salt and freshly ground black pepper
shredded fresh basil, to garnish
grated Parmesan cheese, to serve

1 Heat the oil in a large pan and fry the onion, carrot, celery and garlic over a low heat for about 10 minutes, until softened. Stir frequently. Do not allow the vegetables to colour.

2 Add the beef and cook until it changes colour, breaking up any lumps with a wooden spoon. Pour in the wine. Stir frequently until it has evaporated, then add the milk and continue cooking and stirring until this has evaporated, too.

3 Stir in the tomatoes and tomato purée, with salt and pepper to taste. Simmer the sauce, uncovered, over the lowest possible heat for at least 45 minutes.

4 Bring a large pan of lightly salted water to the boil and cook the pasta until it is *al dente*. Drain and tip into a warmed large bowl. Pour over the sauce and toss to combine. Garnish with basil and serve, with Parmesan cheese handed separately.

Cook's Tip
Don't skimp on the cooking time – it is essential for a full-flavoured Bolognese sauce. Some Italian cooks insist on cooking it for 3–4 hours, so the longer the better.

Fettuccine Bolognese with Baby Tomatoes

This is a versatile meat sauce. You can toss it with freshly cooked pasta – the quantity here is enough for 450g/1lb tagliatelle, spaghetti or any short pasta shapes such as penne or fusilli – or alternatively you can layer it in a baked dish like lasagne.

Serves 4–6

45ml/3 tbsp olive oil
1 onion, finely chopped
1 small carrot, finely chopped
1 celery stick, finely chopped
2 garlic cloves, crushed
400g/14oz minced beef
120ml/4fl oz/ 1/2 cup red wine
200ml/7fl oz/scant 1 cup passata
15ml/1 tbsp tomato purée
5ml/1 tsp dried oregano
15ml/1 tbsp chopped fresh flat leaf parsley
about 350ml/12fl oz/1 1/2 cups beef stock
8 baby Italian tomatoes
450g/1lb fresh fettuccine
salt and freshly ground black pepper
fresh Parmesan, to serve

1 Heat the oil in a large saucepan, add the onion, carrot, celery and garlic, and cook over a low heat, stirring frequently, for 5–7 minutes.

2 Add the minced beef and cook for 5 minutes, stirring frequently and breaking up any lumps in the meat with a wooden spoon. Stir in the wine and mix well.

3 Cook for 1–2 minutes, then add the passata, tomato purée, oregano, parsley and 60ml/4 tbsp of the beef stock. Season with salt and pepper to taste. Stir well and bring to the boil over a moderate heat.

4 Lower the heat, cover the pan and simmer for 30 minutes, stirring from time to time and adding more stock as necessary. Add the tomatoes and simmer for 10 minutes more.

5 Bring a pan of lightly salted water to the boil and cook the fettuccine until *al dente*. Drain, return to the pan and add the sauce. Toss well, then serve with shavings of Parmesan.

Spirali with Rich Meat Sauce

The sauce definitely improves if kept overnight in the fridge. This allows the flavours time enough to mature. There isn't any wine in this meat sauce, but the bacon and redcurrant jelly give it a fine flavour.

Serves 4

15ml/1 tbsp vegetable oil
450g/1lb minced beef
115g/4oz rindless smoked streaky bacon rashers, chopped
1 onion, chopped
2 celery sticks, chopped
150ml/ ¼ pint/ ⅔ cup chicken stock
45ml/3 tbsp tomato purée
1 garlic clove, chopped
45ml/3 tbsp chopped fresh mixed herbs
15ml/1 tbsp redcurrant jelly
350g/12oz/3 cups dried spirali
salt and freshly ground black pepper
chopped fresh oregano, to garnish

1 Heat the oil in a large saucepan. Add the beef and bacon, and cook over a moderate heat, stirring occasionally, for about 10 minutes, until browned.

2 Add the onion and celery, and cook for 5 minutes, stirring occasionally, then tip the contents of the pan into a metal colander and drain off the excess fat. Return the meat mixture to the pan.

3 Stir in the stock, tomato purée, garlic, herbs and redcurrant jelly. Season well, bring to the boil, then lower the heat, cover and simmer for at least 30 minutes, stirring occasionally.

4 Bring a large pan of lightly salted water to the boil and cook the pasta until it is *al dente*. Drain thoroughly and turn it into a large serving bowl. Pour over the sauce and toss to coat. Serve immediately, garnished with chopped fresh oregano.

Variation
You can use sweet mint jelly or chutney instead of the redcurrant jelly.

Bogus Bolognese

This doesn't pretend to be anything like the real thing, but Worcestershire sauce, chilli and chorizo sausages ensure that it is full of flavour and makes a very good family meal.

Serves 4

15ml/1 tbsp vegetable oil
1 onion, chopped
225g/8oz minced beef
5ml/1 tsp mild chilli powder
15ml/1 tbsp Worcestershire sauce
30ml/2 tbsp plain flour
150ml/ ¼ pint/ ⅔ cup beef stock
4 chorizo sausages, sliced
200g/7oz can chopped tomatoes
50g/2oz/ ⅓ cup baby sweetcorn cobs, halved lengthways
15ml/1 tbsp chopped fresh basil
350g/12oz dried spaghetti
salt and freshly ground black pepper
fresh basil sprigs, to garnish

1 Heat the oil in a large saucepan. Add the onion and minced beef, and fry over a moderate heat for 5 minutes, stirring to break up any lumps.

2 Add the chilli powder and cook, stirring constantly, for a further 3 minutes.

3 Stir in the Worcestershire sauce and flour. Cook for 1 minute, stirring constantly, then gradually pour in the stock, stirring constantly. Stir in the sliced sausages, tomatoes, baby sweetcorn and chopped basil. Season with salt and pepper to taste, and bring to the boil. Lower the heat and simmer for 30 minutes.

4 Bring a large pan of lightly salted water to the boil and cook the pasta until it is *al dente*.

5 Drain, place on four individual plates and top with the meat sauce. Garnish with the basil sprigs.

Cook's Tip
Make up the bogus Bolognese sauce and freeze in conveniently sized portions for up to two months.

Pasta with Chicken Liver & Beef Sauce

Chicken livers make the meat sauce wonderfully rich.

Serves 4–6

115g/4oz frozen chicken livers, thawed and drained
50g/2oz/ ¼ cup butter
75g/3oz diced pancetta
1 onion, finely chopped
1 carrot, finely chopped
1 celery stick, finely chopped
225g/8oz lean minced beef
30ml/2 tbsp tomato purée
120ml/4fl oz/ ½ cup white wine
200ml/7fl oz/scant 1 cup beef stock
freshly grated nutmeg
150ml/ ¼ pint/ ⅔ cup double cream
450g/1lb dried tagliatelle, spaghetti or fettuccine
salt and freshly ground black pepper
freshly grated Parmesan cheese, to serve

1 Trim the chicken livers and chop them roughly. Melt the butter in a saucepan and cook the pancetta for 2–3 minutes, until beginning to brown.

2 Add the onion, carrot and celery, and fry over a medium heat for 4–5 minutes, stirring frequently. Stir in the minced beef and brown over a high heat, breaking it up with a spoon.

3 Stir in the chicken livers and cook for 2–3 minutes. Add the tomato purée, mix well and pour in the wine and stock. Season with salt, pepper and nutmeg to taste. Bring to the boil, lower the heat, cover and simmer over a low heat for about 35 minutes, stirring occasionally.

4 Stir in the cream and heat through gently but do not allow the sauce to boil.

5 Bring a large pan of lightly salted water to the boil and cook the pasta until it is *al dente*.

6 Drain well and divide among heated plates or bowls. Top with the meat sauce and serve with plenty of Parmesan.

Cheesy Beef & Pasta Bake

Penne is coated in a cheese sauce and layered with beef in this favourite dish.

Serves 4

30ml/2 tbsp olive oil
3 shallots, chopped
1 garlic clove, crushed
1 celeriac root, diced
115g/4oz/3 cups button mushrooms, chopped
450g/1lb lean minced beef
30ml/2 tbsp red vermouth (optional)
200g/7oz can chopped tomatoes
15ml/1 tbsp tomato purée, dissolved in 45ml/3 tbsp hot water
a sprig of fresh thyme
225g/8oz/2 cups dried penne
300ml/ ½ pint/1 ¼ cups milk
25g/1oz/2 tbsp butter
25g/1oz/2 tbsp plain flour
150g/5oz/1 cup cubed mozzarella cheese
60ml/4 tbsp freshly grated Parmesan cheese
salt and freshly ground black pepper
fresh basil sprigs, to garnish

1 Heat the oil in a pan and fry the shallots, garlic and celeriac for 6 minutes, until softened. Stir in the mushrooms, fry for 2 minutes, then transfer the mixture to a bowl.

2 Add the beef to the pan and fry over a high heat until well browned. Drain off the excess fat and return the vegetables.

3 Pour in the vermouth, if using, tomatoes and tomato purée mixture, then add the thyme and season well. Bring to the boil, cover the pan and simmer gently for about 30 minutes.

4 Preheat the oven to 200°C/400°F/Gas 6. Bring a pan of lightly salted water to the boil and cook the pasta until it is *al dente*.

5 Meanwhile, place the milk, butter and flour in a saucepan. Heat gently, whisking constantly until thick and smooth. Stir in the mozzarella cheese with half the Parmesan.

6 Drain the pasta and stir it into the cheese sauce. Spoon the meat sauce into an ovenproof dish, top with the pasta mixture and sprinkle the remaining Parmesan over the top. Bake for 25 minutes until golden. Garnish with the basil and serve hot.

Three Tomato Bolognese

Although there's only one authentic Bolognese sauce, there are dozens of delicious dishes based on the famous ragoût. This one is well worth trying.

Serves 4–6

30ml/2 tbsp olive oil
1 onion, finely chopped
1 garlic clove, crushed
5ml/1 tsp dried mixed herbs
1.5ml/ ¼ tsp cayenne pepper
350–450g/12oz–1lb minced beef
400g/14oz can chopped tomatoes
45ml/3 tbsp tomato ketchup
15ml/1 tbsp sun-dried tomato purée
5ml/1 tsp Worcestershire sauce
5ml/1 tsp dried oregano
450ml/ ¾ pint/1¾ cups beef or Vegetable Stock
45ml/3 tbsp red wine
400–450g/14oz–1lb dried spaghetti
salt and freshly ground black pepper
freshly grated Parmesan cheese, to serve

1 Heat the olive oil in a saucepan and fry the onion and garlic over a low heat, stirring frequently, for about 5 minutes, until softened. Stir in the mixed herbs and cayenne, and cook for 2–3 minutes more.

2 Add the minced beef and cook gently for about 5 minutes, stirring frequently and breaking up any lumps in the meat with a wooden spoon.

3 Stir in the canned tomatoes, ketchup, sun-dried tomato purée, Worcestershire sauce, oregano and plenty of black pepper. Pour in the stock and red wine, and bring to the boil, stirring. Cover the pan, lower the heat and simmer, stirring occasionally, for 30 minutes.

4 Bring a large pan of lightly salted water to the boil and cook the pasta until it is *al dente*. Drain well and divide among warmed bowls. Taste the sauce and add a little salt if necessary, then spoon it on top of the pasta and sprinkle with a little grated Parmesan. Serve immediately, with extra Parmesan handed separately.

Tagliatelle with Meat Sauce

Using a combination of minced beef and pork with white wine and cream makes for a very rich, sophisticated sauce.

Serves 6–8

450g/1lb fresh or dried tagliatelle
freshly grated Parmesan cheese, to serve

For the meat sauce

25g/1oz/2 tbsp butter
15ml/1 tbsp olive oil
1 onion, finely chopped
2 carrots, finely chopped
2 celery sticks, finely chopped
2 garlic cloves, crushed
130g/4½oz pancetta or rindless streaky bacon, diced
250g/9oz lean minced beef
250g/9oz lean minced pork
120ml/4fl oz/ ½ cup dry white wine
2 x 400g/14oz cans crushed Italian plum tomatoes
475–750ml/16fl oz–1¼ pints/2–3 cups beef stock
100ml/3½fl oz/scant ½ cup double cream
salt and freshly ground black pepper

1 First, make the meat sauce. Heat the butter and oil in a large saucepan and cook the vegetables and the pancetta or bacon over a moderate heat, stirring frequently, for 10 minutes.

2 Add the minced beef and pork, lower the heat and cook gently for 10 minutes, stirring frequently and breaking up any lumps in the meat with a wooden spoon. Season to taste, then stir in the wine. Simmer for 5 minutes.

3 Add the canned tomatoes and 250ml/8fl oz/1 cup of the beef stock and bring to the boil. Stir the sauce well, then lower the heat. Partly cover the pan and simmer very gently for 2 hours. Stir occasionally and add more stock as it is absorbed.

4 Stir the cream into the sauce, then simmer, without a lid, for another 30 minutes, stirring frequently.

5 Bring a large pan of lightly salted water to the boil and cook the pasta until it is *al dente*. Drain it and tip it into a warmed bowl. Pour the sauce over the pasta and toss well. Serve, sprinkled with grated Parmesan.

Individual Pasta Bakes

If you make the meat sauce in advance, assembling these bakes takes very little time.

Serves 4

15ml/1 tbsp olive oil
350g/12oz minced beef
1 onion, chopped
1 garlic clove, chopped
400g/14oz can chopped tomatoes
15ml/1 tbsp dried mixed herbs
30ml/2 tbsp tomato purée
350g/12oz dried rigatoni
fresh basil sprigs, to garnish

For the cheese sauce

50g/2oz/ ¼ cup butter
50g/2oz/ ½ cup plain flour
450ml/ ¾ pint/1 ¾ cups milk
2 egg yolks
50g/2oz/ ⅔ cup freshly grated Parmesan cheese
salt and freshly ground black pepper

1 Heat the olive oil in a large, heavy-based frying pan. Add the beef and fry over a moderate heat, stirring occasionally, for about 10 minutes, until browned. Add the onion and cook for 5 minutes, stirring occasionally.

2 Stir in the garlic, tomatoes, herbs and tomato purée. Bring to the boil, cover and simmer for 30 minutes.

3 Meanwhile, make the cheese sauce. Melt the butter in a small saucepan, stir in the flour and cook for 1–2 minutes, stirring constantly. Gradually add the milk, stirring constantly until the sauce boils and thickens. Whisk in the egg yolks and cheese, and season with salt and pepper to taste.

4 Bring a large pan of lightly salted water to the boil and cook the pasta until it is *al dente*.

5 Drain the pasta well, return it to the clean pan and toss with the meat sauce.

6 Preheat the grill. Divide the pasta mixture among four flameproof dishes. Spoon the cheese sauce over and place under the grill until well browned. Serve immediately, garnished with fresh basil.

Rigatoni with Bresaola & Peppers

Bresaola – cured raw beef – is usually served thinly sliced as an antipasto. Here its almost gamey flavour proves the perfect partner for pasta.

Serves 6

30ml/2 tbsp olive oil
1 small onion, finely chopped
150g/5oz bresaola, cut into thin strips
4 mixed red and orange or yellow peppers, diced
120ml/4fl oz/ ½ cup dry white wine
400g/14oz can chopped tomatoes
450g/1lb/4 cups dried rigatoni
50g/2oz/ ⅔ cup freshly shaved Parmesan cheese
salt and freshly ground black pepper
1 small handful of fresh basil leaves, to garnish

1 Heat the oil in a medium saucepan, and add the onion and bresaola. Cover and cook over a low heat for 5–8 minutes, until the onion has softened. Add the peppers, wine, 5ml/1 tsp salt and plenty of pepper. Stir well, then simmer for 10–15 minutes.

2 Add the canned tomatoes and increase the heat to high. Bring to the boil, stirring, then lower the heat and replace the lid. Simmer gently, stirring occasionally, for 20 minutes, or until the peppers are very soft and the sauce is quite creamy.

3 Bring a pan of lightly salted water to the boil and cook the pasta until it is *al dente*.

4 Drain the cooked pasta and tip it into a warmed bowl. Taste the sauce for seasoning, then pour it over the pasta and add half the Parmesan. Toss well and serve immediately, with the basil leaves and the remaining Parmesan sprinkled on top.

Cook's Tip

Use fresh tomatoes, if you can locate sun-ripened ones that are full of flavour. You'll need about four, and should peel and chop them before adding them to the sauce.

Meatballs with Cream Sauce

Three types of meat make these meatballs extra special.

Serves 6

40g/1½ oz/3 tbsp butter
½ onion, finely chopped
350g/12oz minced beef
115g/4oz minced veal
225g/8oz lean minced pork
1 egg
115g/4oz cooked mashed potatoes
30ml/2 tbsp chopped fresh dill
1 garlic clove, finely chopped
2.5ml/½ tsp ground allspice
1.5ml/¼ tsp grated nutmeg
40g/1½ oz/¾ cup fresh white breadcrumbs, soaked in 175ml/6fl oz/¾ cup milk
about 40g/1½ oz/⅓ cup plain flour
60ml/4 tbsp olive oil
450g/1lb dried tagliatelli
175ml/6fl oz/¾ cup single cream
salt and freshly ground black pepper
fresh dill sprigs, to garnish

1 Melt 25g/1oz/2 tbsp of the butter in a pan and cook the onion over a low heat, until softened. Transfer the onion to a bowl, using a slotted spoon.

2 Add the minced meats, egg, mashed potatoes, dill, garlic, spices and seasoning to the bowl. Add the soaked breadcrumbs and mix well.

3 Shape the mixture into balls about 2.5cm/1in in diameter. Coat them lightly in flour. Heat the oil in a large frying pan and cook the meatballs for 8–10 minutes, until brown on all sides, shaking the pan occasionally.

4 Meanwhile, bring a large pan of lightly salted water to the boil and cook the pasta until it is *al dente*.

5 Using a slotted spoon, transfer the meatballs to a dish and keep them hot. Stir 15ml/1 tbsp flour into the fat in the frying pan. Whisk in the cream, then simmer for 3–4 minutes.

6 Drain the pasta and toss it with the remaining butter. Divide among six warmed plates, top each with a portion of meatballs and sauce. Garnish with dill and serve immediately.

Pasta Timbales

An alternative way to serve pasta for a special occasion. Mixed with minced beef and tomato, and baked in a lettuce parcel, it makes an impressive dish.

Serves 4

8 cos lettuce leaves
fresh basil sprigs, to garnish

For the filling

15ml/1 tbsp vegetable oil
175g/6oz minced beef
15ml/1 tbsp tomato purée
1 garlic clove, crushed
115g/4oz/1 cup dried short-cut macaroni
salt and freshly ground black pepper

For the sauce

25g/1oz/2 tbsp butter
25g/1oz/¼ cup plain flour
250ml/8fl oz/1 cup double cream
30ml/2 tbsp chopped fresh basil

1 Preheat the oven to 180°C/350°F/Gas 4. Make the filling. Heat the oil in a large pan and fry the beef for 7 minutes. Add the tomato purée and garlic, and cook for 5 minutes.

2 Meanwhile, bring a large pan of lightly salted water to the boil and cook the macaroni until it is *al dente*. Drain the macaroni and stir it into the meat sauce.

3 Line four 150ml/¼ pint/⅔ cup ramekins with the cos lettuce leaves, overlapping the sides. Season the meat mixture and spoon it into the lettuce-lined ramekins. Fold the lettuce leaves over the filling. Stand the ramekins in a roasting tin and pour in boiling water to come halfway up the sides. Cover the tin with foil and cook in the oven for 20 minutes.

4 While the timbales are cooking, make the sauce. Melt the butter in a pan. Add the flour and cook, stirring constantly, for 1 minute. Gradually add the cream, stirring until the sauce boils and thickens. Stir in the basil, with salt and pepper to taste.

5 Turn out the timbales on to warmed individual plates and pour the sauce around them. Garnish with the basil sprigs and serve immediately.

Corsican Beef Stew with Macaroni

In Corsica, pasta is often served with gravy and, in this case, a rich beef stew.

Serves 4

25g/1oz/ ½ cup dried mushrooms (ceps or porcini)
6 garlic cloves
900g/2lb stewing beef, cut into 5cm/2in cubes
115g/4oz lardons, or rindless thick streaky bacon cut into strips
45ml/3 tbsp olive oil
2 onions, sliced
300ml/ ½ pint/1 ¼ cups dry white wine
30ml/2 tbsp passata
pinch of ground cinnamon
fresh rosemary sprig
1 bay leaf
225g/8oz/2 cups large macaroni
50g/2oz/ ⅔ cup freshly grated Parmesan cheese
salt and freshly ground black pepper

1 Soak the mushrooms in warm water for 30 minutes. Drain, set them aside and reserve the liquid. Cut three garlic cloves into thin strips and insert them into the beef by making little slices with a sharp knife. Push the lardons or pieces of bacon into the beef with the garlic. Season the meat to taste.

2 Heat the oil in a heavy-based pan and brown the beef in batches. Transfer to a plate. Add the sliced onions to the pan and cook until lightly browned. Crush the remaining garlic and add to the onions. Return the meat to the pan.

3 Stir in the white wine, passata, mushrooms, cinnamon, rosemary and bay leaf. Season with salt and pepper. Cook gently, stirring frequently, for 30 minutes.

4 Strain the mushroom liquid and add it to the stew with enough water to cover. Bring to the boil, cover and simmer very gently for 3 hours, until the meat is very tender.

5 Bring a large pan of lightly salted water to the boil and cook the macaroni until it is *al dente*. Lift the pieces of meat out of the gravy and transfer to a warmed serving platter. Drain the pasta and layer it in a serving bowl with the gravy and two-thirds of the cheese. Serve with the meat and the remaining cheese.

Pastitsio

Macaroni in a cheese sauce is layered with cinnamon and cumin-spiced minced beef to make a Greek version of lasagne.

Serves 4–6

225g/8oz/2 cups dried short-cut macaroni
30ml/2 tbsp olive oil
1 large onion, finely chopped
2 garlic cloves, crushed
450g/1lb minced steak
300ml/ ½ pint/1 ¼ cups beef stock
10ml/2 tsp tomato purée
5ml/1 tsp ground cinnamon
5ml/1 tsp ground cumin
15ml/1 tbsp chopped fresh mint
50g/2oz/ ¼ cup butter
40g/1 ½ oz/ ⅓ cup plain flour
120ml/4fl oz/ ½ cup milk
120ml/4fl oz/ ½ cup natural yogurt
175g/6oz/1 ½ cups grated Kefalotiri cheese
salt and freshly ground black pepper

1 Bring a saucepan of lightly salted water to the boil and cook the macaroni until it is *al dente*. Drain, rinse under cold water and drain again. Set aside. Preheat the oven to 190°C/375°F/ Gas 5.

2 Heat the oil in a frying pan. Add the onion and garlic, and fry over a moderate heat, stirring frequently, for 5 minutes, until softened. Add the minced steak and stir until browned. Stir in the stock, tomato purée, cinnamon, cumin and mint, and season with salt and pepper to taste. Cook gently for 10–15 minutes, until the sauce is thick and flavoursome.

3 Melt the butter in a saucepan. Stir in the flour and cook, stirring constantly, for 1 minute. Gradually add the milk and yogurt, stirring over a low heat until the sauce thickens. Stir in half the cheese, and season with salt and pepper. Stir the macaroni into the cheese sauce.

4 Spread half the macaroni mixture over the base of a large ovenproof dish. Cover with the meat sauce and top with the remaining macaroni. Sprinkle the remaining cheese over the top and bake for 45 minutes or until golden brown on top.

Simple Baked Lasagne

This is a good basic lasagne for a family supper.

Serves 4

30ml/1 tbsp olive oil
1 onion, finely chopped
2 garlic cloves, chopped
1 celery stick, finely chopped
1 carrot, grated
450g/1lb lean minced beef
15–30ml/1–2 tbsp tomato purée
250–350ml/8–12fl oz/1–1½ cups Vegetable Stock
2 bay leaves
400g/14oz no-precook lasagne sheets
75g/3oz/1 cup freshly grated Parmesan cheese
15g/½ oz/1 tbsp butter

For the béchamel sauce

750ml/1¼ pints/3 cups milk
1 bay leaf
3 blades of mace
115g/4oz/ ½ cup butter
75g/3oz/ ¾ cup plain flour
salt and freshly ground black pepper

1 Heat the oil in a large saucepan and fry the onion, garlic and celery until softened. Add the carrot and minced beef, and cook for 10 minutes, then drain off the excess fat.

2 Stir in the tomato purée and 250ml/8fl oz/1 cup of the stock. Add the bay leaves and cook over a low heat for 1–1½ hours, adding more stock as needed.

3 Make the béchamel sauce. Heat the milk in a pan, with the bay leaf and mace, to just below boiling point. Remove from the heat. Leave to infuse for 15 minutes, then scoop out the herbs. Melt the butter in a small pan and stir in the flour. Cook, stirring constantly, for 1 minute. Gradually add the milk, stirring until the sauce boils and thickens. Season to taste.

4 Preheat the oven to 200°C/400°/Gas 6. Spread a large spoonful of the meat sauce over the base of an ovenproof dish. Top with a layer of lasagne, cover with a thin layer of meat sauce, then a layer of béchamel sauce. Sprinkle with a little Parmesan. Repeat the layers, ending with a layer of pasta and béchamel. Sprinkle the rest of the Parmesan over and dot with the butter. Bake for 45 minutes. Allow to stand for 5–10 minutes before serving.

Three-cheese Lasagne

The cheese makes this lasagne quite expensive, so reserve this mouthwatering dish for a special occasion.

Serves 6–8

30ml/2 tbsp olive oil
1 onion, finely chopped
1 carrot, finely chopped
1 celery stick, finely chopped
1 garlic clove, crushed
675g/1½lb lean minced beef
400g/14oz can chopped tomatoes
300ml/ ½ pint/1¼ cups beef stock
300ml/ ½ pint/1¼ cups red wine
30ml/2 tbsp sun-dried tomato purée
10ml/2 tsp dried oregano
9 no-precook lasagne sheets
3 x 150g/5oz packets mozzarella cheese, thinly sliced
450g/1lb/2 cups ricotta cheese
114g/4oz/1⅓ cups freshly grated Parmesan cheese
salt and freshly ground black pepper

1 Heat the oil in a large saucepan. Add the onion, carrot, celery and garlic, and cook over a low heat, stirring occasionally, for 10 minutes, until softened.

2 Add the minced beef and cook until it changes colour, stirring constantly and breaking it up with a wooden spoon. Drain off the excess fat.

3 Add the tomatoes, stock, wine, tomato purée and oregano, and season with salt and pepper to taste. Bring to the boil, stirring constantly. Cover, lower the heat and simmer gently for 1 hour, stirring occasionally.

4 Preheat the oven to 190°C/375°F/Gas 5. Check for seasoning, then ladle one-third of the meat sauce into a 33 x 23cm/13 x 9in ovenproof dish and cover with 3 sheets of lasagne. Arrange one-third of the mozzarella slices over the top, dot with one-third of the ricotta, then sprinkle with one-third of the grated Parmesan.

5 Repeat these layers twice, then bake for 45 minutes, until golden brown and bubbling. Leave to stand for 10 minutes before serving.

Lasagne al Forno

The classic lasagne is great for a special-occasion meal.

Serves 6

45ml/3 tbsp olive oil
500g/1 ¼ lb lean minced beef
75g/3oz diced pancetta
130g/4½ oz chicken livers, trimmed and chopped
1 onion, finely chopped
2 garlic cloves, crushed
150ml/ ¼ pint/ ⅔ cup dry white wine
30–45ml/2–3 tbsp tomato purée
2 x 400g/14oz cans chopped tomatoes
45ml/3 tbsp single cream
about 8–10 fresh lasagne sheets, green or white, precooked if necessary
75g/3oz/1 cup freshly grated Parmesan cheese
salt and freshly ground black pepper
fresh flat leaf parsley sprigs, to garnish

For the white sauce

600ml/1 pint/2½ cups milk
1 bay leaf
1 small onion, sliced
50g/2oz/ ¼ cup butter
40g/1½oz/ ⅓ cup plain flour
freshly grated nutmeg

1 Heat the oil in a large pan. Add the minced beef and brown, stirring and breaking it up with a wooden spoon. Add the pancetta and chicken livers, and cook for 3–4 minutes. Add the onion and garlic, and cook for 5 minutes more. Stir in the wine and cook until well reduced.

2 Stir in the tomato purée and tomatoes, and season with salt and pepper to taste. Bring to the boil, then lower the heat and simmer for 15–20 minutes, until thickened. Stir in the cream, remove from the heat and set aside.

3 Meanwhile, make the white sauce. Pour the milk into a saucepan, and add the bay leaf and sliced onion. Heat gently until the milk is just below boiling point, then remove the pan from the heat and leave to infuse for 10 minutes. Scoop out the bay leaf and onion.

4 Melt the butter in a saucepan and stir in the flour. Cook for 1 minute, stirring constantly, then gradually whisk in the milk until the mixture boils and thickens to a smooth sauce. Season and add nutmeg to taste.

5 Preheat the oven to 190°C/375°F/Gas 5. Spread some meat sauce on the base of a rectangular ovenproof dish. Top with a layer of lasagne. Trickle over some white sauce and sprinkle with Parmesan. Repeat the layers, finishing with a layer made by swirling the last of the two sauces together. Sprinkle liberally with grated Parmesan.

6 Bake the lasagne for about 30 minutes, until bubbling and golden brown. Allow to stand for 10 minutes before cutting. Serve garnished with flat leaf parsley.

Cook's Tip

There's no need to spread out the white sauce – just add it in generous dollops. When you add the sheets of lasagne, press down evenly and the sauce will spread naturally.

New York-style Lasagne

This sophisticated lasagne is made by layering the meat sauce with ricotta, spinach and pepperoni.

Serves 6

400g/14oz fresh spinach
about 8–10 lasagne sheets, green or white, precooked if necessary
125g/4oz thinly sliced pepperoni sausage
500g/1 ¼ lb/2½ cups ricotta cheese, mashed with a fork
50g/2oz/ ⅔ cup freshly grated Parmesan cheese

For the meat sauce

30ml/2 tbsp olive oil
250g/9oz lean minced beef
250g/9oz lean minced pork
1 onion, chopped
2 garlic cloves, crushed
60ml/4 tbsp dry vermouth
400g/14oz can chopped tomatoes
45ml/3 tbsp tomato purée
150ml/ ¼ pint/ ⅔ cup beef stock or water
2.5ml/ ½ tsp dried oregano
salt and freshly ground black pepper

1 Snap off any thick stalks from the spinach, then blanch the leaves in little boiling water until just wilted. Drain and refresh under cold water. Drain again, squeeze dry and chop the leaves.

2 Make the meat sauce. Heat the oil in a large frying pan, add the minced meats and cook over a high heat, stirring to break up any lumps, for about 5 minutes, until well browned. Add the onion and garlic, and cook for 5 minutes more.

3 Add the vermouth and cook over a high heat until reduced. Stir in the remaining sauce ingredients. Bring to the boil, then lower the heat and simmer for 20–30 minutes, until thickened.

4 Preheat the oven to 190°C/375°F/Gas 5. In a large ovenproof dish, layer the meat sauce with the pasta sheets, chopped spinach and sliced sausage. Dot each layer of spinach and sausage with the ricotta and sprinkle with the Parmesan. Finish with a generous topping of Parmesan.

5 Bake for 35–40 minutes, until bubbling and golden. Leave to stand for 10 minutes before serving.

Cannelloni with Carrot & Courgette

A little meat goes a long way when teamed with vegetables as a stuffing for pasta tubes.

Serves 4

15ml/1 tbsp vegetable oil
175g/6oz lean minced beef
2 garlic cloves, crushed
30ml/2 tbsp plain flour
120ml/4fl oz/ ½ cup beef stock
1 carrot, finely chopped
1 yellow courgette, chopped
8 no-precook cannelloni tubes
115g/4oz fresh spinach
salt and freshly ground black pepper

For the sauce

25g/1oz/2 tbsp butter
25g/1oz/ ¼ cup plain flour
250ml/8fl oz/1 cup milk
50g/2oz/ ⅔ cup freshly grated Parmesan cheese

1 Preheat the oven to 180°C/350°F/Gas 4. Heat the oil in a large pan. Add the minced beef and garlic, and cook over a moderate heat, stirring frequently and breaking up the meat with a wooden spoon, for 5 minutes.

2 Stir in the flour and cook, stirring constantly, for 1 minute. Gradually stir in the stock and bring to the boil.

3 Add the carrot and courgette, season with salt and pepper to taste and cook for 10 minutes. Spoon the mixture into the cannelloni tubes and arrange them in a single layer in an ovenproof dish.

4 Snap off any thick stalks from the spinach, then blanch the leaves in a pan containing a small amount of boiling water. When wilted, drain well and spread out on top of the cannelloni tubes.

5 Make the sauce. Melt the butter in a pan. Stir in the flour and cook, stirring constantly, for 1 minute. Gradually add the milk, stirring constantly until the sauce boils and thickens. Add the grated cheese and stir until it melts. Season well.

6 Pour the sauce over the cannelloni and spinach, and bake for 30 minutes. Leave to stand for 5–10 minutes before serving.

Celebration Cannelloni

Serve this rich and substantial dish for a party – it can be made a day ahead up to the baking stage.

Serves 6

15ml/1 tbsp olive oil
1 small onion, finely chopped
450g/1lb lean minced beef
1 garlic clove, finely chopped
5ml/1 tsp dried mixed herbs
120ml/4fl oz/ ½ cup beef stock
1 egg, lightly beaten
75g/3oz cooked ham, finely chopped
45ml/3 tbsp fine fresh white breadcrumbs
150g/5oz/1⅔ cups freshly grated Parmesan cheese
18 no-precook cannelloni tubes
salt and freshly ground black pepper

For the tomato sauce

30ml/2 tbsp olive oil
1 small onion, finely chopped
½ carrot, finely chopped
1 celery stick, finely chopped
1 garlic clove, crushed
400g/14oz can chopped Italian plum tomatoes
250ml/8fl oz/1 cup water
a few sprigs of fresh basil
2.5ml/ ½ tsp dried oregano

For the white sauce

50g/2oz/ ¼ cup butter
50g/2oz/ ½ cup plain flour
900ml/1½ pints/3¾ cups milk
nutmeg

1 Heat the olive oil in a frying pan and cook the onion over a gentle heat, stirring occasionally, until softened.

2 Add the minced beef and garlic, and stir over the heat for 10 minutes, then add the mixed herbs and season with salt and pepper to taste. Moisten with half the stock. Cover and simmer for 25 minutes, stirring from time to time and adding more stock as needed. Leave to cool.

3 Make the tomato sauce. Heat the olive oil in a pan, and cook the vegetables and garlic for 10 minutes. Add the tomatoes, water and herbs, and season with salt and pepper to taste. Bring to the boil, then simmer for 25–30 minutes, stirring occasionally. Process the tomato sauce in a blender or food processor.

4 Stir the egg, ham, breadcrumbs and 90ml/6 tbsp of the grated Parmesan into the meat mixture.

5 Spread a little of the tomato sauce over the base of an ovenproof dish. Using a teaspoon, fill the cannelloni tubes with the meat mixture and place them in a single layer in the dish on top of the tomato sauce. Pour the remaining tomato sauce over the top.

6 Preheat the oven to 190°C/375°F/Gas 5. Make the white sauce. Melt the butter in a medium pan, stir in the flour and cook, stirring constantly, for 1–2 minutes. Gradually add the milk, stirring constantly, until the sauce boils and thickens. Grate in fresh nutmeg to taste, whisk and season.

7 Pour the white sauce over the stuffed cannelloni, then sprinkle with the remaining Parmesan. Bake for 40–45 minutes, or until the cannelloni tubes feel tender when pierced with a skewer. Leave to stand for 5–10 minutes before serving.

Gingered Chicken Noodles

A blend of ginger, spices and coconut milk flavours this delicious supper dish, which is made in minutes.

Serves 4

350g/12oz skinless, boneless chicken breasts
225g/8oz courgettes
275g/10oz aubergine
about 30ml/2 tbsp vegetable oil
5cm/2in piece of fresh root ginger, finely chopped
6 spring onions, sliced
10ml/2 tsp Thai green curry paste
400ml/14fl oz/1⅔ cups coconut milk
475ml/16fl oz/2 cups chicken stock
115g/4oz dried medium egg noodles
45ml/3 tbsp chopped fresh coriander, plus extra, to garnish
15ml/1 tbsp lemon juice
salt and freshly ground black pepper

1 Cut the chicken into bite-size pieces. Halve the courgettes lengthways and roughly chop them. Cut the aubergine into pieces of a similar size.

2 Heat the oil in a large, shallow pan and stir-fry the chicken pieces until golden. Remove with a slotted spoon and drain on kitchen paper.

3 Add a little more oil to the pan, if necessary, and stir-fry the ginger and spring onions for 3 minutes. Add the courgettes and cook for 2–3 minutes, or until beginning to turn golden. Stir in the curry paste and cook for 1 minute.

4 Add the coconut milk, stock and aubergine, then return the chicken to the pan. Simmer for 10 minutes. Add the noodles and cook for a further 5 minutes, or until the chicken is cooked and the noodles are tender. Stir in the coriander and lemon juice, and adjust the seasoning. Serve garnished with the extra chopped fresh coriander.

Cook's Tip
If liked, stir in a little Thai fish sauce just before serving.

Chinese Chicken with Cashew Nuts

Marinating the chicken gives it a really marvellous flavour and makes it melt-in-the-mouth tender.

Serves 4

4 skinless, boneless chicken breasts, 175g/6oz each, sliced into strips
3 garlic cloves, crushed
60ml/4 tbsp soy sauce
30ml/2 tbsp cornflour
225g/8oz dried egg noodles
45ml/3 tbsp groundnut or sunflower oil
15ml/1 tbsp sesame oil
115g/4oz/1 cup roasted cashew nuts
6 spring onions, cut into 5cm/2in pieces and halved lengthways
salt
spring onion curls and a little chopped fresh red chilli, to garnish

1 Put the chicken strips in a bowl and add the garlic, soy sauce and cornflour. Mix until the chicken is well coated. Cover and chill for about 30 minutes.

2 Meanwhile, bring a pan of lightly salted water to the boil. Add the egg noodles. Turn off the heat and leave to stand for 5 minutes. Drain well and reserve.

3 Preheat a wok. Add both oils. When they are hot, add the chilled chicken, with the marinade. Stir-fry over a high heat for 3–4 minutes, or until golden brown.

4 Add the cashew nuts and spring onions to the wok, and stir-fry for 2–3 minutes.

5 Add the drained noodles and toss over the heat for about 2 minutes more, or until the noodles are hot. Serve, garnished with the spring onion curls and chopped chilli.

Cook's Tip
To make spring onion curls, trim the green part and cut off the bulb. Make a series of lengthways cuts in the stem to within 5mm/¼in of one end. Place in iced water until curled.

Sweet & Sour Chicken Noodles

This all-in-one dish is the busy cook's answer to that perennial question of what to cook for supper when time is short and everyone is hungry.

Serves 4

275g/10oz dried egg noodles
15ml/1 tbsp vegetable oil
3 spring onions, chopped
1 garlic clove, crushed
2.5cm/1in piece of fresh root ginger, grated
5ml/1 tsp hot paprika
5ml/1 tsp ground coriander
3 skinless, boneless chicken breasts, sliced
115g/4oz/1 cup sugar snap peas, topped and tailed
115g/4oz/ ⅔ cup baby sweetcorn cobs, halved
225g/8oz/4 cups fresh beansprouts, rinsed
15ml/1 tbsp cornflour
45ml/3 tbsp soy sauce
45ml/3 tbsp lemon juice
15ml/1 tbsp granulated sugar
45ml/3 tbsp chopped fresh coriander, to garnish

1 Bring a large saucepan of lightly salted water to the boil. Add the noodles. Turn off the heat and leave to stand for 5 minutes. Drain well and reserve.

2 Preheat a wok. Add the oil. When it is hot, stir-fry the spring onions until softened. Stir in the garlic, ginger, paprika, ground coriander and chicken slices. Stir-fry for 3–4 minutes.

3 Add the sugar snap peas, sweetcorn and beansprouts. Toss to mix, then cover and steam for 2–3 minutes, until the sugar snap peas are crisp-tender. Add the noodles and toss over the heat.

4 Stir the cornflour, soy sauce, lemon juice and sugar together in a small bowl. Add to the chicken mixture and simmer briefly to thicken. Serve immediately in heated bowls, garnished with chopped fresh coriander.

Cook's Tip
Light soy sauce has a stronger flavour than the sweeter dark variety, but the latter adds more colour to a dish.

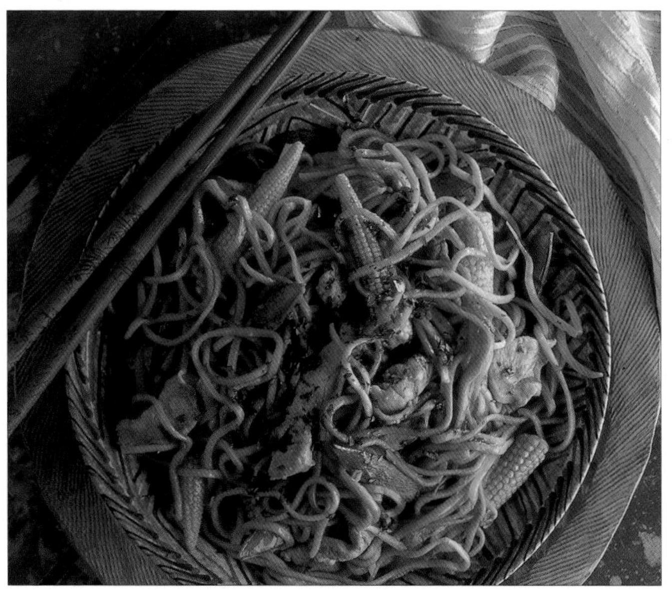

Chicken Chow Mein

Dried egg noodles need very little cooking and are perfect for quick and tasty stir-fried dishes such as this old family favourite.

Serves 4

225g/8oz skinless, boneless chicken breasts
45ml/3 tbsp soy sauce
15ml/1 tbsp rice wine or dry sherry
a few drops of dark sesame oil
350g/12oz dried egg noodles
30ml/2 tbsp vegetable oil
2 garlic cloves, finely chopped
50g/2oz/ ½ cup mangetouts, topped and tailed
115g/4oz/2 cups beansprouts, rinsed
50g/2oz lean ham, finely shredded
4 spring onions, finely chopped
salt and freshly ground black pepper

1 Using a sharp knife, slice the chicken into very fine shreds about 5cm/2in long. Place in a bowl and add 10ml/2 tsp of the soy sauce, with the rice wine or sherry and the sesame oil. Mix well, then set aside.

2 Bring a large pan of lightly salted water to the boil and add the noodles. Turn off the heat and leave to stand for 5 minutes. Drain well and reserve.

3 Preheat a wok and add half the vegetable oil. When it is very hot, add the chicken mixture and stir-fry for 2 minutes, then transfer it to a plate and keep it hot.

4 Wipe the wok clean and heat the remaining oil. Stir in the garlic, mangetouts, beansprouts and shredded ham, and stir-fry for another minute or so. Add the noodles.

5 Toss the noodles over the heat until they are heated through. Add the remaining soy sauce and season with pepper to taste, and salt, if necessary.

6 Return the chicken and any juices to the noodle mixture, add the chopped spring onions and toss the mixture once more. Serve immediately in heated bowls.

Chicken Curry with Rice Vermicelli

Lemon grass gives this South-east Asian curry a wonderful lemony flavour and fragrance.

Serves 4

1 chicken, about 1.5kg/3–3½ lb
225g/8oz sweet potatoes
60ml/4 tbsp vegetable oil
1 onion, finely sliced
3 garlic cloves, crushed
30–45ml/2–3 tbsp Thai curry powder
5ml/1 tsp granulated sugar
10ml/2 tsp fish sauce
600ml/1 pint/2½ cups coconut milk
1 lemon grass stalk, cut in half
350g/12oz rice vermicelli, soaked in hot water until soft
1 lemon, cut into wedges, to serve

For the garnish
115g/4oz/2 cups beansprouts, rinsed
2 spring onions, finely sliced on the diagonal
2 fresh red chillies, seeded and finely sliced
8–10 fresh mint leaves

1 Skin the chicken. Cut the flesh into small pieces and set it aside. Peel the sweet potatoes and cut them into large chunks, about the size of the chicken pieces.

2 Heat half the oil in a large heavy-based pan, and fry the onion and garlic until the onion softens. Add the chicken pieces and stir-fry until they change colour. Stir in the curry powder and sugar. Mix thoroughly, then stir in the fish sauce.

3 Pour in the coconut milk and add the lemon grass. Cook over a low heat for 15 minutes.

4 Meanwhile, heat the remaining oil in a large frying pan. Fry the sweet potatoes until lightly golden. Using a slotted spoon, add them to the chicken. Cook for 10–15 minutes more, or until both the chicken and sweet potatoes are tender.

5 Bring a saucepan of lightly salted water to the boil. Drain the rice vermicelli and add it to the pan. Cook for 3–5 minutes, until tender, then drain well. Place in shallow bowls, with the chicken curry. Garnish with the beansprouts, spring onions, chillies and mint, and serve with the lemon wedges.

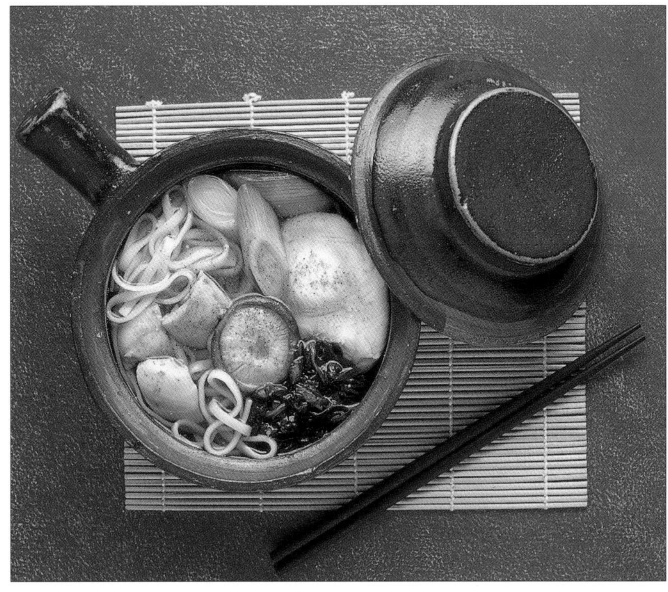

Individual Noodle Casseroles

In Japan, where this recipe originated, these individual casseroles are cooked in earthenware pots.

Serves 4

115g/4oz skinless, boneless chicken thigh, diced
2.5ml/ ½ tsp salt
2.5ml/ ½ tsp sake or dry white wine
2.5ml/ ½ tsp soy sauce
115g/4oz spinach leaves, trimmed
300g/11oz dried udon noodles
1 leek, cut diagonally into 4cm/1½ in slices
4 shiitake mushrooms, stems removed
4 eggs
seven-flavour spice (shichimi), to serve (optional)

For the soup
1.5 litres/2½ pints/6 cups kombu and bonito stock or instant dashi
25ml/5 tsp soy sauce
7.5ml/1½ tsp salt
20ml/4 tsp mirin

1 Put the chicken in a bowl and sprinkle with the salt, sake or wine and soy sauce.

2 Snap off any thick stalks from the spinach. Blanch the leaves in a little boiling water. When wilted, drain, refresh under cold water, drain again and squeeze. Cut into 4cm/1½in lengths.

3 Bring a large pan of lightly salted water to the boil and cook the noodles according to the instructions on the packet, but for 3 minutes less than the suggested cooking time.

4 Meanwhile, in a separate pan, bring the ingredients for the soup to the boil. Add the chicken and leek. Skim the surface, then cook for 5 minutes. Divide the noodles between four individual flameproof casseroles. Pour the soup into the casseroles. Place each casserole over a moderate heat, and divide the shiitake mushrooms among them.

5 Gently break an egg into each casserole. Cover and simmer for 2 minutes. Divide the spinach among the casseroles and simmer for 1 minute more. Serve immediately. Sprinkle seven-flavour spice over the casseroles, if you like.

Bamie Goreng

This fried noodle dish is wonderfully accommodating. You can add extra vegetables, or vary the meat content, depending on what you have to hand, bearing in mind the need to achieve a balance of colours, flavours and textures.

Serves 6–8

450g/1lb dried egg noodles
2 eggs, beaten
90ml/6 tbsp vegetable oil
25g/1oz/2 tbsp butter
2 garlic cloves, crushed
1 skinless, boneless chicken breast, thinly sliced
115g/4oz pork fillet, thinly sliced
115g/4oz calf's liver, trimmed and thinly sliced
115g/4oz cooked peeled prawns
115g/4oz Chinese leaves
2 celery sticks, finely sliced
4 spring onions, shredded
about 60ml/4 tbsp chicken stock
soy sauce
salt and freshly ground black pepper
deep-fried onions and fresh celery leaves, to garnish

1 Bring a large saucepan of lightly salted water to the boil and cook the noodles for 3–4 minutes. Drain, rinse under cold water and drain again. Set aside.

2 Season the eggs with salt and pepper to taste. Heat 5ml/1 tsp of the oil with the butter in a small pan. When the butter has melted, add the eggs and stir over a medium heat until lightly scrambled. Set aside.

3 Preheat a wok and add the remaining vegetable oil. When hot, stir-fry the garlic with the chicken, pork and liver over a medium-high heat for 2–3 minutes, until they have changed colour. Add the prawns, Chinese leaves, celery and spring onions, and toss well.

4 Add the noodles to the wok and toss over the heat until heated through. Moisten with a little stock and flavour with soy sauce to taste. Finally, stir in the scrambled eggs.

5 Garnish the dish with deep-fried onions and fresh celery leaves. Serve immediately.

Special Fried Noodles

This tasty dish from Singapore has much in common with the famous Indonesian Bamie Goreng, but tends to be spicier, thanks to the ginger and chilli sauce.

Serves 4–6

275g/10oz dried egg noodles
1 skinless, boneless chicken breast
115g/4oz lean pork
30ml/2 tbsp vegetable oil
175g/6oz cooked peeled prawns
4 shallots, chopped
2cm/¾ in piece of fresh root ginger, peeled and thinly sliced
2 garlic cloves, crushed
45ml/3 tbsp light soy sauce
5–10ml/1–2 tsp chilli sauce
15ml/1 tbsp rice vinegar
5ml/1 tsp granulated sugar
2.5ml/½ tsp salt
225g/8oz fresh spinach leaves, shredded
3 spring onions, shredded

1 Bring a large pan of lightly salted water to the boil and cook the noodles for 3–4 minutes. Drain, rinse under cold water and drain again. Set aside.

2 Using a very sharp knife, slice the chicken and pork thinly against the grain. Preheat a large wok. Add the vegetable oil. When hot, add the chicken, pork and prawns, and stir-fry for 2–3 minutes. Add the shallots, ginger and garlic, and stir-fry without letting them colour.

3 Add the soy sauce, chilli sauce, vinegar, sugar and salt. Bring to a simmer, add the spinach and spring onions, cover and steam for 3–4 minutes.

4 Add the noodles and toss over the heat until they are hot and all the ingredients are well mixed. Serve at once.

Cook's Tips

- *Put the chicken breast and pork in the freezer for 30 minutes before slicing to firm the meat.*
- *The prawns look more attractive if the heads and shells are removed but the tails are left intact.*

Stir-fried Turkey with Broccoli & Mushrooms

This is a really easy, tasty supper dish.

Serves 4

275g/10oz dried egg noodles
115g/4oz/scant 1 cup broccoli florets
5ml/1 tsp cornflour
45ml/3 tbsp oyster sauce
15ml/1 tbsp dark soy sauce
120ml/4fl oz/ ½ cup chicken stock
10ml/2 tsp lemon juice
45ml/3 tbsp groundnut oil
450g/1lb turkey steaks, cut into thin strips
1 small onion, chopped
2 garlic cloves, crushed
10ml/2 tsp grated fresh root ginger
115g/4oz/1½ cups fresh shiitake mushrooms, sliced
4 baby sweetcorn cobs, halved lengthways
15ml/1 tbsp sesame oil
salt and freshly ground black pepper
4 spring onions

1 Bring a large pan of lightly salted water to the boil and add the noodles. Cover, remove from the heat and leave to stand. Divide the broccoli florets into sprigs and thinly slice the stalks diagonally. Finely chop the white parts of the spring onions and thinly shred the green parts.

2 In a bowl, mix together the cornflour, oyster sauce, soy sauce, stock and lemon juice. Set aside.

3 Preheat a wok. Add 30ml/2 tbsp of the groundnut oil. When hot, stir-fry the turkey for 2 minutes, until golden and crispy at the edges. Remove the turkey from the wok and keep it hot.

4 Add the remaining groundnut oil to the wok and stir-fry the onion, garlic and ginger for 1 minute. Increase the heat, add the broccoli, mushrooms and sweetcorn, and stir-fry for 2 minutes.

5 Return the turkey to the wok, then add the sauce with the seasoning. Cook, stirring for 1 minute, until the sauce has thickened. Stir in the sesame oil. Drain the noodles and serve with the stir-fry. Scatter the spring onion on top.

Duck with Noodles, Pineapple & Ginger

As striking as any still-life, but substantially more satisfying for supper.

Serves 2–3

4 spring onions, chopped
2 boneless duck breasts, skinned
15ml/1 tbsp light soy sauce
175g/6oz dried egg noodles
225g/8oz can pineapple rings
75ml/5 tbsp water
4 pieces of drained Chinese stem ginger in syrup, plus 45ml/3 tbsp syrup from the jar
30ml/2 tbsp cornflour mixed to a paste with a little water
175g/6oz each cooked baby spinach and blanched green beans
¼ each red and green pepper, seeded and cut into thin strips
salt and freshly ground black pepper

1 Select a shallow bowl that fits into your steamer and that will accommodate the duck breasts side by side. Spread out the spring onions in the bowl, arrange the duck breasts on top and drizzle the soy sauce over. Cover with non-stick baking paper. Set the steamer over boiling water and cook the duck breasts for about 1 hour, or until tender. Remove the breasts from the steamer and leave to cool slightly.

2 Cut the breasts into thin slices. Place on a plate, moisten with a little of the cooking juices and keep warm. Strain the remaining juices into a small saucepan and set aside.

3 Bring a large pan of lightly salted water to the boil and cook the noodles until they are just tender.

4 Meanwhile, drain the pineapple, reserving 75ml/5 tbsp of the juice. Add this to the reserved cooking juices, with the measured water. Stir in the ginger syrup, then stir in the cornflour paste and cook, stirring until thickened. Season.

5 Cut the pineapple and ginger into attractive shapes. Drain the noodles and swirl them into nest shapes on individual plates. Add the spinach and beans, then the duck. Top with the pineapple, ginger and peppers. Pour over the sauce and serve.

Cellophane Noodles with Pork

For a quick meal at the end of a long day, this delectably spicy dish has to be high on the list.

Serves 3–4

115g/4oz cellophane noodles
4 dried Chinese black mushrooms
225g/8oz pork fillet, diced
30ml/2 tbsp dark soy sauce
30ml/2 tbsp Chinese rice wine
2 garlic cloves, crushed
15ml/1 tbsp grated fresh root ginger
5ml/1 tsp chilli oil
45ml/3 tbsp groundnut oil
4–6 spring onions, chopped
5ml/1 tsp cornflour blended with 175ml/6fl oz/¾ cup chicken stock
30ml/2 tbsp chopped fresh coriander
salt and freshly ground black pepper
fresh coriander sprigs, to garnish

1 Put the noodles and mushrooms in separate bowls and pour over warm water to cover. Leave to soak for 15–20 minutes until soft, then drain well. Cut the noodles into 12.5cm/5in lengths. Squeeze out any water from the mushrooms, discard the stems and finely chop the caps.

2 Meanwhile, put the pork into a bowl with the soy sauce, rice wine, garlic, ginger and chilli oil. Toss to coat, then set aside for about 15 minutes. Drain, reserving the marinade.

3 Preheat a wok. Add the groundnut oil. When hot, stir-fry the pork and mushrooms for 3 minutes. Add the spring onions and stir-fry for 1 minute. Stir in the cornflour mixture, marinade and seasoning. Cook for about 1 minute.

4 Add the noodles and toss over the heat for about 2 minutes. Stir in the chopped coriander. Taste and adjust the seasoning. Serve, garnished with coriander sprigs.

Cook's Tip
If you haven't got any rice wine, use dry sherry.

Shanghai Noodles with Lap Cheong

The sausages give this simple dish a lovely sweet-savoury flavour.

Serves 4

30ml/2 tbsp vegetable oil
115g/4oz rindless back bacon, cut into bite-size pieces
2 lap cheong sausages, rinsed in warm water, drained and finely sliced
2 garlic cloves, finely chopped
2 spring onions, roughly chopped
225g/8oz Chinese greens or fresh spinach leaves, cut into 5cm/2in pieces
450g/1lb fresh Shanghai noodles
30ml/2 tbsp oyster sauce
30ml/2 tbsp soy sauce
freshly ground black pepper

1 Preheat a wok. Add half the vegetable oil. When it is hot, add the bacon and lap cheong with the garlic and spring onions. Stir-fry over a medium heat for a few minutes, until golden. Using a slotted spoon, remove the mixture from the wok and keep warm.

2 Add the remaining vegetable oil to the wok. When it is hot, add the Chinese greens or spinach leaves and stir-fry over a high heat for about 3 minutes, stirring frequently, until the leaves start to wilt.

3 Add the noodles and return the lap cheong mixture to the wok. Season with oyster sauce, soy sauce and pepper to taste. Toss over the heat until the noodles are heated through. Serve immediately in warmed bowls.

Cook's Tip
Lap cheong are firm, cured waxy sausages, made from pork and cereal, and flavoured with paprika, soy sauce and wine. They are available from Chinese food markets. They can be steamed with rice, chicken or pork, added to an omelette or stir-fried with vegetables. You could also use the slightly sweeter ap yeung cheung, made from preserved duck liver and pork, and flavoured in the same way.

Five-flavour Noodles

The Japanese title for this dish is *Gomoku Yakisoba*, meaning five different ingredients, but you can add as many as you wish.

Serves 4

500g/1¼lb fresh soba noodles
200g/7oz pork fillet, thinly sliced
25ml/1½ tbsp vegetable oil
10ml/2 tsp grated fresh root ginger
1 garlic clove, crushed
200g/7oz green cabbage, roughly chopped
115g/4oz/2 cups beansprouts, rinsed
1 green pepper, seeded and cut into thin strips
1 red pepper, seeded and cut into thin strips
ao-nori seaweed, to garnish (optional)

For the seasoning

60ml/5 tbsp Worcestershire sauce
15ml/1 tbsp soy sauce
15ml/1 tbsp oyster sauce
15ml/1 tbsp granulated sugar
2.5ml/½ tsp salt

1 Bring a large pan of lightly salted water to the boil and cook the noodles until just tender. Drain. Cut the pork into 4cm/1½ in strips and season with salt. Preheat a wok. Add 10ml/2 tsp of the oil. When hot, stir-fry the pork until just cooked, then remove it from the pan.

2 Wipe out the wok and then heat the remaining oil in it. Stir-fry the ginger, garlic and cabbage for 1 minute.

3 Add the beansprouts and stir until softened, then add the green and red peppers, and stir-fry for 1 minute.

4 Return the pork to the wok and add the noodles. Stir in all the seasoning ingredients and toss the mixture over the heat for 2–3 minutes. Serve immediately, sprinkled with the ao-nori seaweed, if using.

Cook's Tip

The seaweed garnish not only looks good, but it adds authenticity to the stir-fry.

Meatballs Laced with Noodles

Wrapping these meatballs in noodles looks tricky, but if you've ever rolled up a ball of wool you'll discover that it is easy enough.

Serves 4

400g/14oz minced pork
2 garlic cloves, finely chopped
30ml/2 tbsp chopped fresh coriander or parsley
15ml/1 tbsp oyster sauce
30ml/2 tbsp fresh white breadcrumbs
1 egg, beaten
175g/6oz fresh thin egg noodles
oil, for deep-frying
salt and freshly ground black pepper
fresh coriander leaves, to garnish
baby spinach leaves and chilli sauce, to serve

1 In a bowl, mix together the pork, garlic, chopped coriander or parsley, oyster sauce, breadcrumbs and egg. Season with salt and pepper, and mix, first with a spoon and then with your hands. Form into balls about the size of a walnut.

2 Bring a large pan of lightly salted water to the boil and cook the noodles for 3 minutes. Drain, rinse under cold running water and drain well.

3 With a meatball in one hand and 3–5 strands of noodles in the other, wrap the noodles securely around the meatball as when winding wool. Wrap the other meatballs in the same way.

4 Heat the oil for deep-frying. Add the meatballs, in batches, and fry until golden brown and cooked through in the centre. As each batch browns, remove with a slotted spoon and drain well on kitchen paper.

5 Serve hot, garnished with fresh coriander leaves, on a bed of baby spinach leaves with chilli sauce.

Cook's Tip

Test the oil by dropping in a cube of day-old bread. It should brown in 30 seconds.

Cantonese Fried Noodles

For this delicious dish, boiled noodles are fried to form a crisp crust, which is topped with beef and stir-fried vegetables.

Serves 2–3

25g/1oz Chinese dried mushrooms
225g/8oz dried egg noodles
60ml/4 tbsp vegetable oil
225g/8oz lean beef steak, sliced into thin strips
1 leek, trimmed and sliced into matchsticks
225g/8oz can bamboo shoots, drained and sliced into matchsticks
150g/5oz Chinese leaves, cut into small diamond shapes
15ml/1 tbsp cornflour
15ml/1 tbsp rice wine or dry sherry
30ml/2 tbsp dark soy sauce
5ml/1 tsp sesame oil
5ml/1 tsp caster sugar

1 Soak the dried mushrooms in a small bowl of warm water for 30 minutes. Meanwhile, bring a pan of lightly salted water to the boil and cook the noodles until tender. Drain, rinse under cold water and drain again. Pat dry with kitchen paper.

2 Drain the mushrooms, reserving 90ml/6 tbsp of the soaking water. Cut off and discard the stems, then slice the caps thinly.

3 Heat half the oil in a large frying pan and sauté the noodles lightly. Press them against the base of the pan until they form a flat, even cake. Cook for 4 minutes, or until crisp underneath, then slide the noodle cake on to a plate. Invert it and return it to the pan. Cook for 3 minutes more, then slide on to the plate again and keep hot.

4 Preheat a wok and add the remaining oil. When hot, stir-fry the beef, mushrooms, leek and bamboo shoots for 2–3 minutes. Add the Chinese leaves and stir-fry for 1–2 minutes.

5 Put the cornflour in a bowl and stir in the reserved soaking water to make a paste. Add to the wok with the remaining ingredients and cook for 15 seconds to thicken. Divide the noodles among 2–3 warmed bowls and pile the stir-fried mixture on top.

Braised Birthday Noodles with Hoi-sin Lamb

It is considered bad luck to cut birthday noodles since this might shorten one's life.

Serves 4

350g/12oz thick dried egg noodles
1kg/2¼ lb neck fillets of lamb
30ml/2 tbsp vegetable oil
15ml/1 tbsp cornflour
30ml/2 tbsp soy sauce
30ml/2 tbsp rice wine
grated rind and juice of ½ orange
15ml/1 tbsp hoi-sin sauce
15ml/1 tbsp wine vinegar
5ml/1 tsp soft light brown sugar
115g/4oz fine green beans
salt and freshly ground black pepper
2 hard-boiled eggs, halved, and 2 spring onions, finely chopped, to garnish

For the marinade

2 garlic cloves, crushed
10ml/2 tsp grated fresh root ginger
30ml/2 tbsp soy sauce
30ml/2 tbsp rice wine
1–2 dried red chillies
30ml/2 tbsp vegetable oil

1 Bring a large pan of lightly salted water to the boil. Add the noodles and cook for 2 minutes only. Drain, rinse under cold water and drain again. Set aside.

2 Cut the lamb into 5cm/2in thick medallions. Mix the ingredients for the marinade in a large shallow dish. Add the lamb and leave to marinate for at least 4 hours or overnight.

3 Heat the oil in a heavy-based pan. Drain the lamb, reserving the marinade, and fry until browned on all sides. Pour over the marinade, and add just enough water to cover. Bring to the boil, skim, then lower the heat and simmer for 40 minutes, or until the meat is tender, adding more water as needed.

4 In a bowl, mix the cornflour and soy sauce, and stir in the rice wine, orange rind and juice, hoi-sin sauce, vinegar and sugar. Stir into the lamb. Add the noodles with the beans. Simmer until cooked. Season. Divide among four large bowls, garnish each with half an egg, sprinkle with spring onions and serve.

Beef & Broccoli Stir-fry

A quick-to-make dish with Eastern appeal.

Serves 4

10ml/2 tsp cornflour
45ml/3 tbsp soy sauce
45ml/3 tbsp ruby port
15ml/1 tbsp sunflower oil
350g/12oz lean beef steak, cut into thin strips
1 garlic clove, crushed
2.5cm/1in piece of fresh root ginger, finely chopped
1 red pepper, seeded and sliced
225g/8oz/1½ cups small broccoli florets
350g/12oz rice vermicelli, soaked in warm water until soft
fresh parsley sprigs, to garnish

1 Mix the cornflour, soy sauce and port in a small bowl.

2 Preheat a wok. Add the oil. When hot, stir-fry the beef, garlic and ginger until the beef is browned. Add the red pepper and broccoli, and stir-fry for 4–5 minutes, until just tender.

3 Stir the cornflour mixture into the wok. Cook, stirring constantly, until the sauce thickens and becomes glossy. Drain the vermicelli, add it to the wok and toss over the heat for 2–3 minutes until heated through. Serve in warmed bowls, garnished with parsley.

Variations

You could use red wine if you do not have port. Try using other vegetables such as mangetouts, sugar snap peas or fresh asparagus instead of the broccoli.

Rice Noodles with Beef & Black Bean Sauce

This is an excellent combination – beef with a chilli sauce tossed with silky smooth rice noodles.

Serves 4

450g/1lb fresh flat rice noodles
60ml/4 tbsp vegetable oil
1 onion, finely sliced
2 garlic cloves, finely chopped
2 slices of fresh root ginger, finely chopped
225g/8oz mixed peppers, seeded and cut into strips
350g/12oz rump steak, finely sliced against the grain
45ml/3 tbsp fermented black beans, rinsed in warm water, drained and chopped
30ml/2 tbsp soy sauce
30ml/2 tbsp oyster sauce
15ml/1 tbsp chilli black bean sauce
15ml/1 tbsp cornflour
120ml/4fl oz/½ cup stock or water
salt and freshly ground black pepper
2 spring onions, finely chopped, and 2 fresh red chillies, seeded and finely sliced, to garnish

1 Rinse the noodles under hot water and drain well. Preheat a wok. Add two tablespoons of the oil. When hot, stir-fry the onion, garlic, ginger and mixed pepper strips for 3–5 minutes. Remove with a slotted spoon and keep hot.

2 Add the remaining oil to the wok. When hot, add the sliced beef and fermented black beans, and stir-fry over a high heat for 5 minutes, or until they are cooked.

3 In a small bowl, mix the soy sauce, oyster sauce and chilli black bean sauce with the cornflour and stock or water until smooth. Add the cornflour paste to the beef mixture in the wok, then stir in the onion mixture. Cook over a medium heat, stirring constantly, for 1 minute.

4 Add the noodles and mix lightly. Toss over a medium heat until the noodles are heated through. Adjust the seasoning if necessary. Serve at once, garnished with the chopped spring onions and chillies.

Spaghetti Olio e Aglio

Proof positive that you don't need numerous ingredients to make a tasty dish.

Serves 4

120ml/4fl oz/ ½ cup olive oil
2 garlic cloves, crushed
450g/1lb dried spaghetti
30ml/2 tbsp fresh parsley, roughly chopped
salt and freshly ground black pepper

1 Heat the olive oil in a medium pan and add the garlic and a pinch of salt. Cook over a low heat, stirring constantly, until golden. Do not allow the garlic to become too brown or it will taste bitter.

2 Meanwhile, bring a large pan of lightly salted water to the boil and cook the spaghetti until *al dente*.

3 Drain the spaghetti well, return it to the clean pan and add the warm – not sizzling – garlic and oil with plenty of black pepper and the parsley. Toss to coat. Serve immediately, in warmed bowls.

Cook's Tips
- *Don't be tempted to serve this with grated Parmesan. Its pure taste would be compromised.*
- *The most commonly exported Italian olive oil comes from Tuscany. It is full-bodied with a slight peppery aftertaste. Ligurian oil has a sweeter and more delicate flavour and is ideal for this dish. Olive oil from the south of Italy has a faint almond-like flavour. It is worth buying the best-quality extra virgin olive oil for this classic Roman dish.*

Spaghettini with Garlic & Chilli Oil

It is essential to use a good-quality virgin olive oil and a brightly coloured red chilli for this simply delicious pasta sauce.

Serves 4

350g/12oz dried spaghettini
75ml/5 tbsp virgin olive oil
3 garlic cloves, finely chopped
1 fresh red chilli, seeded and chopped
75g/3oz/ ¾ cup drained sun-dried tomatoes in oil, chopped
30ml/2 tbsp chopped fresh parsley
salt and freshly ground black pepper
freshly grated Parmesan cheese, to serve

1 Bring a large pan of lightly salted water to the boil. Add the pasta and cook until *al dente*.

2 Towards the end of the cooking time, heat the oil in a large pan. Add the garlic and chilli, and cook gently for 2–3 minutes. Stir in the sun-dried tomatoes and remove from the heat.

3 Drain the pasta and add it to the hot sauce. Return to the heat and cook for 2–3 minutes, tossing the pasta to coat the strands. Season with salt and pepper, and stir in the parsley. Serve in warmed bowls, topped with the grated Parmesan.

Variation
For a smoother sauce and a slight change of flavour, tip the contents of a 200g/7oz jar of sun-dried tomatoes into a food processor, and add 2 smoked garlic cloves and 5–10ml/1–2 tsp dried red chilli flakes. Process to a smooth purée, and season with salt and pepper. Toss with the freshly cooked pasta and serve garnished with 8 sliced stoned black olives.

Garlic & Herb Pasta

Served with plenty of fresh Parmesan cheese, this tasty pasta dish makes a speedy and satisfying supper.

Serves 4

250g/9oz mixed dried egg and spinach tagliatelle
3 garlic cloves, crushed
30ml/2 tbsp drained capers, finely chopped
10ml/2 tsp Dijon mustard
60ml/4 tbsp olive oil
60ml/4 tbsp mixed chopped fresh chives, parsley and oregano
50g/2oz/ ½ cup pine nuts, toasted
15ml/1 tbsp lemon juice
salt and freshly ground black pepper
freshly shaved Parmesan cheese, to serve

1 Bring a large pan of lightly salted water to the boil and cook the pasta until *al dente*.

2 Mix the garlic, capers and mustard in a bowl. Gradually drizzle in the olive oil, whisking constantly until thoroughly combined. Stir in the herbs, pine nuts and lemon juice. Season with salt and plenty of pepper.

3 Drain the pasta and return it to the clean pan. Add the herb dressing and toss until well combined. Serve in warmed bowls, sprinkled with plenty of shaved Parmesan cheese.

Variations

- *You can use the classic combination of* fines herbes *– parsley, chervil, tarragon and chives instead of the mixed herbs suggested here.*
- *For a very herby flavour, if you can get it, serve with grated Sapsago, which is flavoured with melilot.*

Tagliatelle with Fresh Herbs

This is a lovely dish for a light summer lunch when fresh herbs are plentiful.

Serves 4

3 fresh rosemary sprigs
1 small handful of fresh flat leaf parsley
5–6 fresh mint leaves
5–6 fresh sage leaves
8–10 large fresh basil leaves, plus extra to garnish
30ml/2 tbsp extra virgin olive oil
50g/2oz/ ¼ cup butter
1 shallot, finely chopped
2 garlic cloves, finely chopped
pinch of chilli powder
400g/14oz fresh egg tagliatelle
1 bay leaf
120ml/4fl oz/ ½ cup dry white wine
90–120ml/6–8 tbsp Vegetable Stock
salt and freshly ground black pepper

1 Strip the rosemary and parsley leaves from their stalks and chop them with the fresh mint, sage and basil.

2 Heat the olive oil and half the butter in a large, heavy-based saucepan. Add the shallot and garlic, and season with chilli powder to taste. Cook over a very low heat, stirring frequently, for 2–3 minutes.

3 Meanwhile, bring a large pan of lightly salted water to the boil and cook the pasta until *al dente*.

4 Add the chopped herbs and the bay leaf to the shallot mixture and stir for 2–3 minutes. Increase the heat, add the wine and bring to the boil, then boil rapidly for 1–2 minutes until it reduces. Lower the heat, add the vegetable stock and simmer for 1–2 minutes.

5 Drain the pasta and add it to the herb mixture. Toss well to mix, then remove and discard the bay leaf. Season to taste with salt and pepper.

6 Put the remaining butter in a warmed large bowl, tip the dressed pasta into it and toss thoroughly to mix until the butter has melted. Serve immediately, garnished with basil leaves.

Linguine with Rocket

You will often find this traditional Calabrian dish served as a starter in fashionable restaurants. It is very quick and easy to make at home and is worth trying for yourself.

Serves 4

350g/12oz fresh or dried linguine
120ml/4fl oz/½ cup extra virgin olive oil
1 large bunch rocket, about 150g/5oz, stalks removed, leaves shredded or torn
75g/3oz/1 cup freshly grated Parmesan cheese
salt and freshly ground black pepper

1 Bring a large pan of lightly salted water to the boil and cook the pasta until it is *al dente*. Drain.

2 Heat about half the olive oil in the pasta pan, then add the pasta, followed by the rocket. Fry over a medium to high heat, stirring and tossing constantly, for 1–2 minutes, or until the rocket is just wilted, then remove the pan from the heat.

3 Tip the pasta and rocket into a warmed large bowl. Add the freshly grated Parmesan and the remaining olive oil. Add a little salt and black pepper to taste.

4 Toss the mixture quickly to mix and coat the ingredients with the olive oil. Serve immediately.

Cook's Tips

- *Buy rocket by the bunch from the greengrocer or, better still, grow it yourself. Use the leaves when they are young and bright green. In hot weather, rocket leaves quickly turn yellow, and older leaves have a distinctly cabbage-like flavour.*
- *Although cultivated rocket is much less pungent than the wild variety, you may still find its flavour too powerful. If so, blanch the leaves very briefly in boiling water and drain before cooking them in the oil.*

Orecchiette with Tomatoes & Rocket

Serve this hearty dish as a main course with country bread. Some delicatessens and supermarkets sell a farmhouse-style Italian loaf called *pugliese*, which would be perfect.

Serves 4–6

45ml/3 tbsp olive oil
1 small onion, finely chopped
300g/11oz canned chopped Italian plum tomatoes
2.5ml/½ tsp dried oregano
pinch of chilli powder
about 30ml/2 tbsp red wine
2 medium potatoes, diced
300g/11oz/2¾ cups dried orecchiette
2 garlic cloves, finely chopped
150g/5oz rocket, stalks removed, leaves shredded
90g/3½ oz/scant ½ cup ricotta cheese
salt and freshly ground black pepper
freshly grated Pecorino cheese, to serve

1 Heat 15ml/1 tbsp of the olive oil in a pan. Add half the onion and cook, stirring occasionally, for about 5 minutes, until it is softened. Stir in the chopped tomatoes and dried oregano, and season with chilli powder to taste. Pour the red wine over and season with salt and pepper to taste. Cover the pan and simmer for about 15 minutes, stirring occasionally.

2 Bring a large saucepan of lightly salted water to the boil. Add the potatoes and pasta. Stir well and let the water return to the boil. Lower the heat and simmer for about 15 minutes, or until both the potatoes and the pasta are just tender.

3 When the pasta and diced potatoes are almost ready, heat the remaining olive oil in a large, heavy-based pan, add the remaining onion and the garlic, and fry over a medium heat for 2–3 minutes, stirring occasionally.

4 Add the rocket, toss over the heat for about 2 minutes, until wilted, then add the tomato sauce and the ricotta. Mix well.

5 Drain the pasta and potatoes, add both to the pan of sauce and toss to mix. Taste for seasoning and serve immediately in warmed bowls, with grated Pecorino handed separately.

Spaghettini with Roasted Garlic

Roasted garlic tastes sweet and is far milder than you would expect, so a whole head is not so excessive as it might seem.

Serves 4

whole head of garlic
120ml/4fl oz/½ cup extra virgin olive oil, plus extra for brushing
400g/14oz fresh or dried spaghettini
salt and freshly ground black pepper
coarsely shaved Parmesan cheese, to serve

1 Preheat the oven to 180°C/350°F/Gas 4. Place the garlic in an oiled baking tin and roast it for 30 minutes. Set it aside to cool slightly.

2 Bring a pan of lightly salted water to the boil and cook the pasta until it is *al dente*.

3 Slice off the top third of the head of garlic with a sharp knife. Hold the garlic over a bowl and dig out the flesh from each clove with the point of the knife so that it falls into the bowl. Pour in the oil and add plenty of black pepper. Mix well.

4 Drain the pasta and return it to the clean pan. Pour in the oil and garlic mixture, and toss the pasta until all the strands are thoroughly coated. Serve immediately, with shavings of Parmesan handed separately.

Cook's Tip

Although you can now buy roasted garlic in most supermarkets, it is best to roast it yourself for this simple recipe, so that it melts into the olive oil and coats the strands of pasta beautifully. If you can, use the new season's fresh garlic, which is wonderfully plump, tender and sweet. It is usually available from the middle of spring. The purple-skinned variety is considered to have the best flavour.

Rigatoni with Garlic Crumbs

A hot and spicy dish – halve the quantity of chilli if you like a milder flavour.

Serves 4–6

45ml/3 tbsp olive oil
2 shallots, chopped
10ml/2 tsp crushed dried chillies
400g/14oz can chopped tomatoes with garlic and herbs
6 slices of white bread
115g/4oz/ ½ cup butter
2 garlic cloves, chopped
115g/4oz/1½ cups sliced mushrooms
450g/1lb/4 cups dried rigatoni
salt and freshly ground black pepper
fresh herb sprigs, to garnish

1 Heat the oil in a pan. Add the shallots and fry over a low heat, stirring occasionally, for 6–8 minutes, until golden. Add the dried chillies and chopped tomatoes, half-cover and simmer for 20 minutes.

2 Meanwhile, cut the crusts off the bread and discard them. Reduce the bread to crumbs in a food processor. Heat the butter in a frying pan, add the garlic and breadcrumbs, and stir-fry until pale golden and crisp.

3 Stir the mushrooms into the shallot and tomato mixture, season to taste, and leave over a low heat while you cook the pasta.

4 Bring a large pan of lightly salted water to the boil and cook the pasta until it is *al dente*.

5 Drain the pasta, return it to the clean pan and add the sauce. Toss thoroughly. Divide among four warmed bowls, sprinkle with the garlic crumbs, garnish with the herb sprigs and serve immediately.

Variations

Use sliced drained sun-dried tomatoes in oil instead of the mushrooms, if you like, and a whole fresh red chilli, seeded and chopped, instead of the dried chilli.

Cook's Tip

It is better to use day-old bread instead of fresh when making crumbs in a food processor, otherwise the bread may form into clumps.

Chitarra Spaghetti with Butter & Herbs

This is a versatile recipe. You can use just one favourite herb or several – basil, flat leaf parsley, rosemary, thyme, marjoram or sage would also work well. The square-shaped *spaghetti alla chitarra* is traditional with this kind of sauce, but you could use ordinary spaghetti or even linguine.

Serves 4

2 good handfuls of mixed fresh herbs, plus extra herb leaves and flowers, to garnish

400g/14oz fresh or dried spaghetti alla chitarra

115g/4oz/ ½ cup butter

salt and freshly ground black pepper

freshly grated Parmesan cheese, to serve

1 Chop the herbs roughly or finely, whichever you prefer.

2 Bring a large pan of lightly salted water to the boil and cook the pasta until it is *al dente*.

3 When the pasta is almost ready, melt the butter in a large, heavy-based pan. As soon as it sizzles, drain the pasta and add it to the pan, then sprinkle in the herbs, and season with salt and pepper to taste.

4 Toss over a medium heat until the pasta is coated in the butter and herbs. Serve immediately in warmed bowls, sprinkled with extra herb leaves and flowers. Hand around freshly grated Parmesan separately.

Variation

If you like the flavour of garlic with herbs, add 1–2 crushed garlic cloves when melting the butter.

Fusilli with Basil & Parsley

Choose a mixture of plain, spinach and tomato pasta for this recipe.

Serves 4

400g/14oz dried fusilli

For the basil and parsley sauce

2 garlic cloves, crushed

75g/3oz/1 cup pine nuts

50g/2oz/2 cups fresh basil leaves, plus extra to garnish

25g/1oz/ ½ cup fresh flat leaf parsley

150ml/ ¼ pint/ ⅔ cup extra virgin olive oil

salt and freshly ground black pepper

1 Bring a large pan of lightly salted water to the boil and cook the pasta until *al dente*.

2 Meanwhile, make the sauce. Place the garlic, pine nuts, basil and parsley in a blender or food processor. Process briefly to chop and mix. With the motor running, gradually add the olive oil through the lid or feeder tube. Continue to process until the sauce is smooth and creamy.

3 Drain the pasta and return it to the clean pan. Toss well with the sauce, and season to taste with salt and pepper. Serve in warmed bowls, garnished with extra fresh basil leaves.

Cook's Tip

The basil and parsley sauce can be made in advance and will keep for a few days in the fridge.

Variation

You can vary the flavour of the sauce by using fresh coriander instead of the parsley.

Linguine with Pesto

Pesto is traditionally made with a mortar and pestle, but it is much easier to use a food processor.

Serves 5–6

65g/2½ oz/2½ cups fresh basil leaves, plus extra to garnish
3–4 garlic cloves, peeled
45ml/3 tbsp pine nuts
2.5ml/ ½ tsp salt
75ml/5 tbsp olive oil
50g/2oz/ ⅔ cup freshly grated Parmesan cheese
60ml/4 tbsp freshly grated Pecorino cheese
500g/1¼lb fresh or dried linguine
freshly ground black pepper

1 Place the basil, garlic, pine nuts, salt and olive oil in a blender or food processor and process until smooth. Scrape into a bowl and stir in the cheeses. Season with pepper.

2 Bring a large pan of lightly salted water to the boil and cook the pasta until it is *al dente*. Just before draining it, remove about 60ml/4 tbsp of the cooking water and stir it into the basil mixture.

3 Drain the pasta and return it to the clean pan. Add the basil pesto and toss to coat. Serve immediately, garnished with the basil sprigs.

Variations

- *Traditional Ligurian pesto does not contain pine nuts and is made using all Pecorino, rather than a mixture of cheeses. In addition, 75–115g/3–4oz green beans and 75g/3oz/ ¼ cup diced potato are cooked with the pasta.*
- *For a more aromatic pesto, dry-fry the pine nuts in a heavy-based frying pan, stirring frequently, for 1–2 minutes before mixing them with the other ingredients.*
- *For a milder, creamier pesto, stir in 30ml/2 tbsp Greek-style yogurt instead of the pasta water.*
- *For walnut pesto, substitute 25g/1oz/ ¼ cup shelled walnuts for the pine nuts.*

Spaghetti with Rocket Pesto

This is the pesto for real rocket lovers. It is sharp and peppery, and delicious for a summer pasta meal with a glass of chilled white wine.

Serves 4

4 garlic cloves
90ml/6 tbsp pine nuts
2 large handfuls of rocket, about 150g/5oz, stalks removed
50g/2oz/ ⅔ cup freshly grated Parmesan cheese
50g/2oz/ ⅔ cup freshly grated Pecorino cheese
90ml/6 tbsp extra virgin olive oil
400g/14oz fresh or dried spaghetti
salt and freshly ground black pepper
freshly grated Parmesan and Pecorino cheese, to serve

1 Put the garlic and pine nuts in a blender or food processor and process until finely chopped.

2 Add the rocket, Parmesan and Pecorino, and process for 5 seconds. With the motor running, gradually add the olive oil, pouring it through the hole in the lid or the feeder tube. Stop and scrape down the side of the bowl. Season and process for 5–10 seconds more until smooth.

3 Meanwhile, bring a large pan of lightly salted water to the boil and cook the spaghetti until *al dente*.

4 Just before the pasta is ready, scrape the pesto into a large bowl, add 60ml/4 tbsp of the cooking water from the pasta and stir well to mix.

5 Drain the pasta, tip it into the bowl of pesto and toss well. Serve immediately, with the grated cheeses handed separately.

Variation

To temper the flavour of the rocket and make the pesto milder, stir 115g/4oz/ ½ cup ricotta or mascarpone cheese into the pesto before adding the cooking water and tossing the sauce with the pasta.

Spaghetti with Sun-dried Tomato Sauce

There's something totally irresistible about sun-dried tomatoes. All that rich, concentrated, fruity flavour makes them ideal for serving with spaghetti.

Serves 4

350g/12oz dried spaghetti
4 garlic cloves, crushed
10–15 sun-dried tomatoes in oil, drained and roughly chopped
50g/2oz/½ cup stoned black olives
120ml/4fl oz/ ½ cup extra virgin olive oil
3 beefsteak tomatoes, peeled, seeded and chopped
45ml/3 tbsp drained capers
25g/1oz/ ¼ cup chopped fresh basil, plus extra leaves to garnish
salt and freshly ground black pepper

1 Bring a large pan of lightly salted water to the boil and cook the spaghetti until *al dente*.

2 Meanwhile, put the garlic, sun-dried tomatoes and the olives in a food processor or blender. Process until finely chopped. With the motor running, slowly add the olive oil through the hole in the lid, or the feeder tube. Continue processing until thickened and smooth.

3 Scrape the mixture into a mixing bowl. Stir in the chopped fresh tomatoes, capers and chopped basil. Season with salt and pepper to taste.

4 Drain the spaghetti well, return it to the clean pan and add the tomato sauce. Toss well. Serve in warmed bowls, garnished with fresh basil leaves.

Cook's Tip
You can replace some of the olive oil with a little of the oil from the tomatoes for a stronger flavour.

Spirali with Tomato & Cream Cheese Sauce

Treat the family with this inexpensive, easy, but very tasty pasta dish.

Serves 4

30ml/2 tbsp olive oil
1 red onion, thinly sliced
2 garlic cloves, chopped
200g/7oz jar sun-dried tomatoes in oil, drained
30ml/2 tbsp roughly chopped fresh herbs
400g/14oz can chopped tomatoes
350g/12oz dried spirali
60ml/4 tbsp cream cheese
salt and freshly ground black pepper
chopped fresh flat leaf parsley, to garnish

1 Heat the oil in a frying pan and cook the onion, stirring occasionally, for 5 minutes, until slightly softened. Stir in the garlic and sun-dried tomatoes, and cook for 2–3 minutes more. Add the herbs and canned tomatoes, and bring to the boil. Simmer over a low heat until the sauce has thickened.

2 Meanwhile, bring a large pan of lightly salted water to the boil and cook the pasta until it is *al dente*.

3 Add the cream cheese and seasoning to the sauce, and stir over a medium heat until it has been absorbed.

4 Drain the pasta and return it to the clean pan. Add the sauce and toss to coat. Serve in warmed bowls, garnished with chopped flat leaf parsley.

Cook's Tip
Cut the cost of using sun-dried tomatoes in oil. Buy a large bag of dry sun-dried tomatoes from a health-food shop. Soak them overnight in water to cover. Squeeze out the excess moisture, then put them in a jar and cover with virgin olive oil. Add sliced garlic and fresh herbs for extra flavour, and cover with an airtight lid. These will keep for several months in the fridge.

Linguine with Sun-dried Tomato Pesto

Tomato pesto was once a rarity, but is becoming increasingly popular and is absolutely delicious.

Serves 4

25g/1oz/ ⅓ cup pine nuts
25g/1oz/ ⅓ cup freshly grated Parmesan cheese
50g/2oz/ ½ cup drained sun-dried tomatoes in olive oil
1 garlic clove, roughly chopped
60ml/4 tbsp olive oil
350g/12oz fresh or dried linguine
salt and freshly ground black pepper
basil leaves, to garnish
coarsely shaved Parmesan cheese, to serve

1 Put the pine nuts in a small non-stick frying pan and toss them over a low to medium heat for 1–2 minutes, or until they are lightly toasted and golden.

2 Tip the nuts into a food processor. Add the Parmesan, sun-dried tomatoes and garlic, with pepper to taste. Process until finely chopped. With the machine running, gradually add the olive oil through the feeder tube until it has all been incorporated evenly and the mixture is smooth.

3 Bring a large pan of lightly salted water to the boil and cook the pasta until it is *al dente*.

4 Drain the pasta, reserving 60ml/4 tbsp of the cooking water. Tip the pasta into a warmed bowl, add the pesto and the hot water and toss well. Serve in warmed bowls, garnished with basil leaves. Hand round shavings of Parmesan separately.

Cook's Tip

You can make this pesto up to 2 days in advance and keep it in a bowl in the fridge until ready to use. Pour a thin film of olive oil over the pesto in the bowl, then cover the bowl tightly with clear film to prevent the strong smell of the pesto from tainting other foods in the fridge.

Vermicelli with Lemon

Fresh and tangy, this is a good recipe to remember when you're pushed for time, because the sauce can be made in the time it takes to cook the pasta.

Serves 4

350g/12oz dried vermicelli
juice of 2 large lemons
50g/2oz/ ¼ cup butter
200ml/7fl oz/scant 1 cup double cream
115g/4oz/1⅓ cups freshly grated Parmesan cheese, plus extra to serve
salt and freshly ground black pepper

1 Bring a large pan of lightly salted water to the boil and cook the pasta until it is *al dente*.

2 Meanwhile, pour the lemon juice into a heavy-based medium saucepan. Add the butter and cream, then season with salt and pepper to taste.

3 Bring to the boil, then lower the heat and simmer for about 5 minutes, stirring occasionally, until the cream reduces slightly.

4 Drain the pasta and return it to the clean pan. Add the grated Parmesan, then pour over the sauce. Toss quickly over a medium heat until the pasta is evenly coated with the sauce, then divide the mixture among four warmed bowls and serve immediately. Hand extra grated Parmesan separately.

Cook's Tips

- *Lemons vary in the amount of juice they yield. On average, a large fresh lemon will yield 60–90ml/4–6 tbsp. This dish is quite tangy; you can use less juice if you prefer.*
- *A lemon at room temperature will yield more juice than one straight from the fridge.*
- *For an even more lemony taste, you could add a little grated lemon rind to the sauce when you add the butter and cream to the pan in step 2.*

Spaghetti with Fresh Tomato Sauce

This is traditionally made in high summer, when tomatoes are very ripe and sweet. It is deliberately kept simple, so that nothing detracts from the pure tomato flavour.

Serves 4

60ml/4 tbsp olive oil
1 onion, finely chopped
675g/1½ lb ripe Italian plum tomatoes, peeled and chopped
350g/12oz fresh or dried spaghetti
a small handful of fresh basil leaves, shredded
salt and freshly ground black pepper
coarsely shaved Parmesan cheese, to serve

1 Heat the oil in a large pan, add the onion and cook over a low heat, stirring frequently, for about 5 minutes, until softened and lightly coloured. Add the tomatoes, with salt and pepper to taste. Cover and simmer, stirring occasionally, for 30–40 minutes, until thick.

2 Meanwhile, bring a saucepan of lightly salted water to the boil and cook the pasta until it is *al dente*.

3 Drain the pasta, tip it into a warmed bowl, pour the sauce over, add the basil and toss well. Serve in warmed bowls with shaved Parmesan handed separately.

Cook's Tips

- *The Italian plum tomatoes called San Marzano are the best variety to use. When fully ripe, they have thin skins that can be peeled off easily.*
- *To peel tomatoes, cut a cross in the blossom of each one, then plunge them into boiling water for about 30 seconds. Lift them out with a slotted spoon. The skin will have begun to peel back from the crosses and will be easy to remove.*
- *An alternative method is to spear each tomato in turn with a long-handled fork and hold it in a flame, turning it until the skin chars slightly and splits.*

Bucatini with Raw Tomato Sauce

This is a wonderfully simple uncooked tomato sauce that goes well with both long pasta strands and small, chunky shapes.

Serves 4

500g/1¼ lb ripe Italian plum tomatoes
1 large handful fresh basil leaves
75ml/5 tbsp extra virgin olive oil
1 garlic clove, crushed
350g/2oz fresh or dried bucatini
115g/4oz ricotta salata cheese, diced
salt and freshly ground black pepper
coarsely shaved Pecorino cheese, to serve

1 Roughly chop the plum tomatoes, removing the cores and as many of the seeds as you can. Tear the basil leaves into shreds with your fingers.

2 Put the tomatoes, basil, olive oil and garlic in a bowl, and season with salt and pepper to taste. Stir well to mix, cover and then leave at room temperature for 1–2 hours to let the flavours mingle.

3 Bring a large pan of lightly salted water to the boil and cook the pasta until it is *al dente*.

4 Drain the pasta and return it to the clean pan. Add the raw tomato sauce and the ricotta salata, and toss to coat. Serve immediately, with shavings of Pecorino cheese.

Cook's Tips

- *Ricotta salata is a salted and dried version of ricotta cheese made from the whey of Pecorino. It is firmer than the traditional soft white ricotta, with a compact, flaky texture. It can be easily diced, crumbled and even grated. It is available from some delicatessens. If you can't locate it, you can use feta cheese instead.*
- *If fresh plum tomatoes are not available, use vine-ripened tomatoes instead.*

Pasta with Sugocasa & Chilli

Sugocasa consists of crushed Italian tomatoes and comes in bottles or jars. It is coarser than passata, but finer than canned chopped tomatoes and is ideal for quick dishes such as this one.

Serves 4

500g/1lb sugocasa
2 garlic cloves, crushed
150ml/ ¼ pint/ ⅔ cup dry white wine
15ml/1 tbsp sun-dried tomato purée
1 fresh red chilli
350g/12oz dried penne or tortiglioni
60ml/4 tbsp finely chopped fresh flat leaf parsley
salt and freshly ground black pepper
freshly grated Pecorino cheese, to serve

1 Put the sugocasa, garlic, wine, sun-dried tomato purée and whole chilli in a saucepan and bring to the boil. Cover, lower the heat and simmer gently.

2 Bring a large pan of lightly salted water to the boil, add the pasta and cook until *al dente*.

3 Remove the chilli from the sauce. If you want a mere suggestion of heat, discard it. Otherwise, seed and chop some or all of the flesh and return it to the sauce. Stir in half the parsley. Taste for seasoning.

4 Drain the pasta and tip it into a warmed large bowl. Pour the sauce over the pasta and toss to mix. Serve at once, sprinkled with the grated Pecorino and the remaining parsley.

Cook's Tip
Look for sugocasa in delicatessens or supermarkets. It is sometimes labelled "crushed Italian tomatoes". If you can't locate it, use a mixture of canned chopped tomatoes and passata instead.

Penne with Tomatoes & Mozzarella

This is a deliciously light pasta dish, full of fresh flavours. Use buffalo-milk mozzarella, if you can – its flavour is noticeably better.

Serves 4

275g/10oz/2½ cups dried penne
450g/1lb ripe plum tomatoes
275g/10oz mozzarella cheese, drained
60ml/4 tbsp olive oil
15ml/1 tbsp balsamic vinegar
grated rind of 1 lemon
15ml/1 tbsp lemon juice
15 fresh basil leaves, shredded, plus extra, to garnish
salt and freshly ground black pepper

1 Bring a large pan of lightly salted water to the boil and cook the pasta until *al dente*.

2 Meanwhile, cut the tomatoes into quarters and squeeze out the seeds, then chop the flesh into cubes. Cut the mozzarella into pieces of a similar size.

3 Put the olive oil in a bowl and stir in the balsamic vinegar, lemon rind, lemon juice and basil. Stir well, then season with salt and pepper to taste. Add the tomatoes and mozzarella, and leave to stand until the pasta is cooked.

4 Drain the pasta and return it to the clean pan. Add the tomato mixture and toss well. Garnish with the extra basil leaves and serve immediately, if serving hot, or allow to cool to room temperature.

Variation
Add 50g/2oz/ ½ cup black olives and 25g/1oz/ ½ cup chopped, drained sun-dried tomatoes in oil with the fresh tomatoes in step 3. Proceed as the recipe above and serve garnished with 30ml/2 tbsp toasted pine nuts.

Conchiglie with Tomatoes & Rocket

This pretty pasta dish owes its success to the contrast in flavour between sweet cherry tomatoes and peppery rocket.

Serves 4

450g/1lb/4 cups dried conchiglie or farfalle
45ml/3 tbsp olive oil
450g/1lb ripe cherry tomatoes, halved
75g/3oz fresh rocket
salt and freshly ground black pepper
freshly shaved Parmesan cheese, to serve

1 Bring a large pan of lightly salted water to the boil and cook the pasta until it is *al dente*.

2 Heat the oil in a pan, add the tomatoes and cook for barely 1 minute. The tomatoes should only just heat through and not disintegrate.

3 Trim the rocket, removing any tough stems. Wash the leaves, drain well, then pat them dry with kitchen paper.

4 Drain the pasta, return it to the clean pan and add the tomatoes, then the rocket. Carefully stir over the heat to mix and heat through. Season well with salt and pepper. Serve immediately with plenty of shaved Parmesan cheese.

Variations

- *Cut 4 unpeeled red potatoes into eight pieces and cook with the pasta, omitting the tomatoes.*
- *Instead of rocket, use 115g/4oz radicchio di Treviso or 75g/3oz lamb's lettuce (also known as corn salad) or 115g/4 oz spinach.*

Double Tomato Tagliatelle

Sun-dried tomatoes add pungency to this dish, while the grilled fresh tomatoes give it bite.

Serves 4

45ml/3 tbsp olive oil
1 garlic clove, crushed
1 small onion, chopped
60ml/4 tbsp dry white wine
6 drained sun-dried tomatoes in oil, chopped
30ml/2 tbsp chopped fresh parsley
50g/2oz/ ½ cup stoned black olives, halved
4 tomatoes, halved
450g/1lb fresh tagliatelle
salt and freshly ground black pepper
freshly shaved Parmesan cheese, to serve

1 Heat 30ml/2 tbsp of the olive oil in a large, heavy-based saucepan. Add the garlic and onion, and cook over a medium heat, stirring occasionally, for 2–3 minutes, until softened.

2 Stir in the wine, sun-dried tomatoes and parsley. Cook for 2 minutes. Stir in the black olives.

3 Preheat the grill. Put the tomatoes on a tray and brush them with the remaining oil. Grill under a medium heat until cooked through and beginning to brown on top.

4 Meanwhile, bring a large pan of lightly salted water to the boil and cook the tagliatelle until *al dente*.

5 Drain the pasta, return it to the clean pan and toss with the sauce. Serve with the grilled tomatoes, freshly ground black pepper and shavings of Parmesan.

Cook's Tip

Olives marinated in olive oil flavoured with garlic and herbs would go especially well in this dish, but olives in brine are also satisfactory. Spanish and Greek black olives tend to be plumper and juicier than Italian.

Rigatoni with Winter Tomato Sauce

In winter, when fresh tomatoes are not at their best, this is the sauce the Italians serve with their favourite pasta.

Serves 6–8

60ml/4 tbsp olive oil
1 garlic clove, thinly sliced
1 onion, finely chopped
1 carrot, finely chopped
1 celery stick, finely chopped
a few leaves each fresh basil, thyme and oregano or marjoram, plus extra, to garnish
2 x 400g/14oz cans chopped Italian plum tomatoes
15ml/1 tbsp sun-dried tomato purée
5ml/1 tsp granulated sugar
about 90ml/6 tbsp dry red or white wine (optional)
350g/12oz/3 cups dried rigatoni
salt and freshly ground black pepper
coarsely shaved Parmesan cheese, to serve

1 Heat the olive oil in a large, heavy-based saucepan. Add the garlic slices and cook, stirring constantly, over a very low heat for 1–2 minutes.

2 Add the onion, carrot, celery and the fresh herbs. Cook over a low heat, stirring frequently, for 5–7 minutes, until the vegetables have softened and are lightly coloured.

3 Add the canned tomatoes, tomato purée and sugar, and then stir in the wine, if using. Season with salt and pepper to taste. Bring to the boil, stirring constantly, then lower the heat so that the mixture is simmering gently. Cook, uncovered, for about 45 minutes, stirring occasionally, until the vegetables are tender and the sauce has thickened.

4 Bring a large pan of lightly salted water to the boil. Add the pasta and cook until it is *al dente*. Drain it and tip it into a warmed serving bowl.

5 Pour the sauce over the pasta and toss thoroughly. Serve immediately, with shavings of Parmesan handed separately. Garnish with the extra chopped herbs.

Fusilli with Tomato & Balsamic Vinegar

The intense, sweet-sour flavour of balsamic vinegar gives a pleasantly gentle kick to a sauce made with canned tomatoes.

Serves 6–8

2 x 400g/14oz cans chopped Italian plum tomatoes
2 drained sun-dried tomatoes in olive oil, thinly sliced
2 garlic cloves, crushed
45ml/3 tbsp olive oil
5ml/1 tsp granulated sugar
350g/12oz/3 cups fresh or dried fusilli
45ml/3 tbsp balsamic vinegar
salt and freshly ground black pepper
rocket salad, Italian country bread and coarsely shaved Pecorino cheese, to serve

1 Put the canned tomatoes and sun-dried tomatoes in a medium saucepan with the garlic, olive oil and sugar. Season with salt and pepper to taste. Bring to the boil over a medium heat, stirring constantly. Lower the heat and simmer gently for about 30 minutes, until reduced.

2 Meanwhile, bring a large pan of lightly salted water to the boil. Add the pasta and cook until it is *al dente*.

3 Stir the balsamic vinegar into the tomato sauce. Cook for 1–2 minutes more.

4 Drain the pasta and return it to the clean pan. Pour the sauce over and toss well. Serve in warmed bowls, with rocket salad and bread. Offer the shaved Pecorino separately.

Cook's Tip

Balsamic vinegar from Modena is expensive, but its price is an indication of its quality. Cheaper imitations have either not been matured for the requisite minimum of 12 years or are made from red wine vinegar that is coloured and flavoured with caramel. Real balsamic vinegar has a mellow and concentrated flavour.

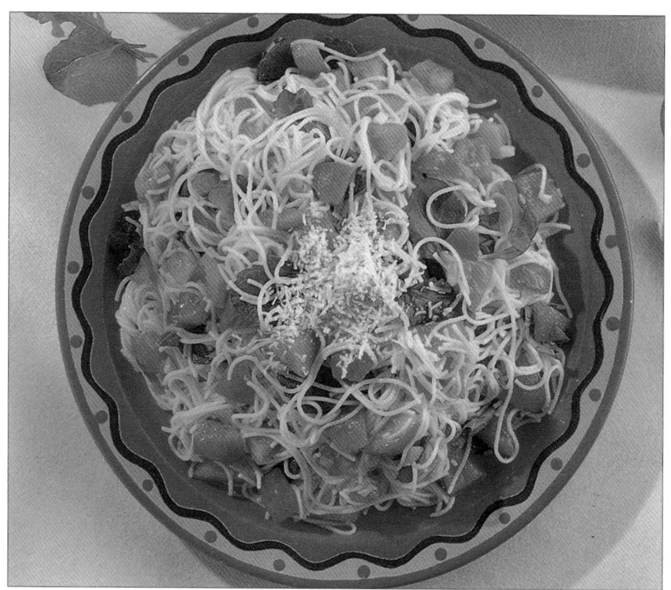

Heavenly Pasta

Delicate angel hair pasta served with a rocket, tomato and lime sauce is a rare treat.

Serves 4

450g/1lb very ripe tomatoes, peeled and chopped
1 small bunch of tender, young rocket leaves
4 garlic cloves, crushed
grated rind of ½ lime
juice of 2 limes
1.5ml/ ¼ tsp Tabasco sauce
350g/12oz capellini (angel hair pasta)
60ml/4 tbsp olive oil
salt and freshly ground black pepper
freshly grated Parmesan cheese, to serve

1 Combine the tomatoes, rocket, garlic, lime rind and juice in a bowl. Stir in the Tabasco sauce and olive oil, then cover and set aside for 20–30 minutes.

2 Bring a large pan of lightly salted water to the boil and cook the pasta until it is *al dente.*

3 Drain the pasta and return it to the clean pan. Add the tomato mixture and toss well. Season with salt and pepper to taste. Add Parmesan cheese to taste, toss again, and serve in warmed bowls, with extra Parmesan on top, if you like.

Cook's Tip

Tabasco sauce is made from chillies, and has a distinctive aroma and hot flavour. The original sauce was made from red chillies, but a green Tabasco, made from jalapeño chillies, is now available. It is slightly milder. There are also many other pepper sauces available.

Variation

You could substitute young sorrel leaves or baby spinach for the rocket, and lemon juice and rind for the lime.

Sun-dried Tomato & Parmesan Carbonara

Classic carbonara contains prosciutto or bacon. This vegetarian version substitutes sun-dried tomatoes, with excellent results. Serve it with a crisp green salad and plenty of fresh, crusty bread.

Serves 4

175g/6oz dried tagliatelle
2 eggs, beaten
150ml/¼ pint/ ⅔ cup double cream
15ml/1 tbsp wholegrain mustard
50g/2oz/ ½ cup sun-dried tomatoes in olive oil, drained and thinly sliced
50g/2oz/ ⅔ cup freshly grated Parmesan cheese
12 fresh basil leaves, shredded, plus whole sprigs, to garnish
salt and freshly ground black pepper

1 Bring a pan of lightly salted water to the boil and cook the pasta until it is *al dente.*

2 Whisk together the eggs, cream and mustard in a bowl. Add plenty of seasoning and whisk again.

3 Drain the pasta and return it to the pan. Add the cream mixture, sun-dried tomatoes, Parmesan and basil. Toss over a very low heat for 1 minute, until the mixture thickens slightly.

4 Adjust the seasoning and serve immediately, garnished with the basil sprigs.

Cook's Tip

You can include additional ingredients, such as lightly fried onion and garlic, fresh or dried mushrooms or black olives, stirring them in with the sun-dried tomatoes in step 3. Whatever extras you include, it is important that the mixture is heated through very quickly so the eggs have no time to scramble.

Paglia e Fieno with Radicchio

This is a light, modern pasta dish of the kind served in fashionable restaurants.

Serves 4

45ml/3 tbsp pine nuts
350g/12oz dried paglia e fieno
45ml/3 tbsp extra virgin olive oil
30ml/2 tbsp sun-dried tomato purée
2 sun-dried tomatoes in olive oil, drained and cut into very thin slivers
40g/1½oz radicchio leaves, finely shredded
4–6 spring onions, thinly sliced into rings
salt and freshly ground black pepper

1 Put the pine nuts in a non-stick frying pan and toss them over a low to medium heat for 1–2 minutes, or until they are lightly toasted and golden. Remove and set aside.

2 Bring two pans of lightly salted water to the boil. Add the spinach flavoured pasta to one pan and the plain egg pasta to the other. Cook until both batches are *al dente*.

3 While the pasta is cooking, heat 15ml/1 tbsp of the olive oil in a pan. Add the sun-dried tomato purée and the sun-dried tomatoes, then stir in 2 ladlefuls of the water used for cooking the pasta. Simmer over a low heat until the sauce has reduced slightly, stirring constantly.

4 Stir in the shredded radicchio, then taste and season if necessary. Keep on a low heat. Drain the paglia e fieno, keeping the colours separate, and return the noodles to the pans in which they were cooked. Add about 15ml/1 tbsp oil to each pan and toss over a medium to high heat until the pasta is glistening with the oil.

5 Arrange a portion of green and white pasta in each of four warmed bowls, then spoon the sun-dried tomato and radicchio mixture in the centre. Sprinkle the spring onions and toasted pine nuts decoratively over the top and serve immediately. Before eating, each diner should toss the sauce ingredients with the pasta to mix well.

Cappelletti with Tomatoes, White Wine & Cream

In this very quick and easy recipe, the sauce coats little filled pasta hats to make a really substantial, creamy supper dish for vegetarians.

Serves 4–6

400ml/14fl oz/1⅔ cups passata
90ml/6 tbsp dry white wine
150ml/¼ pint/⅔ cup double cream
225g/8oz/2½ cups fresh cappelletti
1 small handful of fresh basil leaves
60ml/4 tbsp freshly grated Parmesan cheese
salt and freshly ground black pepper

1 Pour the passata into a pan and stir in the wine. Bring to the boil over a medium heat, then stir in the cream until evenly mixed and bubbling. Lower the heat and simmer.

2 Bring a large pan of lightly salted water to the boil and cook the pasta until *al dente*. Meanwhile, finely shred most of the basil leaves and set aside with the whole leaves.

3 Drain the pasta, return it to the pan and toss it with the grated Parmesan. Pour the sauce over and toss well. Serve sprinkled with the shredded basil and whole basil leaves.

Cook's Tips

- *Cappelletti with a variety of fillings are available from supermarkets and Italian delicatessens.*
- *Other stuffed pasta shapes, such as tortellini, ravioli, or the more unusual sacchettini (little purses) or caramellone (toffees), can be used with this sauce.*
- *The tomato sauce can be made up to a day ahead, then chilled until ready to use. Reheat it gently in a heavy-based saucepan while the pasta is cooking.*

Tagliatelle with Tomatoes & Courgettes

Courgettes add texture and fresh colour to the tagliatelle in this simple dish.

Serves 3–4

225g/8oz wholewheat tagliatelle
30ml/2 tbsp olive oil
1 onion, chopped
2 celery sticks, chopped
1 garlic clove, crushed
2 courgettes, sliced
5–6 ripe tomatoes, peeled and chopped
30ml/2 tbsp sun-dried tomato purée
50g/2oz/ ½ cup flaked almonds, toasted
salt and freshly ground black pepper

1 Bring a large pan of lightly salted water to the boil, add the pasta and cook until *al dente.*

2 Meanwhile, heat the olive oil in another pan. Add the onion, celery and garlic, and cook, stirring frequently, over a gentle heat for 3–4 minutes, or until the onions have softened and are lightly browned.

3 Stir in the courgettes, tomatoes and sun-dried tomato purée. Cook over a low heat, stirring occasionally, for 5 minutes, until the courgettes are crisp-tender, then season with salt and pepper to taste.

4 Drain the pasta, return it to the clean pan and add the sauce. Toss well. Place in a warmed serving dish and scatter the toasted almonds over the top to serve.

Variation
Use banana (yellow) courgettes for a change, or a mixture of both colours.

Pasta with Spring Vegetables

Celebrate the arrival of tender, new-season vegetables with this colourful, creamy pasta dish.

Serves 4

115g/4oz/scant 1 cup broccoli florets
115g/4oz baby leeks, trimmed
225g/8oz asparagus spears, trimmed
1 small fennel bulb
115g/4oz/1 cup fresh or frozen peas
350g/12oz dried penne
40g/1 ½ oz/3 tbsp butter
1 shallot, chopped
45ml/3 tbsp chopped fresh mixed herbs, such as parsley, thyme and sage
300ml/ ½ pint/1 ¼ cups double cream
salt and freshly ground black pepper
freshly grated Parmesan cheese, to serve

1 Divide the broccoli florets into tiny sprigs. Cut the leeks and asparagus diagonally into 5cm/2in lengths. Trim the fennel bulb and remove any tough outer leaves. Cut it into wedges, leaving the layers attached at the root end so the pieces stay intact.

2 Cook each vegetable separately, one after the other, in a large pan of lightly salted boiling water until just tender. Remove each batch of vegetables with a slotted spoon and place them in a bowl. Keep hot. (Using the same water each time for cooking the vegetables creates a simple vegetable stock which is perfect for cooking the pasta.)

3 Bring the water used for cooking the vegetables back to the boil. Add the pasta and cook until *al dente.*

4 Meanwhile, melt the butter in another pan. Add the shallot and fry over a medium heat, stirring occasionally, until softened, but not browned. Stir in the vegetables, with the herbs and cream. Season to taste with salt and pepper, and cook for a few minutes, until thickened.

5 Drain the pasta and return it to the clean pan. Add the sauce and toss lightly. Serve in warmed bowls, topped with Parmesan.

Tagliolini with Asparagus

Tagliolini are very thin home-made egg noodles. They go well with this subtle cream sauce flavoured with asparagus.

Serves 4
450g/1lb fresh asparagus, trimmed
50g/2oz/ 1/4 cup butter
3 spring onions, finely chopped
3–4 fresh mint leaves, finely chopped
150ml/ 1/4 pint/ 2/3 cup double cream
350g/12oz fresh tagliolini or other egg noodles
50g/2oz/ 2/3 cup freshly grated Parmesan cheese
salt and freshly ground black pepper
fresh basil, to garnish

1 Bring a large pan of lightly salted water to the boil. Add the asparagus spears and boil for 4–6 minutes, until just tender.

2 Using a slotted spoon, lift out the asparagus spears. Cut the tips off, and then cut the stalks into 4cm/1 1/2 in pieces. Set the asparagus aside and reserve the pan of cooking water.

3 Melt the butter in a large, heavy-based frying pan. Add the spring onions and mint, and cook over a low heat, stirring occasionally, for 3–4 minutes.

4 Stir in the cream and asparagus, season with salt and pepper to taste, and heat gently, but do not boil.

5 Meanwhile, bring the asparagus cooking water back to the boil and cook the pasta until it is *al dente*.

6 Drain the pasta well, then add it to the sauce in the frying pan. Raise the heat slightly, and mix well. Stir in the Parmesan and serve at once, garnished with basil leaves.

Cook's Tip
If you prefer, stir only half the pasta into the sauce and offer the rest at the table.

Garganelli with Asparagus, Wine & Cream

A lovely recipe for late spring when bunches of fresh young asparagus are on sale in shops and markets everywhere.

Serves 4
350g/12oz fresh young asparagus, trimmed
350g/12oz/3 cups dried garganelli
25g/1oz/2 tbsp butter
200ml/7fl oz/scant 1 cup double cream
30ml/2 tbsp dry white wine
115g/4oz/1 1/3 cups freshly grated Parmesan cheese
30ml/2 tbsp chopped fresh mixed herbs, such as basil, flat leaf parsley, chervil, marjoram and oregano
salt and freshly ground black pepper

1 Cut the asparagus spears diagonally into pieces that are roughly the same length and shape as the garganelli. Keep the tips separate.

2 Bring a large pan of lightly salted water to the boil. Add all but the tips of the asparagus and cook for 2 minutes, then add the tips and cook for 1 minute more. Working quickly, transfer the asparagus to a colander, using a slotted spoon, and rinse under cold water. Set aside to drain.

3 Bring the asparagus cooking water back to the boil and cook the pasta until it is *al dente*.

4 Meanwhile, put the butter and cream in a medium saucepan, season with salt and pepper to taste, and bring to the boil over a low heat. Simmer for a few minutes until the cream has reduced and thickened slightly, then add the asparagus, wine and about half the grated Parmesan. Taste for seasoning and keep on a low heat.

5 Drain the pasta and tip it into a warmed bowl. Pour the sauce over, sprinkle with the fresh herbs and toss well. Serve immediately, topped with the remaining grated Parmesan.

Penne with Artichokes

This sauce is garlicky and richly flavoured, and makes a superb dinner-party starter.

Serves 6

juice of 1 lemon
2 globe artichokes
30ml/2 tbsp olive oil
1 small fennel bulb, thinly sliced, with feathery tops reserved
1 onion, finely chopped
4 garlic cloves, finely chopped
1 handful fresh flat leaf parsley, roughly chopped
400g/14oz can chopped Italian plum tomatoes
150ml/ ¼ pint/ ⅔ cup dry white wine
350g/12oz/3 cups dried penne
10ml/2 tsp capers, chopped
salt and freshly ground black pepper
freshly grated Parmesan cheese, to serve

1 Stir half the lemon juice into a bowl of cold water. Cut off the artichoke stalks, then discard the outer leaves. Cut off the tops of the inner leaves so that the base remains. Cut the base in half lengthways, then prise the choke out of the centre with the tip of a knife and discard. Cut the artichokes lengthways into 5mm/ ¼ in slices, adding them to the bowl of acidulated water.

2 Bring a large pan of water to the boil. Add a pinch of salt, then drain the artichokes and add them immediately to the water. Boil for 5 minutes, drain and set aside.

3 Heat the oil in a large pan and cook the fennel, onion, garlic and parsley over a low heat, for 10 minutes.

4 Add the tomatoes and wine, with salt and pepper. Bring to the boil, stirring, then simmer for 15 minutes. Stir in the artichokes, replace the lid and simmer for 10 minutes more.

5 Meanwhile, bring a pan of lightly salted water to the boil and cook the pasta until it is *al dente*. Stir the capers into the tomato sauce, then add the remaining lemon juice.

6 Tip the pasta into a warmed large bowl, pour the sauce over and toss. Serve immediately, garnished with the reserved fennel fronds. Hand around a bowl of grated Parmesan separately.

Pasta with Coriander & Grilled Aubergines

Pasta with a piquant sauce of coriander and lime is superb with succulent grilled aubergines.

Serves 2

15g/½ oz/ ½ cup coriander leaves
30ml/2 tbsp pine nuts
30ml/2 tbsp freshly grated Parmesan cheese
3 garlic cloves
juice of ½ lime
105ml/7 tbsp olive oil
225g/8oz/2 cups dried cellentani or other pasta shapes
1 large aubergine
salt and freshly ground black pepper

1 Process the coriander leaves, pine nuts, Parmesan, garlic, lime juice and 60ml/4 tbsp of the olive oil in a food processor or blender for 30 seconds, until almost smooth.

2 Bring a pan of lightly salted water to the boil, and cook the pasta until it is *al dente*.

3 Meanwhile, cut the aubergine in half lengthways, then cut each half into 5mm/ ¼in slices. Layer the aubergine strips in a colander with salt and leave to stand for 30 minutes over a plate to catch any juices. Rinse off the excess salt under cold water, and drain.

4 Spread the slices out on a baking sheet, brush with half the remaining oil, and season well with salt and black pepper.

5 Grill the aubergine slices for about 4 minutes. Turn them over and brush them with the remaining oil. Season as before. Grill for 4 minutes more.

6 Drain the pasta, tip it into a warmed bowl and toss with the coriander sauce. Serve with the grilled aubergine slices.

Pasta with Aubergine & Tomato Sauce

This pasta recipe was popular long before roasted vegetables become fashionable. It is delicious.

Serves 4

2 medium aubergines, about 225g/8oz each, diced small
45ml/3 tbsp olive oil
275g/10oz/2½ cups dried macaroni or fusilli
50g/2oz/⅔ cup grated Pecorino cheese
salt and freshly ground black pepper
shredded fresh basil leaves, to garnish

For the tomato sauce

30ml/2 tbsp olive oil
1 onion, finely chopped
400g/14oz can chopped tomatoes
10ml/2 tsp balsamic vinegar

1 Preheat the oven to 220°C/425°F/Gas 7. Make the sauce. Heat the oil in a large pan and fry the onion gently until softened. Add the tomatoes and season. Bring to the boil, lower the heat, cover and simmer for 20 minutes. Stir the sauce and add a little water if it gets too thick. Remove from the heat.

2 Spread out the diced aubergine in a roasting tin, add the oil and toss to coat. Roast for 20–25 minutes, turning the pieces every 4–5 minutes with a fish slice so that they brown evenly.

3 Bring a large pan of lightly salted water to the boil and cook the pasta until it is *al dente*.

4 Drain the pasta thoroughly and return it to the clean pan. Reheat the sauce and stir in the vinegar. Add it to the pasta with half the roasted aubergine and half the Pecorino. Toss to mix, then taste for seasoning.

5 Spoon the mixture into a warmed large serving dish and top with the remaining roasted aubergine. Scatter the shredded basil leaves over the top, followed by the remaining grated Pecorino. Serve at once.

Spaghetti with Aubergines & Ricotta

Do try to locate ricotta salata for this classic dish. Its slight saltiness is the ideal match for the richness of the deep-fried aubergines.

Serves 4–6

60ml/4 tbsp olive oil
1 garlic clove, roughly chopped
450g/1lb ripe plum tomatoes, peeled and chopped
vegetable oil for shallow frying
1 large aubergine, about 350g/12oz, diced small
400g/14oz fresh or dried spaghetti
1 handful fresh basil leaves, shredded
115g/4oz ricotta salata cheese, coarsely grated
salt and freshly ground black pepper

1 Heat the olive oil in a pan, add the garlic and cook over a low heat, stirring constantly, for 1–2 minutes. Stir in the tomatoes, then season with salt and pepper to taste. Cover and simmer for 20 minutes.

2 Meanwhile, heat the oil for shallow frying in a frying pan and fry the aubergine cubes, in batches, for 4–5 minutes, until tender and lightly browned. As each batch cooks, remove it with a slotted spoon and drain on kitchen paper.

3 Bring a large pan of lightly salted water to the boil and cook the pasta until it is *al dente*. Meanwhile, stir the fried aubergine into the tomato sauce and warm through. Taste and adjust the seasoning, if necessary.

4 Drain the pasta and tip it into a warmed bowl. Add the sauce, with the shredded basil and a generous handful of the grated ricotta salata. Toss well and serve immediately, with the remaining ricotta sprinkled on top.

Cook's Tip

In Italy, this dish is known as spaghetti alla Bellini and is named after the Sicilian composer. It is sometimes also called spaghetti alla Norma, after his opera.

Penne with Aubergine & Goat's Cheese

Substantial and richly flavoured, this makes a good choice for a winter supper.

Serves 6
45ml/3 tbsp olive oil
15g/ ½ oz/1 tbsp butter
2 aubergines, about 275g/10oz each, cubed
1 garlic clove, chopped
500ml/17fl oz/generous 2 cups passata
15ml/1 tbsp tomato purée
350g/12oz/3 cups dried penne
115g/4oz firm goat's cheese, cubed
45ml/3 tbsp shredded fresh basil
salt and freshly ground black pepper

1 Heat half the olive oil and butter in a large, heavy-based pan. Add the aubergine cubes and fry, stirring frequently, until just golden on all sides, adding more oil and butter if needed.

2 Stir in the garlic, passata and tomato purée. Bring to the boil, then lower the heat and simmer for 15–20 minutes, until thickened. Season generously.

3 Bring a large pan of lightly salted water to the boil and cook the pasta until it is *al dente*. Drain well and tip into a warmed serving bowl.

4 Add the aubergine sauce, goat's cheese and basil to the pasta and toss well. Serve immediately.

Cook's Tip
Montrachet would be a good choice of cheese for this dish. It has a mild, creamy flavour. Made in Burgundy in France, it is ripened for only a few days, wrapped in vine leaves or chestnut leaves. It is usually sold still wrapped in the leaves.

Penne with Aubergine & Mint Pesto

This splendid variation on the classic Italian pesto uses fresh mint rather than basil for a different flavour.

Serves 4
2 large aubergines, about 275g/10oz each
450g/1lb/4 cups dried penne
50g/2oz/ ½ cup walnut halves

For the pesto
25g/1oz/1 cup fresh mint leaves
15g/ ½ oz/ ½ cup flat leaf parsley
40g/1 ½ oz/ ⅓ cup walnuts
40g/1 ½oz/ ½ cup freshly grated Parmesan cheese
2 garlic cloves
90ml/6 tbsp olive oil
salt and freshly ground black pepper

1 Cut the aubergines lengthways into 1cm/ ½ in slices, then cut the slices again crossways to give short strips.

2 Layer the aubergine strips in a colander with salt and leave to stand for 30 minutes over a plate to catch any juices. Rinse off the excess salt under cold water, and drain.

3 Make the pesto. Place the mint, parsley, walnuts, Parmesan and garlic in a food processor, and blend until smooth. With the motor running, gradually add the oil through the feeder tube in a thin, continuous stream until the mixture amalgamates. Season with salt and pepper to taste.

4 Bring a large pan of lightly salted water to the boil and cook the penne for 8 minutes. Add the aubergine strips and cook for 3 minutes more.

5 Drain the pasta and aubergine strips, and return the mixture to the clean pan. Add the pesto and walnut halves, and toss until combined. Serve immediately.

Cook's Tip
Choose aubergines with glossy, unblemished skins. They should feel firm and heavy for their size.

Green Pasta with Avocado Sauce

Avocados make a rich and creamy sauce, which looks very effective on spinach-flavoured tagliatelle.

Serves 6

3 ripe tomatoes
2 large ripe avocados
450g/1lb dried spinach-flavoured tagliatelle
25g/1oz/2 tbsp butter, plus extra for tossing the pasta
1 garlic clove, crushed
350ml/12fl oz/1½ cups double cream
dash of Tabasco sauce
salt and freshly ground black pepper
freshly grated Parmesan cheese and soured cream, to serve

1 Cut the tomatoes in half and remove the cores. Squeeze out the seeds and cut the tomatoes into dice. Set aside.

2 Cut the avocados in half, take out the stones and remove the peel. Chop the flesh roughly.

3 Bring a pan of lightly salted water to the boil and cook the pasta until it is *al dente*.

4 Meanwhile, melt the butter in a saucepan and add the garlic. Cook over a low heat for 1 minute, then add the cream and chopped avocados. Increase the heat and cook for 5 minutes, stirring constantly to break up the avocados.

5 Add the diced tomatoes and season to taste with salt, pepper and a little Tabasco sauce.

6 Drain the pasta, return it to the clean pan and toss it with a knob of butter. Divide it among four warmed bowls and spoon over the sauce. Sprinkle with grated Parmesan and top each portion with a spoonful of soured cream.

Variation
Use snipped chives instead of the soured cream topping if you prefer a less rich dish.

Buckwheat Noodles with Cabbage

This is a very unusual pasta dish. The buckwheat noodles used are unique to Valtellina in the Italian Alps, where the dish originated.

Serves 6

400g/14oz savoy cabbage, cut into 1cm/½ in strips
2 potatoes, cut into 5mm/¼ in slices
400g/14oz dried pizzoccheri (Italian buckwheat noodles)
75g/3oz/6 tbsp butter
a generous bunch of fresh sage leaves, shredded
2 garlic cloves
200g/7oz Fontina cheese, rind removed and thinly sliced
30–45ml/2–3 tbsp freshly grated Parmesan cheese, plus extra to serve
salt

1 Bring a very large saucepan of lightly salted water to the boil. Add the cabbage and potatoes, and boil for 5 minutes.

2 Add the pasta, stir well and let the water return to the boil. Lower the heat and simmer for 15 minutes, or until the pasta is *al dente*.

3 A few minutes before the pasta is ready, melt the butter in a small saucepan. Add the sage and whole garlic cloves, and fry gently until the garlic is golden and sizzling. Lift the garlic out of the pan and discard it. Set the flavoured butter aside.

4 Drain the pasta and vegetables. Pour a quarter of the mixture into a warmed large bowl and arrange about a third of the Fontina slices on top. Repeat these layers until all the ingredients have been used, then sprinkle with the grated Parmesan. Pour the sage and garlic butter over the top and serve immediately, with extra Parmesan handed separately.

Cook's Tip
Packets of dried pizzoccheri pasta are available from good Italian delicatessens.

Pasta with Savoy Cabbage & Gruyère

This is an inexpensive and simple dish with a surprising texture and flavour. The cabbage retains some crispness and contrasts beautifully with the pasta.

Serves 4

25g/1oz/2 tbsp butter, plus extra for greasing
350g/12oz fresh or dried tagliatelle
1 small savoy or green cabbage, thinly sliced
1 small onion, chopped
15ml/1 tbsp chopped fresh parsley
150ml/ ¼ pint/ ⅔ cup single cream
50g/2oz/ ½ cup grated Gruyère or Cheddar cheese
about 300ml/ ½ pint/1 ¼ cups hot Vegetable Stock
salt and freshly ground black pepper

1 Preheat the oven to 180°C/350°F/Gas 4 and grease a large ovenproof dish with butter. Bring a large pan of lightly salted water to the boil and cook the pasta until it is *al dente*.

2 Meanwhile, place the cabbage in a mixing bowl. Melt the butter in a small frying pan and fry the onion until softened. Add it to the cabbage and mix well.

3 Drain the pasta and add it to the cabbage mixture, with the parsley. Mix well and then pour into the prepared dish.

4 Beat together the single cream and grated Gruyère or Cheddar cheese in a large jug, then stir in the hot stock. Season well and pour the mixture over the cabbage and pasta, so that it comes about halfway up the dish. If necessary, add a little more stock.

5 Cover tightly with foil or a lid and bake for 30–35 minutes, until the cabbage is crisp-tender and the stock is bubbling. Remove the lid for the last 5 minutes of the cooking time to brown the top.

Penne Rigati with Cauliflower

Give cauliflower cheese a twist by adding your favourite pasta shapes.

Serves 6

1 medium cauliflower, separated into florets
500g/1 ¼ lb/5 cups dried penne rigati or other short pasta
500ml/17fl oz/generous 2 cups milk
1 bay leaf
50g/2oz/ ¼ cup butter
50g/2oz/ ½ cup plain flour
75g/3oz/1 cup freshly grated Parmesan or Cheddar cheese
salt and freshly ground black pepper

1 Bring a large pan of lightly salted water to the boil and cook the cauliflower florets for 8–10 minutes, until they are just tender, but still firm to the bite. Remove them from the pan with a strainer or slotted spoon. Chop the cauliflower into bite-size pieces and set aside.

2 Bring the cooking water back to the boil and cook the pasta until it is *al dente*.

3 Heat the milk with the bay leaf, either in a pan on top of the stove or in the microwave. Melt the butter in a heavy-based pan. Add the flour, and cook, stirring constantly, for 1–2 minutes. Remove the bay leaf from the milk. Gradually add the milk to the butter and flour mixture, stirring constantly, until the sauce boils and thickens.

4 Stir the cheese into the sauce, then fold in the cauliflower. Season with plenty of salt and pepper.

5 Drain the pasta and return it to the clean pan. Add the cheese and cauliflower sauce, and toss to mix. Serve at once, in warmed bowls.

Cook's Tip

Save some of the cheese for topping the pasta, if you like, or offer extra at the table.

Tagliatelle with Spinach & Garlic Cheese

The most unlikely combinations can prove surprisingly successful, a fact that is amply illustrated in this delicious dish. Italian pasta and spinach, Chinese soy sauce and cheese are mixed here to make this wonderful and mouthwatering dish.

Serves 4

225g/8oz fresh leaf spinach, trimmed
225g/8oz dried tagliatelle, preferably mixed colours
30ml/2 tbsp light soy sauce
75g/3oz garlic and herb cheese
45ml/3 tbsp milk
salt and freshly ground black pepper

1 Remove any tough stalks from the spinach, then wash the leaves well in cold water. Place them in a heavy-based pan with just the water that clings to the leaves. Cover the pan tightly and cook the spinach until it has just wilted. Drain it very well, using the back of a wooden spoon to press out the excess liquid. Chop the leaves roughly with kitchen scissors.

2 Bring a large pan of lightly salted water to the boil and cook the pasta until it is *al dente*.

3 Meanwhile, put the spinach in a frying pan and stir in the soy sauce over a low heat. Add the garlic and herb cheese, and stir in the milk. Bring slowly to the boil, stirring constantly until smooth. Season to taste with salt and pepper.

4 Drain the pasta, return it to the clean pan and pour over the sauce. Toss to mix, then serve in warmed bowls.

Variations

- *This dish would also work well with watercress, sorrel, rocket or radicchio instead of spinach.*
- *If you don't like garlic, use unflavoured boursin or crumbled feta and stir in 15ml/1 tbsp chopped fresh herbs.*

Fusilli with Peppers & Onions

Grilled peppers have a delicious smoky flavour, and look very colourful in this simple dish.

Serves 4

2 large peppers
400g/14oz/3½ cups dried fusilli
90ml/6 tbsp olive oil
1 large red onion, thinly sliced
2 garlic cloves, crushed
45ml/3 tbsp finely chopped fresh parsley
salt and freshly ground black pepper
freshly grated Parmesan cheese, to serve

1 Preheat the grill. Cut the peppers in half, remove the cores and seeds, and place them cut side down in the grill pan. Grill until the skins have blistered and begun to char.

2 Put the peppers in a bowl, cover with several layers of kitchen paper and set aside for 10 minutes. Peel off the skins and slice the flesh into thin strips.

3 Bring a large pan of lightly salted water to the boil and cook the pasta until it is *al dente*.

4 Heat the oil in a frying pan. Add the onion and fry over a medium heat, stirring frequently, until it is translucent. Stir in the garlic and cook for 2 minutes over a low heat.

5 Add the peppers and mix gently. Stir in about 45ml/3 tbsp of the pasta cooking water. Stir in the parsley and season the mixture with salt and pepper to taste.

6 Drain the pasta. Tip it into the pan with the vegetables, and toss thoroughly to coat. Serve in warmed bowls, with the Parmesan passed separately.

Cook's Tip

Use red and yellow peppers, or mix red with orange. For a dramatic effect, look out for dark purple peppers.

Eliche with Chargrilled Peppers

This is a dish for high summer when peppers and tomatoes ripen naturally and are plentiful. It is equally good cold as a salad.

Serves 4

3 large peppers (red, yellow and orange)
350g/12oz/3 cups fresh or dried eliche
1–2 garlic cloves, finely chopped
4 ripe Italian plum tomatoes, peeled, seeded and diced
50g/2oz/ ½ cup stoned black olives, halved or quartered lengthways
60m 1¼ tbsp extra virgin olive oil
a handful of fresh basil leaves
salt and freshly ground black pepper

1 Preheat the grill. Cut the peppers in half, remove the cores and seeds, and place them cut side down in the grill pan. Grill until the skins have blistered and begun to char.

2 Put the peppers in a bowl, cover with several layers of kitchen paper and set aside for 10 minutes.

3 Bring a large pan of lightly salted water to the boil and cook the pasta until it is *al dente*.

4 While the pasta is cooking, peel the peppers, slice the flesh thinly and place it in a large bowl.

5 Add the garlic, tomatoes, olives and olive oil to the peppers. Mix lightly, then add salt and pepper to taste.

6 Drain the cooked pasta and tip it into the bowl. Add the basil leaves. Toss thoroughly to mix and serve immediately in warmed bowls.

Variation

A few strips of sun-dried tomatoes would give this even more flavour. Choose the type in oil, and use some of the oil in the dressing, if you like.

Capellini with Peppers & Mangetouts

The vegetables in this pretty, summery dish are barely cooked – rather, they are just heated through. As a result, they stay lovely and crisp, providing a contrast to the tender pasta.

Serves 4

350g/12oz dried capellini
15ml/1 tbsp groundnut oil
30ml/2 tbsp cornflour
30ml/2 tbsp water
15ml/1 tbsp vegetable oil
3 garlic cloves, finely chopped
175ml/6fl oz/ ¾ cup Vegetable Stock
45ml/3 tbsp dry sherry
30ml/2 tbsp sesame oil
15ml/1 tbsp light soy sauce
5ml/1 tsp chilli sauce
2.5ml/ ½ tsp caster sugar
2.5ml/ ½ tsp Szechuan peppercorns, crushed
1 red pepper, seeded and cut into strips
1 yellow pepper, seeded and cut into strips
115g/4oz mangetouts, trimmed and halved
10 button mushrooms, thinly sliced
3 spring onions
pared rind of 1 orange, thinly shredded, to garnish

1 Bring a large pan of lightly salted water to the boil and cook the pasta until it is *al dente*. Drain in a colander, then transfer to a large bowl and stir in the groundnut oil.

2 Put the cornflour in a small bowl and stir in the measured water to make a smooth paste.

3 Preheat a wok or large, heavy-based frying pan and add the vegetable oil. When it is hot, add the garlic and stir-fry for about 20 seconds. Add the vegetable stock, sherry, sesame oil, soy sauce, chilli sauce, sugar and Szechuan peppercorns. Bring to the boil, stirring constantly. Pour in the cornflour mixture, stirring all the time until slightly thickened.

4 Add the pasta and vegetables to the wok. Toss over the heat for about 2 minutes, or until the mixture is hot. Serve at once, garnished with the orange rind.

Spaghetti with Pepper & Tomato Sauce

Look out for packs of mixed peppers, which are ideal for making this quick and easy supper dish.

Serves 4

30ml/2 tbsp olive oil
2 onions, chopped
1 red pepper, seeded and cut into strips
1 green pepper, seeded and cut into strips
1 yellow pepper, seeded and cut into strips
3 tomatoes, peeled, seeded and chopped
1 garlic clove, chopped
15ml/1 tbsp chopped fresh oregano
350g/12oz dried spaghetti
salt and freshly ground black pepper
fresh oregano strips, to garnish

1 Heat the oil in a large, heavy-based pan. Add the onions and peppers, and fry over a medium heat, stirring frequently, for 10 minutes, until softened.

2 Stir in the tomatoes, garlic and chopped oregano. Season with plenty of salt and pepper, and bring to the boil, stirring frequently. Lower the heat and leave to simmer while you cook the pasta.

3 Bring a large pan of lightly salted water to the boil and cook the pasta until it is *al dente*.

4 Drain the pasta thoroughly and return it to the clean pan. Add the sauce and toss well. Serve immediately, garnished with the oregano sprigs.

Cook's Tip
For an even quicker sauce, use already cut pepper strips that you can buy in jars of olive oil. Fry the chopped onion for 3–5 minutes in step 1, then drain the peppers and add them in step 2.

Strozzapretti with Courgette Flowers

This pretty, summery dish is strewn with colourful courgette flowers, but you can make it even if you don't have the flowers.

Serves 4

50g/2oz/ 1/4 cup butter
30ml/2 tbsp extra virgin olive oil
1 small onion, thinly sliced
200g/7oz small courgettes, cut into thin julienne
1 garlic clove, crushed
10ml/2 tsp finely chopped fresh marjoram
350g/12oz/3 cups dried strozzapretti
a large handful of courgette flowers, thoroughly washed and dried
salt and freshly ground black pepper
thin shavings of Parmesan cheese, to serve

1 Heat the butter and half the olive oil in a pan, and cook the onion over a low heat, stirring occasionally, until softened. Add the courgettes, garlic and marjoram, and season with salt and pepper to taste. Mix well. Cook for 5–8 minutes until the courgettes have softened but are not coloured, turning them over from time to time.

2 Meanwhile, bring a pan of lightly salted water to the boil and cook the pasta until it is *al dente*.

3 Set aside a few whole courgette flowers for the garnish, then roughly shred the rest and add them to the courgette mixture. Stir to mix and taste for seasoning.

4 Drain the pasta, tip it into a warmed large bowl and add the remaining oil. Toss thoroughly, add the courgette mixture and toss again. Top with Parmesan and the reserved courgette flowers, and serve immediately.

Cook's Tip
Strozzapretti or "priest stranglers" are short pasta shapes from Modena. You can buy packets of them in Italian delicatessens, or use gemelli, a similar kind of twisted pasta.

Paglia e Fieno

The title of this dish translates as "straw and hay" which refers to the yellow and green colours of the pasta when mixed together. Using fresh peas makes all the difference to this dish.

Serves 4

450g/1lb dried paglia e fieno (egg- and spinach-flavoured tagliatelle)
50g/2oz/ ¼ cup butter
900g/2lb fresh peas in the pod, shelled
200ml/7fl oz/scant 1 cup double cream
50g/2oz/ ⅔ cup freshly grated Parmesan cheese, plus extra to serve
freshly grated nutmeg
salt and freshly ground black pepper

1 Bring a large pan of lightly salted water to the boil and cook the pasta until it is *al dente*.

2 Meanwhile, melt the butter in a heavy-based saucepan and add the peas. Sauté for 2–3 minutes, stirring occasionally, then stir in 150ml/ ¼ pint/ ⅔ cup of the cream. Bring to the boil, then lower the heat and simmer until slightly thickened.

3 Drain the pasta and add it to the pan containing the cream and pea sauce. Toss briefly to mix.

4 Pour in the remaining cream. Add the cheese, and season to taste with salt, pepper, and a little grated nutmeg. Toss over a gentle heat until well coated and heated through. Serve immediately, with extra Parmesan cheese.

Variation
Sautéed mushrooms make a good addition.

Tagliatelle with Baby Vegetables

Make this in the spring, when there are plenty of baby vegetables in markets or on farm stalls.

Serves 4

30ml/2 tbsp olive oil
115g/4oz baby carrots, halved lengthways
115g/4oz baby aubergines, halved lengthways
115g/4oz baby courgettes, halved lengthways
2 garlic cloves, chopped
15ml/1 tbsp chopped fresh rosemary, plus fresh rosemary sprigs to garnish
300ml/ ½ pint/1 ¼ cups single cream
350g/12oz fresh tagliatelle
salt and freshly ground black pepper

1 Heat the oil in a large, heavy-based frying pan. Add the carrots, aubergines, courgettes, garlic and chopped rosemary, and cook over a gentle heat, covered, for 20–30 minutes, until browned, stirring occasionally.

2 Remove the pan from the heat and stir in the cream, scraping any sediment from the base of the pan. Season to taste with salt and pepper. Return the pan to a low heat and cook for about 4 minutes more until heated through.

3 Meanwhile, bring a large pan of lightly salted water to the boil and cook the pasta until *al dente*.

4 Drain the pasta thoroughly and return it to the clean pan. Add the vegetable mixture and toss thoroughly to coat. Serve immediately, garnished with fresh rosemary.

Variation
Mix and match the vegetables, according to what is available in the shops. If you are lucky enough to take part in an organic box scheme, ask your supplier for the youngest, freshest vegetables around. Patty pan squash, mangetouts or baby parsnips could be used. Just make sure that the total quantity is about 350g/12oz.

Garganelli with Spring Vegetables

A light, buttery sauce marries young fresh vegetables and pasta to make a dish that would be ideal for a simple lunch.

Serves 4

350g/12oz fresh young asparagus, trimmed
4 young carrots
1 bunch spring onions
150g/5oz/1¼ cups shelled fresh peas
350g/12oz/3 cups dried garganelli
75g/3oz/6 tbsp unsalted butter, diced
60ml/4 tbsp dry white wine
a few sprigs each of fresh flat leaf parsley, mint and basil, leaves stripped and chopped
salt and freshly ground black pepper
freshly grated Parmesan cheese, to serve

1 Cut off the asparagus tips, holding the knife at a slant. Set the tips aside. Cut the stems on the diagonal into 4cm/1½ in pieces.

2 Cut the carrots and spring onions on the diagonal into 4cm/1½in pieces.

3 Bring a large pan of lightly salted water to the boil and add the asparagus stems, carrots and peas. Bring back to the boil, then simmer for 5 minutes. Add the asparagus tips and simmer for 3 minutes more. Using a slotted spoon, transfer the cooked vegetables to a bowl.

4 Bring the water used for cooking the vegetables back to the boil and cook the pasta until it is *al dente*.

5 Meanwhile, melt the butter in a large, heavy-based frying pan. Add the cooked vegetables, with the white wine, and season with salt and pepper to taste. Toss over a medium to high heat until the wine has reduced and the vegetables are glistening with melted butter.

6 Drain the pasta and tip it into a warmed large bowl. Add the dressed vegetables, the spring onions and the herbs, and toss well. Serve immediately, with freshly grated Parmesan.

Capellini with Rocket & Mangetouts

A light but filling pasta dish, with the added pepperiness of fresh rocket.

Serves 4

250g/9oz dried capellini
225g/8oz mangetouts
175g/6oz rocket
50g/2oz/½ cup pine nuts, roasted
30ml/2 tbsp freshly grated Parmesan cheese
salt and freshly ground black pepper

1 Bring a large pan of lightly salted water to the boil and cook the pasta until *al dente*. Meanwhile, carefully top and tail the mangetouts.

2 As soon as the pasta is cooked, drop the rocket and mangetouts into the pan. Drain immediately.

3 Tip the pasta mixture into a warmed bowl, and add the pine nuts and Parmesan. Season and toss to coat. Serve at once.

Capellini with Spinach & Feta

An ideal supper dish for warm evenings when you don't feel like cooking much.

Serves 6

375g/12oz dried capellini
300g/11oz mangetouts
275g/10oz baby spinach leaves
30ml/2 tbsp chopped fresh oregano or marjoram
115g/4oz feta cheese, crumbled
salt and freshly ground black pepper

1 Bring a large pan of lightly salted water to the boil and cook the pasta until *al dente*. Meanwhile, carefully top and tail the mangetouts.

2 As soon as the pasta is cooked, drop the spinach and mangetouts into the pan, then drain immediately.

3 Tip the pasta mixture into a warmed bowl and add the oregano or marjoram, and feta. Season, toss well and serve.

Trenette with Pesto, French Beans & Potatoes

Potatoes are almost as good with pesto as is pasta, so any recipe that combines all three ingredients is bound to be a winner.

Serves 4

about 40 fresh basil leaves
2 garlic cloves, thinly sliced
25ml/1½ tbsp pine nuts
45ml/3 tbsp freshly grated Parmesan cheese, plus extra to serve
30ml/2 tbsp freshly grated Pecorino cheese, plus extra to serve
60ml/4 tbsp extra virgin olive oil
2 potatoes, total weight about 250g/9oz
100g/3½ oz French beans
350g/12oz dried trenette
salt and freshly ground black pepper

1 Put the basil leaves, garlic, pine nuts and cheeses in a blender or food processor, and process for about 5 seconds. Add half the olive oil and a pinch of salt, and process for 5 seconds more. Stop the machine, remove the lid and scrape down the side of the bowl. Add the remaining olive oil and process for 5–10 seconds.

2 Peel the potatoes and cut each one in half lengthways. Slice each half crossways into 5mm/ ¼in thick slices. Top and tail the beans, then cut them into 2cm/ ¾in pieces. Bring a large pan of lightly salted water to the boil. Add the potatoes and beans, and boil, uncovered, for 5 minutes.

3 Add the pasta, bring the water back to the boil, stir well, then cook until the pasta is *al dente*.

4 Meanwhile, put the pesto in a large bowl and thin it with 45–60ml/3–4 tbsp of the water used for cooking the pasta.

5 Drain the pasta and vegetables, add them to the pesto and toss well. Serve immediately on warmed plates, with extra grated Parmesan and Pecorino handed separately.

Pasta with Green Vegetable Medley

Tossed with freshly cooked pasta, this mixture of tender green vegetables and tomatoes is ideal for a fresh and light lunch or supper.

Serves 4

2 carrots
1 courgette
75g/3oz French beans
1 small leek
2 ripe Italian plum tomatoes
a handful of fresh flat leaf parsley
25g/1oz/2 tbsp butter
45ml/3 tbsp extra virgin olive oil
2.5ml/ ½ tsp granulated sugar
115g/4oz/1 cup frozen peas
450g/1lb fresh or dried penne rigate or other pasta shapes
salt and freshly ground black pepper

1 Dice the carrots and courgette finely. Top and tail the French beans, then cut them into 2cm/ ¾in lengths. Slice the leek thinly. Peel and dice the tomatoes. Chop the parsley and set it aside.

2 Melt the butter in the oil in a medium pan, and add the prepared leek and carrots. Sprinkle the sugar over and fry, stirring frequently, for about 5 minutes.

3 Stir in the courgette, French beans, peas and plenty of salt and pepper. Cover and cook gently until the vegetables are tender, stirring occasionally.

4 Meanwhile, bring a large pan of lightly salted water to the boil. Add the pasta and cook until *al dente*.

5 Stir the parsley and chopped plum tomatoes into the vegetable mixture and adjust the seasoning. Drain the pasta, return it to the clean pan and add the vegetable mixture. Toss well and serve at once.

Variations

Use fresh peas when they are in season, or substitute mangetouts for the frozen peas and baby corn cobs for the green beans.

Spaghetti with Ratatouille Sauce

Rich, colourful and robust, this famous Provençal vegetable ratatouille makes a superb sauce for spaghetti or shaped pasta.

Serves 4

30ml/2 tbsp olive oil
1 onion, sliced
1 garlic clove, chopped
2 courgettes, sliced
1 large aubergine, cut into large chunks
30ml/2 tbsp tomato purée
400g/14oz can chopped tomatoes
30ml/2 tbsp chopped fresh mixed herbs
350g/12oz dried spaghetti
salt and freshly ground black pepper
fresh flat leaf parsley sprigs, to garnish
freshly grated Parmesan cheese, to serve

1 Heat the oil in a large, heavy-based pan. Add the onion and fry over a medium heat, stirring frequently, for 5 minutes. Add the garlic, courgettes and aubergine, and cook for 2 minutes more, stirring occasionally.

2 Stir in the tomato purée, chopped tomatoes and mixed herbs, and season with salt and pepper to taste. Bring to the boil, then lower the heat and simmer, stirring occasionally, for 20–30 minutes, until the mixture has thickened and the vegetables are very tender.

3 Meanwhile, bring a large pan of lightly salted water to the boil and cook the pasta until it is *al dente*.

4 Drain the pasta well, return it to the clean pan and add the ratatouille. Toss to coat. Serve immediately in warmed bowls, garnished with the fresh flat leaf parsley. Hand around a bowl of freshly grated Parmesan cheese.

Variation
For extra colour and flavour, add a sliced orange pepper with the onion in step 1.

Pappardelle Tossed with Grilled Vegetables

A hearty dish to be eaten with crusty bread and washed down with a robust red wine.

Serves 4

1 aubergine
2 courgettes
1 red pepper
8 garlic cloves, unpeeled
about 150ml/ ¼ pint/ ⅔ cup extra virgin olive oil
450g/1lb dried pappardelle
salt and freshly ground black pepper
a few fresh thyme sprigs, to garnish

1 Preheat the grill. Slice the aubergine and courgettes lengthways. Cut the pepper in half, cut out the stalk and white pith, and scrape out the seeds. Slice the pepper lengthways into eight pieces.

2 Arrange the vegetables and unpeeled garlic cloves in a single layer in a grill pan. Brush liberally with some of the oil and season with salt and pepper. Grill until the vegetables are slightly charred and the garlic is soft, turning once.

3 Set the garlic cloves aside to cool slightly. Put the grilled vegetables in a bowl, add the remaining olive oil and toss well to coat. Pop the garlic flesh out of the skins and add it to the vegetable mixture.

4 Bring a large pan of lightly salted water to the boil and cook the pasta until *al dente*. Drain well, return to the clean pan and add the vegetable mixture. Serve immediately, garnished with the thyme.

Cook's Tips
- *Try barbecuing the vegetables for a really smoky flavour.*
- *If you can locate baby aubergines and courgettes, so much the better. Use 2–3 aubergines and about 6 courgettes.*

Conchiglie with Roasted Vegetables

Nothing could be simpler than tossing pasta with roasted vegetables. The flavour is superb.

Serves 4–6

1 red pepper, seeded and cut into 1cm/½in squares
1 yellow or orange pepper, seeded and cut into 1cm/½ in squares
1 small aubergine, roughly diced
2 courgettes, roughly diced
75ml/5 tbsp extra virgin olive oil
15ml/1 tbsp chopped fresh flat leaf parsley
5ml/1 tsp dried oregano or marjoram
250g/9oz baby Italian plum tomatoes, halved lengthways
2 garlic cloves, roughly chopped
350–400g/12–14oz/3–3½ cups dried conchiglie
salt and freshly ground black pepper
4–6 fresh marjoram or oregano flowers, to garnish

1 Preheat the oven to 190°C/375°F/Gas 5. Put the peppers, aubergine and courgettes in a bowl, add 45ml/3 tbsp of the olive oil and stir to coat the vegetables. Tip them into a large roasting tin and spread them out. Sprinkle the fresh and dried herbs over the vegetables. Add salt and pepper to taste, and stir well. Roast for 30 minutes, stirring two or three times.

2 Stir the halved tomatoes and chopped garlic into the vegetable mixture, then roast for 20 minutes more, stirring once or twice.

3 Meanwhile, bring a large pan of lightly salted water to the boil and cook the pasta until *al dente*.

4 Drain the pasta and tip it into a warmed bowl. Add the vegetables with any liquid in the roasting tin. Add the remaining oil and toss well. Serve the pasta and vegetables hot in warmed bowls, sprinkling each portion with a few herb flowers.

Variation
This mixture makes a marvellous filling for pitta pockets, especially if you use small pasta shapes.

Vermicelli Frittata

A frittata is a flat, baked omelette. It is absolutely delicious cold. Cut into wedges, it makes excellent picnic fare.

Serves 4–6

50g/2oz dried vermicelli
6 eggs
60ml/4 tbsp double cream
a handful of fresh basil leaves, shredded
a handful of fresh flat leaf parsley, chopped
75g/3oz/1 cup freshly grated Parmesan cheese
25g/1oz/2 tbsp butter
15ml/1 tbsp olive oil
1 onion, finely sliced
3 large pieces of drained bottled roasted red pepper, cut into strips
1 garlic clove, crushed
salt and freshly ground black pepper
rocket leaves, to serve

1 Preheat the oven to 190°C/375°F/Gas 5. Bring a small pan of lightly salted water to the boil and cook the pasta until *al dente*.

2 Meanwhile, beat the eggs with the cream and herbs in a bowl. Whisk in about two-thirds of the grated Parmesan and add salt and pepper to taste.

3 Drain the pasta well and allow to cool; snip it into short lengths. Add it to the egg mixture and whisk again. Set aside.

4 Melt the butter in the oil in a large non-stick frying pan that can be safely used in the oven. Fry the onion over a low heat, for 5 minutes, until softened. Add the peppers and garlic.

5 Pour the egg and pasta mixture into the pan and stir to make sure that the pasta is evenly distributed. Cook over a low to medium heat, without stirring, for 3–5 minutes, or until the frittata is just set underneath.

6 Sprinkle over the remaining Parmesan and transfer the pan to the oven. Bake for 5 minutes, or until set. Before serving, leave to stand for at least 5 minutes. Cut into wedges and serve warm or cold with rocket.

Pasta with Caponata

The Sicilians have an excellent sweet and sour vegetable dish called *caponata*, which goes wonderfully well with pasta.

Serves 4

60ml/4 tbsp extra virgin olive oil
8 shallots, peeled
2 garlic cloves, crushed
1 large red pepper, sliced
1 medium aubergine, cut into sticks
2 medium courgettes, cut into sticks
450ml/ ¾ pint/ 1¾ cups tomato juice
150ml/ ¼ pint/ ⅔ cup water
30ml/2 tbsp balsamic vinegar
juice of 1 lemon
15ml/1 tbsp granulated sugar
30ml/2 tbsp sliced stoned black olives
30ml/2 tbsp drained capers
400g/14oz fresh or dried tagliatelle
salt and freshly ground black pepper

1 Heat the oil in a large saucepan. Add the shallots, garlic and red pepper, and fry over a low heat, stirring occasionally, for 5 minutes. Stir in the aubergine and courgettes and fry, stirring occasionally, for a further 5 minutes.

2 Stir in the tomato juice and water. Bring to the boil, stirring occasionally, then add the vinegar, lemon juice, sugar, olives and capers. Season with salt and pepper to taste and simmer over a fairly low heat while you cook the pasta.

3 Bring a large pan of lightly salted water to the boil and cook the pasta until it is *al dente*.

4 Drain the pasta, return it to the clean pan and add the caponata. Serve at once in warmed bowls.

Cook's Tip
It is worth buying genuine balsamic vinegar for this dish, as it has a unique sweet-sour flavour. Otherwise, use a good-quality red wine vinegar.

Vegetable & Macaroni Bake

A tasty change from macaroni cheese, this recipe is delicious served with steamed fresh vegetables.

Serves 6

225g/8oz/2 cups wholewheat macaroni
225g/8oz leeks, sliced
45ml/3 tbsp Vegetable Stock
225g/8oz broccoli florets
50g/2oz/4 tbsp butter
50g/2oz/ ½ cup plain wholemeal flour
900ml/1½ pints/3¾ cups milk
150g/5oz/1¼ cups grated mature Cheddar cheese
5ml/1 tsp prepared English mustard
350g/12oz can sweetcorn kernels, drained
25g/1oz/ ½ cup fresh wholemeal breadcrumbs
30ml/2 tbsp chopped fresh parsley
2 tomatoes, cut into eighths
salt and freshly ground black pepper

1 Preheat the oven to 200°C/400°F/Gas 6. Bring a large saucepan of lightly salted water to the boil, add the macaroni and cook until *al dente*.

2 Meanwhile, combine the leeks and stock in a small pan. Cover and cook for about 10 minutes, until the leeks are tender.

3 Bring a small pan of water to the boil and blanch the broccoli for 2 minutes. Drain the pasta, then the leeks and broccoli.

4 Melt the butter in a large pan, stir in the flour and cook for 1–2 minutes, stirring constantly. Gradually add the milk, stirring constantly until the sauce boils and thickens.

5 Remove the pan from the heat, add 115g/4oz/1 cup of the grated cheese and stir until it has melted. Stir in the pasta, leeks, broccoli, mustard and sweetcorn. Season to taste with salt and pepper, and mix thoroughly. Transfer the mixture to an ovenproof dish.

6 Mix the remaining cheese, breadcrumbs and parsley together, and sprinkle over the surface. Arrange the tomatoes on top and then bake for 30–40 minutes, until golden brown and bubbling.

Spinach & Ricotta Conchiglione

Few pasta fillings are more pleasing than this mixture of chopped spinach and ricotta.

Serves 4

350g/12oz dried conchiglione
450ml/ ¾ pint/scant 2 cups passata
275g/10oz frozen chopped spinach, thawed
50g/2oz white bread, crusts removed, crumbled
120ml/4fl oz/ ½ cup milk
60ml/4 tbsp olive oil
250g/9oz/1 ½ cups ricotta cheese
pinch of freshly grated nutmeg
1 garlic clove, crushed
2.5ml/ ½ tsp black olive paste (optional)
25g/1oz/ ⅓ cup freshly grated Parmesan cheese
25g/1oz/ ⅓ cup pine nuts
salt and freshly ground black pepper

1 Bring a large saucepan of lightly salted water to the boil and cook the pasta until *al dente*. Drain, refresh under cold water, drain again and reserve until needed.

2 Pour the passata into a nylon sieve placed over a bowl. Place the spinach in another sieve and press out any excess liquid with the back of a spoon.

3 Place the bread, milk and 45ml/3 tbsp of the oil in a food processor and process to combine. Add the spinach and ricotta, and season with salt, pepper and nutmeg. Process briefly to mix.

4 Discard the liquid that has drained from the passata. Tip the thicker liquid that remains in the sieve into the clean bowl and stir in the garlic, remaining oil and olive paste, if using. Spread this mixture evenly over the base of an ovenproof dish.

5 Preheat the oven to 180°C/350°F/Gas 4. Spoon the spinach mixture into the conchiglione. Arrange them over the sauce and cover the dish with foil.

6 Bake for about 15 minutes, until the pasta and sauce are both hot. Remove the foil, scatter with Parmesan cheese and pine nuts, and brown under a hot grill.

Home-made Ravioli

It is a pleasure to make your own fresh pasta by hand.

Serves 4–6

200g/7oz/1 ¾ cups strong plain flour
5ml/ ½ tsp salt
15ml/1 tbsp olive oil
2 eggs, beaten
melted butter, to serve
fresh basil, to garnish

For the filling

15ml/1 tbsp olive oil
1 small red onion, finely chopped
1 small green pepper, finely chopped
1 carrot, coarsely grated
50g/2oz/ ½ cup walnuts, chopped
115g/4oz/ ½ cup ricotta cheese
30ml/2 tbsp freshly grated fresh Parmesan or Pecorino cheese, plus extra to serve
15ml/1 tbsp chopped fresh marjoram or basil
salt and freshly ground black pepper

1 Make the filling. Heat the oil in a small pan and fry the onion, pepper and carrot for 5 minutes, then allow to cool. Mix with the walnuts, cheeses, herbs and seasoning.

2 Place the flour, salt, oil and eggs in a food processor. Pulse to combine. Transfer the dough to a floured surface and knead for 5 minutes. Wrap in clear film and leave to rest for 20 minutes.

3 Divide the dough in half and roll out each piece on a floured surface to a thickness of about 5mm/ ¼ in. Working with one piece of dough at a time, fold it into three and re-roll. Repeat this up to six times until it is smooth and no longer sticky.

4 Keep the rolled dough under clean, dry dish towels while you fold and roll the second piece. Place small scoops of the filling in neat rows about 5cm/2in apart on the surface. Brush in between with a little water and then place the first pasta sheet on the top. Press down well between the rows then, using a ravioli or pastry cutter, cut into squares.

5 Bring a large pan of lightly salted water to the boil and cook the ravioli, in batches if necessary, for 4–5 minutes. Drain well. Toss in a little melted butter. Serve with extra cheese and basil.

Coriander Ravioli with Pumpkin Filling

A stunning herb pasta with a superb creamy pumpkin and roast garlic filling.

Serves 4–6

200g/7oz/1¾ cups strong unbleached white flour
2 eggs, beaten
pinch of salt
45ml/3 tbsp fresh coriander
coriander sprigs and crushed coriander seeds, to garnish

For the filling

4 garlic cloves, unpeeled
450g/1lb pumpkin, peeled and seeds removed
115g/4oz/⅔ cup ricotta cheese
4 pieces of drained sun-dried tomatoes in oil, finely chopped, plus 30ml/2 tbsp of the oil from the jar
freshly ground black pepper

1 Preheat the oven to 200°C/400°F/Gas 6. Place the flour, eggs, salt and coriander in a food processor. Pulse to combine. Transfer the dough to a floured board and knead for 5 minutes. Wrap in clear film and leave to rest for 20 minutes.

2 Put the garlic on a baking sheet and bake for 10–15 minutes, until softened. Steam the pumpkin for 5–8 minutes until tender. Drain well and put in a bowl. Pop the garlic cloves out of their skins and mash them into the pumpkin with the ricotta and drained sun-dried tomatoes. Season with black pepper.

3 Divide the pasta into four pieces and flatten slightly. Using a pasta machine, on its thinnest setting, roll out each piece. Leave the sheets of pasta on a clean dish towel. Using a 7.5cm/3in crinkle-edged round cutter, stamp out 36 rounds. Top 18 of the rounds with a teaspoonful of filling, brush the edges with water and place another round of pasta on top. Press firmly around the edges to seal.

4 Bring a large pan of water to the boil, add the ravioli and cook for 4–5 minutes. Drain well and tip into a warmed bowl. Add the reserved tomato oil and toss gently. Garnish with the coriander sprigs and seeds, and serve.

Ravioli with Cheese & Herbs

Home-made ravioli can be slightly fiddly, but they are well worth the effort.

Serves 4–6

200g/7oz/1¾ cups strong unbleached white flour
2 eggs, beaten
pinch of salt
semolina, to coat
75g/3oz/6 tbsp butter, melted, to serve

For the filling

225g/8oz/1 cup full-fat soft cheese
1 garlic clove, crushed
90ml/6 tbsp chopped fresh herbs

1 Place the flour, eggs and salt in a food processor. Pulse to combine, then transfer the dough to a lightly floured surface and knead for 5 minutes, until smooth.

2 Divide the dough into four pieces and flatten slightly. Using a pasta machine, on its thinnest setting, roll out each piece. Leave the sheets on clean dish towels to dry slightly.

3 Meanwhile, make the filling. Mix the soft cheese with the garlic and 60ml/4 tbsp of the herbs. Season to taste.

4 Place small scoops of the filling on one of the pasta sheets, keeping them in neat rows, about 4cm/1½in apart. Brush the pasta with water, place another sheet on top and press down around each scoop of filling. Cut out the ravioli, toss them in semolina and leave to rest for 15 minutes. Make more ravioli in the same way.

5 Bring a large pan of lightly salted water to the boil and cook the ravioli, in batches, for 4–5 minutes. Drain and toss with the melted butter. Sprinkle with the remaining herbs and serve.

Variation

Fill the ravioli with a mixture of full-fat soft cheese and crumbled Gorgonzola; omit the garlic and herbs. Sprinkle the cooked ravioli with toasted pine nuts.

Spinach & Dolcelatte Ravioli

The filling for these ravioli is superb and does justice to the home-made pasta.

Serves 4–6

200g/7oz/1¾ cups strong unbleached white flour
2 eggs, beaten
pinch of salt
melted butter, chopped fresh parsley and Parmesan shavings, to serve

For the filling

225g/8oz fresh spinach leaves
25g/1oz/2 tbsp butter
1 small onion, finely chopped
25g/1oz/⅓ cup freshly grated Parmesan cheese
40g/1½ oz dolcelatte cheese, crumbled
salt and freshly ground black pepper

1 Place the flour, beaten eggs and salt in a food processor. Pulse to combine, then transfer the dough to a lightly floured surface and knead for 5 minutes, until smooth.

2 Divide the pasta into four pieces and flatten slightly. Using a pasta machine, on its thinnest setting, roll out each piece. Leave the sheets on clean dish towels to dry slightly.

3 Meanwhile, make the filling. Wash the spinach, then place it in a heavy-based pan with just the water that clings to the leaves. Cover and cook until wilted, then drain well, pressing out the excess liquid. Chop finely and put in a bowl. Melt the butter in a small pan and fry the onion until soft. Add to the spinach with the cheeses. Season well and leave to cool.

4 Place small scoops of the filling on one of the pasta sheets in neat rows about 4cm/1½in apart. Brush the pasta with water, place another sheet on top and press down around each scoop of filling. Cut out the ravioli. Make more ravioli in the same way, then leave them all to rest for 15 minutes.

5 Bring a large pan of lightly salted water to the boil and cook the ravioli for 4–5 minutes. Drain well, then toss with melted butter and parsley. Divide among four warmed serving plates, scatter with shavings of Parmesan and serve.

Ravioli with Swiss Chard

Only the leaves of the chard are used for this tasty dish.

Serves 4–6

200g/7oz/1¾ cups strong unbleached white flour
2 eggs, beaten
pinch of salt

For the filling

350g/12oz Swiss chard
60ml/4 tbsp water
115g/4oz/⅔ cup ricotta cheese
45ml/3 tbsp freshly grated Parmesan cheese
pinch of freshly grated nutmeg
milk (optional)
salt and freshly ground black pepper

For the sauce

75g/3oz/6 tbsp butter
leaves from 5–6 fresh sage sprigs

1 Place the flour, eggs and salt in a food processor. Pulse to combine, then transfer the dough to a lightly floured surface and knead for 5 minutes, until smooth.

2 Divide the pasta into four pieces and flatten slightly. Using a pasta machine, on its thinnest setting, roll out each piece. Leave the sheets on clean dish towels to dry slightly.

3 Meanwhile, make the filling. Trim the chard, separating the leaves from the stems. Chop the leaves finely and place them in a heavy-based pan with the water. Cover and cook until wilted, then drain well, pressing out the excess liquid. Mash the ricotta with the Parmesan, nutmeg and seasoning. Add the chard and mix well. If the mixture seems a bit thick, add a little milk.

4 Place small scoops of the filling on one of the pasta sheets in neat rows about 4cm/1½in apart. Brush the pasta with water, place another sheet on top and press down around each scoop of filling. Cut out the ravioli. Make more ravioli in the same way, then leave them all to rest for 15 minutes.

5 Bring a large pan of lightly salted water to the boil and cook the ravioli for 4–5 minutes. Meanwhile, make the sauce by melting the butter with the sage leaves. Drain the ravioli well and arrange in warmed dishes. Spoon on the sauce and serve.

Sardinian Ravioli

Known as *culurgiones*, these ravioli, with their unusual mashed potato and mint filling, are from northern Sardinia. Here, they are gratinéed in the oven with butter and cheese, but they are often served dressed with a tomato sauce.

Serves 4–6

300g/11oz/2¾ cups strong white flour
3 eggs, beaten
5ml/1 tsp salt
50g/2oz/¼ cup butter
50g/2oz/⅔ cup freshly grated Pecorino cheese

For the filling

2 potatoes, each about 200g/7oz, diced
65g/2½oz/generous ⅔ cup freshly grated hard salty Pecorino cheese
75g/3oz soft fresh Pecorino cheese
1 egg yolk
1 large bunch fresh mint, leaves removed and chopped
good pinch of saffron powder
salt and freshly ground black pepper

1 First, make the filling. Cook the potatoes in salted boiling water for 15–20 minutes, or until soft. Drain the potatoes and tip into a bowl, then mash until smooth. Leave until cold.

2 Add both the cheeses, the egg yolk, mint and saffron to the mashed potatoes, and season with salt and pepper to taste. Stir well to mix.

3 Place the flour, eggs and salt in a food processor. Pulse to combine, then transfer the dough to a lightly floured surface and knead for 5 minutes, until smooth.

4 Using a pasta machine, roll out one-quarter of the pasta into a 90cm–1 metre/36–39in strip. Cut the strip with a sharp knife into two 45–50cm/18–20in lengths.

5 With a fluted 10cm/4in biscuit cutter, cut out 4–5 discs from one of the pasta strips. Put a mound of filling on one side of each disc. Brush the edges with water, then fold the dough over the filling to make what looks like a miniature pasty. Pleat the curved edge on each ravioli to seal.

6 Put the ravioli on floured dish towels, sprinkle with flour and leave to dry. Repeat the process to make more ravioli.

7 Preheat the oven to 190°C/375°F/Gas 5. Bring a large pan of lightly salted water to the boil and cook the ravioli, in batches if necessary, for 4–5 minutes. Meanwhile, melt the butter in a small saucepan.

8 Drain the ravioli, tip them into a large ovenproof dish and pour the melted butter over them. Sprinkle with the grated Pecorino and bake in the oven for 10–15 minutes, until golden and bubbly. Allow to stand for 5 minutes before serving.

Tortelli with Squash Stuffing

Winter squash come in all shapes and sizes. Some, like Munchkins and Mama Mia have delectable flesh, which tastes great with pasta.

Serves 4–6

300g/11oz/2¾ cups strong white flour
3 eggs, beaten
5ml/1 tsp salt
melted butter and freshly grated Parmesan cheese, to serve

For the filling

1kg/2¼ lb winter squash (weight with shell)
75g/3oz/1½ cups amaretti biscuits, crushed
2 eggs, beaten
75g/3oz/1 cup freshly grated Parmesan cheese
pinch of freshly grated nutmeg
fresh white breadcrumbs (optional)
salt and freshly ground black pepper

1 Preheat the oven to 190°C/375°F/Gas 5. Make the filling. Cut the squash into wedges, leaving the skin on. Place these in a roasting tin, cover and bake for 30–45 minutes, until the flesh is soft. Scoop it into a food processor and process until smooth.

2 Scrape the squash purée into a bowl and add the biscuit crumbs, eggs, Parmesan and nutmeg. Season with salt and pepper. If the mixture is too sloppy, add 15–30g/1–2 tbsp of the breadcrumbs. Set aside.

3 Place the flour, eggs and salt in the clean food processor. Pulse to combine, then transfer the dough to a lightly floured surface and knead for 5 minutes. Roll it out very thinly, by hand or in a pasta machine.

4 Place tablespoons of filling every 6cm/2½in along a sheet of pasta in rows 5cm/2in apart. Moisten. Cover with another sheet and press down gently. Use a fluted pastry wheel to cut between the rows to form rectangles. Leave to dry for 30 minutes.

5 Bring a large pan of lightly salted water to the boil and cook the tortelli in batches for 4–5 minutes. Drain and place in warmed dishes. Spoon the melted butter over, sprinkle with Parmesan and serve immediately.

Stuffed Conchiglione

This makes an excellent vegetarian main course, but would also be a good choice for a dinner-party starter.

Serves 4
20 dried conchiglione
25g/1oz/2 tbsp butter
1 small onion, finely chopped
275g/10oz fresh spinach leaves, trimmed, washed and shredded
1 garlic clove, crushed
1 sachet of saffron powder
freshly grated nutmeg
250g/9oz/1½ cups ricotta cheese
1 egg
50g/2oz/⅔ cup freshly grated Parmesan cheese
salt and freshly ground black pepper

For the sauce
60ml/4 tbsp olive oil
1 onion, chopped
1 celery stick, chopped
1 carrot, finely chopped
1 garlic clove, sliced
4–5 fresh basil leaves
2 x 400g/14oz cans chopped tomatoes
15ml/1 tbsp tomato purée
90ml/6 tbsp red wine
300ml/½ pint/1 cup Vegetable Stock
105ml/7 tbsp double cream

1 Bring a large pan of lightly salted water to the boil and cook the pasta shells for 10 minutes. Drain the shells, return them to the pan and cover with cold water.

2 Make the sauce. Heat the oil in a heavy-based pan. Add the onion, celery, carrot and garlic, and fry over a medium heat, stirring occasionally, for 10 minutes, until soft.

3 Add the basil, tomatoes, tomato purée and red wine, bring to the boil, then lower the heat and simmer for 45 minutes, until thick and flavoursome.

4 Meanwhile, melt the butter in a pan. Add the onion and cook gently, stirring occasionally, for 10 minutes, until softened.

5 Add the spinach, garlic and saffron, then grate in plenty of nutmeg and stir in salt and pepper to taste. Cook, stirring frequently, for 5–8 minutes, until the spinach is tender.

6 Drain the spinach well, tip it into a bowl and beat in the ricotta and egg. Preheat the oven to 190°C/375°F/Gas 5.

7 Purée the tomato sauce in a food processor, then make it up to 750ml/1¼ pints/3 cups with the stock. Stir in the cream.

8 Spread about half the sauce over the bases of four individual gratin dishes. Drain the pasta shells and fill them with the spinach mixture, using a teaspoon. Arrange five shells in the centre of each dish, spoon the remaining sauce over, then cover with the Parmesan. Bake for 10–12 minutes. Leave to stand for 5 minutes before serving.

Pasta Pie

This is an excellent supper dish, and children absolutely love it.

Serves 4
30ml/2 tbsp olive oil
1 small onion, finely chopped
400g/14oz can chopped tomatoes
15ml/1 tbsp sun-dried tomato purée
5ml/1 tsp dried mixed herbs
5ml/1 tsp dried oregano or basil
5ml/1 tsp granulated sugar
175g/6oz/1½ cups dried conchiglie
30ml/2 tbsp freshly grated Parmesan cheese
30ml/2 tbsp dried breadcrumbs
salt and freshly ground black pepper

For the white sauce
25g/1oz/2 tbsp butter
25g/1oz/¼ cup plain flour
600ml/1 pint/2½ cups milk
1 egg

1 Heat the oil in a large pan and cook the onion until softened. Stir in the tomatoes. Fill the empty can with water and pour it into the pan, then stir in the tomato purée, herbs and sugar.

2 Add salt and pepper to taste, and bring to the boil, stirring. Cover the pan, lower the heat and simmer, stirring occasionally, for 10–15 minutes.

3 Preheat the oven to 190°C/375°F/Gas 5. Bring a pan of lightly salted water to the boil and cook the pasta until it is *al dente*.

4 Meanwhile, make the white sauce. Melt the butter in a pan, add the flour and cook, stirring, for 1 minute. Gradually add the milk, stirring constantly until the sauce boils and thickens.

5 Drain the pasta and tip it into an ovenproof dish. Stir in the tomato sauce. Beat the egg into the white sauce, then pour the sauce over the pasta mixture.

6 Level the surface, sprinkle it with grated Parmesan and breadcrumbs, and bake for 15–20 minutes, or until the topping is golden brown and the cheese is bubbling. Allow to stand for about 10 minutes before serving.

Baked Vegetable Lasagne

Vegetable lasagne became a bit of a cliché when restaurants began catering for vegetarians, but it can be a very tasty dish.

Serves 8

30ml/2 tbsp olive oil
1 medium onion, very finely chopped
500g/1 ¼lb tomatoes, chopped
75g/3oz/6 tbsp butter
675g/1 ½lb/8 cups wild mushrooms, sliced
2 garlic cloves, finely chopped
juice of ½ lemon
12–16 fresh lasagne sheets, precooked if necessary
175g/6oz/2 cups freshly grated Parmesan cheese
salt and freshly ground black pepper

For the white sauce

50g/2oz/ ¼ cup butter
50g/2oz/ ½ cup plain flour
900ml/1 ½ pints/3¾ cups hot milk

1 Preheat the oven to 200°C/400°F/Gas 6. Heat the oil in a pan and sauté the onion until translucent. Add the tomatoes and cook for 6–8 minutes, stirring often. Season and set aside.

2 Heat half the butter in a frying pan and cook the mushrooms until the juices run. Add the garlic, lemon juice and seasoning. Cook until the liquid has almost completely evaporated and the mushrooms are starting to brown. Set aside.

3 Make the white sauce. Melt the butter in a pan, add the flour and cook, stirring, for 1–2 minutes. Gradually add the hot milk, stirring until the sauce boils and thickens.

4 Spread a spoonful of the white sauce over the base of an ovenproof dish and cover it with 3–4 sheets of lasagne. Add a thin layer of mushrooms, then one of white sauce. Sprinkle with a little Parmesan. Make another layer of pasta, spread with a thin layer of the tomato mixture, then add a layer of white sauce. Sprinkle with cheese. Repeat the layers, ending with a layer of pasta thickly coated with white sauce, saving some cheese.

5 Sprinkle with the remaining Parmesan cheese, dot with the remaining butter and bake for 20 minutes, until bubbling.

Leek & Chèvre Lasagne

An unusual and lighter than average lasagne using a soft French goat's cheese.

Serves 6

2 red peppers
1 large aubergine, sliced
30ml/2 tbsp olive oil
3 leeks, thinly sliced
200g/7oz chèvre, broken into pieces
6–8 fresh lasagne sheets, precooked if necessary
50g/2oz/ ⅔ cup freshly grated Parmesan cheese
salt and freshly ground black pepper

For the sauce

50g/2oz/ ¼ cup butter
50g/2oz/ ½ cup plain flour
900ml/1 ½ pints/3¾ cups milk
2.5ml/ ½ tsp ground bay leaves
freshly grated nutmeg
freshly parsley, to garnish

1 Cut the peppers in half and remove the cores and seeds. Place them cut side down in a grill pan, and grill until blistered and beginning to char. Put them in a bowl, cover with several layers of kitchen paper and set aside.

2 Lightly salt the aubergine slices, lay them in a colander to drain for 30 minutes, then rinse and pat dry with kitchen paper.

3 Heat the oil in a large frying pan and fry the leeks gently for about 5 minutes until softened. Add the aubergine slices and fry them until softened. Peel the roasted peppers and slice them into strips.

4 Make the sauce. Melt the butter in a pan, add the flour and cook for 1–2 minutes, stirring constantly. Gradually add the milk, stirring constantly until the sauce boils and thickens. Stir in the bay leaves and add grated nutmeg, salt and pepper to taste.

5 Preheat the oven to 190°C/375°F/Gas 5. Layer the vegetables, chèvre, lasagne sheets and sauce in a large ovenproof dish, making at least two layers of each and ending with a thick layer of the sauce. Sprinkle with the Parmesan and bake for 45 minutes. Leave to stand for 5–10 minutes before serving, cut into slices, garnished with parsley.

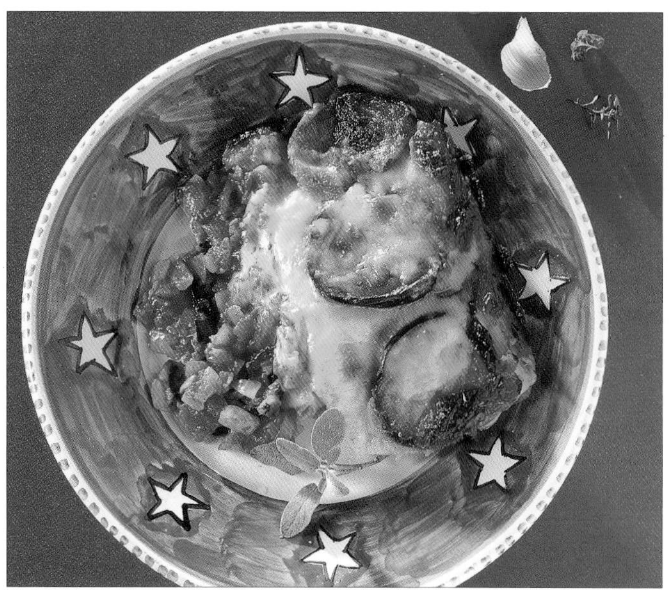

Aubergine Lasagne

Aubergines are very satisfying vegetables and give substance to this tasty bake.

Serves 4

3 medium aubergines, sliced
75ml/5 tbsp olive oil
2 large onions, finely chopped
2 x 400g/14oz cans chopped tomatoes
5ml/1 tsp dried mixed herbs
2–3 garlic cloves, crushed
6 no-precook lasagne sheets
salt and freshly ground black pepper

For the cheese sauce
25g/1oz/2 tbsp butter
25g/1oz/¼ cup plain flour
300ml/ ½ pint/1 ¼ cups milk
2.5ml/ ½ tsp prepared English mustard
115g/4oz/1 cup grated mature Cheddar
15ml/1 tbsp freshly grated Parmesan cheese

1 Layer the aubergine slices in a colander, sprinkling each layer lightly with salt. Leave to stand for 30 minutes, then rinse well and pat dry with kitchen paper.

2 Heat 60ml/4 tbsp of the oil in a large pan, fry the aubergine slices until soft and drain on kitchen paper. Add the remaining oil to the pan, cook the onions for 5 minutes, then stir in the tomatoes, herbs, garlic and seasoning. Bring to the boil, then cover the pan and simmer the mixture for 30 minutes.

3 Meanwhile, make the cheese sauce. Melt the butter in a pan, stir in the flour and cook for 1–2 minutes, stirring constantly. Gradually add the milk, stirring until the sauce boils and thickens. Stir in the mustard, cheeses and seasoning.

4 Preheat the oven to 200°C/400°F/Gas 6. Arrange half the aubergines in the base of a large ovenproof dish and spoon over half the tomato sauce. Arrange three sheets of lasagne on top. Make a second layer in the same way. Spoon over the cheese sauce, cover the dish with foil and bake for 30 minutes. Remove the foil for the last 10 minutes to brown the crust. Leave to stand for 5–10 minutes before serving.

Spinach, Walnut & Gruyère Lasagne

This nutty lasagne introduces a delicious combination of flavours.

Serves 8

45ml/3 tbsp walnut oil
1 large onion, chopped
225g/8oz celeriac, finely chopped
1 large garlic clove, finely chopped
2.5ml/ ½ tsp granulated sugar
115g/4oz/1 cup chopped walnuts
300ml/ ½ pint/1 ¼ cups passata
150ml/ ¼ pint/ ⅔ cup Dubonnet
350g/12oz no-precook spinach lasagne sheets
30ml/2 tbsp chopped fresh basil
salt and freshly ground black pepper

For the spinach sauce
75g/3oz/6 tbsp butter
30ml/2 tbsp walnut oil
1 medium onion, chopped
75g/3oz/ ¾ cup plain flour
5ml/1 tsp dried mustard
1.2 litres/2 pints/5 cups milk
225g/8oz/2 cups grated Gruyère cheese
freshly grated nutmeg
450g/1lb frozen spinach, thawed and puréed

1 Heat the oil in a pan and sauté the onion and celeriac for 8–10 minutes. Add the garlic to the pan and cook for about 1 minute, then add the sugar, walnuts, passata and Dubonnet. Season to taste. Simmer, uncovered, for 25 minutes.

2 Make the spinach sauce. Melt the butter with the oil and cook the onion for 5 minutes. Stir in the flour and cook, stirring, for 1 minute, then add the mustard powder and milk, stirring vigorously until the sauce boils and thickens. Remove from the heat and stir in three-quarters of the Gruyère. Season with salt, pepper and nutmeg. Finally, stir in the spinach.

3 Preheat the oven to 180°C/350°F/Gas 4. Spread a layer of the spinach sauce on the base of a large ovenproof dish. Top with a little walnut and tomato sauce, then add a layer of lasagne sheets. Continue until the dish is full, ending with a layer of either sauce. Sprinkle the remaining Gruyère over the top, followed by the basil. Bake for 45 minutes. Leave to stand for 5–10 minutes before serving.

Mushroom Bolognese

A quick – and exceedingly tasty – vegetarian version of the classic Italian meat dish. Use cultivated or wild mushrooms, or a mixture.

Serves 4

15ml/1 tbsp olive oil
1 onion, chopped
1 garlic clove, crushed
450g/1lb/6 cups mushrooms
15ml/1 tbsp tomato purée
400g/14oz can chopped tomatoes
15ml/1 tbsp chopped fresh oregano, plus extra to garnish
450g/1lb fresh spaghetti
salt and freshly ground black pepper
shavings of Parmesan cheese, to serve

1 Heat the oil in a large, heavy-based pan. Add the chopped onion and garlic, and cook over a medium heat, stirring occasionally, for 2–3 minutes.

2 Meanwhile, trim the mushroom stems neatly, then cut each mushroom into quarters. Add the mushrooms to the pan and cook over a high heat for 3–4 minutes, stirring occasionally.

3 Stir in the tomato purée, chopped tomatoes and oregano. Lower the heat, cover and cook for 5 minutes.

4 Meanwhile, bring a large pan of lightly salted water to the boil and cook the pasta until *al dente*.

5 Season the mushroom sauce with salt and pepper to taste. Drain the pasta, tip it into a bowl and add the mushroom mixture. Toss thoroughly to mix. Serve in warmed bowls, topped with shavings of Parmesan and a sprinkling of extra chopped fresh oregano.

Cook's Tip
If you prefer to use dried pasta, make this the first thing that you cook. It will take 10–12 minutes, during which time you can make the mushroom mixture. Use 350g/12oz dried pasta.

Tagliatelle with Mushrooms

This is a lovely, moist dish with loads of flavour. It is also pleasingly low in fat.

Serves 4

1 small onion, finely chopped
2 garlic cloves, crushed
150ml/ ¼ pint/ ⅔ cup Vegetable Stock, preferably home-made
225g/8oz/3 cups mixed fresh mushrooms, such as field, chestnut, oyster or chanterelles, quartered
60ml/4 tbsp white or red wine
10ml/2 tsp tomato purée
15ml/1 tbsp soy sauce
225g/8oz fresh sun-dried tomato and herb tagliatelle
5ml/1 tsp chopped fresh thyme
30ml/2 tbsp chopped fresh parsley
salt and freshly ground black pepper
shavings of Parmesan cheese, to serve (optional)

1 Put the onion and garlic into a pan with the stock. Cover and cook over a medium heat for 5 minutes, or until tender.

2 Stir in the mushrooms, wine, tomato purée and soy sauce. Cover and cook for 5 minutes.

3 Remove the lid from the pan and increase the heat. Bring to the boil and boil until the liquid has reduced by half. Season with salt and pepper to taste.

4 Meanwhile, bring a large pan of lightly salted water to the boil and cook the pasta until it is *al dente*.

5 Drain the pasta, return it to the clean pan and toss lightly with the mushroom mixture and chopped herbs. Serve at once, with shavings of Parmesan cheese, if you like.

Cook's Tip
Mushrooms are best eaten as fresh as possible, as they do not store well and quickly lose their texture. Cultivated varieties will keep in the fridge for up to three days; wild mushrooms for one to two days. Never store them in a plastic bag.

Tagliatelle with Chanterelles

Simplicity is the key to the success of this attractive and sophisticated dish.

Serves 4

about 50g/2oz/ ¼ cup butter
225–350g/8–12oz/3–4 cups chanterelle mushrooms
15ml/1 tbsp plain flour
150ml/ ¼ pint/ ⅔ cup milk
90ml/6 tbsp crème fraîche
15ml/1 tbsp chopped fresh parsley
275g/10oz fresh tagliatelle
salt and freshly ground black pepper

1 Melt 40g/1½ oz/3 tbsp of the butter in a large, heavy-based frying pan. Add the mushrooms and fry for about 2–3 minutes over a gentle heat until the juices begin to run, then increase the heat and cook until the liquid has almost evaporated. Using a slotted spoon, transfer the mushrooms to a bowl.

2 Stir the flour into the liquid remaining in the pan, adding a little more butter if necessary. Cook, stirring constantly, for about 1 minute and then gradually add the milk, stirring until the sauce boils and thickens.

3 Stir in the crème fraîche and parsley, and return the mushrooms to the pan. Season with salt and pepper to taste, and stir well. Leave over the lowest possible heat while you cook the pasta.

4 Bring a large pan of lightly salted water to the boil and cook the pasta until it is *al dente*.

5 Drain well, return to the clean pan and pour over the mushroom sauce. Toss lightly and serve on warmed plates.

Cook's Tip
It is important to clean chanterelles thoroughly. Brush gently with a soft brush, then hold each one by the stalk and let cold water run under the gills to dislodge hidden grit and dirt. Shake gently to dry.

Tortellini with Mushroom & Cheese Sauce

A rich sauce of mushrooms and three cheeses coats mouthwatering filled pasta.

Serves 4

450g/1lb ricotta-and-spinach-filled tortellini
50g/2oz/ ¼ cup butter
2 garlic cloves, chopped
225g/8oz/3 cups field or button mushrooms, sliced
15ml/1 tbsp plain flour
175ml/6fl oz/ ¾ cup milk
50g/2oz/⅔ cup freshly grated Parmesan cheese
50g/2oz/ ½ cup grated Fontina cheese
115g/4oz/ ⅔ cup ricotta cheese
60ml/4 tbsp single cream
30ml/2 tbsp snipped fresh chives
salt and freshly ground black pepper

1 Bring a large pan of lightly salted water to the boil and cook the tortellini until they are *al dente*.

2 Melt the butter in a large, heavy-based frying pan, and fry the garlic and mushrooms for about 5 minutes until browned. Using a slotted spoon, remove the mushrooms from the pan and place them in a bowl.

3 Add the flour to the butter remaining in the frying pan, and cook, stirring constantly, for 1 minute. Gradually add the milk, stirring constantly, until the sauce boils and thickens.

4 Stir in the Parmesan, Fontina and ricotta cheeses, and heat gently until they have melted into the sauce. Return the mushrooms to the sauce and stir in the cream and chives. Season with salt and pepper to taste.

5 Drain the pasta and tip it into a large serving bowl. Pour over the sauce and toss gently to coat. Serve immediately.

Cook's Tip
You can use either plain or spinach-flavoured tortellini.

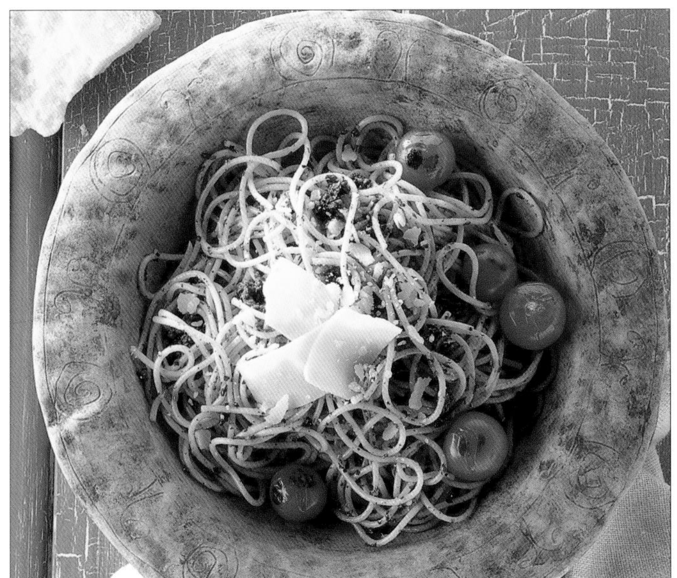

Spaghetti with Black Olive & Mushroom Sauce

Spaghetti gets star treatment, thanks to a rich pungent sauce topped with sweet cherry tomatoes.

Serves 4

15ml/1 tbsp olive oil
1 garlic clove, chopped
225g/8oz/3 cups mushrooms, chopped
150g/5oz/1¼ cups stoned black olives, roughly chopped
30ml/2 tbsp chopped fresh parsley
1 fresh red chilli, seeded and chopped
225g/8oz cherry tomatoes
450g/1lb dried spaghetti
slivers of Parmesan cheese, to serve

1 Heat the olive oil in a large, heavy-based saucepan. Add the garlic and cook, stirring occasionally, for 1 minute over a low heat. Increase the heat slightly, stir in the mushrooms, cover and cook for 5 minutes.

2 Tip the mushroom mixture into a blender or food processor and add the olives, parsley and red chilli. Process the mixture until smooth.

3 Heat an ungreased frying pan and add the cherry tomatoes. Shake the pan gently until the tomato skins start to split. Lower the heat to the lowest setting to keep the tomatoes hot while you cook the pasta.

4 Bring a large pan of lightly salted water to the boil and cook the pasta until it is *al dente*.

5 Drain the pasta, return it to the pan and add the olive mixture. Toss over the heat until the pasta is coated and the sauce is hot. Serve on warmed plates, topped with the tomatoes and garnished with slivers of Parmesan.

Spaghetti with Mixed Mushroom & Basil Sauce

Taking its inspiration from Stroganoff, this mushroom and soured cream sauce is very good with spaghetti.

Serves 4

50g/2oz/¼ cup butter
1 onion, chopped
350g/12oz/5 cups mixed mushrooms, such as brown, flat and button, sliced
1 garlic clove, chopped
350g/12oz dried spaghetti
300ml/½ pint/1¼ cups soured cream
30ml/2 tbsp chopped fresh basil
50g/2oz/⅔ cup freshly grated Parmesan cheese, plus extra to serve
salt and freshly ground black pepper
torn flat leaf parsley, to garnish

1 Melt the butter in a large, heavy-based frying pan. Add the onion and fry over a low heat, stirring occasionally, for about 10 minutes, until softened.

2 Add the mushrooms and garlic to the pan and fry, stirring occasionally, for 10 minutes, until softened.

3 Meanwhile, bring a large pan of lightly salted water to the boil and cook the pasta until *al dente*.

4 Stir the soured cream into the mushroom mixture, with the basil and Parmesan. Season with plenty of salt and pepper, cover and heat through.

5 Drain the pasta and tip it into a warmed serving bowl. Add the mushroom and basil sauce, and toss thoroughly to mix. Garnish with the flat leaf parsley. Serve immediately with plenty of Parmesan cheese.

Variation
Tarragon also complements mushrooms. As it is very pungent, use only 15ml/1 tbsp chopped fresh tarragon.

Mushroom & Chilli Carbonara

Dried porcini mushrooms intensify the flavour of this simple dish, while chilli flakes add a spicy undertone.

Serves 4

15g/½oz dried porcini mushrooms
300ml/ ½ pint/1¼ cups hot water
225g/8oz dried spaghetti
25g/1oz/2 tbsp butter
15ml/1 tbsp olive oil
1 garlic clove, crushed
225g/8oz/3 cups button or chestnut mushrooms, sliced
5ml/1 tsp dried chilli flakes
2 eggs
300ml/ ½ pint/1¼ cups single cream
salt and freshly ground black pepper
freshly grated Parmesan cheese and chopped fresh parsley, to garnish

1 Put the dried mushrooms in a bowl. Add the hot water and soak for 15 minutes, then drain and reserve the soaking liquid.

2 Bring a large pan of lightly salted water to the boil and cook the spaghetti until it is *al dente*. Drain, rinse under cold water and drain again.

3 Melt the butter in the olive oil in a large, heavy-based saucepan and sauté the garlic for 30 seconds. Add the mushrooms, including the drained porcini, and the dried chilli flakes, and stir well. Cook over a medium heat for about 2 minutes, stirring occasionally.

4 Increase the heat. Pour in the reserved mushroom soaking liquid, bring to the boil and cook over a high heat until the mushroom liquid has reduced slightly.

5 Beat the eggs and cream in a bowl and season well. Add the cooked spaghetti to the mushroom mixture in the pan and heat through.

6 Add the egg mixture and toss over the heat for just long enough to cook it lightly and coat the pasta. Serve in warmed bowls, sprinkled with the Parmesan and parsley.

Pasta & Wild Mushroom Mould

A crisp crumb coating contrasts beautifully with the tender pasta and mushrooms in this bake.

Serves 4–6

600ml/1 pint/2½ cups milk
1 bay leaf
1 small onion stuck with 6 cloves
15g/ ½ oz dried porcini mushrooms
300ml/ ½ pint/1¼ cups hot water
200g/7oz/1¾ cups dried pasta shapes
50g/2oz/ ¼ cup butter
45ml/3 tbsp fresh white breadcrumbs
10ml/2 tsp dried mixed herbs
40g/1½oz/ ⅓ cup plain flour
60ml/4 tbsp freshly grated Parmesan cheese
freshly grated nutmeg
2 eggs, beaten
30ml/2 tbsp olive oil
350g/12oz/4 cups button mushrooms, sliced
2 garlic cloves, crushed
30ml/2 tbsp chopped fresh parsley
salt and freshly ground black pepper

1 Pour the milk into a pan, and add the bay leaf and clove-studded onion. Bring to just below the boil, then remove the pan from the heat and set aside for 15 minutes.

2 Meanwhile, put the porcini mushrooms in a second bowl, pour over the hot water and soak for 15 minutes.

3 Meanwhile, bring a large pan of lightly salted water to the boil and cook the pasta until it is *al dente*.

4 Melt the butter in a saucepan over a low heat and use a little to brush the inside of a large oval pie dish. Mix the breadcrumbs and dried mixed herbs together, and use them to coat the inside of the dish.

5 Remove the onion and bay leaf from the milk and discard. Stir the flour into the remaining melted butter, cook over a low heat, stirring constantly, for 1 minute, then gradually add the milk, stirring constantly until the sauce boils and thickens.

6 Stir the cheese into the sauce, and season with nutmeg, salt and pepper to taste. Drain the pasta and stir it into the sauce. Cool for 5 minutes, then beat in the eggs.

7 Drain the porcini, reserving the soaking liquid. Heat the oil in a pan and fry the porcini, button mushrooms and garlic over a medium heat, stirring occasionally, for about 3 minutes. Season with salt and pepper to taste, stir in the reserved soaking liquid and cook over a high heat until it has reduced a little. Stir in the chopped parsley.

8 Preheat the oven to 190°C/375°F/Gas 5. Spoon a layer of the pasta mixture into the crumb-coated dish. Sprinkle over a thin layer of the mushrooms. Repeat the layers until all the ingredients are used up, finishing with a layer of the pasta mixture. Cover with a sheet of greased foil and transfer to the oven. Bake for 30 minutes. Allow to stand for 5 minutes before turning out to serve.

Pasta with Mushrooms & Sun-dried Tomatoes

Served with warm ciabatta, this makes an excellent vegetarian supper dish.

Serves 4

15g/½oz dried porcini mushrooms
175ml/6fl oz/¾ cup hot water
45ml/3 tbsp olive oil
2 garlic cloves, finely chopped
a handful of fresh flat leaf parsley, roughly chopped
2 large pieces sun-dried tomato in olive oil, drained and sliced into thin strips
120ml/4fl oz/½ cup dry white wine
225g/8oz/3 cups chestnut mushrooms, thinly sliced
475ml/16fl oz/2 cups Vegetable Stock
450g/1lb/4 cups dried short pasta shapes
salt and freshly ground black pepper
rocket and fresh flat leaf parsley, to garnish

1 Put the porcini mushrooms in a bowl, pour the hot water over and soak for 15 minutes. Tip into a sieve set over a bowl and squeeze the porcini to release as much liquid as possible. Reserve the strained soaking liquid. Chop the porcini finely.

2 Heat the oil in a frying pan and cook the garlic, parsley, sun-dried tomato strips and porcini over a low heat, stirring frequently, for about 5 minutes. Stir in the wine, simmer for a few minutes until reduced, then add the chestnut mushrooms. Pour in the stock and simmer for 15–20 minutes more until the liquid has reduced and the sauce is quite thick and rich.

3 Meanwhile, bring a large pan of lightly salted water to the boil and cook the pasta shapes until they are *al dente*.

4 Taste the mushroom sauce for seasoning. Drain the pasta, reserving a little of the cooking liquid, and tip it into a warmed large bowl. Add the mushroom sauce and toss well, thinning the sauce if necessary with some of the pasta cooking water. Serve immediately, sprinkled with chopped rocket and parsley.

Fusilli with Wild Mushrooms & Herbs

A very rich dish with an earthy flavour and lots of garlic, this makes an ideal main course, especially if it is followed by a crisp green salad of mixed leaves.

Serves 4

½ x 275g/10oz jar wild mushrooms in olive oil
25g/1oz/2 tbsp butter
225g/8oz/3 cups fresh wild mushrooms, sliced if large
5ml/1 tsp finely chopped fresh thyme
5ml/1 tsp finely chopped fresh marjoram or oregano, plus extra herbs to serve
4 garlic cloves, crushed
350g/12oz/3 cups fresh or dried fusilli
200ml/7fl oz/scant 1 cup double cream
salt and freshly ground black pepper

1 Drain about 15ml/1 tbsp of the oil from the bottled mushrooms into a medium saucepan. Slice or chop the fresh mushrooms into bite-size pieces, if they are large.

2 Add the butter to the oil in the pan and heat until sizzling. Add the bottled and fresh mushrooms, thyme, marjoram or oregano and garlic, and season with salt and pepper to taste. Simmer, stirring frequently, for 10 minutes, or until the fresh mushrooms are soft and tender.

3 Meanwhile, bring a large pan of lightly salted water to the boil and cook the fusilli until they are *al dente*.

4 As soon as the mushrooms are cooked, increase the heat to high and toss the mixture with a wooden spoon to drive off any excess liquid. Pour in the double cream and bring to the boil, stirring constantly, then taste and add more salt and pepper if necessary.

5 Drain the pasta and tip it into a warmed bowl. Pour the sauce over and toss well. Serve immediately, sprinkled with extra fresh marjoram or oregano leaves.

Tagliarini with White Truffle

There is nothing quite like the fragrance and flavour of the Italian white truffle. This simple style of serving it is one of the best ways to enjoy it.

Serves 4
350g/12oz fresh tagliarini
75g/3oz/6 tbsp unsalted butter, diced
60ml/4 tbsp freshly grated Parmesan cheese
freshly grated nutmeg
1 small white truffle, about 25–40g/1–1½ oz
salt and freshly ground black pepper

1 Bring a large pan of lightly salted water to the boil and cook the pasta until it is *al dente*.

2 Drain the pasta thoroughly and tip it into a warmed large bowl. Add the diced butter and grated Parmesan. Grate in a little nutmeg, and add salt and pepper to taste. Toss well until the pasta is coated in melted butter and cheese.

3 Divide the pasta equally among four warmed bowls and carefully shave paper-thin slivers of the white truffle on top. Serve immediately.

Cook's Tip
White Italian truffles can be bought during the months of September and October from specialist food shops and delicatessens. They are very expensive, however, and there are some alternative ways of getting the flavour of truffles without the expense. Some Italian delicatessens sell "truffle cheese", which is a mountain of cheese with shavings of truffle in it, and this can be used instead of the Parmesan and fresh truffle in this recipe. Another alternative is to toss hot pasta in truffle oil and serve it with freshly grated Parmesan. Canned and bottled truffles and – a less expensive alternative – truffle pieces are also available. Use the oil to flavour egg or rice dishes.

Cheat's Lasagne with Mixed Mushrooms

This vegetarian version of lasagne requires neither baking nor the preparation of various sauces and fillings.

Serves 4
40g/1½ oz/⅔ cup dried porcini mushrooms
60ml/4 tbsp olive oil
1 large garlic clove, chopped
375g/13oz/5 cups mixed mushrooms, including brown cap, field, shiitake and wild varieties, roughly sliced
175ml/6fl oz/¾ cup dry white wine
90ml/6 tbsp canned chopped tomatoes
2.5ml/½ tsp granulated sugar
8 fresh lasagne sheets
40g/1½ oz/½ cup freshly grated Parmesan cheese
salt and freshly ground black pepper
fresh basil leaves, to garnish

1 Place the porcini in a bowl and cover with boiling water. Leave to soak for 15 minutes, then drain and rinse.

2 Heat the oil in a large, heavy-based frying pan and sauté the porcini over a high heat for 5 minutes until the edges are just crisp. Reduce the heat, add the garlic and fresh mushrooms. Sauté for 5 minutes more, until tender, stirring occasionally.

3 Add the wine and cook for 5–7 minutes until reduced. Stir in the tomatoes, sugar and seasoning and cook over a medium heat for about 5 minutes, until thickened.

4 Meanwhile, bring a large pan of lightly salted water to the boil and cook the lasagne until it is *al dente*. Drain.

5 To serve, spoon a little of the mushroom sauce on to each of four warm serving plates. Place a sheet of lasagne on top and spoon a quarter of the remaining mushroom sauce over each serving. Sprinkle with some Parmesan and top with another pasta sheet. Sprinkle with black pepper and the remaining Parmesan, and garnish with the basil leaves.

Pasta with Courgette & Walnut Sauce

For the best flavour, use the youngest, freshest courgettes you can find for this tasty dish, preferably ones from your own garden.

Serves 4

65g/2½ oz/5 tbsp butter
1 large Spanish-type onion, halved and thinly sliced
450g/1lb courgettes, very thinly sliced
350g/12oz dried short pasta shapes such as penne or fusilli
50g/2oz/ ½ cup walnuts, coarsely chopped
45ml/3 tbsp chopped fresh parsley
30ml/2 tbsp single cream
salt and freshly ground black pepper
freshly grated Parmesan cheese, to serve

1 Melt the butter in a frying pan. Add the onion, cover and cook over a low heat for 5 minutes, then add the courgettes.

2 Stir well, cover again and continue to cook over a low heat until the vegetables are very soft, stirring occasionally.

3 Meanwhile, bring a large pan of lightly salted water to the boil and cook the pasta until it is *al dente*.

4 While the pasta is cooking, add the walnuts, parsley and cream to the courgette mixture and stir well. Season with salt and pepper to taste.

5 Drain the pasta and return it to the clean pan. Add the courgette sauce and mix well. Serve in warmed bowls, with freshly grated Parmesan to sprinkle on top of each portion.

Cook's Tip

The onions and courgettes should not be fried, but rather "sweated" in the butter. A gentle heat is used and, because there is a lid on the pan, the technique resembles steaming.

Penne with Broccoli & Pecans

This sauce is absolutely delicious with pasta and can also be spread on slices of fresh or grilled ciabatta.

Serves 4

275g/10oz/2½ cups dried penne
450g/1lb fresh broccoli, cut into equal-size florets

For the sauce

50g/2oz/ ½ cup pecan nuts
30ml/2 tbsp fresh brown breadcrumbs
75g/3oz/1½ cups roughly chopped fresh parsley
120ml/4fl oz/ ½ cup extra virgin olive oil
30ml/2 tbsp single cream
salt and freshly ground black pepper

1 First make the sauce. Place the pecans, breadcrumbs and parsley in a blender or food processor and process for 20 seconds. With the motor running, gradually add the olive oil through the lid or feeder tube to make a slightly textured paste. Add the cream, season with salt and pepper to taste, and process briefly to mix.

2 Bring a large pan of lightly salted water to the boil and cook the pasta until it is *al dente*.

3 Steam the broccoli florets for about 3 minutes, until they are tender but retain a little crunch.

4 Drain the pasta, place in a bowl and mix with the broccoli. Spoon on to warmed serving plates and pour the sauce over.

Variation

You can substitute hazelnuts for the pecans. Roast them first by spreading them out on a grill pan and placing them under a medium heat until they are golden. Shake the pan from time to time and watch them closely, because they burn readily. Let them cool slightly, then tip them into a clean dish towel and rub off the skins before using them in the sauce. Serve with spirali instead of penne.

Farfalle with Fennel & Walnut Sauce

A scrumptious blend of walnuts and crisp steamed fennel, this always goes down well.

Serves 4

75g/3oz/¾ cup walnuts
1 garlic clove
25g/1oz/1 cup fresh flat leaf parsley, stalks removed
115g/4oz/½ cup ricotta cheese
450g/1lb dried farfalle
450g/1lb fennel bulbs, trimmed and thinly sliced
chopped walnuts, to garnish

1 Place the walnuts, garlic and parsley in a food processor. Pulse until roughly chopped. Transfer to a bowl and stir in the ricotta.

2 Bring a large pan of lightly salted water to the boil and cook the pasta until it is *al dente*.

3 Meanwhile, steam the fennel for 4–5 minutes, until just tender but still crisp.

4 Drain the pasta, return it to the clean pan, and add the walnut mixture and the fennel. Toss well and sprinkle with the extra chopped walnuts. Serve immediately.

Cook's Tip
When preparing the fennel, cut off and reserve the feathery fronds. Use them as an extra garnish, if you like.

Variation
As they have a special affinity with fennel, you could substitute pistachio nuts for the walnuts.

Tagliatelle with Olive & Pecan Sauce

This is an unusual sauce that would make this dish a spectacular first course at a dinner party.

Serves 4–6

2 thick slices wholemeal bread
300ml/½ pint/1¼ cups milk
275g/10oz/2½ cups pecan nuts
115g/4oz/1 cup stoned black olives
1 garlic clove, crushed
50g/2oz/⅔ cup freshly grated Parmesan cheese
90ml/6 tbsp olive oil, plus extra for tossing the pasta
150ml/¼ pint/⅔ cup double cream
450g/1lb fresh or dried tagliatelle
30ml/2 tbsp chopped fresh parsley
salt and freshly ground black pepper

1 Preheat the oven to 190°C/375°F/Gas 5. Cut the crusts off the bread. Put the slices in a shallow bowl and pour over the milk. Leave to soak until all the milk is absorbed.

2 Spread the pecans on a baking sheet and toast in the oven for 5 minutes. Leave to cool.

3 Place the soaked bread, pecans, olives, garlic, Parmesan and olive oil in a food processor and blend until smooth. Season to taste with salt and pepper. Add the cream and process briefly again to mix.

4 Bring a large pan of lightly salted water to the boil and cook the pasta until it is *al dente*. Drain well and toss with a little olive oil. Divide the pasta equally among individual bowls and place a generous spoonful of sauce on each portion. Sprinkle with chopped parsley and serve immediately.

Variation
Pecans tend to be rather expensive. For economy, substitute walnut pieces.

Pasta with Nut & Cream Sauce

Based on a classic Italian recipe, this has a strong, nutty flavour, and should be accompanied by a salad of dressed leaves.

Serves 4

50g/2oz/ ½ cup walnut pieces
50g/2oz/ ½ cup hazelnuts
350g/12oz dried fusilli lunghi or spaghetti
25g/1oz/2 tbsp butter
300ml/ ½ pint/1¼ cups single cream
50g/2oz/1 cup fresh white breadcrumbs
25g/1oz/ ⅓ cup freshly grated Parmesan cheese
pinch of freshly grated nutmeg
salt and freshly ground black pepper
fresh rosemary sprigs, to garnish

1 Preheat the grill. Spread the walnuts and hazelnuts in an even layer in the grill pan and place under a medium heat for about 5 minutes, shaking the pan occasionally, until they are evenly toasted and golden.

2 Let the nuts cool slightly, tip them into a clean dish towel and rub off the skins. Chop the nuts roughly and set them aside.

3 Bring a large pan of lightly salted water to the boil and cook the pasta until it is *al dente*.

4 Meanwhile, heat the butter and cream in a saucepan until the butter is melted. Stir in the breadcrumbs and nuts, and heat gently, stirring constantly, for 2 minutes, until thickened. Add the Parmesan, nutmeg and seasoning to taste. Stir over a low heat until the cheese has melted.

5 Drain the pasta thoroughly and tip it into a bowl. Add the sauce and toss to coat. Serve immediately, garnished with the fresh rosemary.

Variation
Try using different cheeses in the walnut sauce. Gorgonzola or Roquefort could be used instead of Parmesan, or even Stilton.

Macaroni with Hazelnut & Coriander Sauce

This is a very simple recipe. The reason it works so well is because the warm, earthy flavour of the nuts is balanced by the exotic taste of the coriander.

Serves 4

50g/2oz/ ½ cup hazelnuts
350g/12oz short-cut macaroni
2 garlic cloves, halved
1 bunch fresh coriander
90ml/6 tbsp olive oil
salt and freshly ground black pepper
fresh coriander sprigs, to garnish

1 Preheat the grill. Spread out the hazelnuts in the grill pan and place them under a medium heat, shaking the pan occasionally, for 5 minutes, or until toasted and golden.

2 Let the hazelnuts cool slightly, then tip them into a clean dish towel and rub off the skins.

3 Bring a large pan of lightly salted water to the boil and cook the macaroni until it is *al dente*.

4 Meanwhile, put the nuts in a food processor and chop them finely, then add the garlic, coriander and 5ml/1 tsp salt. Process until the coriander is chopped, then, with the motor running, gradually add 75ml/5 tbsp of the oil through the feeder tube, until the mixture forms a thick sauce. Season with salt and pepper to taste.

5 Heat the remaining olive oil in a saucepan and add the sauce. Fry very gently, stirring all the time, for about 1 minute, until heated through.

6 Drain the pasta thoroughly and stir it into the sauce. Toss well to coat. Serve immediately, garnished with fresh coriander.

Butter Bean & Pesto Pasta

Buy good quality, ready-made pesto, rather than making your own. Pesto forms the basis of several very tasty sauces, and it is especially delicious with butter beans.

Serves 4

225g/8oz/2 cups dried pasta shapes, preferably mixed colours
400g/14oz can butter beans, drained
45ml/3 tbsp pesto
150ml/ 1/4 pint/ 2/3 cup single cream
30ml/2 tbsp extra virgin olive oil
freshly grated nutmeg

To serve

45ml/3 tbsp pine nuts
sprigs of fresh basil
freshly grated Parmesan cheese (optional)

1 Bring a large pan of lightly salted water to the boil and cook the pasta until it is *al dente*.

2 Meanwhile, put the beans in a saucepan, and stir in the pesto and cream. Heat gently, stirring occasionally, until the mixture simmers. Stir in 15–30ml/1–2 tbsp of the pasta cooking water to thin the sauce if necessary.

3 Drain the pasta and return it to the clean pan. Toss with the olive oil. Grate in a little nutmeg, then add the bean mixture and toss until well mixed.

4 Serve in warmed bowls, topped with the pine nuts and garnished with the basil sprigs. Offer grated Parmesan cheese for sprinkling, if you like.

Variations

- *Other beans may be used instead of the butter beans. Borlotti or cannellini would work well.*
- *For a change of flavour, use red pesto, made with sun-dried tomatoes, rather than traditional basil pesto.*

Fusilli with Lentil & Cheese Sauce

Lentils make a good sauce for pasta, with plenty of body and flavour. This is a delicious and filling supper dish, ideal for winter nights.

Serves 4

75g/2 1/2 oz/ 1/3 cup green lentils
15ml/1 tbsp olive oil
1 onion, chopped
1 garlic clove, chopped
1 carrot, cut into matchsticks
350g/12oz/3 cups dried fusilli
15ml/1 tbsp tomato purée
15ml/1 tbsp chopped fresh oregano
150ml/ 1/4 pint/ 2/3 cup Vegetable Stock
225g/8oz/2 cups grated Cheddar cheese, plus extra to serve
salt and freshly ground black pepper

1 Pick over the lentils. Put them in a pan with cold water to cover generously. Bring to the boil and cook for 25–30 minutes, until tender. Drain and set aside.

2 Heat the oil in a large frying pan, and fry the onion and garlic over a medium heat, stirring occasionally, for 3 minutes. Add the carrot and cook for a further 5 minutes.

3 Bring a pan of lightly salted water to the boil and cook the pasta until it is *al dente*.

4 Meanwhile, stir the lentils, tomato purée and oregano into the vegetable mixture, cover and cook for 2 minutes.

5 Stir in the stock, and season with salt and pepper to taste. Cover and simmer for 10 minutes. Stir in the cheese.

6 Drain the pasta thoroughly and stir it into the sauce to coat. Serve in warmed bowls, and hand round plenty of extra grated cheese separately.

Cook's Tip

Many vegetarians swear that adding a little yeast extract to lentils brings out their flavour. Try it and see.

Lasagne Rolls

Perhaps this dish has a more elegant presentation than ordinary vegetarian lasagne, but it is just as tasty.

Serves 4

8–10 fresh lasagne sheets
225g/8oz fresh spinach
115g/4oz/1¾ cups mushrooms, sliced
Lentil Bolognese
115g/4oz mozzarella cheese, thinly sliced
freshly grated Parmesan cheese, to serve

For the sauce

40g/1½ oz/⅓ cup plain flour
40g/1½ oz/3 tbsp butter
600ml/1 pint/2½ cups milk
freshly grated nutmeg
salt and freshly ground black pepper

1 Bring a large pan of lightly salted water to the boil and cook the lasagne until it is *al dente*. Drain and allow to cool.

2 Cook the spinach, in just the water clinging to the leaves after washing, for 2 minutes over a low heat. Add the sliced mushrooms and cook, stirring occasionally, for a further 2 minutes. Drain very well, pressing out all the excess moisture, and chop roughly.

3 Lay out the pasta sheets and spread with the lentil bolognese, spinach, mushrooms and mozzarella slices. Roll up each one and place in a single layer in a large ovenproof dish with the join down.

4 To make the sauce, put the flour, butter and milk into a saucepan and gradually bring to the boil, stirring continuously until the sauce is thick and smooth. Lower the heat. Simmer for 2 minutes, then season with salt and pepper, and stir in grated nutmeg to taste.

5 Preheat the grill. Pour the sauce over the pasta, sprinkle over the Parmesan and brown under the grill. Serve immediately.

Spirali with Soured Cream Sauce

Entertaining unexpected guests need never be a problem while you have easy recipes such as this one at your command.

Serves 4

350g/12oz/3 cups dried spirali
25g/1oz/2 tbsp butter
1 onion, chopped
1 garlic clove, chopped
15ml/1 tbsp chopped fresh oregano
300ml/½ pint/1¼ cups soured cream
75g/3oz/¾ cup grated mozzarella cheese
75g/3oz/¾ cup grated Bel Paese cheese
5 sun-dried tomatoes in oil, drained and sliced
salt and freshly ground black pepper

1 Bring a large pan of lightly salted water to the boil and cook the pasta until it is *al dente*.

2 Meanwhile, melt the butter in a large frying pan and fry the onion over a medium heat, stirring frequently, for 8 minutes, until softened. Add the garlic and cook for 1 minute.

3 Stir in the oregano and soured cream, and heat gently until almost boiling. Stir in the mozzarella and Bel Paese, and heat gently, stirring occasionally, until the cheeses have melted. Add the sliced sun-dried tomatoes and season to taste.

4 Drain the pasta and tip it into a serving bowl. Pour over the sauce and toss well to coat. Serve immediately.

Variation

Use leeks, shallots or an Italian white onion instead of an ordinary brown onion.

Lentil Bolognese

This is a really useful, tasty and nutritious sauce to serve with pasta.

Serves 6

45ml/3 tbsp olive oil
1 onion, chopped
2 garlic cloves, crushed
2 carrots, coarsely grated
2 celery sticks, chopped
115g/4oz/⅔ cup red lentils
115g/4oz can chopped tomatoes
30ml/2 tbsp tomato purée
450ml/¾ pint/scant 2 cups stock
15ml/1 tbsp fresh marjoram, chopped, or 5ml/1 tsp dried marjoram
salt and black pepper

1 Heat the olive oil in a large, heavy-based pan. Add the onion, garlic, carrots and celery, and fry over a low heat, stirring occasionally, until soft.

2 Stir in the lentils, tomatoes, tomato purée, stock and marjoram, season to taste, and bring to the boil. Lower the heat, then simmer for 20 minutes until thick.

Fettuccine all'Alfredo

A classic dish from Rome, Fettuccine all'Alfredo is simply pasta tossed with double cream, butter and freshly grated Parmesan cheese. It is incredibly quick and simple, perfect for a midweek supper.

Serves 4

450g/1lb dried fettuccine
25g/1oz/2 tbsp butter
200ml/7fl oz/scant 1 cup double cream
50g/2oz/ ⅔ cup freshly grated Parmesan cheese, plus extra to serve
freshly grated nutmeg
salt and freshly ground black pepper
fresh dill sprigs or chopped fresh flat leaf parsley to garnish

1 Bring a large pan of lightly salted water to the boil and cook the pasta. Allow slightly less time than usual; it should be almost *al dente*, but still slightly firm.

2 Meanwhile, melt the butter with 150ml/ ¼ pint/ ⅔ cup of the cream in a heavy-based saucepan. Bring to the boil, then lower the heat and simmer for 1 minute, until slightly thickened. Leave over the lowest possible heat.

3 Drain the pasta very well and add it to the cream sauce. Keeping the heat low, toss the pasta in the sauce.

4 Add the remaining cream with the Parmesan, and season with salt and pepper to taste. Grate in a little nutmeg. Toss until well coated and heated through. Serve immediately, garnished with dill or parsley and with extra freshly grated Parmesan.

Cook's Tip
While fettuccine is traditional, this sauce also goes well with tagliatelle. Pasta shapes, such as penne, rigatoni or farfalle, are also suitable.

Creamy Pasta with Parmesan Curls

Several perfectly formed curls of Parmesan give a plate of creamy pasta a lift.

Serves 4–6

250g/9oz/2¼ cups dried campanelle
250g/9oz tub mascarpone cheese
200ml/7fl oz/scant 1 cup crème fraîche
75g/3oz/1 cup freshly grated Parmesan cheese
115g/4oz/2 cups sun-dried tomatoes in oil, drained and thinly sliced
salt and freshly ground black pepper

To garnish
1 piece of Parmesan cheese, about 175g/6oz

1 Unless you are an old hand at making Parmesan curls, do this first, before cooking the pasta. Holding a swivel-blade vegetable peeler at a 45° angle, draw it steadily across the block of Parmesan cheese to form a curl. Make several curls, depending on the number of guests being served.

2 Bring a large pan of lightly salted water to the boil and cook the pasta until it is *al dente*.

3 Meanwhile, put the mascarpone and crème fraîche in a second saucepan and heat gently until the mascarpone has melted. Add the Parmesan and sun-dried tomatoes, and cook over a low heat for 5 minutes. Season with plenty of black pepper and a little salt.

4 Drain the pasta, return it to the clean pan and pour the sauce over. Toss to mix thoroughly. Serve immediately on warmed individual plates, adding a few Parmesan curls to garnish each portion.

Cook's Tip
Mascarpone is a very rich cheese, containing 90 per cent fat. A lighter version, called fiorello light, is now being made. While this is suitable for the health-conscious on a low-fat diet, it is not so delicious as the genuine article.

Spaghetti with Feta

We tend to think of pasta as being essentially Italian, but Greeks love it too, especially with feta and tomatoes.

Serves 2–3
115g/4oz dried spaghetti
30ml/2 tbsp extra virgin olive oil
1 garlic clove
8 cherry tomatoes, halved
a little freshly grated nutmeg
75g/3oz feta cheese, crumbled
15ml/1 tbsp chopped fresh basil
a few black olives, to serve

1 Bring a large pan of lightly salted water to the boil and cook the pasta until it is *al dente*. Drain it in a colander.

2 Heat the olive oil in the clean pan. Add the whole garlic clove and cook it over a low heat for 1–2 minutes. Add the tomatoes, increase the heat and fry them for 1 minute, then remove the garlic and discard.

3 Toss in the spaghetti, season with the nutmeg, salt and pepper to taste, then stir in the crumbled feta and basil. Toss over the heat to warm the pasta through. Serve in warmed bowls, topped with olives.

Variation
Substitute small pasta shapes for the spaghetti or break the long strands into smaller pieces. Omit the cherry tomatoes. Cut and reserve the tops off four to six beefsteak tomatoes and scoop out the flesh with a teaspoon, leaving the "shell" intact. Place the tomato "shells" upside down on kitchen paper to drain for 20 minutes. Cook the tomato flesh in the garlic-flavoured oil and combine with the other ingredients, including the olives, as described in the recipe. Pile the tossed pasta into the tomato "shells", replace the tops and arrange in an ovenproof dish. Drizzle with a little olive oil and bake in a preheated oven at 190°C/375°F/Gas 5 for 25–30 minutes. In traditional Greek style, serve warm, rather than hot.

Tagliatelle with Gorgonzola Sauce

Some dishes are destined to become firm favourites. Without question, this one falls into that category.

Serves 4
25g/1oz/2 tbsp butter, plus extra for tossing the pasta
225g/8oz Gorgonzola cheese
150ml/ ¼ pint/ ⅔ cup double cream
5ml/1 tsp cornflour
30ml/2 tbsp dry vermouth
15ml/1 tbsp chopped fresh sage
450g/1lb fresh or dried tagliatelle
salt

1 Melt the butter in a heavy-based saucepan. Stir in 175g/6oz of the crumbled Gorgonzola and about one-third of the cream. Stir over a very gentle heat for 2–3 minutes, until the cheese has melted.

2 Mix the cornflour to a paste with the vermouth and add this to the pan with the remaining cream. Whisk over the heat until smooth, then stir in the sage. Keep warm over the lowest possible heat, whisking occasionally.

3 Bring a large pan of lightly salted water to the boil and cook the pasta until it is *al dente*.

4 Drain the pasta, return it to the pan and toss with a knob of butter. Divide among four warmed bowls, top with the sauce and sprinkle over the remaining cheese. Serve immediately.

Cook's Tip
When buying Gorgonzola, avoid cheese that is hard in texture or sour smelling.

Variation
Substitute crumbled Stilton for the Gorgonzola and white port for the vermouth.

Castiglioni with Parmesan Sauce

This is an extremely quick and simple sauce, perfect for anyone in a hurry.

Serves 4

450g/1lb/4 cups dried castiglioni
50g/2oz/¼ cup butter
300ml/½ pint/1¼ cups double cream
175g/6oz/2 cups freshly grated Parmesan cheese
30ml/2 tbsp pine nuts, toasted
salt and freshly ground black pepper
finely shredded fresh flat leaf parsley, to garnish

1 Bring a large pan of lightly salted water to the boil and cook the pasta until it is *al dente*.

2 Meanwhile, heat the butter and cream in a saucepan and stir in half the Parmesan. Heat gently, stirring occasionally, until the Parmesan has melted. Keep the sauce warm.

3 Drain the pasta and tip it into a large serving bowl. Add the remaining Parmesan, season with salt and pepper, if needed, and toss until coated. Pour over the sauce and toss again. Sprinkle on the pine nuts and serve immediately, garnished with parsley.

Cook's Tip

Double cream does not usually curdle when heated, unless there are other very acid ingredients present, such as lemon juice. It can even be boiled without problems. However, it should always be heated gently to avoid the possibility of curdling. Lower fat dairy products, such as single cream, smetana and yogurt, are more likely to curdle and are not, therefore, suitable substitutes.

Variation

If you are unable to find castiglioni – round pasta shapes with scalloped edges – you could use conchiglie instead.

Penne with Courgettes & Goat's Cheese

The mild, almost buttery flavour of courgettes is enlivened by the addition of sharp goat's cheese.

Serves 4

350g/12oz/3 cups dried penne
60ml/4 tbsp olive oil
2 garlic cloves, chopped
2 large courgettes, sliced
225g/8oz goat's cheese with herbs, diced
30ml/2 tbsp chopped fresh oregano, plus oregano sprigs to garnish
salt and freshly ground black pepper

1 Bring a large pan of lightly salted water to the boil and cook the pasta until it is *al dente*.

2 Meanwhile, heat the oil in a large, heavy-based frying pan. Add the garlic and courgettes, and cook over a gentle heat, stirring occasionally, for 10 minutes.

3 Add the goat's cheese and chopped oregano, and toss over the heat for 1 minute, until heated through.

4 Drain the pasta thoroughly and return it to the clean pan. Add the courgette mixture and toss well. Season to taste with salt and pepper. Serve in warmed bowls, garnished with the oregano sprigs.

Variations

- *Diced feta cheese, with its sharp, salty taste, is a good alternative to goat's cheese.*
- *Use smoked, rather than herb-flavoured, goat's cheese.*
- *Substitute 175g/6oz shelled fresh or frozen broad beans for the courgettes. Cook them in 175ml/6fl oz/¾ cup simmering Vegetable Stock, then stir them briefly with the garlic in step 2.*
- *Substitute 2 medium carrots for 1 of the courgettes. Slice and cook with the courgette, as above.*

Paglia e Fieno with Walnuts & Gorgonzola

Cheese and nuts are popular ingredients for pasta sauces. This dish is very rich, so reserve for a dinner-party starter.

Serves 4

275g/10oz dried paglia e fieno
25g/1oz/2 tbsp butter
5ml/1 tsp finely chopped fresh sage
115g/4oz torta di Gorgonzola cheese, diced
45ml/3 tbsp mascarpone cheese
75ml/5 tbsp milk
50g/2oz/½ cup walnut halves, ground
30ml/2 tbsp freshly ground Parmesan cheese
freshly ground black pepper

1 Bring a large pan of lightly salted water to the boil and cook the pasta until it is *al dente*.

2 Meanwhile, melt the butter in a large pan over a low heat, add the sage and stir. Sprinkle in the Gorgonzola and mascarpone, and stir until they start to melt. Stir in the milk.

3 Sprinkle in the walnuts and Parmesan, and add plenty of black pepper. Continue to stir over a low heat until the mixture forms a creamy sauce. Do not allow it to boil or the nuts will taste bitter. Do not cook the sauce for longer than a few minutes or the nuts will discolour it.

4 Drain the pasta, tip it into a warmed bowl, then add the sauce and toss well. Serve immediately, with more black pepper ground on top.

Cook's Tip
Ready-ground nuts are sold in packets in supermarkets, but you will get a better flavour if you buy walnut halves and grind them yourself in a food processor.

Pipe with Ricotta, Saffron & Spinach

Serve this fairly rich dish in small quantities. Omit the saffron, with its quite strong flavour, if you like.

Serves 4–6

300g/11oz/2¾ cups dried pipe
300–350g/11–12oz fresh spinach leaves
freshly grated nutmeg
250g/9oz/generous 1 cup ricotta cheese
1 small pinch of saffron strands soaked in 60ml/4 tbsp warm water
salt and freshly ground black pepper
freshly grated Pecorino cheese, to serve

1 Bring a large pan of lightly salted water to the boil and cook the pasta until it is *al dente*.

2 Meanwhile, wash the spinach and put the leaves in a pan with only the water that clings to the leaves. Season with freshly grated nutmeg, with salt and pepper to taste.

3 Cover the pan and cook over a medium to high heat, shaking the pan occasionally, for 5 minutes, until the spinach is wilted and tender. Tip into a colander, press it to extract as much liquid as possible, then roughly chop it.

4 Put the ricotta in a large bowl. Strain in the saffron water. Add the spinach, beat well to mix, then add a ladleful or two of the pasta cooking water to loosen the mixture. Season to taste with salt and pepper.

5 Drain the pasta and add it to the ricotta mixture. Toss well. Serve in warmed bowls, sprinkled with Pecorino.

Cook's Tip
For the best results, use fresh white ricotta, which is sold by weight in Italian delicatessens.

Fusilli with Mascarpone & Spinach

Simply delicious – that sums up this combination of a creamy, green sauce with tender pasta.

Serves 4

350g/12oz/3 cups dried fusilli
50g/2oz/ ¼ cup butter
1 onion, chopped
1 garlic clove, chopped
30ml/2 tbsp fresh thyme leaves
225g/8oz frozen leaf spinach, thawed and drained
225g/8oz/1 cup mascarpone cheese
salt and freshly ground black pepper
fresh thyme sprigs, to garnish

1 Bring a large pan of lightly salted water to the boil and cook the pasta until it is *al dente*.

2 Meanwhile, melt the butter in a large, heavy-based saucepan. Add the onion and fry over a low heat, stirring occasionally, for 4–5 minutes, until softened.

3 Stir in the garlic, thyme and spinach, and season with salt and pepper to taste. Heat gently, stirring occasionally, for about 5 minutes, until heated through.

4 Stir in the mascarpone and heat gently until melted and heated through.

5 Drain the pasta thoroughly and return it to the clean pan. Add the sauce and toss until well coated. Serve immediately, garnished with the fresh thyme.

Variations

Use a mixture of cheeses instead of plain mascarpone. Mash together equal quantities of mascarpone and Gorgonzola or Roquefort or mix together equal quantities of mascarpone and grated Parmesan or Pecorino. Alternatively, replace the mascarpone with torta di Gorgonzola, which consists of layers of Gorgonzola and mascarpone.

Tagliatelle with Mozzarella & Asparagus Sauce

Tender asparagus tips look very impressive surrounded by ribbons of tender pasta.

Serves 4

225g/8oz asparagus tips
350g/12oz dried tagliatelle
115g/4oz/ ½ cup butter
1 onion, chopped
1 garlic clove, chopped
30ml/2 tbsp Vegetable Stock or water
150ml/ ¼ pint/ ⅔ cup double cream
75g/3oz mozzarella cheese, grated
salt and freshly ground black pepper
fresh flat leaf parsley sprigs, to garnish

1 Bring a large pan of lightly salted water to the boil. Add the fresh asparagus and cook for 5–10 minutes, until tender. Lift out the asparagus tips with a slotted spoon and set them aside.

2 Bring the pan of water back to the boil and cook the pasta until it is *al dente*.

3 Meanwhile, melt the butter in a large frying pan and fry the onion with the garlic over a low heat for 5 minutes, until softened. Stir in the stock or water.

4 Pour in the cream and bring to the boil, stirring. Add the asparagus. Simmer for 2 minutes, stirring occasionally.

5 Add the mozzarella cheese and simmer for 1 minute more. Season with salt and pepper to taste.

6 Drain the pasta and tip it into a bowl. Add the sauce and toss to coat. Serve immediately, garnished with the parsley.

Cook's Tip

Fresh asparagus is still quite seasonal, so keep your eyes open for it, and cook it in this delicious sauce when it is at its best.

Lemon & Parmesan Capellini with Herb Bread

Cream thickened with Parmesan cheese and flavoured with lemon rind makes a superb and unusual sauce for pasta.

Serves 2

½ Granary baguette
50g/2oz/ ¼ cup butter, softened
1 garlic clove, crushed
30ml/2 tbsp chopped fresh herbs
225g/8oz fresh or dried capellini
250ml/8fl oz/1 cup single cream
75g/3oz/1 cup freshly grated Parmesan cheese
finely grated rind of 1 lemon
salt and freshly ground black pepper
chopped fresh parsley and grated lemon rind (optional), to garnish

1 Preheat the oven to 200°C/400°F/Gas 6. Cut the baguette into thick slices.

2 Put the butter in a bowl and beat in the garlic and herbs. Spread thickly over each slice of bread.

3 Reassemble the baguette. Wrap in foil, support on a baking sheet and bake for 10 minutes.

4 Meanwhile, bring a large pan of lightly salted water to the boil and cook the pasta until it is *al dente*.

5 Pour the cream into another pan and bring to the boil. Stir in the Parmesan and lemon rind. The sauce should thicken in about 30 seconds.

6 Drain the pasta, return it to the clean pan and toss with the sauce. Season to taste and sprinkle with a little chopped fresh parsley and grated lemon rind, if liked. Serve immediately with the hot herb bread.

Cook's Tip
It is best to buy unwaxed lemons if the rind is to be grated.

Penne with Fennel Concassé & Blue Cheese

The aniseed flavour of the fennel makes it the perfect partner for pasta in a rich tomato sauce, especially when topped with tasty blue cheese.

Serves 2

1 fennel bulb
30ml/2 tbsp extra virgin olive oil
1 shallot, finely chopped
225g/8oz/2 cups dried penne or other pasta shapes
300ml/ ½ pint/1 ¼ cups passata
pinch of granulated sugar
5ml/1 tsp chopped fresh oregano
115g/4oz blue cheese
salt and freshly ground black pepper

1 Cut the fennel bulb in half. Cut away the hard core and root. Slice the fennel thinly, then cut the slices into strips.

2 Heat the oil in a small saucepan. Add the fennel and shallot, and cook for 2–3 minutes over a high heat, stirring occasionally.

3 Meanwhile, bring a large pan of lightly salted water to the boil and cook the pasta until it is *al dente*.

4 Add the passata, sugar and oregano to the fennel mixture. Cover the pan and simmer gently for 10–12 minutes, until the fennel is tender. Add salt and pepper to taste.

5 Drain the pasta and return it to the clean pan. Toss with the sauce. Serve immediately in warmed bowls, with the blue cheese crumbled over the top.

Cook's Tip
For a mild flavour, choose a cheese such as dolcelatte or mycella. If you prefer a stronger taste, use Fourme d'Ambert, Bavarian blue or Stilton.

Pasta from Pisa

Nothing could be simpler than hot pasta tossed with fresh ripe tomatoes, ricotta and sweet basil. Serve it on a hot summer's day, as it is surprisingly refreshing.

Serves 4–6

350g/12oz/3 cups dried conchiglie
130g/4½ oz/⅔ cup ricotta cheese
6 ripe Italian plum tomatoes, diced small
2 garlic cloves, crushed
a handful of fresh basil leaves, shredded, plus extra basil leaves to garnish
60ml/4 tbsp extra virgin olive oil
salt and freshly ground black pepper

1 Bring a large pan of lightly salted water to the boil and cook the pasta until it is *al dente*.

2 Meanwhile, put the ricotta in a large bowl and mash it with a fork until smooth.

3 Add the tomatoes, garlic and basil, season with salt and pepper to taste and mix well. Add the olive oil and whisk thoroughly. Taste for seasoning.

4 Drain the cooked pasta, tip it into the ricotta and tomato mixture and toss thoroughly to mix. Garnish with extra basil leaves and serve immediately.

Variations

- *An avocado is the ideal ingredient for adding extra colour and flavour to this pasta dish. Halve, stone and peel, then dice the flesh. Toss it with the hot pasta at the last minute to avoid discoloration of the flesh.*
- *Substitute diced mozzarella cheese for the ricotta and garnish with black olives.*
- *Use fresh mint leaves instead of the basil.*

Penne with Rocket & Mozzarella

Like a warm salad, this pasta dish is very quick and easy to make – perfect for an *al fresco* summer lunch.

Serves 4

400g/14oz/3½ cups fresh or dried penne
6 ripe Italian plum tomatoes, peeled, seeded and diced
2 x 150g/5oz packets mozzarella cheese, drained and diced
4 large handfuls of rocket, total weight about 150g/5oz
75ml/5 tbsp extra virgin olive oil
salt and freshly ground black pepper

1 Bring a large pan of lightly salted water to the boil and cook the pasta until it is *al dente*.

2 Meanwhile, put the tomatoes, mozzarella, rocket and olive oil into a large bowl, season with a little salt and pepper to taste, and toss well to mix.

3 Drain the cooked pasta and tip it into the bowl. Toss well to mix and serve immediately.

Cook's Tip

As with all simple recipes, the success of this dish depends upon having the freshest and best-quality ingredients. It is worth looking for mozzarella di bufala. Make sure that you buy only tender young rocket with no yellowing or damaged leaves. Sun-ripened tomatoes have the sweetest flavour; if in doubt about the quality, buy vine tomatoes.

Variation

Unless the rocket leaves are very young, they can be quite peppery. For a less peppery taste, use basil leaves instead of rocket, or a mixture of the two.

Baked Macaroni Cheese

A few refinements turn a family favourite into a dish that would be ideal for a supper with friends.

Serves 4

275g/10oz/2½ cups dried short-cut macaroni
2 leeks, chopped
50g/2oz/¼ cup butter
50g/2oz/½ cup plain flour
900ml/1½ pints/3¼ cups milk
225g/8oz/2 cups grated mature Cheddar cheese
30ml/2 tbsp fromage frais
5ml/1 tsp wholegrain mustard
50g/2oz/1 cup fresh white breadcrumbs
25g/1oz/¼ cup grated double Gloucester cheese
salt and freshly ground black pepper
15ml/1 tbsp chopped fresh parsley, to garnish

1 Preheat the oven to 180°C/350°F/Gas 4. Bring a large pan of lightly salted water to the boil and cook the macaroni with the leeks until the macaroni is *al dente*. Drain, rinse under cold water and set aside.

2 Heat the butter in a saucepan, add the flour and cook for 1–2 minutes, stirring constantly. Gradually add the milk, stirring constantly until the sauce boils and thickens. Add the Cheddar cheese, fromage frais and mustard, mix well and season with salt and pepper to taste.

3 Stir the drained macaroni and leeks into the cheese sauce and pile into a greased ovenproof dish. Level the top with the back of a spoon, and sprinkle over the breadcrumbs and double Gloucester cheese.

4 Bake for 35–40 minutes. Serve immediately, garnished with the fresh parsley.

Variations
Use broccoli or cauliflower instead of leeks, or leave out the vegetables altogether and arrange tomato slices around the rim of the bake, with the crumb mixture confined to the centre.

Macaroni with Four Cheeses

Rich and creamy, this is a deluxe macaroni cheese that goes well with either a tomato and basil salad or dressed green leaves.

Serves 4

250g/9oz/2¼ cups short-cut macaroni
50g/2oz/¼ cup butter
50g/2oz/½ cup plain flour
600ml/1 pint/2½ cups milk
120ml/4fl oz/½ cup double cream
90ml/6 tbsp dry white wine
50g/2oz/½ cup grated Gruyère or Emmental cheese
50g/2oz Fontina cheese, diced small
50g/2oz Gorgonzola cheese, crumbled
75g/3oz/1 cup freshly grated Parmesan cheese
salt and freshly ground black pepper
green salad, to serve

1 Preheat the oven to 180°C/350°F/Gas 4. Bring a large pan of lightly salted water to the boil and cook the macaroni until it is *al dente*.

2 Meanwhile, melt the butter in a heavy-based saucepan over a low heat. Add the flour and cook, stirring constantly, for 1–2 minutes. Add the milk a little at a time, whisking vigorously after each addition. Stir in the cream, followed by the dry white wine. Bring to the boil, stirring constantly. Cook, stirring continuously, until the sauce thickens, then remove the pan from the heat.

3 Add the Gruyère or Emmental, the Fontina, Gorgonzola and about one-third of the grated Parmesan to the sauce. Stir well to mix in the cheeses, then taste for seasoning, and add salt and pepper if necessary.

4 Drain the pasta well and tip it into an ovenproof dish. Pour the sauce over the pasta and mix well, then sprinkle the remaining Parmesan over the top.

5 Transfer the dish to the oven and bake for 25–30 minutes, or until golden brown. Serve hot with a green salad.

Macaroni & Blue Cheese

This comforting dish is ideal for serving on a chilly autumn evening, or after Christmas, when you may well have the remains of a whole Stilton.

Serves 6

butter, for greasing
450g/1lb/4 cups dried short-cut macaroni
50g/2oz/ 1/4 cup butter
75g/3oz/ 2/3 cup plain flour
1.2 litres/2 pints/5 cups hot milk
225g/8oz Stilton cheese, crumbled
salt and freshly ground black pepper

1 Preheat the oven to 180°C/350°F/Gas 4. Grease a shallow 33 x 23cm/13 x 9in ovenproof dish.

2 Bring a large pan of lightly salted water to the boil and cook the macaroni until *al dente*. Drain the macaroni and rinse under cold running water. Drain well again, place in a large bowl and set aside.

3 Melt the butter in a heavy-based pan, add the flour and cook over a low heat for 1–2 minutes, stirring constantly. Gradually add the hot milk, whisking constantly until the sauce boils and thickens. Season with salt and pepper to taste.

4 Stir the sauce into the macaroni. Add three-quarters of the crumbled Stilton and stir well. Transfer the macaroni mixture to the prepared dish and spread evenly.

5 Sprinkle the remaining cheese evenly over the surface. Bake for about 25 minutes, until the macaroni is bubbling hot. Brown the surface under a hot grill, if you like.

Macaroni Cheese with Winter Vegetables

Leeks and celeriac add extra flavour to an ever-popular supper dish.

Serves 4

225g/8oz/2 cups dried short-cut macaroni
50g/2oz/ 1/4 cup butter
2 leeks, chopped
1 small celeriac root, diced
75ml/5 tbsp plain flour
750ml/1 1/4 pints/3 cups milk
200g/7oz/scant 2 cups grated mature Cheddar cheese
45ml/3 tbsp fresh white breadcrumbs
salt and freshly ground black pepper

1 Preheat the oven to 200°C/400°F/Gas 6. Bring a large pan of lightly salted water to the boil and cook the macaroni until it is *al dente*.

2 Meanwhile, melt the butter in a separate pan, add the leeks and celeriac, and cook over a medium heat, stirring occasionally, for 4 minutes.

3 Stir in the flour, and cook, stirring constantly, for 1 minute. Gradually add the milk, stirring constantly until the sauce boils and thickens.

4 Remove the sauce from the heat. Drain the macaroni well and add it to the sauce, with most of the cheese. Season to taste. Pour the macaroni mixture into an ovenproof dish.

5 Mix the breadcrumbs with the remaining cheese, then sprinkle the mixture over the dish. Bake for 20–25 minutes, until the topping is golden.

Cook's Tip

Heat the milk before you make the sauce, if you like. It will be absorbed more easily by the flour mixture, and the sauce will be less likely to form lumps.

Macaroni Cheese Pie

Macaroni cheese is incredibly popular in the Caribbean, and appears in numerous guises.

Serves 4

225g/8oz/2 cups dried short-cut macaroni
40g/1½oz/3 tbsp butter, plus extra for greasing
45ml/3 tbsp plain flour
450ml/¾ pint/scant 2 cups milk
5ml/1 tsp mild prepared mustard
2.5ml/½ tsp ground cinnamon
175g/6oz/1½ cups mature Cheddar cheese, grated
1 egg, beaten
4 spring onions, finely chopped
40g/1½oz/3 tbsp canned chopped tomatoes
115g/4oz/⅔ cup fresh or drained canned sweetcorn kernels
salt and freshly ground black pepper
chopped fresh parsley, to garnish

1 Preheat the oven to 180°C/350°F/Gas 4. Bring a large pan of lightly salted water to the boil and cook the macaroni until *al dente*. Rinse under cold water and drain.

2 Melt 25g/1oz/2 tbsp of the butter in a pan and stir in the flour. Cook for 1–2 minutes, stirring. Gradually add the milk, whisking constantly until the sauce boils and thickens.

3 Stir in the mustard, cinnamon and two-thirds of the cheese. Cook gently, stirring frequently, until the cheese has melted, then remove from the heat and whisk in the egg. Set aside.

4 Melt the remaining butter in a small frying pan and cook the spring onions, chopped plum tomatoes and sweetcorn over a gentle heat for 5–10 minutes. Season to taste.

5 Tip half the cooked macaroni into a greased ovenproof dish. Pour over half the cheese sauce and mix well, then spoon the tomato and sweetcorn mixture over the macaroni.

6 Stir the remaining macaroni into the remaining cheese sauce, then spread this carefully over the tomato and sweetcorn mixture. Top with the rest of the cheese. Bake for 45 minutes, or until the top is golden and bubbling. Garnish with the parsley.

Macaroni Soufflé

This is generally a great favourite with children, and is rather like a light and fluffy macaroni cheese.

Serves 3–4

75g/3oz/¾ cup dried short-cut macaroni
75g/3oz/6 tbsp butter
45ml/3 tbsp dried breadcrumbs
5ml/1 tsp ground paprika
40g/1½oz/⅓ cup plain flour
300ml/½ pint/1¼ cups milk
75g/3oz/¾ cup grated Cheddar or Gruyère cheese
50g/2oz/⅔ cup freshly grated Parmesan cheese
3 eggs, separated
salt and freshly ground black pepper

1 Preheat the oven to 150°C/300°F/Gas 2. Bring a pan of lightly salted water to the boil and cook the macaroni until *al dente*.

2 Melt the butter in a pan. Use a little of it to coat the insides of a 1.2 litre/2 pint/5 cup soufflé dish, then coat evenly with the breadcrumbs, shaking out any excess.

3 Heat the butter remaining in the pan and stir in the paprika and flour. Cook for 1 minute, stirring. Gradually add the milk, stirring until the sauce boils and thickens. Add the grated cheeses, stirring until melted, then season well.

4 Remove the pan from the heat, let the sauce cool slightly, then beat in the egg yolks. Whisk the egg whites until they form soft peaks and spoon one-quarter into the sauce mixture, beating it gently to loosen it up.

5 Using a large metal spoon, carefully fold in the rest of the egg whites. Gently fold in the macaroni. Transfer the mixture to the prepared soufflé dish. Bake in the centre of the oven for about 40–45 minutes, until the soufflé has risen and is golden brown.

Cook's Tip
Make sure you serve this as soon as it is cooked or it will sink dramatically. The middle should wobble very slightly.

Tortellini with Cream, Butter & Cheese

This is a wonderfully self-indulgent but extremely quick alternative to macaroni cheese.

Serves 4–6

450g/1lb/4 cups fresh tortellini
50g/2oz/ ¼ cup butter, plus extra for greasing
300ml/ ½ pint/1 ¼ cups double cream
115g/4oz piece of fresh Parmesan cheese
freshly grated nutmeg
salt and freshly ground black pepper
fresh oregano sprigs, to garnish

1 Bring a large pan of lightly salted water to the boil and cook the tortellini until *al dente*.

2 Meanwhile, melt the butter in a heavy-based pan over a low heat and stir in the cream. Bring to the boil and cook for 2–3 minutes, until slightly thickened.

3 Grate the Parmesan cheese and stir three-quarters of it into the sauce until melted. Season to taste with salt, pepper and nutmeg. Preheat the grill.

4 Drain the pasta well and spoon it into a buttered flameproof serving dish. Pour over the sauce, sprinkle over the remaining cheese and place under the grill until brown and bubbling. Serve immediately, garnished with oregano.

Variations

- *Add 15ml/1 tbsp finely chopped fresh oregano or 30ml/2 tbsp finely chopped fresh parsley to the sauce and omit the grated nutmeg.*
- *Use mature Gouda or Edam instead of Parmesan.*
- *Substitute Manchego for the Parmesan and stir 15–30ml/1–2 tbsp chopped almonds into the sauce before pouring it over the pasta.*

Baked Tortellini with Three Cheeses

Serve this delectable dish straight from the oven while the cheese is still runny.

Serves 4–6

450g/1lb/4 cups fresh tortellini
350g/12oz/1½ cups ricotta cheese
2 eggs, beaten
25g/1oz/2 tbsp butter
25g/1oz/1 cup fresh basil leaves
115g/4oz smoked mozzarella cheese, grated
60ml/4 tbsp freshly grated Parmesan cheese
salt and freshly ground black pepper

1 Preheat the oven to 190°C/375°F/Gas 5. Bring a large pan of lightly salted water to the boil and cook the tortellini until they are *al dente*.

2 Mash the ricotta in a large bowl with a fork. Beat in the eggs and season well with salt and pepper.

3 Use the butter to grease an ovenproof dish. Spoon in half the tortellini, pour over half the ricotta mixture and cover with half the basil leaves.

4 Cover with the smoked mozzarella and most of the remaining basil, reserving a sprig or two for the garnish. Top with the rest of the tortellini and spread over the remaining ricotta mixture.

5 Sprinkle evenly with the Parmesan cheese. Transfer to the oven and bake for 35–45 minutes, or until golden brown and bubbling. Decorate with the reserved basil and serve.

Cook's Tip

Fresh tortellini with a huge variety of fillings are widely available from supermarkets and delicatessens. A three-cheese, sun-dried tomato or ricotta and spinach filling would go very well in this dish. Plain, spinach-flavoured and tomato-flavoured tortellini are all suitable. Other filled pasta, such as agnolotti or cappelletti, could also be used.

Agnolotti with Taleggio & Marjoram

The filling for these little half-moons is very simple, but the combination of flavours is delicious.

Serves 6–8

300g/11oz/2¾ cups strong white flour
3 eggs, beaten
5ml/1 tsp salt
350–400g/12–14oz Taleggio cheese
about 30ml/2 tbsp finely chopped fresh marjoram, plus extra to garnish
salt and freshly ground black pepper
115g/4oz/½ cup hot melted butter and freshly grated Parmesan cheese, to serve

1 Place the flour, eggs and salt in a food processor. Pulse to combine. Transfer the dough to a floured surface and knead for 5 minutes, until smooth. Using a pasta machine, roll out one-quarter of the dough into a strip 90cm–1m/39in–1yd long. Cut the strip into two 45–50cm/18–20in lengths.

2 Cut 8–10 little cubes of Taleggio and space them evenly along one side of one of the pasta strips. Sprinkle each Taleggio cube with marjoram and pepper to taste. Brush a little water around each cube of cheese, then fold the plain side of the pasta strip over them.

3 Starting from the folded edge, press gently around each cube with your fingertips, pushing the air out. Sprinkle lightly with flour. Using half of a 5cm/2in fluted round ravioli or biscuit cutter, cut around each cube to make a half-moon shape. The folded edge should be the straight edge.

4 Put the agnolotti on floured dish towels, sprinkle lightly with flour and leave to dry while making more agnolotti.

5 Bring a large pan of lightly salted water to the boil and cook the agnolotti until *al dente*.

6 Drain the agnolotti and divide them equally among six to eight warmed large bowls. Drizzle sizzling hot butter over them and sprinkle with Parmesan and marjoram. Hand around more grated Parmesan separately.

Pansotti with Herbs & Cheese

Pasta triangles with a ricotta and herb filling, pansotti taste wonderful with a walnut sauce.

Serves 6–8

300g/11oz/2¾ cups strong white flour
3 eggs, beaten
5ml/1 tsp salt
25g/1oz/1 cup chopped fresh herbs
115g/4oz/½ cup hot melted butter and freshly grated Parmesan cheese, to serve

For the filling

250g/9oz/generous 1 cup ricotta cheese
150g/5oz/1½ cups freshly grated Parmesan cheese
1 large handful fresh basil leaves, finely chopped
1 large handful fresh flat leaf parsley, finely chopped
a few sprigs fresh marjoram or oregano, leaves removed and finely chopped
1 garlic clove, crushed
1 small egg
salt and freshly ground black pepper

For the sauce

115g/4oz/1 cup walnuts
1 garlic clove, halved
60ml/4 tbsp extra virgin olive oil
120ml/4fl oz/½ cup double cream

1 Place the flour, eggs, salt and herbs in a food processor. Pulse to combine, then transfer the dough to a lightly floured surface and knead for 5 minutes, until smooth.

2 Make the filling. Mash the ricotta in a bowl. Add the Parmesan, herbs, garlic and egg, and beat well. Season to taste.

3 Make the sauce. Put the walnuts, garlic and oil in a food processor, and process to a paste, then add up to 120ml/4fl oz/½ cup warm water through the feeder tube to slacken the consistency. Spoon the mixture into a large bowl and beat in the cream.

4 Using a pasta machine, roll out one-quarter of the pasta into a 90cm–1m/36in–1yd strip. Cut the strip with a sharp knife into two 45–50cm/18–20in lengths.

5 Using a 5cm/2in square ravioli cutter, cut 8–10 squares from one of the pasta strips. Put a mound of filling in the centre of each square. Brush a little water around the edge of the dough, then fold each square diagonally in half over the filling to make a triangle. Press gently to seal.

6 Spread out the pansotti on clean floured dish towels, sprinkle lightly with flour and leave to dry. Make more pansotti in the same way.

7 Bring a large pan of lightly salted water to the boil and cook the pansotti until *al dente*. Meanwhile, add a ladleful of the pasta cooking water to the walnut sauce to thin it down.

8 Drain the pansotti and tip them into the bowl of walnut sauce. Drizzle the hot melted butter over them, toss well, then sprinkle with grated Parmesan. Serve immediately, with more grated Parmesan handed separately.

Ravioli with Four Cheese Sauce

This has a smooth, rich sauce that coats the pasta very evenly.

Serves 4

350g/12oz/3 cups fresh ravioli
50g/2oz/ 1/4 cup butter
50g/2oz/ 1/2 cup plain flour
450ml/ 3/4 pint/scant 2 cups milk
50g/2oz fresh Parmesan cheese
50g/2oz Edam cheese
50g/2oz Gruyère cheese
50g/2oz Fontina cheese
salt and freshly ground black pepper
chopped fresh flat leaf parsley, to garnish

1 Bring a large pan of lightly salted water to the boil and cook the pasta until it is *al dente*.

2 Meanwhile, melt the butter in a saucepan over a low heat. Stir in the flour and cook for 1–2 minutes, stirring constantly. Gradually add the milk, stirring constantly until the sauce boils and thickens.

3 Grate all the cheeses and stir them into the sauce until they are just beginning to melt. Remove the pan from the heat and season the sauce with salt and pepper to taste.

4 Drain the ravioli thoroughly and tip it into a large serving bowl. Pour over the sauce and toss to coat. Serve immediately, garnished with the chopped fresh parsley.

Cook's Tips

• Buy the ravioli from your favourite fresh pasta retailer, or make your own, following the instructions in the Techniques section. Alternatively, serve the sauce over tortellini.

• The sauce would go well with almost all vegetarian fillings, from mushrooms to sun-dried tomatoes.

• As the cheeses are such a feature of the recipe, it is worth buying them from a delicatessen, if possible, rather than plastic-wrapped from a supermarket. Buy the Parmesan in a single piece rather than ready grated.

Spicy Cheese Lasagne

Adding a chilli and hot pepper flakes peps up a dish that is sometimes in danger of being a bit bland.

Serves 8

50g/2oz/ 1/4 cup butter, plus extra for greasing
1 large onion, finely chopped
3 garlic cloves, crushed
1 small fresh green chilli
50g/2oz/ 1/2 cup plain flour
1 litre/1 3/4 pints/4 cups milk
2 x 400g/14oz cans chopped tomatoes
1 large courgette, sliced
2.5ml/ 1/2 tsp hot red pepper flakes
12–16 fresh lasagne sheets, precooked if necessary, or no-precook dried lasagne
350g/12oz/3 cups grated mature Cheddar cheese
salt and freshly ground black pepper
fresh parsley, to garnish

1 Preheat the oven to 190°C/375°F/Gas 5. Grease a large ovenproof dish.

2 Melt the butter in a large pan. Add the onion, garlic and chilli, and cook over a low heat, stirring occasionally, for about 5 minutes, until softened.

3 Stir in the flour and cook for 1–2 minutes, stirring constantly. Gradually add the milk, stirring constantly until the sauce boils and thickens.

4 Stir the tomatoes, courgette and hot pepper flakes into the sauce. Season with salt and pepper.

5 Spoon a little of the sauce into the prepared ovenproof dish and spread it evenly over the base. Cover with a layer of lasagne sheets.

6 Add one-third of the remaining sauce and one-third of the grated cheese. Repeat the layers until all the ingredients have been used.

7 Bake for about 45 minutes, until the top is golden. Leave to stand for 10 minutes before serving garnished with parsley.

Soft Fried Noodles

This is a very basic dish that may be served as an accompaniment or on those occasions when you are feeling a little peckish and fancy something simple.

Serves 4–6
350g/12oz dried egg noodles
30ml/2 tbsp vegetable oil
30ml/2 tbsp finely chopped spring onions
soy sauce, to taste
salt and freshly ground black pepper

1 Bring a large pan of lightly salted water to the boil and cook the noodles until just tender. Drain, rinse under cold running water and drain again thoroughly.

2 Preheat a wok. Pour in the vegetable oil and swirl it around. Add the spring onions and stir-fry for 30 seconds over a medium heat. Add the drained noodles, stirring gently to separate the strands.

3 Reduce the heat to low and stir-fry the noodles, turning and tossing constantly, until they are heated through and lightly browned and crisp on the outside, but still soft and tender inside. Long chopsticks are ideal for turning the noodles, or use two wooden spatulas.

4 Tip the noodles into a warmed serving dish and season with soy sauce, salt and pepper. Serve at once.

Variations

- *If you want to add protein, break an egg into the noodles and stir until lightly scrambled.*
- *The noodles are also good tossed with a dollop of chilli black bean sauce.*
- *For a more substantial dish, stir-fry 115g/4oz/scant 1 cup very thinly sliced cauliflower florets before cooking the spring onions. Add 15ml/1 tbsp yellow bean sauce and 10ml/2 tsp brown sugar, and heat through just before serving.*

Loopy Noodle Nests

Serve these with stir-fries or as a crunchy snack.

Makes 4–6 nests
175g/6oz flat ribbon noodles
oil, for deep-frying

1 Bring a large pan of lightly salted water to the boil and cook the noodles until *al dente*. Drain, rinse under cold water and drain again. Blot dry on kitchen paper.
2 Heat the oil for deep-frying to 190°C/375°F. Using a spoon and fork, swirl the noodles into nests.
3 Carefully lower each nest in turn into the oil. Deep-fry for about 3–4 minutes, or until golden. Drain on kitchen paper.

Noodles with Ginger & Coriander

Here is a simple noodle dish that goes well with most oriental dishes. It can also be served as a snack for 2–3 people.

Serves 2–6
a handful of fresh coriander sprigs
225g/8oz dried egg noodles
45ml/3 tbsp groundnut oil
5cm/2in piece of fresh root ginger, peeled and cut into fine shreds
6–8 spring onions, cut into shreds
30ml/2 tbsp light soy sauce
salt and freshly ground black pepper

1 Strip the leaves from the coriander stalks. Pile them on a chopping board and coarsely chop them using a cleaver or large sharp knife.

2 Bring a large pan of lightly salted water to the boil and cook the noodles until they are just tender. Drain, rinse under cold water and drain again. Return to the clean pan and toss with 15ml/1 tbsp of the oil.

3 Preheat a wok until hot, add the remaining oil and swirl it around. Add the ginger and stir-fry for a few seconds, then add the noodles and spring onions. Stir-fry over a medium heat for 3–4 minutes, until hot.

4 Sprinkle over the soy sauce and chopped coriander, and season with salt and pepper to taste. Toss well, transfer to a warmed bowl and serve at once.

Cook's Tip

Many of the dried egg noodles available are sold in skeins or bundles. As a guide, allow 1 skein of noodles per person as an average portion for a main dish.

Noodles Primavera

As tasty as it is colourful, this is a substantial dish destined to become a favourite with all the family.

Serves 4

225g/8oz dried broad rice noodles
115g/4oz/scant 1 cup broccoli florets
1 carrot, thinly sliced lengthways
225g/8oz asparagus, trimmed and cut into 5cm/2in lengths
1 red or yellow pepper, seeded and cut into strips
50g/2oz baby corn cobs
50g/2oz/ ½ cup sugar snap peas, topped and tailed
45ml/3 tbsp vegetable oil
15ml/1 tbsp chopped fresh root ginger
2 garlic cloves, chopped
2 spring onions, finely chopped
450g/1lb tomatoes, chopped
1 bunch of rocket leaves
soy sauce, to taste
salt and freshly ground black pepper

1 Soak the noodles in hot water for about 30 minutes, until soft. Drain.

2 Bring a large pan of lightly salted water to the boil and blanch the broccoli florets for 1 minute. Lift out with a slotted spoon, refresh under cold water, drain and set aside.

3 Repeat this process in turn with the carrot, asparagus, red or yellow pepper, baby corn cobs and sugar snap peas, keeping all the vegetables separate.

4 Preheat a wok, add the oil and swirl it around. Add the ginger, garlic and spring onions, and stir-fry for 30 seconds over a medium heat. Then add the tomatoes and stir-fry for 2–3 minutes.

5 Add the noodles to the wok and toss over the heat for 3 minutes to heat through. Toss in the blanched vegetables and rocket leaves. Season with soy sauce, salt and pepper to taste, and cook, stirring and tossing all the time, until the vegetables are tender and the dish is piping hot. Transfer to a warmed serving bowl and serve immediately.

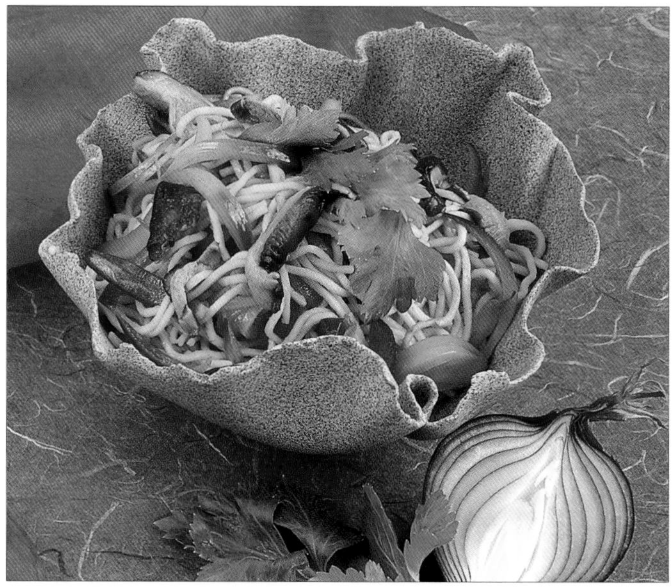

Oriental Vegetable Noodles

Fresh shiitake mushrooms and sesame oil are authentic oriental ingredients in this tasty stir-fry, but it is Italian balsamic vinegar that gives it the edge.

Serves 6

500g/1¼lb fine dried egg noodles
1 red onion
115g/4oz/1½ cups fresh shiitake mushrooms
15ml/1 tbsp vegetable oil
45ml/3 tbsp dark soy sauce
15ml/1 tbsp balsamic vinegar
10ml/2 tsp caster sugar
5ml/1 tsp salt
15ml/1 tbsp sesame oil
celery leaves, to garnish

1 Bring a large saucepan of lightly salted water to the boil. Add the egg noodles and cook briefly until they are just tender. Drain thoroughly.

2 Thinly slice the red onion and the shiitake mushrooms. Preheat a wok, then add the vegetable oil and swirl it around. When the oil is hot, add the onion and mushrooms, and stir-fry for 2 minutes.

3 Add the noodles to the wok with the soy sauce, balsamic vinegar, sugar and salt. Toss them over the heat for 2–3 minutes, then add the sesame oil. Transfer to a warmed bowl and serve at once, garnished with the celery leaves.

Cook's Tip

Shiitake mushrooms have a unique flavour and texture. Originating in the East, they are now widely cultivated in Europe and the United States. The caps are velvety and tan in colour, sometimes with light veins or faint white spots. The stems are often quite tough and may need to be removed before cooking. Otherwise, simply wipe the mushrooms with kitchen paper. Do not wash them otherwise they will absorb more moisture. There is also no need to peel them. Shiitake mushrooms should be cooked gently and briefly, as prolonged cooking tends to make them tough and unpalatable.

Crispy Noodles with Mixed Vegetables

In this dish, rice vermicelli noodles are deep-fried until crisp, then tossed into a colourful selection of stir-fried vegetables.

Serves 3–4

2 large carrots
2 courgettes
4 spring onions
115g/4oz yard-long beans or green beans
115g/4oz dried vermicelli rice noodles or cellophane noodles
groundnut oil, for deep-frying
2.5cm/1in piece of fresh root ginger, shredded
1 fresh red chilli, sliced
115g/4oz/1½ cups fresh shiitake or button mushrooms, thickly sliced
a few Chinese cabbage leaves, coarsely shredded
75g/3oz/⅓ cup beansprouts
30ml/2 tbsp light soy sauce
30ml/2 tbsp Chinese rice wine or dry sherry
5ml/1 tsp granulated sugar
30ml/2 tbsp roughly torn coriander leaves

1 Cut the carrots and courgettes into fine sticks. Shred the spring onions into similar-size pieces. Trim the beans. If using yard-long beans, cut them into short lengths. Break the noodles into lengths of about 7.5cm/3in.

2 Half-fill a wok with oil and heat it to 180°C/350°F. Deep-fry the noodles, a handful at a time for 1–2 minutes, until puffed and crispy. Lift out with a spider or slotted spoon and drain on kitchen paper. Carefully pour off all but 30ml/2 tbsp of the oil.

3 Reheat the oil in the wok. When hot, add the beans and stir-fry for 2–3 minutes. Add the ginger, chilli, mushrooms, carrots and courgettes, and stir-fry for 1–2 minutes.

4 Add the Chinese cabbage, beansprouts and spring onions. Stir-fry for 1 minute, then add the soy sauce, rice wine or sherry and sugar. Cook, stirring, for about 30 seconds.

5 Add the noodles and coriander, and toss, taking care not to crush the noodles. Pile on a warm serving plate and serve.

Noodle Cakes with Vegetables

Slightly crisp noodle cakes topped with vegetables make a superb dish.

Serves 4

175g/6oz dried egg vermicelli
15ml/1 tbsp vegetable oil
2 garlic cloves, finely chopped
115g/4oz/⅔ cup baby corn cobs, halved lengthways
115g/4oz/1½ cups fresh shiitake mushrooms, halved
3 celery sticks, sliced
1 carrot, diagonally sliced
115g/4oz/1 cup mangetouts
75g/3oz/¾ cup drained canned sliced bamboo shoots
15ml/1 tbsp cornflour, mixed to a paste with 15ml/1 tbsp water
15ml/1 tbsp dark soy sauce
5ml/1 tsp caster sugar
300ml/½ pint/1¼ cups Vegetable Stock
salt and freshly ground white pepper
spring onion curls, to garnish

1 Bring a saucepan of lightly salted water to the boil and cook the egg vermicelli briefly until just tender. Drain, refresh under cold water, drain again, then dry thoroughly on kitchen paper.

2 Heat 2.5ml/½ tsp of the oil in a non-stick frying pan. When it is very hot, spread half the noodles over the base. Fry for 2–3 minutes until the noodles are lightly toasted and have stuck together to form a cake. Carefully turn this over, fry the other side, then slide the noodle cake on to a heated serving plate. Make a second cake from the remaining noodles. Keep hot.

3 Heat the remaining oil in the clean pan, then fry the garlic for a few seconds. Add the corn cobs and mushrooms, and stir-fry for 3 minutes over a medium heat. Add the celery, carrot, mangetouts and bamboo shoots. Stir-fry for 2 minutes, or until the vegetables are crisp-tender.

4 Stir in the cornflour paste, soy sauce, sugar and stock. Cook, stirring, until the sauce thickens. Season with salt and white pepper to taste.

5 Divide the vegetable mixture among the noodle cakes, garnish with the spring onion curls and serve immediately. Each noodle cake serves two people.

Fried Noodles with Beancurd

Fried potatoes and beancurd (tofu) are both excellent vehicles for the spicy flavours in this unusual stir-fry.

Serves 4

2 eggs
60ml/4 tbsp vegetable oil
5ml/1 tsp chilli powder
5ml/1 tsp ground turmeric
1 large onion, finely sliced
2 fresh red chillies, seeded and finely sliced
15ml/1 tbsp soy sauce
2 large cooked potatoes, cut into small cubes
6 pieces of fried beancurd (tofu), sliced
225g/8oz/4 cups beansprouts
115g/4oz green beans, blanched
350g/12oz fresh thick egg noodles
salt and freshly ground black pepper
sliced spring onions, to garnish

1 Beat the eggs lightly in a bowl. Heat an omelette pan and grease it lightly with a little of the oil. Use half the egg mixture to make a thin omelette. Slide it on to a plate, blot it with kitchen paper, roll it up and cut it into narrow strips. Make a second omelette in the same way and slice. Set the omelette strips aside for the garnish.

2 In a cup, mix together the chilli powder and turmeric. Form a paste by stirring in a little water.

3 Preheat a wok and swirl in the remaining oil. Add the onion and stir-fry over a medium heat until soft. Reduce the heat and add the chilli paste, sliced chillies and soy sauce. Stir-fry for 2–3 minutes.

4 Add the potatoes and stir-fry for about 2 minutes, mixing them well with the chillies. Add the beancurd, then the beansprouts, green beans and noodles.

5 Gently stir-fry over a low heat until the noodles are evenly coated and heated through. Take care not to break up the potatoes or the beancurd. Season with salt and pepper to taste. Serve hot, garnished with the reserved omelette strips and spring onion slices.

Chinese Mushrooms with Cellophane Noodles

Red fermented beancurd adds extra flavour to this hearty vegetarian dish.

Serves 4

115g/4oz Chinese dried mushrooms
25g/1oz dried wood ears
115g/4oz dried beancurd (tofu)
30ml/2 tbsp vegetable oil
2 garlic cloves, finely chopped
2 slices of fresh root ginger, finely chopped
10 Szechuan peppercorns, crushed
15ml/1 tbsp red fermented beancurd (tofu)
½ star anise
pinch of granulated sugar
15–30ml/1–2 tbsp soy sauce
50g/2oz cellophane noodles, soaked in hot water until soft
salt

1 Soak the Chinese mushrooms and wood ears separately in bowls of hot water for 30 minutes. Break the dried beancurd into small pieces and soak it in water, following the instructions on the packet.

2 Strain the mushrooms, reserving the liquid. Squeeze as much liquid from the mushrooms as possible, then discard the mushroom stems. Cut the cups in half if they are large.

3 The wood ears should swell to five times their original size. Drain them, rinse thoroughly and drain again. Cut off any gritty parts, then cut each wood ear into two or three pieces.

4 Heat the oil in a heavy-based pan. Add the garlic, ginger and Szechuan peppercorns. Fry for a few seconds, then add the mushrooms and red fermented beancurd. Mix lightly and fry, stirring occasionally, for 5 minutes.

5 Add the reserved mushroom liquid to the pan, with sufficient water to cover the mushrooms completely. Add the star anise, sugar and soy sauce, then cover and simmer for 30 minutes.

6 Add the chopped wood ears and reconstituted beancurd pieces to the pan. Cover and cook for about 10 minutes.

7 Drain the cellophane noodles, add them to the mixture and cook for 10 minutes more, until tender, adding more liquid if necessary. Add salt to taste and serve.

Cook's Tip
Brick red in colour, red fermented beancurd (tofu) has a very strong, cheesy flavour, and is fermented with salt, red rice and rice wine. Look out for it in Chinese food stores.

Variation
If you can't find Szechuan peppercorns, then use ordinary black ones instead.

Fried Noodles with Beansprouts & Asparagus

Soft fried noodles contrast beautifully with crisp beansprouts and asparagus.

Serves 2

115g/4oz dried egg noodles
60ml/4 tbsp vegetable oil
1 small onion, chopped
2.5cm/1in piece of fresh root ginger, peeled and grated
2 garlic cloves, crushed
175g/6oz young asparagus, trimmed
115g/4oz/2 cups beansprouts
4 spring onions, sliced
45ml/3 tbsp soy sauce
salt and freshly ground black pepper

1 Bring a large pan of lightly salted water to the boil and cook the noodles briefly until they are just tender. Drain and toss in 30ml/2 tbsp of the oil.

2 Preheat a wok, add the remaining oil and swirl it around. When it is very hot, add the onion, ginger and garlic, and stir-fry over a medium heat for 2–3 minutes. Add the asparagus and stir-fry for 2–3 minutes more.

3 Add the noodles and beansprouts, and stir-fry for 2 minutes, then stir in the spring onions and soy sauce. Season with salt and pepper, if necessary, stir-fry for 1 minute, then transfer to a warmed bowl. Serve at once.

Cook's Tip

The beansprouts on sale in supermarkets and Chinese food stores are usually those of mung beans. However, the sprouts of a wide variety of beans, peas and seeds are also edible and can be home-grown in a large jar or a special sprouter. Aduki beans, chick-peas, lentils, soya beans, alfalfa seeds, poppy seeds, sesame seeds, pumpkin seeds and sunflower seeds are all suitable for sprouting. Store fresh sprouts in a covered container in the fridge for up to a week.

Somen Noodles with Saffron Sauce

It is unusual to find somen noodles teamed with asparagus, but the partnership works remarkably well.

Serves 4

450g/1lb young asparagus
pinch of saffron strands
30ml/2 tbsp boiling water
25g/1oz/2 tbsp butter
2 shallots, finely chopped
30ml/2 tbsp white wine
250ml/8fl oz/1 cup double cream
grated rind and juice of ½ lemon
115g/4oz/1 cup peas
350g/12oz dried somen noodles
½ bunch fresh chervil, roughly chopped
salt and freshly ground black pepper

1 Cut off the asparagus tips, then slice the remaining spears into short rounds. Steep the saffron in the boiling water in a cup or small bowl.

2 Melt the butter in a saucepan, add the shallots and cook over a low heat, stirring occasionally, for 3 minutes, until soft.

3 Stir in the white wine, cream and saffron infusion. Bring to the boil, lower the heat and simmer gently for 5 minutes, or until the sauce thickens to a coating consistency. Add the grated lemon rind and juice, and season with salt and pepper to taste.

4 Bring a large pan of lightly salted water to the boil. Cook the asparagus tips for 2 minutes, scoop them out with a slotted spoon and add them to the sauce.

5 Cook the peas and asparagus rounds in the boiling water until just tender. Scoop them out and add them to the sauce.

6 Let the water return to the boil and cook the somen noodles until just tender. Drain, return to the clean pan and pour the sauce over the top.

7 Toss the noodles with the sauce and vegetables, adding the chervil, and more salt and pepper if needed. Serve at once, in warmed plates.

Somen Noodles with Courgettes

This is a colourful dish packed with lots of flavour – absolutely perfect for a midweek family supper. Pumpkin or patty pan squash can be used instead of the courgettes.

Serves 4

2 yellow courgettes
2 green courgettes
60ml/4 tbsp pine nuts
60ml/4 tbsp extra virgin olive oil
2 shallots, finely chopped
2 garlic cloves, finely chopped
30ml/2 tbsp bottled capers, rinsed and drained
4 drained sun-dried tomatoes in oil, cut into strips
300g/11oz dried somen noodles
60ml/4 tbsp chopped mixed fresh herbs
grated rind of 1 lemon
50g/2oz/⅔ cup freshly grated Parmesan cheese
salt and freshly ground black pepper

1 Slice the courgettes diagonally into rounds, making them roughly the same thickness as the noodles, then cut the slices into matchsticks.

2 Toast the pine nuts in an ungreased frying pan over a medium heat until golden in colour.

3 Heat half the oil in a large frying pan. Add the shallots and garlic, and fry until fragrant. Push the shallot mixture to one side of the pan, add the remaining oil and, when hot, stir-fry the courgettes until soft.

4 Stir thoroughly to incorporate the shallot mixture and add the capers, sun-dried tomatoes and pine nuts. Remove the pan from the heat.

5 Bring a large pan of lightly salted water to the boil and cook the noodles until just tender. Drain well.

6 Toss the noodles into the courgette mixture and add the herbs, lemon rind and Parmesan. Season with salt and pepper to taste, and toss over the heat for 1–2 minutes. Transfer to a warmed serving bowl and serve immediately.

Somen Noodles with Baked Cherry Tomatoes

This summery dish is bursting with flavour. Baking the cherry tomatoes slowly strengthens their taste. If you can find yellow cherry tomatoes, use a mixture of red and yellow for an extra-special touch.

Serves 4–6

1kg/2¼lb cherry tomatoes
3 garlic cloves, finely sliced
1 bunch of fresh basil
120ml/4fl oz/½ cup extra virgin olive oil
450g/1lb dried somen noodles
salt and freshly ground black pepper
shavings of Parmesan cheese and tiny basil sprigs, to garnish

1 Preheat the oven to 180°C/350°F/Gas 4. Cut the tomatoes in half and arrange them, cut side up, in a single layer in an ovenproof dish. Season with salt and pepper to taste, and sprinkle with sliced garlic.

2 Strip the basil leaves from the stems, then arrange half of them over the tomatoes. Drizzle half the olive oil over the top. Bake the tomatoes for 1–1½ hours. Set aside in a cool place until ready to serve.

3 Just before serving, bring a large pan of lightly salted water to the boil and cook the somen noodles until just tender. Drain well, tip into a bowl and toss lightly with the baked tomatoes and their juices.

4 Add the remaining basil, with more olive oil and seasoning. Serve at once, garnished with Parmesan shavings and a few basil sprigs.

Cook's Tip
Take care when tossing the mixture that you don't break up the baked tomatoes too much.

Rice Noodles with Vegetable Chilli Sauce

Vegetable chilli is often served with jacket potatoes or rice. Teaming it with noodles is inspirational.

Serves 4

15ml/1 tbsp sunflower oil
1 onion, chopped
2 garlic cloves, crushed
1 fresh red chilli, seeded and finely chopped
1 red pepper, seeded and diced
2 carrots, finely chopped
175g/6oz/1 cup baby corn cobs, halved
225g/8oz can sliced bamboo shoots, rinsed and drained
400g/14oz can red kidney beans, rinsed and drained
300ml/ ½ pint/1 ¼ cups passata
15ml/1 tbsp soy sauce
5ml/1 tsp ground coriander
250g/9oz dried rice noodles
30ml/2 tbsp chopped fresh parsley, plus parsley sprigs, to garnish
salt and freshly ground black pepper

1 Heat the sunflower oil in a large, heavy-based pan. Add the onion, garlic, chilli and red pepper, and cook over a medium heat, stirring occasionally, for 5 minutes.

2 Stir in the carrots, corn cobs, bamboo shoots, kidney beans, passata, soy sauce and ground coriander.

3 Bring to the boil, then cover, lower the heat and simmer gently for 30 minutes, until the vegetables are tender, stirring occasionally. Season with salt and pepper to taste.

4 Meanwhile, put the rice noodles in a bowl and pour over sufficient boiling water to cover them. Stir with a fork and leave to stand for 3–4 minutes, or according to the packet instructions. Drain, then rinse with boiling water and drain thoroughly again.

5 Stir the parsley into the sauce. Spoon the noodles on to warmed serving plates and top with the sauce. Garnish with the parsley and serve immediately.

Vegetable & Egg Noodle Ribbons

Serve this elegant, colourful dish with a tossed green salad as a light lunch for four or as a starter for six to eight people.

Serves 4–8

1 large carrot
2 courgettes
50g/2oz/ ¼ cup butter
15ml/1 tbsp olive oil
6 fresh shiitake mushrooms, thinly sliced
50g/2oz/ ½ cup frozen peas, thawed
350g/12oz broad dried egg noodles
10ml/2 tsp chopped mixed herbs (such as marjoram, chives and basil)
salt and freshly ground black pepper
25g/1oz Parmesan cheese, to serve (optional)

1 Using a vegetable peeler, carefully slice thin strips from the carrot and from the courgettes.

2 Heat the butter with the olive oil in a large frying pan. Add the carrot and shiitake mushrooms, and fry, stirring frequently, for 2 minutes. Add the courgettes and peas, and stir-fry until the courgettes are cooked, but still crisp. Season with salt and pepper to taste.

3 Meanwhile, bring a large pan of lightly salted water to the boil and cook the noodles briefly until just tender. Drain them well and tip them into a warmed serving bowl. Add the vegetables and toss to mix.

4 Sprinkle over the fresh herbs and season to taste. If using the Parmesan cheese, grate or shave it over the top. Toss lightly and serve immediately.

Cook's Tip

The noodles you want here are the Chinese broad flat ribbons, which are available from Oriental markets. However, pappardelle could be used instead.

Spicy Vegetable Chow Mein

Ten minutes is all the time it takes to make this simply delicious snack.

Serves 3

225g/8oz dried egg noodles
115g/4oz French beans
30–45ml/2–3 tbsp vegetable oil
2 garlic cloves, crushed
1 onion, chopped
1 small red pepper, seeded and chopped
1 small green pepper, seeded and chopped
1 celery stick, finely chopped
2.5ml/ ½ tsp Chinese five-spice powder
1 vegetable stock cube, crumbled
2.5ml/ ½ tsp freshly ground black pepper
15ml/1 tbsp soy sauce
salt

1 Bring a large pan of lightly salted water to the boil and cook the noodles briefly until they are just tender. Drain and spread out on a large plate to cool.

2 Blanch the French beans in lightly salted boiling water for 1 minute, then remove and drain.

3 Preheat a wok. Swirl in the oil and stir-fry the French beans, garlic, onion, peppers and celery, tossing them together to mix.

4 Stir in the five-spice powder and crumble in the stock cube. Stir in the black pepper and cook for 3 minutes.

5 Stir in the noodles and soy sauce. Toss the mixture over the heat for 2–3 minutes, until the noodles have heated through and are coated in the sauce. Transfer to a warmed serving bowl and serve at once.

Cook's Tip
Chinese five-spice powder is a mixture of star anise, pepper, fennel, cloves and cinnamon. It is available from supermarkets and Chinese food stores. When buying, make sure you have Chinese powder, as Indian five-spice powder is different.

Chow Mein with Cashew Nuts

It is the lemon sauce that makes this chow mein extra special.

Serves 4

225g/8oz dried egg noodles
30ml/2 tbsp vegetable oil
50g/2oz/ ½ cup cashew nuts
2 carrots, cut into matchsticks
3 celery sticks, cut into matchsticks
1 green pepper, seeded and cut into thin strips
225g/8oz/4 cups beansprouts
salt
30ml/2 tbsp toasted sesame seeds, to garnish

For the lemon sauce
30ml/2 tbsp light soy sauce
15ml/1 tbsp dry sherry
150ml/ ¼ pint/ ⅔ cup Vegetable Stock
grated rind and juice of 2 lemons
15ml/1 tbsp granulated sugar
10ml/2 tsp cornflour

1 Stir all the ingredients for the lemon sauce together in a jug. Bring a large pan of lightly salted water to the boil and cook the noodles until they are just tender. Drain and spread out on a plate to dry.

2 Preheat a wok and swirl in the oil. Add the cashew nuts, toss them quickly over a high heat until golden, then remove them with a slotted spoon and drain on kitchen paper.

3 Add the carrots and celery to the wok, and stir-fry over a medium heat for 4–5 minutes. Add the green pepper and beansprouts, and stir-fry for 2–3 minutes more.

4 Using a slotted spoon or spider, lift the vegetables out of the wok and set them aside on a plate. Pour the lemon sauce mixture into the wok and cook, stirring constantly, for about 2 minutes, until it is thick.

5 Return the vegetables to the pan, add the noodles and toss over the heat until heated through.

6 Finally, add the cashew nuts and toss them with the noodles and vegetables. Serve immediately on heated plates, with the toasted sesame seeds sprinkled on top.

Peanut Noodles

Add any of your favourite vegetables to this dish, which can be made quickly for a great midweek supper.

Serves 4

200g/7oz medium dried egg noodles
30ml/2 tbsp vegetable oil
2 garlic cloves, crushed
1 large onion, roughly chopped
1 red pepper, seeded and roughly chopped
1 yellow pepper, seeded and roughly chopped
3 courgettes, roughly chopped
150g/5oz/1 ¼ cups roasted unsalted peanuts, roughly chopped
chopped fresh chives, to garnish

For the dressing

60ml/4 tbsp extra virgin olive oil
grated rind and juice of 1 lemon
1 fresh red chilli, seeded and finely chopped
45ml/3 tbsp snipped fresh chives, plus extra to garnish
15–30ml/1–2 tbsp balsamic vinegar
salt and freshly ground black pepper

1 First, make the dressing. Whisk the olive oil, grated lemon rind and 45ml/3 tbsp of the lemon juice in a jug or a small bowl, then add the chilli, chives, plenty of seasoning and balsamic vinegar to taste. Whisk again.

2 Bring a large pan of lightly salted water to the boil. Add the noodles and cook briefly until just tender, or according to the instructions on the packet. Drain thoroughly.

3 Preheat a wok and swirl in the oil. Add the garlic and onion, and stir-fry over a medium heat for 3 minutes, or until beginning to soften.

4 Add the red and yellow peppers and courgettes, and stir-fry until they are just tender. Add the peanuts and stir-fry for 1 minute more.

5 Toss the noodles into the vegetable mixture and stir-fry to heat through. Add the dressing, stir to coat and transfer to a warmed serving bowl. Serve immediately, garnished with the chopped fresh chives.

Thai Noodles with Chinese Chives

This recipe requires a little time for preparation, but the cooking time is very fast.

Serves 4

350g/12oz dried rice noodles
1cm/ ½in piece of fresh root ginger, grated
30ml/2 tbsp light soy sauce
45ml/3 tbsp vegetable oil
225g/8oz Quorn, diced
2 garlic cloves, crushed
1 large onion, cut into thin wedges
115g/4oz fried beancurd (tofu), thinly sliced
1 fresh green chilli, seeded and finely sliced
175g/6oz/3 cups beansprouts
115g/4oz Chinese chives, cut into 5cm/2in lengths
50g/2oz/ ½ cup roasted peanuts, ground
30ml/2 tbsp dark soy sauce
30ml/2 tbsp chopped fresh coriander

1 Place the noodles in a large bowl, cover with water and soak for 20–30 minutes, then drain.

2 Mix the ginger, light soy sauce and 15ml/1 tbsp of the oil in a bowl. Stir in the Quorn and set aside for 10 minutes. Drain, reserving the marinade.

3 Preheat a wok, swirl in half the remaining oil and fry the garlic for a few seconds. Do not let it brown. Add the Quorn and stir-fry for 3–4 minutes. Transfer it to a plate and set aside

4 Heat the remaining oil in the wok and stir-fry the onion for 3–4 minutes, until softened and tinged with brown. Add the beancurd and chilli, stir-fry briefly and then add the noodles. Toss over the heat for 4–5 minutes.

5 Add the beansprouts, Chinese chives and most of the ground peanuts, reserving a little for the garnish. Stir well, then add the Quorn, the dark soy sauce and the reserved marinade. Toss the mixture over the heat for 1–2 minutes to heat through.

6 Spoon on to warmed serving plates. Garnish with the remaining ground peanuts and the chopped fresh coriander. Serve immediately.

Buckwheat Noodles with Goat's Cheese

The earthy flavour of buckwheat goes well with peppery rocket and creamy goat's cheese in this tasty supper dish.

Serves 4

75g/3oz/ ¾ cup hazelnuts
350g/12oz buckwheat noodles
50g/2oz/ ¼ cup butter
2 garlic cloves, finely chopped
4 shallots, sliced
a large handful of rocket leaves
175g/6oz goat's cheese
salt and freshly ground black pepper

1 Preheat the grill. Spread out the hazelnuts in the grill pan and place them under a medium heat until they are golden brown. Watch them closely, as they tend to burn easily. Tip the nuts into a clean dish towel and rub off the skins. Set aside.

2 Bring a large pan of lightly salted water to the boil and cook the noodles until they are just tender. Drain well.

3 Heat the butter in a large, heavy-based frying pan. Add the garlic and shallots, and cook over a medium heat, stirring constantly, for 2–3 minutes, until the shallots are soft.

4 Add the hazelnuts and fry, stirring constantly, for about 1 minute. Add the rocket leaves and, when they start to wilt, toss in the noodles and heat them through.

5 Season with salt and pepper to taste. Crumble in the goat's cheese and serve immediately.

Variations

- *Substitute watercress, sorrel or spinach for the rocket.*
- *You could use fresh wholemeal noodles instead of the buckwheat noodles.*

Indian Mee Goreng

This is a truly international dish combining a mixture of traditional Indian, Chinese and Western ingredients.

Serves 4–6

450g/1lb fresh yellow egg noodles
60–90ml/4–6 tbsp vegetable oil
150g/5oz firm beancurd (tofu), cubed
2 eggs
30ml/2 tbsp water
1 onion, sliced
1 garlic clove, crushed
15ml/1 tbsp light soy sauce
30–45ml/2–3 tbsp tomato ketchup
15ml/1 tbsp chilli sauce (or to taste)
1 large cooked potato, diced
4 spring onions, shredded
1–2 fresh green chillies, seeded and finely sliced
salt and freshly ground black pepper

1 Bring a large pan of water to the boil and cook the fresh egg noodles for just 2 minutes. Drain, rinse under cold water, drain again and set aside.

2 Heat 30ml/2 tbsp of the oil in a large, heavy-based frying pan. Add the beancurd and fry the cubes over a medium heat until golden brown. Lift them out with a slotted spoon and set aside.

3 In a jug, beat the eggs with the water and add a little salt and pepper. Pour the mixture into the oil remaining in the frying pan and make an omelette. Flip over, cook the other side, then slide the omelette out of the pan. Blot the surface with kitchen paper, roll it up and slice it thinly.

4 Preheat a wok. Swirl in the remaining oil, and stir-fry the onion and garlic for 2–3 minutes. Add the drained noodles, soy sauce, ketchup and chilli sauce. Toss well over a medium heat for 2 minutes, then add the diced potato. Reserve a few spring onions for the garnish and stir the rest into the noodles with the chillies and the beancurd.

5 When the mixture is piping hot, stir in the omelette strips. Transfer to a warmed platter, garnish with the remaining spring onions and serve immediately.

Teriyaki Soba Noodles

Japanese soba noodles are made from buckwheat flour, which gives them a unique texture and colour. They are excellent with tofu and asparagus.

Serves 4

350g/12oz dried soba noodles
45ml/3 tbsp vegetable oil
200g/7oz asparagus tips
10ml/2 tsp sesame oil
225g/8oz block of firm tofu
2 spring onions, cut into thin strips
1 carrot, cut into matchsticks
2.5ml/ ½ tsp dried chilli flakes
15ml/1 tbsp sesame seeds
salt and freshly ground black pepper

For the teriyaki sauce

60ml/4 tbsp dark soy sauce
60ml/4 tbsp Japanese sake or dry sherry
60ml/4 tbsp mirin
5ml/1 tsp caster sugar

1 Bring a large pan of lightly salted water to the boil and cook the soba noodles briefly until they are just tender. Drain, rinse under cold running water and drain again.

2 Heat about 30ml/2 tbsp of the vegetable oil in a griddle pan and cook the asparagus for 8–10 minutes, turning frequently, until tender and browned. Using tongs, transfer to a bowl and toss with the sesame oil.

3 Preheat a wok. Swirl in the remaining vegetable oil. When it is very hot, add the tofu and fry for 8–10 minutes, until golden and crisp on all sides. Carefully lift it out of the wok and leave it to drain on kitchen paper. Cut into 1cm/½in slices.

4 Make the teriyaki sauce. Mix the soy sauce, sake or sherry, mirin and sugar together, then heat the mixture in the wok.

5 Toss in the noodles and stir to coat them in the sauce. Heat for 1–2 minutes, then add the tofu and asparagus, and toss lightly to mix. Spoon into warmed serving bowls. Scatter the spring onions and carrot matchsticks on top, and sprinkle with the chilli flakes and sesame seeds. Serve immediately.

Stir-fried Beancurd with Noodles

This is a satisfying dish, which is both tasty and easy to make. It looks and smells wonderfully appetizing and will quickly become a firm family favourite.

Serves 4

225g/8oz firm beancurd (tofu)
groundnut oil, for deep-frying
175g/6oz medium dried egg noodles
15ml/1 tbsp sesame oil
5ml/1 tsp cornflour
10ml/2 tsp dark soy sauce
30ml/1 tbsp Chinese rice wine or dry sherry
5ml/1 tsp granulated sugar
6–8 spring onions, cut diagonally into 2.5cm/1in lengths
3 garlic cloves, sliced
1 fresh green chilli, seeded and sliced
115g/4oz Chinese cabbage leaves, coarsely shredded
50g/2oz/1 cup beansprouts
50g/2oz/ ½ cup cashew nuts, toasted

1 Pat the beancurd dry with kitchen paper then cut it into 2.5cm/1in cubes. Half-fill a wok with groundnut oil and heat to 180°C/350°F, or until a cube of day-old bread browns in 30 seconds. Deep-fry the beancurd cubes, in batches, for 1–2 minutes, until golden and crisp. Drain on kitchen paper. Carefully pour all but 30ml/2 tbsp of the oil from the wok.

2 Bring a large pan of lightly salted water to the boil and cook the noodles briefly until they are just tender. Rinse them under cold water and drain well. Put them in a bowl, add 10ml/2 tsp of the sesame oil and toss to coat. Set aside.

3 In a bowl, mix the cornflour with the soy sauce, rice wine or sherry, sugar and remaining sesame oil.

4 Reheat the oil in the wok and add the spring onions, garlic, chilli, Chinese cabbage and beansprouts. Stir-fry over a medium heat for 1–2 minutes.

5 Add the beancurd with the noodles and sauce. Cook, stirring constantly, for about 1 minute, until well mixed. Sprinkle over the cashew nuts. Serve at once.

Thai Vegetables with Noodles

Serve this as a vegetarian supper on its own or as an accompaniment.

Serves 4

225g/8oz dried egg noodles
15ml/1 tbsp sesame oil
45ml/3 tbsp groundnut oil
2 garlic cloves, thinly sliced
2.5cm/1in piece of fresh root ginger, finely chopped
2 fresh red chillies, seeded and sliced
115g/4oz broccoli, broken into small florets
115g/4oz/⅔ cup baby corn cobs
175g/6oz/2 cups shiitake mushrooms, sliced
1 bunch spring onions, sliced
115g/4oz pak choi, shredded
115g/4oz/2 cups beansprouts
15–30ml/1–2 tbsp dark soy sauce
salt and freshly ground black pepper

1 Bring a large pan of lightly salted water to the boil and cook the noodles briefly until they are just tender. Drain them thoroughly, tip them into a bowl and toss them with the sesame oil. Set aside.

2 Preheat a wok, add the groundnut oil and swirl it around. Add the garlic and ginger, and stir-fry over a medium heat for 1 minute. Add the chillies, broccoli, corn cobs and mushrooms, and stir-fry for 2 minutes more.

3 Add the spring onions, shredded pak choi and beansprouts, and stir-fry for another 2 minutes. Add the drained noodles with the soy sauce and pepper to taste.

4 Toss the mixture over a high heat for 2–3 minutes, until the ingredients are well mixed and have heated through. Transfer to a warmed serving dish and serve at once.

Variations

- *If preferred, you can use shredded Chinese cabbage instead of pak choi.*
- *Substitute oyster mushrooms for the shiitake.*

Sesame Noodles with Spring Onions

This simple but very tasty dish can be prepared and cooked in a few minutes.

Serves 4

2 garlic cloves, roughly chopped
30ml/2 tbsp Chinese sesame paste
15ml/1 tbsp dark sesame oil
30ml/2 tbsp soy sauce
30ml/2 tbsp Chinese rice wine or dry sherry
15ml/1 tbsp clear honey
a pinch of Chinese five-spice powder
350g/12oz dried noodles
4 spring onions, thinly sliced diagonally
50g/2oz/1 cup beansprouts
7.5cm/3in piece of cucumber, cut into matchsticks
15ml/1 tbsp toasted sesame seeds
salt and freshly ground black pepper

1 Put the garlic, sesame paste, sesame oil, soy sauce, Chinese rice wine or sherry, honey and five-spice powder with a pinch each of salt and pepper in a blender or food processor. Process until smooth.

2 Bring a large pan of lightly salted water to the boil and cook the noodles briefly until just tender. Drain the noodles and tip them into a warmed serving bowl.

3 Add the garlic and sesame paste to the hot noodles, with the spring onions, and toss to coat. Top with the beansprouts, cucumber and sesame seeds, and serve.

Cook's Tip

If you can't find Chinese sesame paste, use tahini paste, available from supermarkets and delicatessens, or use smooth peanut butter instead.

Noodles with Braised Leaves

Use Chinese leaves or white cabbage for this tasty dish.

Serves 4

225g/8oz dried egg noodles
5ml/1 tsp sesame oil
45ml/3 tbsp groundnut oil
6 dried red chillies, seeded and chopped
2.5ml/½ tsp Szechuan peppercorns
450g/1lb Chinese leaves, coarsely shredded
15ml/1 tbsp rice vinegar
15ml/1 tbsp granulated sugar
15ml/1 tbsp light soy sauce
salt

1 Bring a pan of lightly salted water to the boil and cook the noodles briefly until they are just tender. Drain them well, then tip into a bowl and toss them with the sesame oil. Set aside.
2 Preheat a wok, add the groundnut oil and swirl it around. Add the chopped chillies and Szechuan peppercorns, and stir-fry for 15 seconds. Add the Chinese leaves and stir-fry over a medium heat for about 1 minute. Season to taste with a pinch of salt and stir-fry for 1 further minute.
3 Stir in the vinegar, sugar, soy sauce and noodles, and stir over the heat for 1 minute, until piping hot. Serve immediately.

Tomato Noodles with Fried Egg

Topping each portion of noodles with a fried egg adds protein, and, when the yolk is pierced, makes a marvellous contribution to the sauce.

Serves 4

350g/12oz medium-thick dried egg noodles
60ml/4 tbsp vegetable oil
2 garlic cloves, crushed
4 shallots, chopped
2.5ml/ ½ tsp chilli powder
5ml/1 tsp paprika
2 carrots, finely diced
115g/4oz/1½ cups button mushrooms, quartered
50g/2oz/ ½ cup peas, thawed if frozen
15ml/1 tbsp tomato ketchup
10ml/2 tsp tomato purée
butter, for frying
4 eggs
salt and freshly ground black pepper

1 Bring a large pan of lightly salted water to the boil and cook the noodles briefly until just tender. Drain, rinse under cold running water and drain again.

2 Preheat a wok, add the oil and swirl it around. When it is hot, add the garlic, shallots, chilli powder and paprika. Stir-fry for about 1 minute, then add the carrots, mushrooms and peas. Continue to stir-fry until the vegetables are cooked.

3 Stir the tomato ketchup and tomato purée into the vegetable mixture. Add the noodles and toss over a medium heat until they are heated through and have taken on the reddish tinge of the paprika and tomato.

4 Meanwhile, melt the butter in a large frying pan and fry the eggs. Season the noodle mixture, divide it among four warmed serving plates and top each portion with a fried egg.

Variations
- *For a change, poach the eggs, rather than fry them.*
- *Beat the eggs together and make 2–3 omelettes, then roll them up and cut into thin strips.*

Curry Fried Noodles

On its own, beancurd tastes fairly bland, but it absorbs the flavour of the curry spices quite wonderfully.

Serves 4

60ml/4 tbsp vegetable oil
30–45ml/2–3 tbsp curry paste
225g/8oz smoked beancurd (tofu), cut into 2.5cm/1in cubes
225g/8oz green beans, cut into 2.5cm/1in lengths
1 red pepper, seeded and cut into fine strips
350g/12oz rice vermicelli, soaked in hot water until soft
15ml/1 tbsp soy sauce
salt and freshly ground black pepper

To serve

sliced spring onions
chopped fresh red chillies
lime wedges

1 Preheat a wok, add half the oil and swirl it around. Stir-fry the curry paste for a few minutes. Add the beancurd and fry the cubes until they are golden brown. Using a slotted spoon, remove them from the wok, drain on kitchen paper and set them aside until needed.

2 Heat the remaining oil in the wok, add the green beans and red pepper, and stir-fry over a medium heat for 3–4 minutes, until crisp-tender. It may be necessary to moisten them with a little water.

3 Drain the noodles and add them to the wok. Continue to stir-fry until the noodles are heated through, then return the curried beancurd to the wok. Season with soy sauce, salt and pepper to taste.

4 Transfer the mixture to a warmed serving dish. Sprinkle with the spring onions and chillies, and serve immediately, with the lime wedges on the side.

Variation
Add 3–4 dried Chinese mushrooms, soaked in hot water for 30 minutes then drained, with the green beans in step 2.

Tuna & Mixed Vegetable Pasta

Mushrooms, tuna and pasta make a tasty combination, and the fat content is satisfyingly low.

Serves 4

15ml/1 tbsp olive oil
175g/6oz/2 cups sliced button mushrooms
1 garlic clove, crushed
½ red pepper, seeded and chopped
15ml/1 tbsp tomato purée
300ml/ ½ pint/1 ¼ cups tomato juice
115g/4oz/1 cup frozen peas
15–30ml/1–2 tbsp drained pickled green peppercorns, crushed
275g/10oz/2½ cups wholewheat pasta shapes
200g/7oz can tuna chunks in brine, drained
6 spring onions, diagonally sliced
salt

1 Heat the olive oil in a heavy-based saucepan. Add the mushrooms, garlic and red pepper, and sauté gently over a low heat until softened.

2 Stir in the tomato purée, then add the tomato juice, peas and some or all of the crushed peppercorns, depending on how spicy you would like the sauce. Bring to the boil, lower the heat and simmer.

3 Bring a large pan of lightly salted water to the boil and cook the pasta until *al dente*.

4 When the pasta is almost ready, add the tuna to the sauce and heat through gently. Stir in the spring onions. Drain the pasta, tip it into a heated bowl and pour over the sauce. Serve at once.

Variations

- *Substitute 115g/4oz/⅔ cup frozen or canned sweetcorn kernels for the peas.*
- *Use canned or flaked smoked mackerel fillets instead of the canned tuna.*

Conchiglie with Tomato & Tuna Sauce

The trick with low-fat food is to make it as flavoursome as you can, using aromatics, herbs and extra flavourings such as capers.

Serves 6

1 medium onion, finely chopped
1 celery stick, finely chopped
1 red pepper, seeded and diced
1 garlic clove, crushed
150ml/ ¼ pint/ ⅔ cup Vegetable Stock
400g/14oz can chopped tomatoes
15ml/1 tbsp tomato purée
10ml/2 tsp caster sugar
15ml/1 tbsp chopped fresh basil
15ml/1 tbsp chopped fresh parsley
450g/1lb/4 cups dried conchiglie
400g/14oz can tuna in brine, drained
30ml/2 tbsp bottled capers in vinegar, drained
salt and freshly ground black pepper

1 Put the onion, celery, red pepper and garlic into a large non-stick pan. Add the vegetable stock, bring to the boil and cook over a medium heat for about 5 minutes, or until most of the stock has evaporated and very little liquid remains.

2 Stir in the tomatoes, tomato purée, sugar, basil and parsley. Season to taste with salt and pepper, and bring to the boil over a medium heat.

3 Lower the heat and simmer the sauce for 30 minutes until thickened, stirring occasionally.

4 Meanwhile, bring a large pan of lightly salted water to the boil and cook the pasta until *al dente*. Drain thoroughly and transfer to a warm serving dish.

5 Flake the tuna into large chunks and add it to the sauce with the capers. Heat gently, stirring occasionally but without breaking up the fish, for 1–2 minutes. Pour over the pasta, toss gently and serve at once.

Pasta with Tuna, Capers & Anchovies

This piquant sauce could be made without tomatoes – just heat the oil, add the other ingredients and heat through gently before tossing with the pasta.

Serves 4

15ml/1 tbsp olive oil
2 garlic cloves, crushed
2 x 400g/14oz cans chopped tomatoes
400g/14oz can tuna in brine, drained
6 drained canned anchovy fillets
30ml/2 tbsp drained bottled capers in vinegar
30ml/2 tbsp chopped fresh basil
450g/1lb/4 cups dried rigatoni, penne or garganelli
salt and freshly ground black pepper
fresh basil sprigs, to garnish

1 Heat the olive oil in a heavy-based saucepan. Add the garlic and cook over a medium heat until golden, but not browned. Lower the heat, stir in the tomatoes and simmer for about 25 minutes, until thickened.

2 Flake the tuna and cut the anchovies in half. Stir the fish into the sauce with the capers and chopped basil. Season well with salt and pepper.

3 Bring a large pan of lightly salted water to the boil and cook the pasta until it is *al dente*.

4 Drain the pasta well, return to the clean pan and toss with the sauce. Serve immediately in warmed bowls, garnished with the fresh basil sprigs.

Cook's Tip

Olive oil is high in monounsaturated fats and so is a healthy choice. However, if you want to cut the fat content of this dish still further, omit it and coat the base of the pan very thinly with light spray oil.

Salmon Pasta with Parsley Sauce

Delicately flavoured and with a lovely colour, salmon makes a surprisingly substantial meal, especially when tossed with pasta shapes.

Serves 4

450g/1lb salmon fillet, skinned
150g/5oz/⅔ cup very low-fat fromage frais
45ml/3 tbsp finely chopped parsley
finely grated rind of ½ orange
225g/8oz/2 cups dried penne or spirali
175g/6oz cherry tomatoes, halved
salt and freshly ground black pepper

1 Cut the salmon into bite-size pieces, arrange on a heatproof plate and cover with foil. Mix the fromage frais, parsley and orange rind in a bowl, and stir in pepper to taste.

2 Bring a large pan of lightly salted water to the boil, add the pasta and return to the boil. Lower the heat, place the plate of salmon on top and simmer for 10–12 minutes, or until both the pasta and salmon are cooked.

3 Lift off the plate of salmon and drain the pasta well. Put the pasta in a bowl and toss with the fromage frais mixture until coated. Add the tomatoes and salmon, and toss again, taking care not to break up the fish too much. Serve hot or cold.

Cook's Tip

Salmon is an oily fish and contains 8–12 per cent fat, mostly in the form of Omega 3 fatty acids, which are believed to be beneficial in helping to prevent coronary heart disease. In this recipe, the fat content of the fish is counterbalanced by using very low-fat or even virtually fat-free fromage frais.

Penne with Salmon & Dill

Rosé wine accentuates the colour of the salmon and gives this simple dish a hint of sophistication.

Serves 6

350g/12oz fresh salmon fillet, skinned
115g/4oz sliced smoked salmon
350g/12oz/3 cups dried penne
1–2 shallots, finely chopped
115g/4oz/1½ cups button mushrooms, quartered
150ml/ ¼ pint/ ⅔ cup rosé wine
150ml/ ¼ pint/ ⅔ cup fish stock
150ml/ ¼ pint/ ⅔ cup low-fat crème fraîche
30ml/2 tbsp chopped fresh dill
salt and freshly ground black pepper
fresh dill sprigs, to garnish

1 Cut the fresh salmon into 2.5cm/1in cubes. Cut the smoked salmon into 1cm/ ½in strips and set aside.

2 Bring a large pan of lightly salted water to the boil and cook the pasta until it is *al dente*.

3 Meanwhile, put the shallots and mushrooms into a non-stick pan and pour in the rosé wine. Bring to the boil over a medium heat and cook for about 5 minutes, or until the wine has reduced almost completely.

4 Pour in the fish stock and crème fraîche, and stir until smooth. Add the fresh salmon, cover the pan and simmer gently over a low heat for 2–3 minutes, or until the salmon is cooked.

5 Drain the pasta and tip it into a warmed serving dish. Add the smoked salmon and dill to the sauce, season to taste with salt and pepper, and pour over the pasta. Toss lightly to mix. Serve at once, garnished with the dill sprigs.

Variation
Use fresh and smoked trout instead of the salmon. Substitute red wine for the rosé, as trout does not have the same delicate pink colouring as salmon.

Tagliatelle with Smoked Trout & Dill

This light pasta dish can also be made with canned tuna or salmon in brine as a store-cupboard alternative for a midweek supper.

Serves 4

350g/12oz fresh or dried tagliatelle
275g/10oz smoked trout fillet, skinned and flaked
225g/8oz cherry tomatoes, halved
150g/5oz/ ⅔ cup low-fat fromage frais or natural yogurt
30ml/2 tbsp chopped fresh dill
30ml/2 tbsp chopped fresh chives
salt and freshly ground black pepper

1 Bring a large pan of lightly salted water to the boil and cook the pasta until *al dente*. Drain well and return to the clean pan.

2 Toss the flaked trout into the hot pasta, and add the tomatoes and fromage frais or yogurt.

3 Heat gently, without boiling, then stir in the herbs and season with black pepper to taste. Spoon into warmed bowls and serve immediately.

Cook's Tip
Low-fat fromage frais can frequently be used in place of cream in sauces, so consider this low-fat option in other recipes too.

Variation
Substitute pappardelle for the tagliatelle and smoked mackerel for the smoked trout. Omit the cherry tomatoes and add strips of red pepper instead. Toss the dressed pasta with finely diced cucumber rather than dill.

Fusilli with Smoked Trout

Curly strands of fusilli in a sauce that tastes deceptively creamy are topped with crisp-tender vegetables and smoked fish to make a dish that tastes every bit as good as it looks.

Serves 4–6

2 carrots, cut into matchstick strips
1 leek, cut into matchstick strips
2 celery sticks, cut into matchstick strips
150ml/ ¼ pint/ ⅔ cup Vegetable Stock
225g/8oz smoked trout fillets, skinned and cut into strips
200g/7oz/scant 1 cup low-fat cream cheese
150ml/ ¼ pint/ ⅔ cup medium sweet white wine or fish stock
15ml/1 tbsp chopped fresh dill or fennel
225g/8oz dried fusilli lunghi
salt and freshly ground black pepper
fresh dill sprigs, to garnish

1 Put the carrots, leek and celery into a pan. Pour in the vegetable stock Bring to the boil and cook over a high heat for 4–5 minutes, until the vegetables are tender and most of the stock has evaporated. Remove the pan from the heat and add the smoked trout.

2 To make the sauce, put the cream cheese and white wine or fish stock into a large pan, and whisk over a low heat until smooth. Season to taste with salt and pepper. Add the chopped dill or fennel.

3 Bring a large pan of lightly salted water to the boil and cook the pasta until *al dente*.

4 Drain the pasta well and add it to the pan with the sauce. Toss lightly, then transfer to a warmed serving bowl. Top with the cooked vegetables and trout. Serve immediately, garnished with dill sprigs.

Variation
Use smoked monkfish instead of trout.

Smoked Trout Cannelloni

Simmering vegetables in stock instead of frying them in fat or oil produces tasty, moist results.

Serves 4–6

1 large onion, finely chopped
1 garlic clove, crushed
60ml/4 tbsp Vegetable Stock
2 x 400g/14oz cans chopped tomatoes
2.5ml/ ½ tsp dried mixed herbs
1 smoked trout, about 400g/14oz
75g/3oz/ ¾ cup frozen peas, thawed
75g/3oz/1 ½ cups fresh white breadcrumbs
16 cannelloni tubes
salt and freshly ground black pepper

For the cheese sauce
25g/1oz/2 tbsp low-fat spread
25g/1oz/ ¼ cup plain flour
350ml/12fl oz/1 ½ cups skimmed milk
freshly grated nutmeg
45ml/3 tbsp freshly grated Parmesan cheese

1 Put the onion, garlic and stock in a large pan. Cover and cook for 3 minutes. Remove the lid and continue to cook, stirring occasionally, until the stock has reduced entirely. Stir in the tomatoes and dried herbs. Simmer, uncovered, for 10 minutes more, or until very thick.

2 Meanwhile, skin the fish, flake the flesh and discard the bones. Put the fish in a bowl and stir in the tomato mixture, peas and breadcrumbs, and season to taste. Leave to cool slightly.

3 Preheat the oven to 190°C/375°F/Gas 5. Spoon the filling into the cannelloni tubes and arrange them in a single layer in an ovenproof dish.

4 Make the sauce. Put the low-fat spread, flour and milk into a pan and cook over a medium heat, whisking constantly until the sauce thickens. Simmer for 2–3 minutes, stirring all the time. Season to taste with salt, pepper and nutmeg.

5 Pour the sauce over the cannelloni and sprinkle with the Parmesan. Bake for 35–40 minutes, or until the top is golden and bubbling. Leave to stand for 5–10 minutes before serving.

Smoked Haddock in Parsley Sauce

Perfect for a family supper, this would be lovely with roasted tomatoes.

Serves 4

450g/1lb smoked haddock fillet
1 small leek or onion, thickly sliced
300ml/ ½ pint/1 ¼ cups skimmed milk
1 bouquet garni (bay leaf, thyme and parsley stalks)
225g/8oz/2 cups dried conchiglie
25g/1oz/2 tbsp low-fat spread
25g/1oz/ ¼ cup plain flour
30ml/2 tbsp chopped fresh parsley
salt and freshly ground black pepper
toasted flaked almonds, to serve (optional)

1 Remove the skin and any bones from the haddock. Put it into a pan with the leek or onion, milk and bouquet garni. Bring to simmering point, cover and cook gently for 8–10 minutes, until the fish flakes easily when tested with the tip of a sharp knife.

2 Strain, reserving the cooking liquid, and discard the bouquet garni. Flake the fish and set it aside with the leek or onion.

3 Bring a large pan of lightly salted water to the boil and cook the pasta until it is *al dente*.

4 Meanwhile, put the low-fat spread and flour in a pan. Whisk in the milk used for cooking the fish. Bring to the boil over a low heat, whisking until smooth. Season with salt and pepper to taste, and add the flaked fish and leek or onion.

5 Drain the pasta thoroughly and tip it into a warmed serving bowl. Add the sauce and chopped parsley. Toss well. Serve at once. Scatter with toasted almonds, if you like.

Cook's Tip

Skin frozen fish when it is only partially thawed. Slide the tip of a knife under the skin to loosen, grip it firmly and pull it off.

Hot Spicy Prawns with Campanelle

Marinated prawns and grilled turkey rashers make this pasta dish a treat that's hard to beat.

Serves 4–6

225g/8oz cooked tiger prawns, peeled
1–2 garlic cloves, crushed
finely grated rind of 1 lemon
15ml/1 tbsp lemon juice
1.5ml/ ¼ tsp red chilli paste or a large pinch of dried ground chilli
15ml/1 tbsp light soy sauce
150g/5oz smoked turkey rashers
225g/8oz dried campanelle
2 shallots, finely chopped
90ml/6 tbsp white wine
60ml/4 tbsp fish stock
4 firm ripe tomatoes, peeled, seeded and chopped
30ml/2 tbsp chopped fresh parsley
salt and freshly ground black pepper

1 In a non-metallic bowl, mix the prawns with the garlic, lemon rind and juice, chilli paste or ground chilli and soy sauce. Season to taste with salt and pepper, cover and set aside to marinate for at least 1 hour.

2 Meanwhile, grill the turkey rashers under a preheated moderate grill for about 3–4 minutes. Drain them on kitchen paper, then dice them.

3 Bring a large pan of lightly salted water to the boil and cook the pasta until *al dente*.

4 Meanwhile, put the shallots and wine in a large pan and bring to the boil over a medium heat, then simmer until the shallots are soft and only about half of the wine remains.

5 Add the prawns, together with their marinade, and bring to the boil over a high heat. Stir in the smoked turkey and fish stock. Heat through for 1 minute.

6 Drain the pasta and add it to the pan with the chopped tomatoes and parsley. Toss thoroughly, transfer to a warmed bowl and serve immediately.

Mixed Summer Pasta

A pretty sauce with plenty of flavour makes this a perfect dish for supper on a warm summer evening.

Serves 4

115g/4oz French beans, cut into 2.5cm/1in pieces
350g/12oz dried fusilli lunghi
15ml/1 tbsp olive oil
½ fennel bulb, sliced
1 bunch spring onions, sliced diagonally
115g/4oz yellow cherry tomatoes
115g/4oz red cherry tomatoes
30ml/2 tbsp chopped fresh dill
225g/8oz cooked peeled prawns
15ml/1 tbsp lemon juice
15ml/1 tbsp wholegrain mustard
60ml/4 tbsp very low-fat fromage frais
salt and freshly ground black pepper
fresh dill sprigs, to garnish

1 Bring a large pan of lightly salted water to the boil and cook the beans for 5 minutes, until tender. Lift out with a slotted spoon, refresh under cold water and drain again. Set aside.

2 Bring the water back to the boil, add the pasta and cook until it is *al dente*.

3 Meanwhile, heat the oil in a large non-stick frying pan. Add the fennel and spring onions, and fry, stirring occasionally, for about 5 minutes.

4 Stir in the cherry tomatoes and fry for 5 minutes more, stirring occasionally.

5 Add the dill and prawns to the pan, cook for 1 minute, then stir in the lemon juice, mustard, fromage frais and beans. Season to taste and simmer for 1 minute.

6 Drain the pasta and add it to the prawn and vegetable sauce. Toss well. Serve immediately, garnished with the fresh dill.

Saffron & Seafood Pappardelle

This resembles a Breton fish stew, and the broad ribbons of tender pasta make a welcome bonus.

Serves 4

a large pinch of saffron strands
4 sun-dried tomatoes, chopped
5ml/1 tsp fresh thyme
60ml/4 tbsp hot water
225g/8oz baby squid
225g/8oz monkfish fillet
2–3 garlic cloves, crushed
2 small onions, quartered
1 small fennel bulb, trimmed and sliced
150ml/¼ pint/⅔ cup white wine
12 large raw prawns in their shells
225g/8oz fresh pappardelle
salt and freshly ground black pepper
30ml/2 tbsp chopped fresh parsley, to garnish

1 Put the saffron, sun-dried tomatoes and thyme into a bowl. Pour over the hot water. Leave to soak for 30 minutes.

2 Pull the head from the body of each squid and remove the quill. Cut the tentacles from the head and rinse these under cold water. Pull off the outer skin, then cut the body into 5mm/¼in rings. Cut the monkfish into 2.5cm/1in cubes.

3 Bring a large pan of lightly salted water to the boil. Put the garlic, onions and fennel into a separate pan and pour over the wine. Cover and simmer for 5 minutes until tender.

4 Add the monkfish to the onion mixture, then pour in the sun-dried tomato mixture. Cover and cook for 3 minutes, then add the prawns in their shells and squid. Cover and cook over a low heat for 1–2 minutes. Do not overcook or the squid will toughen. Season to taste with salt and pepper.

5 Meanwhile, add the pasta to the pan of boiling water and cook until *al dente*.

6 Drain the pasta, divide it among four warmed dishes and top with the fish and shellfish sauce. Sprinkle with the chopped parsley and serve at once.

Spaghetti with White Clam Sauce

This is a low-fat version of one of Italy's most famous pasta dishes.

Serves 4

1kg/2¼lb fresh clams
120ml/4fl oz/ ½ cup dry white wine
350g/12oz dried spaghetti
30ml/2 tbsp olive oil
2 whole garlic cloves, peeled
45ml/3 tbsp chopped fresh flat leaf parsley
salt and freshly ground black pepper

1 Scrub the clams under cold running water, discarding any that are open or that do not close when sharply tapped against the work surface.

2 Put the clams in a large pan, add the wine, then cover the pan tightly and place it over a high heat. Cook, shaking the pan frequently, for about 5 minutes, until the clams are opened.

3 Using a slotted spoon, transfer the clams to a bowl, discarding any that have failed to open. Strain the liquid and set it aside. Put 12 clams in their shells to one side for the garnish, then remove the rest from their shells.

4 Bring a large pan of lightly salted water to the boil and cook the pasta until it is *al dente*.

5 Meanwhile, heat the oil in a deep pan. Fry the whole garlic cloves over a medium heat until golden, crushing them with the back of a spoon. Remove the garlic with a slotted spoon and discard.

6 Add the shelled clams to the garlic-flavoured oil and moisten them with some of the strained liquid from the clams. Season with plenty of pepper. Cook for 1–2 minutes, gradually adding more liquid as the sauce reduces. Stir in the parsley and cook for a further 1–2 minutes.

7 Drain the pasta, add it to the pan and toss well. Serve in individual dishes, garnished with the reserved clams.

Black Pasta with Raw Vegetables

Black pasta derives its colour from the addition of squid ink and looks very dramatic with the colourful vegetables. The avocado will push up the fat content, so leave it out if you prefer.

Serves 4

3 garlic cloves, crushed
15ml/1 tbsp white tarragon vinegar
5ml/1 tsp Dijon mustard
30ml/2 tbsp extra virgin olive oil
5ml/1 tsp finely chopped fresh thyme
1 yellow pepper, seeded
1 red pepper, seeded
225g/8oz mangetouts, topped and tailed
6 radishes
4 ripe plum tomatoes, peeled and seeded
½ avocado (optional)
275g/10oz dried black pasta
salt and freshly ground black pepper
12 fresh basil leaves, to garnish

1 Make a dressing by whisking the garlic, vinegar, mustard, olive oil and chopped thyme together in a large bowl. Season to taste with salt and black pepper.

2 Cut the red and yellow peppers into diamond shapes, halve the mangetouts and slice the radishes.

3 Dice the tomatoes. Peel, stone and slice the avocado, if using. Place all the vegetables in a bowl and add the dressing, stirring thoroughly to mix.

4 Bring a large pan of lightly salted water to the boil and cook the pasta until *al dente*.

5 Drain and tip the pasta into a large shallow serving dish. Cover with the dressed vegetables and serve immediately, garnished with basil leaves.

Variation

Instead of black pasta, you could use Japanese soba or buckwheat noodles, which have a nutty flavour and texture.

Pasta with Scallops in Warm Green Tartare Sauce

When you are trying not to eat too much fat, sauces can be the thing you miss most. Here is a deliciously creamy dish that won't compromise your conscience.

Serves 4
12 large scallops
350g/12oz dried black tagliatelle
60ml/4 tbsp white wine
150ml/ 1/4 pint/ 2/3 cup fish stock
lime wedges and parsley sprigs, to garnish

For the tartare sauce
120ml/4fl oz/ 1/2 cup low-fat crème fraîche
10ml/2 tsp wholegrain mustard
2 garlic cloves, crushed
30–45ml/2–3 tbsp freshly squeezed lime juice
60ml/4 tbsp chopped fresh parsley
30ml/2 tbsp snipped chives
salt and freshly ground black pepper

1 Slice the scallops in half, horizontally. Keep any corals whole. Set aside.

2 To make the tartare sauce, mix the crème fraîche, mustard, garlic, lime juice and herbs in a bowl. Season with salt and pepper to taste.

3 Bring a large pan of lightly salted water to the boil and cook the pasta until it is *al dente*.

4 Meanwhile, put the white wine and fish stock into a pan. Heat to simmering point. Add the scallops and cook very gently for 3–4 minutes (no longer or they will become tough).

5 Lift out the scallops with a slotted spoon. Boil the wine and stock to reduce by half, then add the tartare sauce to the pan. Heat gently, replace the scallops and cook for 1 minute.

6 Drain the pasta and divide it among four warmed bowls. Spoon the scallops and sauce over, garnish with lime wedges and parsley, and serve.

Devilled Crab Conchiglione

Large pasta shells are perfect for stuffing, and this is a really tasty filling.

Serves 4
350g/12oz/3 cups dried conchiglione
200g/7oz/scant 1 cup low-fat cream cheese
150ml/ 1/4 pint/ 2/3 cup skimmed milk
2.5ml/1/2 tsp ground paprika
5ml/1 tsp Dijon mustard
15ml/1 tbsp dried breadcrumbs
10ml/2 tsp freshly grated Parmesan cheese

For the filling
1 shallot, finely chopped
1 celery stick, finely chopped
1/2 small red pepper, seeded and finely chopped
45ml/3 tbsp white wine
45ml/3 tbsp low-fat crème fraîche
2 x 175g/6oz cans crab meat in brine, drained
45ml/3 tbsp fresh white breadcrumbs
30ml/2 tbsp freshly grated Parmesan cheese
15ml/1 tbsp Dijon mustard
2.5ml/ 1/2 tsp red chilli paste
salt and freshly ground black pepper

1 To make the filling, put the shallot, celery, red pepper and wine into a small pan, cover and cook gently for 3–4 minutes, until the vegetables are tender and little of the wine remains. Remove the pan from the heat and stir in the crème fraîche, crab meat, fresh breadcrumbs, Parmesan, mustard and chilli paste. Season, if necessary.

2 Bring a large pan of lightly salted water to the boil and cook the conchiglione, in batches if necessary, until *al dente*. Drain well, then arrange upside-down on a clean dish towel to dry.

3 Put the cream cheese, milk, paprika and mustard into a small pan. Heat gently and whisk until smooth. Season to taste. Pour the sauce into a large ovenproof dish.

4 Preheat the oven to 220°C/425°F/Gas 7. Fill the conchiglione with the crab mixture, and arrange them on top of the sauce. Mix the dried breadcrumbs and Parmesan, and sprinkle on top. Cover the dish with foil and bake for 15 minutes. Uncover and return to the oven for 5 minutes more. Serve at once.

Spaghetti with Turkey Ragoût

Turkey mince is much lower in fat than most other meats and makes an excellent basis for a low-fat pasta meal.

Serves 4
450g/1lb minced turkey
1 medium onion, finely diced
1 medium carrot, diced
1 celery stick, diced
400g/14oz can chopped tomatoes
15ml/1 tbsp tomato purée
5ml/1 tsp dried oregano
2 bay leaves, plus extra to garnish
225g/8oz dried spaghetti
salt and freshly ground black pepper

1 In a non-stick pan, dry-fry the minced turkey with the diced onion over a medium heat, stirring frequently, until the mince is lightly coloured.

2 Stir in the carrot and celery, and cook, stirring constantly, for 5–8 minutes.

3 Add the tomatoes, tomato purée, dried oregano and bay leaves. Bring to the boil, lower the heat, cover and simmer for 40 minutes, until the sauce is thick and full of flavour. Season to taste with salt and pepper.

4 Meanwhile, bring a large pan of lightly salted water to the boil and cook the spaghetti until *al dente*.

5 Drain well, divide among warmed bowls, spoon the ragoût over and serve immediately garnished with bay leaves.

Cook's tip
If you can't find minced turkey, use lean pork, lamb or beef mince and pour off all the fat from the pan before adding the vegetables.

Piquant Chicken with Spaghetti

Morsels of tender chicken in a mouthwatering sauce make this a popular dish for all the family.

Serves 4
1 onion, finely chopped
1 carrot, diced
1 garlic clove, crushed
300ml/ ½ pint/1 ¼ cups Vegetable Stock
4 small skinless, boneless chicken breasts
1 bouquet garni
115g/4oz/1 ½ cups button mushrooms, thinly sliced
5ml/1 tsp balsamic vinegar
½ cucumber, peeled and cut into batons
350g/12oz dried spaghetti
2 firm ripe tomatoes, peeled, seeded and chopped
30ml/2 tbsp low-fat crème fraîche
15ml/1 tbsp chopped fresh parsley
15ml/1 tbsp snipped chives
salt and freshly ground black pepper

1 Put the onion, carrot, garlic and stock into a pan, and add the chicken breasts and bouquet garni. Bring to the boil, lower the heat, cover and simmer gently for 15–20 minutes, or until tender. Transfer the chicken to a plate and cover with foil.

2 Strain the cooking liquid into a clean pan, discarding the vegetables and flavourings. Add the sliced mushrooms and balsamic vinegar, and simmer for 2–3 minutes, until tender. Using a slotted spoon, lift out the mushrooms and set them aside. Boil the stock until it is reduced by half.

3 Meanwhile, bring a large pan of lightly salted water to the boil. Add the cucumber, cook for 20 seconds, then lift out and set aside. Add the pasta to the boiling water and cook it until it is *al dente*.

4 Cut the chicken breasts into bite-size pieces and stir them into the reduced stock, with the chopped tomatoes, crème fraîche, cucumber, parsley and chives. Season with salt and pepper to taste.

5 Drain the pasta, tip it into a warmed serving dish and spoon over the piquant chicken. Serve at once.

Low-fat Spaghetti alla Carbonara

Smoked turkey rashers make a good substitute for bacon in this new look at an old favourite.

Serves 4

150g/5oz smoked turkey rashers
1 medium onion, chopped
1–2 garlic cloves, crushed
150ml/ ¼ pint/ ⅔ cup Vegetable Stock or defatted chicken stock
450g/1lb chilli and garlic-flavoured spaghetti
150ml/ ¼ pint/ ⅔ cup dry white wine
200g/7oz/scant 1 cup low-fat cream cheese
30ml/2 tbsp chopped fresh parsley
salt and freshly ground black pepper
shavings of Parmesan cheese, to serve

1 Cut the turkey rashers into 1cm/ ½in strips. Dry-fry in a non-stick pan over a medium heat for 2–3 minutes.

2 Add the onion, garlic and stock to the pan. Bring to the boil, lower the heat, cover and simmer while you cook the pasta.

3 Bring a large pan of lightly salted water to the boil and cook the pasta until it is *al dente*.

4 Meanwhile, add the wine to the turkey mixture and bring to the boil. Boil rapidly until reduced by half.

5 Whisk the cream cheese into the turkey mixture, beating until smooth. Season to taste with salt and pepper.

6 Drain the pasta, return it to the clean pan, and add the sauce and the chopped parsley. Toss well. Serve immediately in warmed bowls, with shavings of Parmesan.

Cook's Tip
Add the cream cheese gradually, a spoonful at a time, when making the sauce.

Turkey & Pasta Bake

Low in fat, turkey is a good choice for healthy family meals. Here it is combined with smoked turkey rashers, vegetables and rigatoni and topped with cheese before being baked in the oven.

Serves 4

275g/10oz minced turkey
150g/5oz smoked turkey rashers, chopped
1–2 garlic cloves, crushed
1 onion, finely chopped
2 carrots, diced
30ml/2 tbsp tomato purée
300ml/ ½ pint/1 ¼ cups defatted chicken stock
225g/8oz/2 cups dried rigatoni
30ml/2 tbsp freshly grated Parmesan cheese
salt and freshly ground black pepper

1 Dry-fry the minced turkey in a non-stick pan over a medium heat, breaking up any large pieces with a wooden spoon, until well browned all over.

2 Add the chopped turkey rashers, garlic, onion, carrots, tomato purée and stock. Bring to the boil, cover and simmer for 1 hour until tender. Season, if necessary.

3 Preheat the oven to 180°C/350°F/Gas 4. Bring a large pan of lightly salted water to the boil and cook the pasta until *al dente*.

4 Drain thoroughly, return to the clean pan and mix with the turkey sauce.

5 Spoon the pasta mixture into a shallow ovenproof dish and sprinkle with the freshly grated Parmesan. Bake for 20–30 minutes. Let stand for 5 minutes before serving.

Cook's Tip
To remove the fat from home-made chicken stock, let it cool, then chill it overnight in the fridge. The fat will solidify on top and will easily be lifted off.

Penne with Spinach

If you love spinach you'll really enjoy this moist and appetizing pasta dish.

Serves 4

225g/8oz fresh spinach leaves
150g/5oz smoked turkey rashers
350g/12oz/3 cups dried penne, preferably mixed colours
1 garlic clove, crushed
1 small onion, finely chopped
½ small red pepper, seeded and finely chopped
1 small fresh red chilli, seeded and chopped
150ml/ ¼ pint/ ⅔ cup Vegetable Stock
45ml/3 tbsp low-fat crème fraîche
30ml/2 tbsp freshly grated Parmesan cheese, plus extra to garnish
crusty bread, to serve

1 Preheat the grill. Wash the spinach leaves and remove the hard central stalks. Shred the leaves finely and set them aside.

2 Cook the smoked turkey rashers under a preheated moderate grill for 3–4 minutes, until lightly browned. Let them cool a little, then chop them finely.

3 Bring a large pan of lightly salted water to the boil and cook the pasta until it is *al dente*.

4 Meanwhile, put the garlic, onion, red pepper and chilli into a large frying pan. Pour over the stock, cover and cook for about 5 minutes, or until the onion is tender. Add the prepared spinach and cook quickly for 2–3 minutes until it has wilted.

5 Drain the pasta and return it to the clean pan. Add the spinach mixture, the crème fraîche and the grated Parmesan. Toss gently but thoroughly, then pile on warmed plates, sprinkle with the chopped turkey and top with the extra Parmesan. Serve immediately with crusty bread.

Variation
Substitute rocket for the spinach, omit the chilli and add a finely chopped, peeled and seeded tomato.

Pasta Bonbons

For a special occasion, these pretty little pasta packages would be a fine choice.

Serves 4–6

1 quantity of Basic Pasta Dough
flour, for dusting
1 egg white, beaten
salt and freshly ground black pepper

For the filling
1 small onion, finely chopped
1 garlic clove, crushed
150ml/ ¼ pint/ ⅔ cup defatted chicken stock
225g/8oz minced turkey
2–3 fresh sage leaves, chopped
2 drained canned anchovy fillets

For the sauce
150ml/ ¼ pint/ ⅔ cup defatted chicken stock
200g/7oz/scant 1cup low-fat cream cheese
15ml/1 tbsp lemon juice
5ml/1 tsp caster sugar
2 tomatoes, peeled, seeded and finely diced
½ red onion, finely chopped
6 small cornichons (pickled gherkins), sliced

1 Make the filling. Put the onion, garlic and stock into a pan. Bring to the boil, cover and simmer for 5 minutes, until the onion is tender. Uncover and boil for about 5 minutes, or until the stock has reduced to 30ml/2 tbsp.

2 Add the minced turkey and stir it over the heat until lightly coloured. Add the sage and anchovy fillets, and season to taste with salt and pepper. Cook uncovered for 5 minutes, until all the liquid has been absorbed. Leave to cool.

3 Divide the pasta dough in half. Roll one half into thin sheets and cut into 9 x 6cm/3½ x 2½in rectangles. Lay these on a lightly floured dish towel and repeat with the remaining dough.

4 Place a heaped teaspoon of the filling on the centre of each rectangle, brush the surrounding dough with beaten egg white and roll up the pasta to make bonbons or small crackers, pinching in the ends. Transfer to a floured dish towel and leave to rest for 1 hour before cooking.

5 To make the sauce, put the stock, cream cheese, lemon juice and sugar into a pan. Heat gently and whisk until smooth. Add the diced tomatoes, onion and cornichons, and leave over a low heat while you cook the bonbons.

6 Bring a large pan of lightly salted water to the boil and cook the bonbons, in batches, for 5 minutes. As each batch becomes tender, lift out the bonbons with a slotted spoon, drain well and drop into the sauce. When all the bonbons have been added, simmer them in the sauce for 2–3 minutes. Serve in warmed bowls, spooning a little sauce over each bonbon.

Cook's Tip
Allow plenty of time for making these. The bonbons need to rest for at least an hour before being cooked.

Rolled Stuffed Cannelloni

For tender, rustic-looking cannelloni, roll your own. Use lasagne sheets rather than rigid cannelloni tubes.

Serves 4

12 fresh or dried lasagne sheets
fresh basil leaves, to garnish

For the filling

2–3 garlic cloves, crushed
1 small onion, finely chopped
150ml/ ¼ pint/ ⅔ cup white wine
450g/1lb minced turkey
15ml/1 tbsp dried basil
15ml/1 tbsp dried thyme
40g/1½ oz/ ¾ cup fresh white breadcrumbs
salt and freshly ground black pepper

For the sauce

25g/1oz/2 tbsp low-fat margarine
25g/1oz/ ¼ cup plain flour
300ml/ ½ pint/1¼ cups skimmed milk
4 sun-dried tomatoes, soaked in warm water until soft, then drained and chopped
15ml/1 tbsp mixed chopped fresh herbs
30ml/2 tbsp freshly grated Parmesan cheese

1 First, make the filling. Put the garlic, onion and half the wine into a large pan. Cover and cook over a low heat for 5 minutes, then increase the heat and add the turkey. Cook it quickly, breaking up any lumps with a wooden spoon, until all the liquid has evaporated.

2 Lower the heat, and add the remaining wine and the herbs. Cover and cook for 20 minutes.

3 Draw the pan off the heat, stir in the breadcrumbs and season with salt and pepper to taste. Set aside to cool.

4 Bring a large pan of lightly salted water to the boil and cook the lasagne sheets, in batches if necessary, until *al dente*. Drain thoroughly, rinse in cold water and drain again. Pat dry on a clean dish towel.

5 Lay each lasagne sheet in turn on a board. Spoon turkey mixture along one short edge and roll it up to make a tube, encasing the filling. Cut the tubes in half.

6 Preheat the oven to 200°C/400°F/Gas 6. Make the sauce. Put the margarine, flour and skimmed milk into a pan, and whisk over a low heat until smooth. Add the tomatoes and mixed herbs, and season to taste with salt and pepper.

7 Spoon a thin layer of the sauce into a large, shallow ovenproof dish and arrange a layer of cannelloni on top, seam side down. Spoon a layer of sauce over the top, and cover with another layer of cannelloni and the remaining sauce. Sprinkle with grated Parmesan.

8 Bake for 10–15 minutes until lightly browned. Serve at once, garnished with fresh basil leaves.

Low-fat Lasagne

Serve this delicious lasagne with a garnish of mixed salad leaves.

Serves 6–8

1 large onion, chopped
2 garlic cloves, crushed
500g/1¼ lb minced turkey
450ml/ ¾ pint/1¾ cups passata
5ml/1 tsp mixed dried herbs
200g/7oz no-precook dried green lasagne sheets
200g/7oz/scant 1 cup low-fat cottage cheese
225g/8oz frozen leaf spinach, thawed and drained

For the sauce

25g/1oz/2 tbsp low-fat margarine
25g/1oz/ ¼ cup plain flour
300ml/ ½ pint/1¼ cups skimmed milk
25g/1oz/ ⅓ cup freshly grated Parmesan cheese
1.5ml/ ¼ tsp freshly grated nutmeg
salt and freshly ground black pepper
salad leaves and tomatoes, to serve

1 Put the onion, garlic and minced turkey into a non-stick saucepan. Cook over a medium heat, stirring with a wooden spoon to break up any lumps, for 5 minutes or until the turkey is lightly browned.

2 Add the passata and dried herbs, and season with salt and pepper to taste. Bring to the boil, then lower the heat. Cover and simmer for 30 minutes.

3 To make the sauce, put the margarine, flour and skimmed milk in a pan and whisk constantly over a low heat until the sauce boils and thickens. Stir in the Parmesan until melted. Stir in the nutmeg, and season with salt and pepper to taste.

4 Preheat the oven to 190°C/375°F/Gas 5. Layer the turkey mixture, lasagne sheets, cottage cheese and spinach in an ovenproof dish, starting and ending with a layer of turkey.

5 Spoon the cheese sauce evenly over the top and bake for 45–50 minutes, or until golden and bubbling. Leave to stand for 10–15 minutes before serving with salad leaves and tomatoes.

Tagliatelle with Milanese Sauce

Mushrooms and lean ham in a rich tomato sauce make a tasty topping for tagliatelle.

Serves 4

1 onion, finely chopped
1 celery stick, finely chopped
1 red pepper, seeded and diced
1–2 garlic cloves, crushed
150ml/ 1/4 pint/ 2/3 cup Vegetable Stock
400g/14oz can chopped tomatoes
15ml/1 tbsp tomato purée
10ml/2 tsp caster sugar
5ml/1 tsp mixed dried herbs
350g/12oz dried tagliatelle, preferably mixed colours
115g/4oz/1 1/2 cups button mushrooms, sliced
60ml/4 tbsp white wine
60ml/4 tbsp lean cooked ham, diced
salt and freshly ground black pepper
15ml/1 tbsp chopped fresh parsley, to garnish

1 Put the chopped onion, celery, pepper and garlic in a non-stick pan. Add the stock, bring to the boil and cook over a medium heat for 5 minutes.

2 Stir in the tomatoes, tomato purée, sugar and dried herbs. Season to taste with salt and pepper. Bring to the boil, then lower the heat and simmer, stirring occasionally, for 30 minutes, until thick.

3 Bring a large pan of lightly salted water to the boil and cook the pasta until it is *al dente*.

4 Meanwhile, put the mushrooms into a heavy-based pan with the white wine, cover and cook over a medium heat for 3–4 minutes, until the mushrooms are tender and all the wine has been absorbed.

5 Stir the mushrooms into the tomato sauce, then add the diced ham.

6 Drain the pasta well and tip it into a warmed serving dish. Spoon the sauce over, garnish with the chopped parsley and serve immediately.

Home-made Tortellini

When you make your own tortellini, you are in control of the fat content.

Serves 4–6

115g/4oz lean smoked ham
115g/4oz skinless, boneless chicken breast
900ml/1 1/2 pints/3 3/4 cups Vegetable Stock
bunch of fresh coriander
30ml/2 tbsp grated Parmesan cheese, plus extra for serving
1 egg, beaten, plus egg white for brushing
1 quantity Basic Pasta Dough
flour, for dusting
salt and freshly ground black pepper

1 Cut the ham and chicken into large chunks and put them into a saucepan with 150ml/ 1/4 pint/ 2/3 cup of the stock. Strip the leaves from the coriander. Set some aside for the garnish and chop the rest. Add the stalks to the pan. Bring to the boil, cover and simmer for 20 minutes, until the chicken is tender. Set aside to cool slightly.

2 Drain the ham and chicken, reserving the stock, and mince finely. Put the mixture into a bowl and add the Parmesan, beaten egg and chopped coriander. Season to taste.

3 Roll the pasta into thin sheets, then cut it into 4cm/1 1/2in squares. Put 2.5ml/ 1/2 tsp of filling on each. Brush the edges with egg white and fold each square into a triangle. Press out any air and seal firmly.

4 To make the tortellini, curl each triangle around the tip of a forefinger and press two ends together firmly. Lay the tortellini on a lightly floured dish towel to dry out a little for 30 minutes before cooking.

5 Strain the reserved stock into a large pan and add the remainder. Bring to the boil. Lower the heat slightly and add the tortellini. Cook for 5 minutes. Then turn off the heat, cover the pan and leave to stand for 20–30 minutes. Serve in warmed soup plates with some of the stock. Garnish with the reserved coriander leaves. Serve grated Parmesan separately.

Ham-filled Paprika Ravioli

Use a ravioli tray to shape these tasty supper treats.

Serves 4

225g/8oz cooked smoked ham
60ml/4 tbsp mango chutney
1 quantity of Basic Pasta Dough, with 5ml/1 tsp ground paprika added
egg white, beaten
flour, for dusting
1–2 garlic cloves, crushed
1 celery stick, sliced
2–3 sun-dried tomatoes
1 fresh red chilli, seeded and chopped
150ml/ ¼ pint/ ⅔ cup red wine
400g/14oz can chopped tomatoes
5ml/1 tsp chopped fresh thyme, plus extra to garnish
10ml/2 tsp caster sugar
salt and freshly ground black pepper

1 Remove all traces of fat from the ham, place it with the mango chutney in a food processor or blender and mince the mixture finely.

2 Roll the pasta into very thin sheets and lay one piece over a ravioli tray, fitting it carefully into the depressions. Put a teaspoonful of the ham filling into each of the depressions. Brush around the edges of each ravioli with egg white. Cover with another sheet of pasta and press the edges well together to seal.

3 Using a rolling pin, roll over the top of the dough to cut and seal each pocket. Transfer the ravioli to a floured dish towel and leave to rest for 1 hour before cooking.

4 Put the garlic, celery, sun-dried tomatoes, chilli, wine, canned tomatoes and thyme into a pan. Bring to the boil, lower the heat, cover and simmer for 15–20 minutes. Season with salt, pepper and sugar.

5 Bring a large pan of lightly salted water to the boil and cook the ravioli, in batches if necessary, for 4–5 minutes. Drain thoroughly. Spoon a little of the sauce on to each of four warmed serving plates and arrange the ravioli on top. Sprinkle with fresh thyme and serve at once.

Low-fat Cannelloni

A few simple changes make this version of cannelloni the healthier choice.

Serves 4

2 garlic cloves, crushed
2 x 400g/14oz cans chopped tomatoes
10ml/2 tsp soft light brown sugar
15ml/1 tbsp shredded fresh basil
15ml/1 tbsp chopped fresh marjoram
12–16 dried cannelloni tubes
50g/2oz low-fat mozzarella cheese, diced
25g/1oz/ ¼ cup grated mature Cheddar cheese
25g/1oz/ ½ cup fresh white breadcrumbs
salt and freshly ground black pepper
fresh flat leaf parsley, to garnish

For the filling

450g/1lb frozen chopped spinach
large pinch of freshly grated nutmeg
115g/4oz cooked lean ham, very finely chopped
200g/7oz/ scant 1 cup low-fat cottage cheese

1 Put the garlic, canned tomatoes, sugar and herbs into a pan, bring to the boil and cook, uncovered, for 30 minutes, stirring occasionally, until fairly thick.

2 Make the filling. Put the spinach into a pan, cover and cook slowly until thawed. Break up with a fork, then increase the heat to drive off any water. Season with salt, pepper and nutmeg. Spoon the spinach into a bowl, let it cool slightly, then add the chopped ham and cottage cheese.

3 Preheat the oven to 180°C/350°F/Gas 4. Pipe or spoon the filling into each tube of uncooked cannelloni.

4 Spoon half the tomato sauce into the base of an ovenproof dish. Arrange the cannelloni in a single layer on top. Scatter over the mozzarella and cover with the rest of the sauce.

5 Sprinkle over the Cheddar cheese and breadcrumbs. Bake for 30–40 minutes, browning the top under a hot grill if necessary. Garnish with the parsley and serve.

Low-fat Spaghetti Bolognese

Mushrooms are a gift to the health-conscious cook, as long as they are cooked in wine and not fat.

Serves 8

1 medium onion, chopped
2–3 garlic cloves, crushed
300ml/ ½ pint/1 ¼ cups defatted beef or chicken stock
450g/1lb minced turkey or extra lean beef
2 x 400g/14oz cans chopped tomatoes
5ml/1 tsp dried basil
5ml/1 tsp dried oregano
60ml/4 tbsp tomato purée
450g/1lb/6 cups button mushrooms, sliced
150ml/ ¼ pint/ ⅔ cup red wine
450g/1lb dried spaghetti
salt and freshly ground black pepper

1 Put the chopped onion and crushed garlic in a pan and pour in half of the stock. Bring to the boil and cook for 5 minutes, until the onion is tender and very little stock remains.

2 Add the turkey or beef and cook over a medium heat for 5 minutes, breaking up any lumps with a fork.

3 Stir in the chopped tomatoes, herbs, remaining beef or chicken stock and tomato purée, and bring to the boil. Lower the heat, cover and simmer for about 1 hour.

4 Meanwhile, put the button mushrooms into a non-stick frying pan with the wine, bring to the boil and cook for 5 minutes, or until the wine has been absorbed. Add the cooked mushrooms to the meat sauce and season to taste with salt and freshly ground black pepper. Keep the sauce hot while you cook the pasta.

5 Bring a large pan of lightly salted water to the boil and cook the spaghetti until it is *al dente*. Drain thoroughly. Transfer to individual warmed plates, top with the meat sauce and serve.

Chilli Mince & Pipe Rigate

Cheer up a chilly evening with this hearty, warming and colourful dish.

Serves 6

450g/1lb extra lean minced beef
1 onion, finely chopped
2–3 garlic cloves, crushed
1–2 fresh red chillies, seeded and finely chopped
400g/14oz can chopped tomatoes
45ml/3 tbsp tomato purée
5ml/1 tsp mixed dried herbs
450ml/ ¾ pint/1 ¾ cups water
450g/1lb/4 cups dried pipe rigate
400g/14oz can red kidney beans, drained
salt and freshly ground black pepper

1 Dry-fry the minced beef in a heavy-based non-stick saucepan over a medium heat, breaking up any lumps with a wooden spoon, until browned all over. Drain off any fat that has run from the meat.

2 Add the onion, garlic and chillies, and lower the heat. Cover and cook gently, stirring occasionally, for 5 minutes.

3 Stir in the tomatoes, tomato purée, herbs, and measured water. Bring to the boil, then lower the heat and simmer for 1½ hours. Season to taste with salt and pepper and set aside to cool slightly.

4 Bring a large pan of lightly salted water to the boil and cook the pasta until it is *al dente*.

5 Meanwhile, stir the kidney beans into the meat sauce and heat through, stirring occasionally, for about 10 minutes.

6 Drain the pasta and arrange it on warmed plates. Pile the sauce in the centre and serve immediately.

Cook's Tip
If you make the sauce the day before, it will be even more flavoursome and you can also skim off any residual fat.

Round Ravioli with Bolognese Sauce

Tender ravioli and a richly flavoured, low-fat sauce – what more could anyone wish for?

Serves 6

225g/8oz/1 cup low-fat cottage cheese
30ml/2 tbsp grated Parmesan cheese, plus extra for serving
1 egg white, beaten, plus extra for brushing
1.5ml/ ¼ tsp freshly grated nutmeg
1 quantity of Basic Pasta Dough
flour, for dusting
salt and freshly ground black pepper

For the Bolognese Sauce

1 medium onion, finely chopped
1 garlic clove, crushed
150ml/ ¼ pint/ ⅔ cup defatted beef stock
350g/12oz extra lean minced beef
120ml/4fl oz/ ½ cup red wine
30ml/2 tbsp tomato purée
400g/14oz can chopped tomatoes
2.5ml/ ½ tsp chopped fresh rosemary
1.5ml/ ¼ tsp ground allspice

1 To make the filling, mix the cottage cheese, grated Parmesan and egg white in a bowl, add the nutmeg, and season with salt and pepper to taste.

2 Roll the pasta into thin sheets. To make the ravioli, place small amounts of filling (about 5ml/1 tsp) in rows on half the pasta sheets at intervals of 5cm/2in.

3 Brush beaten egg white around each mound of filling. Top each sheet of filled pasta with a sheet of plain pasta and press between each pocket to remove any air and seal firmly.

4 Using a fluted ravioli or pastry cutter, stamp out rounds from the filled pasta and place these on a floured dish towel to dry while you make the sauce.

5 Put the onion and garlic in a pan. Add the stock and cook over a medium heat until most of it has been absorbed. Stir in the beef and cook quickly to brown, breaking up any lumps with a fork.

6 Stir in the wine, tomato purée, chopped tomatoes, rosemary and allspice, and bring to the boil. Lower the heat and simmer, stirring occasionally, for 1 hour. Adjust the seasoning to taste.

7 Bring a large pan of lightly salted water to the boil and cook the ravioli, in batches if necessary, until *al dente*. Drain thoroughly. Serve topped with the Bolognese sauce. Hand grated Parmesan cheese separately.

Cook's Tip

If you buy steak in a piece and mince it yourself, you will be sure that it is lean. Although supermarkets often label minced beef "extra lean" or "premium quality", these terms have no legal meaning. As a general rule, the lighter the colour of the mince, the more fat it contains.

Spinach Tagliarini with Chicken & Asparagus

With its delicate colours and fresh flavours, this would be a good choice for an *al fresco* supper in early summer.

Serves 4–6

2 skinless, boneless chicken breasts
15ml/1 tbsp light soy sauce
30ml/2 tbsp sherry
30ml/2 tbsp cornflour
8 spring onions, trimmed and cut diagonally into 2.5cm/1in slices
1–2 garlic cloves, crushed
needle shreds of rind of ½ lemon
150ml/ ¼ pint/ ⅔ cup defatted chicken stock
5ml/1 tsp caster sugar
30ml/2 tbsp lemon juice
225g/8oz slender asparagus spears, trimmed and cut in 7.5cm/3in lengths
450g/1lb fresh tagliarini
salt and freshly ground black pepper

1 Place the chicken breasts between two sheets of clear film and flatten each of them to a thickness of about 5mm/ ¼in with a rolling pin or the flat side of a meat mallet.

2 Cut the chicken across the grain into 2.5cm/1in strips. Put these into a bowl and add the soy sauce, sherry and cornflour, and season with plenty of salt and pepper. Toss well to coat each piece.

3 Put the chicken, spring onions, garlic and lemon rind in a large non-stick frying pan. Add the stock and bring to the boil, stirring constantly until thickened. Stir in the caster sugar, lemon juice and asparagus. Simmer over a low heat, stirring occasionally, for 4–5 minutes until tender.

4 Meanwhile, bring a large pan of lightly salted water to the boil and cook the pasta until *al dente*.

5 Drain the tagliarini thoroughly. Divide it among warmed serving plates, and spoon over the chicken and asparagus sauce. Serve immediately.

Pasta Napoletana

Classic cooked tomato sauce makes a healthy choice, when served with pasta and not too much Parmesan cheese.

Serves 4

900g/2lb fresh ripe red tomatoes
1 medium onion, chopped
1 medium carrot, diced
1 celery stick, diced
150ml/ ¼ pint/ ⅔ cup dry white wine
1 fresh parsley sprig
a pinch of caster sugar
15ml/1 tbsp chopped fresh oregano
450g/1lb/4 cups pappardelle or lasagnette
salt and freshly ground black pepper
freshly grated Parmesan cheese, to serve
fresh basil, to garnish

1 Peel the tomatoes, chop them roughly and put them in a pan. Add the onion, carrot, celery, wine, parsley sprig and sugar, and mix well. Bring to the boil, then lower the heat and simmer, half-covered, for 45 minutes, until very thick, stirring occasionally.

2 Remove and discard the parsley sprig. Transfer the tomato sauce to a blender or food processor and process until smooth, then return it to the clean pan. Stir in the oregano, season to taste with salt and pepper, and heat through gently.

3 Meanwhile, bring a large pan of lightly salted water to the boil and cook the pasta until it is *al dente*.

4 Drain the pasta thoroughly and return it to the clean pan. Add the sauce and toss to mix. Serve in warmed bowls, with grated Parmesan cheese, garnished with basil.

Cook's Tips

- *Fresh Italian plum tomatoes are best for this sauce, especially if they have been home grown.*
- *The sauce can be puréed by rubbing it through a fine strainer with the back of a wooden spoon.*

Lasagnette with Tomato & Red Wine Sauce

A classic sauce that is simply delicious served with curly pasta. It needs no extra accompaniments.

Serves 4

15ml/1 tbsp olive oil
1 onion, chopped
30ml/2 tbsp tomato purée
5ml/1 tsp mild paprika
2 x 400g/14oz cans chopped tomatoes
pinch of drained oregano
300ml/ ½ pint/1 ¼ cups dry red wine
large pinch of caster sugar
350g/12oz dried lasagnette or other long pasta
salt and freshly ground black pepper
chopped fresh flat leaf parsley, to garnish
Parmesan cheese shavings, to serve

1 Heat the oil in a large, heavy-based frying pan. Add the onion and fry over a low heat, stirring occasionally, for 10 minutes, until softened. Stir in the tomato purée and paprika, and cook for 3 minutes.

2 Add the tomatoes, oregano, wine and sugar, and season with salt and pepper to taste. Bring to the boil, lower the heat and simmer for 20 minutes, until the sauce has reduced and thickened, stirring occasionally.

3 Meanwhile, bring a large pan of lightly salted water to the boil and cook the pasta until it is *al dente*.

4 Drain the pasta, return to the clean pan and toss with the tomato sauce. Serve in warmed bowls, garnished with chopped parsley and with Parmesan shavings sprinkled on top.

Variation

Add 225g/8oz cooked peeled prawns to the tomato sauce about 2 minutes before serving – just long enough to heat through without becoming tough.

Tagliatelle with Tomato & Mushroom Sauce

Adding a little pancetta gives a lot of extra concentrated flavour to the sauce.

Serves 4

25g/1oz/½ cup dried Italian mushrooms (porcini)
175ml/6fl oz/¾ cup hot water
900g/2lb tomatoes, peeled, seeded and chopped
1.5ml/1/4 tsp dried hot chilli flakes
2 slices of pancetta or rindless unsmoked back bacon, cut into thin strips
1 large garlic clove, finely chopped
350g/12oz dried tagliatelle or fettuccine
5ml/1 tsp olive oil
salt and freshly ground black pepper
freshly grated Parmesan cheese, to serve

1 Put the dried mushrooms in a bowl and pour over the hot water to cover. Leave to soak for 20 minutes.

2 Meanwhile, put the tomatoes in a saucepan and add the chilli flakes. Bring to the boil, lower the heat and simmer, stirring occasionally, for 30–40 minutes, or until thick.

3 When the mushrooms have finished soaking, lift them out and squeeze them over the bowl. Set them aside. Carefully pour the soaking liquid into the tomatoes through a muslin-lined strainer, leaving any sandy grit in the base of the bowl. Simmer the tomato sauce for 15 minutes more.

4 Meanwhile, place the pancetta or bacon strips in a non-stick frying pan and dry-fry over a low heat until golden but not crisp. Add the garlic and mushrooms, and dry-fry for 3 minutes, stirring. Add to the tomato sauce and mix well. Season with salt and pepper, and keep hot.

5 Bring a large pan of lightly salted water to the boil and cook the pasta until it is *al dente*. Drain it well and return it to the pan. Toss with the oil. Divide among warmed plates, spoon the sauce on top and serve with Parmesan cheese.

Penne with Broccoli & Chilli

Chunky, with just enough "bite" to provide an interesting contrast to the broccoli, penne are perfect in this easy dish.

Serves 4

350g/12oz/3 cups dried penne
450g/1lb/generous 3 cups small broccoli florets
30ml/2 tbsp Vegetable Stock
1 garlic clove, crushed
1 small fresh red chilli, sliced, or 2.5ml/½ tsp chilli sauce
60ml/4 tbsp low-fat natural yogurt
30ml/2 tbsp toasted pine nuts or cashews
salt and freshly ground black pepper

1 Bring a pan of lightly salted water to the boil and add the pasta. When the water returns to the boil, place the broccoli in a steamer basket set over the top. Cover and cook for 8–10 minutes, until both the pasta and the broccoli are just tender.

2 When the pasta is almost ready, heat the stock in a separate pan, and add the garlic and chilli or chilli sauce. Stir over a low heat for 2–3 minutes.

3 Drain the pasta and stir it into the flavoured stock, with the broccoli and yogurt. Season to taste with salt and pepper, tip into a warmed serving bowl and sprinkle with the toasted nuts. Serve immediately.

Variations
• *You could substitute green Tabasco sauce for the chilli if you like a "kick" of spice, but prefer something a little milder.*
• *For a slightly richer taste, you could use smetana instead of low-fat yogurt.*

Farfalle with Red Pepper Sauce

A quick and easy sauce that tastes great with pasta.

Serves 4

450g/1lb/4 cups dried farfalle
2 large red peppers, seeded and finely diced
1 garlic clove, crushed
3 ripe tomatoes, peeled, seeded and chopped
120ml/4fl oz/½ cup Vegetable Stock
5ml/1 tsp balsamic vinegar
salt and freshly ground black pepper
chopped fresh herbs, to garnish

1 Bring a large pan of lightly salted water to the boil and cook the pasta until it is *al dente*.
2 Meanwhile, make the sauce. Set about 45ml/3 tbsp of the diced red pepper aside for the garnish. Put the rest in a pan with the garlic, tomatoes and stock. Bring to the boil, then lower the heat and simmer, stirring occasionally, until the mixture is thick. Stir in the balsamic vinegar and season to taste.
3 Drain the pasta, tip it into a warmed bowl and toss with the red pepper sauce. Garnish with the reserved red pepper and chopped herbs, and serve.

Fettuccine with Broccoli & Garlic

In this recipe, broccoli is mashed with wine and Parmesan to make a tasty coating sauce.

Serves 4

3–4 garlic cloves, crushed
350g/12oz/2½ cups broccoli florets
150ml/¼ pint/⅔ cup defatted chicken stock
60ml/4 tbsp white wine
30ml/2 tbsp chopped fresh basil
60ml/4 tbsp freshly grated Parmesan cheese
350g/12oz fresh or dried fettuccine or tagliatelle
salt and freshly ground black pepper
fresh basil leaves, to garnish

1 Put the garlic, broccoli and stock into a large saucepan. Bring to the boil over a medium heat and cook for 5 minutes, or until the broccoli is tender, stirring from time to time.

2 Mash with a fork or potato masher until the broccoli is roughly chopped. Stir in the white wine, chopped basil and Parmesan. Season to taste with salt and pepper, and leave over a low heat while you cook the pasta.

3 Bring a large pan of lightly salted water to the boil and cook the fettuccine or tagliatelle until *al dente*.

4 Drain the pasta well and return to the pan. Pour over half the broccoli sauce and toss gently. Divide among warmed plates, top with the remaining broccoli sauce, garnish with the basil leaves and serve immediately.

Cook's Tip

When buying broccoli, look for stems that are neither dry and wrinkled nor woody, with tightly packed, dark green flowerheads. There should be no sign of yellowing. It is best eaten on the day of purchase and cannot be kept, even in a cool dark place, for more than a couple of days without the flowerheads turning yellow.

Tagliatelle with Broccoli & Spinach

This is an excellent vegetarian supper dish. It is nutritious and filling and needs no accompaniment.

Serves 4

2 heads of broccoli
450g/1lb fresh spinach leaves, stalks removed
freshly grated nutmeg
450g/1lb fresh or dried egg tagliatelle
15ml/1 tbsp extra virgin olive oil
juice of ½ lemon
salt and freshly ground black pepper
freshly grated Parmesan cheese, to serve

1 Put the broccoli in the basket of a steamer, cover and steam over boiling water for 10 minutes.

2 Add the spinach to the broccoli, cover and steam for 4–5 minutes, or until both the vegetables are tender. Towards the end of the cooking time, sprinkle them with freshly grated nutmeg, and season with salt and pepper to taste. Transfer the vegetables to a colander.

3 Top up the water in the steamer and add salt. Bring to the boil, then cook the pasta until *al dente*. Meanwhile, chop the broccoli and spinach.

4 Drain the pasta. Heat the oil in the pasta pan, add the pasta and chopped vegetables, and toss over a medium heat until evenly mixed. Sprinkle in some of the lemon juice and plenty of black pepper, then taste and add more lemon juice, salt and nutmeg if you like. Serve immediately, sprinkled with freshly grated Parmesan and black pepper.

Variations

- *To add both texture and protein, garnish the finished dish with one or two handfuls of toasted pine nuts.*
- *Add a sprinkling of dried, crushed red chillies with the black pepper in step 4.*

Wholemeal Pasta with Caraway Cabbage

Crunchy cabbage and Brussels sprouts are perfect partners for pasta in this healthy dish. Caraway seeds and cabbage are a classic combination. Not only do their flavours complement each other, but caraway is also an aid to digestion and reduces the odour of cabbage when it is cooking.

Serves 6

3 onions, roughly chopped
400ml/14fl oz/1⅔ cups Vegetable Stock
350g/12oz round white cabbage, roughly chopped
350g/12oz Brussels sprouts, trimmed and halved
10ml/2 tsp caraway seeds
15ml/1 tbsp chopped fresh dill
200g/7oz/1¾ cups fresh or dried wholemeal spirali
salt and freshly ground black pepper
fresh dill sprigs, to garnish

1 Put the onions in a large saucepan and add half the stock. Bring to the boil, cover and cook over a low heat for about 10 minutes, stirring often, until the onion has softened and most of the liquid has been absorbed.

2 Add the cabbage and Brussels sprouts, and cook over a high heat, stirring, for 2–3 minutes, then stir in the caraway seeds and chopped dill.

3 Pour in the remaining vegetable stock, and season with salt and pepper to taste. Cover and simmer over a low heat for about 10 minutes, until the cabbage and Brussels sprouts are crisp-tender.

4 Meanwhile, bring a large pan of lightly salted water to the boil and cook the pasta until *al dente*.

5 Drain the pasta, tip it into a bowl and add the cabbage mixture. Toss lightly, adjust the seasoning and serve immediately, garnished with dill sprigs.

Tagliatelle & Vegetable Ribbons

Courgettes and carrots are cut into thin, delicate ribbons so that when they are cooked and tossed with tagliatelle they look like coloured pasta.

Serves 4

2 large courgettes
2 large carrots
250g/9oz fresh egg tagliatelle
15ml/1 tbsp extra virgin olive oil
flesh of 3 roasted garlic cloves, plus extra roasted garlic cloves, to serve (optional)
salt and freshly ground black pepper

1 With a vegetable peeler, cut the courgettes and carrots into long thin ribbons. Bring a large pan of lightly salted water to the boil and add the courgette and carrot ribbons. Boil for 30 seconds, then lift out the vegetable ribbons with a slotted spoon and set them aside.

2 Add the tagliatelle to the boiling water and cook until it is *al dente*.

3 Drain the pasta and return it to the pan. Add the vegetable ribbons, oil and garlic, and season with salt and pepper to taste. Toss over a medium to high heat until well mixed. Serve immediately, with extra roasted garlic, if you like.

Cook's Tip

Roasted garlic has a surprisingly mild and sweet flavour. To roast garlic, put a whole head of garlic on a lightly oiled baking sheet and drizzle a little extra olive oil over it. Place in a preheated 180°C/350°F/Gas 4 oven and roast for about 30–45 minutes. Remove the garlic from the oven and set it aside. When cool enough to handle, dig out the flesh from the cloves with the point of a knife, or simply squeeze the soft flesh from the individual cloves with your fingers. Individual cloves can be roasted in the same way, brushed with a little olive oil and cooked for about 20 minutes.

Pasta with Low-fat Pesto Sauce

Unlike traditional pesto, which is made with lashings of olive oil, this simple sauce is relatively low in fat but still full of flavour.

Serves 4

225g/8oz/2 cups dried pasta shapes, such as fusilli or farfalle
50g/2oz/1 cup fresh basil leaves
25g/1oz/ ½ cup fresh parsley sprigs
1 garlic clove, crushed
25g/1oz/ ¼ cup pine nuts
115g/4oz/ ½ cup curd cheese or very low-fat fromage frais
30ml/2 tbsp freshly grated Parmesan cheese
salt and freshly ground black pepper
few sprigs of fresh basil, to garnish

1 Bring a large pan of lightly salted water to the boil and cook the pasta until *al dente*.

2 Meanwhile, put half the basil and half the parsley into a food processor or blender. Add the garlic, pine nuts and curd cheese or fromage frais, and process until smooth.

3 Add the remaining basil and parsley, with the Parmesan, and season with salt and pepper to taste. Process until the herbs are finely chopped.

4 Toss the pasta with the pesto and serve immediately on warmed plates, garnished with fresh basil sprigs.

Cook's Tip
Fromage frais is a kind of curd cheese made from skimmed pasteurized cow's milk. Sometimes, it is enriched with cream to give it a firmer texture. However, this also gives it a rather higher fat content of about eight per cent. Look for the softer type that is labelled "virtually fat-free", which has zero fat, or the slightly firmer low-fat fromage frais which contains some fat. Make sure that you do not buy sweetened fromage frais which contains added sugar.

Farfalle with Grilled Pepper Sauce

This healthy vegetarian dish is packed with vitamin C and full of flavour.

Serves 4

4 peppers, preferably mixed colours, halved and seeded
3 plum tomatoes, peeled and chopped
1 red onion, thinly sliced
1 garlic clove, thinly sliced
350g/12oz/3 cups dried farfalle or other shapes
salt and freshly ground black pepper
30ml/2 tbsp grated Parmesan cheese, to garnish (optional)

1 Preheat the grill. Place the peppers, cut side down, in a grill pan and place under high heat until the skins have blistered and begun to char. Put them in a bowl and cover with several layers of kitchen paper. Set aside for 10–15 minutes.

2 Meanwhile, place the chopped tomatoes, onion and garlic in a heavy-based pan over a low heat. Bring to simmering point, cover and cook gently, stirring occasionally, for about 8–10 minutes, until the onion is tender and the sauce has thickened.

3 Peel the skin from the peppers and slice the flesh thinly. Stir them into the tomato sauce, heat gently, and season with salt and pepper to taste. Leave the pan over a low heat while you cook the pasta.

4 Bring a large pan of lightly salted water to the boil and cook the pasta until *al dente*.

5 Drain the pasta well and transfer to four warmed bowls. Top with the pepper sauce and serve, sprinkled with Parmesan cheese, if using.

Cook's Tip
Grilling the peppers not only makes them easy to peel, it also imparts a delicious flavour to the flesh, making it sweeter and less acerbic than when it is raw.

Torchiette with Tossed Vegetables

Cooking the pasta in water flavoured by the vegetables gives it a fresh taste.

Serves 4

225g/8oz thin asparagus spears, trimmed and cut in half
115g/4oz/1 cup mangetouts, topped and tailed
115g/4oz/⅔ cup baby corn cobs
225g/8oz whole baby carrots, trimmed
1 small red pepper, seeded and chopped
8 spring onions, sliced
225g/8oz/2 cups dried torchiette or other pasta shapes
150ml/1/4 pint/⅔ cup low-fat cottage cheese
150ml/¼ pint/⅔ cup low-fat natural yogurt
15ml/1 tbsp lemon juice
15ml/1 tbsp chopped fresh parsley
15ml/1 tbsp snipped chives
skimmed milk (optional)
salt and freshly ground black pepper

1 Bring a large pan of lightly salted water to the boil. Add the asparagus spears and cook for 2 minutes.

2 Add the mangetouts and cook for 2 minutes more. Using a slotted spoon, transfer the vegetables to a colander, rinse them under cold water, drain and set aside.

3 Bring the water in the pan back to the boil, add the corn cobs, carrots, red pepper and spring onions, and cook until tender. Lift out with a slotted spoon. Drain in a colander, then rinse and drain again.

4 Bring the water back to the boil and add the pasta. Cook it until it is *al dente*.

5 Meanwhile, put the cottage cheese, yogurt, lemon juice, parsley and chives into a food processor or blender and process until smooth. Thin the sauce with skimmed milk, if necessary, and season to taste with salt and pepper.

6 Drain the pasta, return it to the clean pan, and add the vegetables and cottage cheese sauce. Toss lightly and serve immediately in warmed bowls.

Pasta with Tomato Sauce & Roasted Vegetables

This scrumptious dish also tastes good cold, and makes great picnic fare.

Serves 4

1 aubergine
2 courgettes
1 large onion
2 peppers, preferably red or yellow, seeded
450g/1lb plum tomatoes
2–3 garlic cloves, roughly chopped
30ml/2 tbsp olive oil
300ml/½ pint/1¼ cups passata
8 black olives, halved and stoned (optional)
350g/12oz/3 cups dried pasta shapes, such as rigatoni or penne
salt and freshly ground black pepper
60ml/4 tbsp shredded fresh basil and four sprigs basil leaves, to garnish

1 Preheat the oven to 240°C/475°F/Gas 9. Cut the aubergine, courgettes, onion, peppers and tomatoes into large chunks. Discard the tomato seeds.

2 Spread out the vegetables in a large roasting tin. Sprinkle the garlic and oil over the vegetables, and stir and turn to mix evenly. Season to taste with salt and pepper.

3 Roast the vegetables for 30 minutes, or until they are soft and have begun to char around the edges. Stir halfway through the cooking time.

4 Scrape the vegetable mixture into a pan. Stir in the passata and olives, if using, and heat gently.

5 Bring a large pan of lightly salted water to the boil and cook the pasta until it is *al dente*.

6 Drain the pasta and return it to the clean pan. Add the sauce and toss to mix well. Serve immediately in a warmed bowl, sprinkled with the shredded basil and garnished with a basil sprig.

Pasta with Roasted Pepper & Tomato Sauce

Add other vegetables, such as French beans, courgettes or even chick-peas, to make this delicious sauce even more substantial.

Serves 4

2 medium red peppers
2 medium yellow peppers
1 fresh red chilli, seeded
15ml/1 tbsp olive oil
1 medium onion, sliced
2 garlic cloves, crushed
400g/14oz can chopped tomatoes
10ml/2 tsp balsamic vinegar
450g/1lb/4 cups dried conchiglie or spirali
salt and freshly ground black pepper

1 Preheat the oven to 200°C/400°F/Gas 6. Spread out the peppers and chilli in a roasting tin, and roast for 30 minutes or until softened and beginning to char. Remove the tin from the oven and cover with several layers of kitchen paper.

2 Meanwhile, heat the oil in a non-stick pan. Add the onion and garlic, and cook over a low heat, stirring occasionally, for about 5 minutes, until soft and golden.

3 When the peppers and chilli are cool enough to handle, rub off the skins. Cut them in half, remove the seeds and chop the flesh roughly.

4 Stir the chopped peppers and chilli into the onion mixture, then add the tomatoes. Bring to the boil, lower the heat and simmer for 10–15 minutes until slightly thickened and reduced. Stir in the vinegar, and season to taste with salt and freshly ground black pepper.

5 Meanwhile, bring a large pan of lightly salted water to the boil and cook the pasta until *al dente*.

6 Drain the pasta well and add it to the sauce. Toss thoroughly to mix, then serve immediately in warmed bowls.

Tagliatelle with "Hit-the-pan" Salsa

It is possible to make a hot, filling meal within just 15 minutes with this quick-cook salsa sauce.

Serves 2

115g/4oz fresh tagliatelle
15ml/1 tbsp extra virgin olive oil
1 garlic clove, crushed
4 spring onions, sliced
1 green chilli, halved, seeded and sliced
3 large tomatoes, roughly chopped
juice of 1 orange
30ml/2 tbsp fresh parsley, chopped
salt and freshly ground black pepper
freshly grated Parmesan cheese

1 Bring a large pan of lightly salted water to the boil and cook the pasta until it is *al dente*. Drain and place in a large bowl. Add about 5ml/1 tsp of the oil and toss to coat. Season well with salt and pepper.

2 Preheat a wok, swirl in the remaining oil and, when it is hot, stir-fry the garlic, onions and chilli for 1 minute. The pan should sizzle as they cook.

3 Add the tomatoes, orange juice and parsley. Season to taste with salt and pepper. Add the tagliatelle and toss over the heat until heated through. Divide among warmed individual plates and serve immediately with Parmesan cheese.

Cook's Tip

When squeezing citrus fruits, make sure that they are at room temperature, as they will then yield more juice than they would straight from the fridge.

Variation

You could use any pasta shape for this recipe. The sauce would be particularly good with large rigatoni or linguini and would also work well with filled fresh pasta, such as ravioli or tortellini.

Tagliatelle with Sun-dried Tomatoes

Choose plain sun-dried tomatoes for this sauce, instead of those preserved in oil, as they would increase the fat content.

Serves 4

1 garlic clove, crushed
1 celery stick, finely sliced
115g/4oz/2 cups sun-dried tomatoes, finely chopped
90ml/6 tbsp red wine
8 plum tomatoes
350g/12oz dried tagliatelle
salt and freshly ground black pepper

1 Put the garlic, celery, sun-dried tomatoes and wine into a large saucepan. Cook over a low heat, stirring occasionally, for 15 minutes.

2 Meanwhile, plunge the plum tomatoes into a saucepan of boiling water for 1 minute, then into cold water. Slip off their skins. Cut the tomatoes in half, scoop out the seeds and roughly chop the flesh.

3 Stir the plum tomatoes into the sun-dried tomato mixture, and season to taste with salt and pepper. Leave the pan over a low heat while you cook the pasta.

4 Bring a large pan of lightly salted water to the boil and cook the tagliatelle until it is *al dente*.

5. Drain the pasta well and return to the clean pan. Add half the tomato sauce and toss thoroughly to coat. Divide among warmed individual plates and top with the remaining sauce. Serve immediately.

Cook's Tip
This dish looks particularly attractive made with a mixture of plain, spinach-flavoured and tomato-flavoured tagliatelle. It is also delicious with wholemeal pasta.

Ratatouille Penne

Marinated beancurd adds interest to a popular vegetarian dish.

Serves 6

1 small aubergine
2 courgettes, thickly sliced
200g/7oz firm beancurd (tofu), cubed
45ml/3 tbsp dark soy sauce
1 garlic clove, crushed
20ml/4 tsp sesame seeds
1 small red pepper, seeded and sliced
1 onion, finely chopped
1–2 garlic cloves, crushed
150ml/ ¼ pint/ ⅔ cup Vegetable Stock
3 firm ripe tomatoes, peeled, seeded and quartered
15ml/1 tbsp chopped fresh mixed herbs
225g/8oz/2 cups dried penne
salt and freshly ground black pepper

1 Cut the aubergine into 2.5cm/1in cubes. Put these into a colander with the courgettes, sprinkle with salt and leave over the sink to drain for 30 minutes.

2 Put the beancurd in a bowl and add the soy sauce, garlic and half the sesame seeds. Stir, cover and marinate for 30 minutes.

3 Put the pepper, onion, garlic and stock into a pan. Bring to the boil, cover and cook for 5 minutes, until the vegetables are tender. Remove the lid and boil until the stock has evaporated.

4 Rinse the aubergine and courgettes, drain and add to the pan, with the tomatoes and herbs. Cook for 10–12 minutes, until the aubergine and courgettes are tender, adding a little water if the mixture becomes too dry. Season to taste.

5 Meanwhile, bring a large pan of lightly salted water to the boil and cook the pasta until it is *al dente*. Drain thoroughly, return to the clean pan, and add the vegetable mixture and marinated beancurd, with any liquid left in the bowl. Toss lightly, then tip into a heated serving bowl and keep hot.

6 Spread out the remaining sesame seeds in a non-stick frying pan and quickly dry-fry them until golden. Sprinkle them over the pasta dish and serve.

Pappardelle & Provençal Sauce

The flavours of the south of France are captured in this simple dish.

Serves 4

2 small red onions, peeled
150ml/ ¼ pint/ ⅔ cup Vegetable Stock
1–2 garlic cloves, crushed
60ml/4 tbsp red wine
2 courgettes, cut into fingers
1 yellow pepper, seeded and sliced
400g/14oz can chopped tomatoes
10ml/2 tsp chopped fresh thyme
5ml/1 tsp caster sugar
350g/12oz fresh pappardelle
salt and freshly ground black pepper
fresh thyme and 6 stoned black olives, roughly chopped, to garnish

1 Cut each onion into eight wedges, leaving the root end intact to hold them together during cooking. Put into a pan with the stock and garlic. Bring to the boil, lower the heat, cover and simmer for 5 minutes, until tender.

2 Add the red wine, courgettes, yellow pepper, tomatoes, chopped thyme and caster sugar, and season with salt and pepper to taste. Bring to the boil and cook over a low heat for 5–7 minutes, gently shaking the pan occasionally to coat all the vegetables with the sauce.

3 Meanwhile, bring a large pan of lightly salted water to the boil and cook the pasta until it is *al dente*.

4 Drain the pasta well, tip it into a warmed serving dish and top with the vegetable mixture. Garnish with the fresh thyme and chopped black olives, and serve immediately.

Cook's Tip
When making the sauce, do not overcook the vegetables, as the dish is much nicer if they have a slightly crunchy texture to contrast with the tender pasta.

Sweet & Sour Peppers with Farfalle

This Moroccan-inspired recipe has unusual ingredients, but the combination of flavours works very well.

Serves 4–6

1 red pepper
1 yellow pepper
1 orange pepper
1 garlic clove, crushed
30ml/2 tbsp drained bottled capers
30ml/2 tbsp raisins
5ml/1 tsp wholegrain mustard
grated rind and juice of 1 lime
5ml/1 tsp clear honey
30ml/2 tbsp chopped fresh coriander
225g/8oz/2 cups dried farfalle
salt and freshly ground black pepper
shavings of Parmesan cheese, to serve (optional)

1 Cut the peppers into quarters, at the same time removing the stalks and seeds. Bring a large pan of water to the boil. Add the peppers and cook over a medium heat for 10–15 minutes, until tender.

2 Drain, rinse under cold water and drain again. Peel away the skin and cut the flesh lengthways into strips.

3 Put the garlic, capers, raisins, mustard, lime rind and juice, honey and coriander into a bowl and whisk together. Season with salt and pepper to taste.

4 Bring a large pan of lightly salted water to the boil and cook the pasta until it is *al dente*.

5 Drain the pasta thoroughly, return it to the clean pan and add the reserved peppers and dressing. Toss over a low heat for 1–2 minutes, then tip into warmed serving bowls. Serve with a few shavings of Parmesan cheese, if you like.

Tagliatelle with Pea Sauce, Asparagus & Broad Beans

When you're tired of tomatoes, try this creamy pea sauce, which tastes great with a mixture of pasta and vegetables.

Serves 4

15ml/1 tbsp olive oil
1 garlic clove, crushed
6 spring onions, sliced
225g/8oz/2 cups frozen peas, thawed
350g/12oz fresh young asparagus, trimmed
30ml/2 tbsp chopped fresh sage, plus extra leaves to garnish
finely grated rind of 2 lemons
450ml/¾ pint/1¾ cups Vegetable Stock or water
225g/8oz/1½ cups frozen broad beans, thawed
450g/1lb fresh or dried tagliatelle
60ml/4 tbsp low-fat natural yogurt

1 Heat the oil in a pan. Add the garlic and spring onions, and cook over a low heat for 2–3 minutes, until softened.

2 Add the peas and one-third of the asparagus, together with the sage, lemon rind and stock or water. Bring to the boil, lower the heat and simmer for 10 minutes, until tender.

3 Transfer to a blender or food processor and process until smooth, then scrape the mixture into a pan. Pop the broad beans out of their skins and add them to the pan.

4 Cut the remaining asparagus into 5cm/2in lengths, trimming off any tough fibrous stems. Bring a large pan of lightly salted water to the boil, add the asparagus and cook for 2 minutes. Lift out with a slotted spoon and add to the pan of sauce. Reheat gently, stirring occasionally, while you cook the pasta.

5 Let the water return to the boil and add the tagliatelle. Cook until *al dente*.

6 Drain the pasta and return it to the clean pan. Add the yogurt and toss lightly. Divide among warmed plates and top with the sauce. Garnish with the extra sage leaves and serve.

Chinese Ribbons

This is a colourful Chinese-style dish, easily prepared using pasta instead of Chinese noodles.

Serves 4

1 medium carrot
2 small courgettes
175g/6oz runner or other green beans
175g/6oz baby corn cobs
450g/1lb dried ribbon pasta, such as tagliatelle
5ml/1 tsp sesame oil
15ml/1 tbsp corn oil
salt
1cm/½in piece of fresh root ginger, peeled and finely chopped
2 garlic cloves, finely chopped
90ml/6 tbsp yellow bean sauce
6 spring onions, sliced into 2.5cm/1in lengths
30ml/2 tbsp dry sherry
5ml/1 tsp sesame seeds

1 Slice the carrot and courgettes diagonally into chunks. Slice the beans diagonally. Cut the baby corn cobs diagonally in half.

2 Bring a large pan of lightly salted water to the boil and cook the pasta until it is *al dente*.

3 Drain the pasta well, return to the clean pan and add the sesame oil. Toss to coat.

4 Preheat a wok, then swirl in the corn oil. When it is hot, add the ginger and garlic, and stir-fry over a medium heat for 30 seconds, then add the carrots, beans, courgettes and corn cobs, and stir-fry for 3–4 minutes.

5 Stir in the yellow bean sauce. Stir-fry for 2 minutes, add the spring onions, sherry and pasta. Toss over the heat until piping hot. Divide among warmed bowls and serve immediately, sprinkled with sesame seeds.

Cook's Tip

Sesame oil has a strong nutty flavour and a distinctive aroma. It is generally used as a flavouring, rather than as a cooking oil.

Low-fat Tagliatelle with Mushrooms

Mushrooms cooked in stock, with wine and soy sauce have a superb flavour, and make a very good topping for fresh pasta. In addition, they contain no fat and no cholesterol at all.

Serves 4

1 small onion, finely chopped
2 garlic clove, crushed
150ml/ ¼ pint/ ⅔ cup Vegetable Stock
225g/8oz/3 cups mixed fresh mushrooms, quartered if large
60ml/4 tbsp white wine
10ml/2 tsp tomato purée
15ml/1 tbsp soy sauce
225g/8oz fresh sun-dried tomato and herb tagliatelle
5ml/1 tsp chopped fresh thyme
30ml/2 tbsp chopped fresh parsley
salt and freshly ground black pepper
shavings of Parmesan cheese, to serve (optional)

1 Put the onion and garlic into a pan with the stock. Cover and cook over a medium heat for 10 minutes, or until tender.

2 Add the mushrooms, wine, tomato purée and soy sauce. Cover and cook for 5 minutes, then remove the lid from the pan and boil until the liquid has reduced by half.

3 Bring a large pan of lightly salted water to the boil and cook the pasta until it is *al dente*.

4 Meanwhile, stir the chopped fresh herbs into the mushroom mixture, and season with salt and pepper to taste.

5 Drain the pasta thoroughly, return it to the clean pan and add the mushroom mixture. Toss lightly and serve in warmed bowls, with the Parmesan, if you like.

Cook's Tip
Use cultivated or wild mushrooms, such as field, chestnut, oyster and chanterelle, or a mixture.

Tagliatelle with Spinach Gnocchi

Celebrate the sensible way with this sophisticated dish that looks and tastes indulgent but is relatively low in fat.

Serves 4–6

450g/1lb dried tagliatelle, preferably mixed colours
shavings of Parmesan cheese, to garnish

For the spinach gnocchi
450g/1lb frozen chopped spinach
1 small onion, finely chopped
1 garlic clove, crushed
1.5ml/¼ tsp freshly grated nutmeg
400g/14oz/1¾ cups low-fat cottage cheese
115g/4oz/1 cup dried white breadcrumbs
flour, for dusting
75g/3oz/ ¾ cup semolina or plain flour
50g/2oz/ ⅔ cup freshly grated Parmesan cheese
3 egg whites

For the tomato sauce
1 onion, finely chopped
1 celery stick, finely chopped
1 red pepper, seeded and diced
1 garlic clove, crushed
150ml/ ¼ pint/ ⅔ cup Vegetable Stock
400g/14oz can chopped tomatoes
15ml/1 tbsp tomato purée
10ml/2 tsp caster sugar
5ml/1 tsp dried oregano
salt and freshly ground black pepper

1 First, make the tomato sauce. Put the chopped onion, celery, pepper and garlic into a non-stick pan. Add the stock, bring to the boil and cook over a medium heat for 5 minutes, or until the vegetables are tender.

2 Stir in the tomatoes, tomato purée, sugar and oregano. Season to taste with salt and pepper, and bring to the boil. Lower the heat and simmer, stirring occasionally, for 30 minutes, until thickened.

3 Meanwhile, make the gnocchi. Put the frozen spinach, onion and garlic into a pan, cover and cook over a low heat until the spinach has thawed. Remove the lid and increase the heat to drive off any moisture. Season with salt, pepper and nutmeg to taste. Transfer the spinach mixture to a bowl and set aside to cool completely.

4 Add the cottage cheese, breadcumbs, semolina or flour, Parmesan and egg whites to the spinach mixture, and mix. Using two dessertspoons, shape the mixture into about 24 ovals and place them on a lightly floured tray. Place in the fridge for 30 minutes.

5 Bring a large shallow pan of lightly salted water to the boil, then lower the heat to a gentle simmer. Add the gnocchi in batches. As soon as they rise to the surface, after about 5 minutes, remove them with a slotted spoon and drain them thoroughly. Keep the cooked gnocchi hot.

6 Bring another large pan of salted water to the boil and cook the pasta until *al dente*. Drain thoroughly. Transfer to warmed serving plates, top with the spinach gnocchi and spoon over the tomato sauce. Scatter with shavings of Parmesan cheese and serve at once.

Macaroni Cheese with Smoked Turkey

Using skimmed milk and reduced-fat cheese really does make a difference when you are trying to eat more healthily.

Serves 4

1 medium onion, chopped
150ml/ ¼ pint/ ⅔ cup Vegetable Stock
225g/8oz dried short-cut macaroni
25g/1oz/2 tbsp low-fat spread
40g/1½oz/ ⅓ cup plain flour
300ml/ ½ pint/1¼ cups skimmed milk
50g/2oz/½ cup grated reduced-fat Cheddar cheese
5ml/1 tsp prepared mustard
4 smoked turkey rashers, cut in half
2–3 firm tomatoes, sliced
a few fresh basil leaves
15ml/1 tbsp freshly grated Parmesan cheese
salt and freshly ground black pepper

1 Put the onion and stock into a non-stick pan. Bring to the boil and cook over a low heat for 5–6 minutes, until the stock has reduced entirely and the onion is translucent.

2 Bring a large pan of lightly salted water to the boil and cook the macaroni until *al dente*.

3 Meanwhile, put the low-fat spread, flour and milk into a heavy-based pan and whisk together over a medium heat until thickened and smooth. Stir in the grated Cheddar and mustard, and season to taste with salt and pepper.

4 Drain the macaroni and stir it into the cheese sauce, with the cooked onion. Spoon the mixture into a flameproof dish.

5 Preheat the grill. Arrange the turkey rashers and tomatoes so that they overlap on top of the macaroni cheese. Tuck the basil leaves over the tomatoes. Lightly sprinkle with Parmesan.

6 Place under the hot grill until the turkey rashers are cooked and the tomatoes are lightly browned. Serve at once.

Spaghetti with Mixed Bean Chilli

Chick-peas and three different types of bean make this a hearty dish, ideal for coming home to after a long walk on a winter's day.

Serves 6

1 onion, finely chopped
1–2 garlic cloves, crushed
1 large fresh green chilli, seeded and chopped
150ml/ ¼ pint/ ⅔ cup Vegetable Stock
400g/14oz can chopped tomatoes
30ml/2 tbsp tomato purée
120ml/4fl oz/ ½ cup red wine
5ml/1 tsp dried oregano
200g/7oz French beans, sliced
400g/14oz can red kidney beans, drained
400g/14oz can cannellini beans, drained
400g/14oz can chick-peas, drained
450g/1lb dried spaghetti
salt and freshly ground black pepper

1 Put the chopped onion, garlic and chilli into a non-stick pan and pour in the stock. Bring to the boil and cook over a medium heat for 10 minutes, until the onion is tender.

2 Stir in the tomatoes, tomato purée, wine and oregano, and season with salt and pepper to taste. Bring to the boil, lower the heat, cover and simmer the sauce for 20 minutes.

3 Cook the French beans in boiling, salted water for about 5–6 minutes, until tender. Drain thoroughly.

4 Add all the beans and the chick-peas to the sauce, and simmer for a further 10 minutes. Meanwhile, bring a large pan of lightly salted water to the boil and cook the spaghetti until *al dente*. Drain thoroughly. Transfer to a serving dish and top with the chilli. Serve immediately.

Cook's Tip
Use a packet of chilli seasoning mix instead of the fresh chilli, if you like. Simply stir it into the sauce with the tomatoes.

Spinach Ravioli Crescents

Impress your guests with these pretty pasta pasties filled with vegetables and cottage cheese.

Serves 4–6

1 bunch of spring onions, finely chopped
1 carrot, coarsely grated
2 garlic cloves, crushed
200g/7oz/scant 1 cup low-fat cottage cheese
15ml/1 tbsp chopped fresh dill, plus extra to garnish
25g/1oz/ ⅓ cup freshly grated Parmesan cheese
6 halves sun-dried tomatoes, finely chopped
1 quantity of Basic Pasta Dough, flavoured with spinach
beaten egg white, for brushing
flour, for dusting
salt and freshly ground black pepper

1 Put the spring onions, carrot, garlic and cottage cheese into a bowl. Add the chopped dill and Parmesan, then stir in two-thirds of the chopped sun-dried tomatoes. Season to taste with salt and pepper, and set aside.

2 Roll the spinach pasta into thin sheets and cut it into 7.5cm/3in rounds with a fluted ravioli or pastry cutter.

3 Place a spoon of filling in the centre of each pasta round. Brush the edges with egg white, then fold each round in half to make crescents. Press the edges together to seal. Transfer to a floured dish towel to rest for 1 hour before cooking.

4 Bring a large pan of lightly salted water to the boil and cook the crescents in batches until they are just tender. Drain well.

5 Place the crescents on warmed serving plates and sprinkle over the remaining sun-dried tomatoes. Garnish with the extra chopped dill. Serve immediately.

Cook's Tip
Spinach-flavoured pasta not only looks pretty and complements the other ingredients, but it also seals better than plain pasta.

Vegetarian Cannelloni

Cannelloni is great for entertaining as it can be prepared in advance and popped into the oven when guests arrive.

Serves 4–6

1 onion, finely chopped
2 garlic cloves, crushed
2 carrots, coarsely grated
2 celery sticks, finely chopped
150ml/ ¼ pint/ ⅔ cup Vegetable Stock
115g/4oz/ ½ cup red lentils
400g/14oz can chopped tomatoes
30ml/2 tbsp tomato purée
2.5ml/½ tsp ground ginger
5ml/1 tsp chopped fresh thyme
5ml/1 tsp chopped fresh rosemary
40g/1½oz/3 tbsp low-fat spread
40g/1½oz/ ⅓ cup plain flour
600ml/1 pint/2½ cups skimmed milk
1 bay leaf
a large pinch of freshly grated nutmeg
16–18 cannelloni tubes
25g/1oz/ ¼ cup grated reduced-fat Cheddar cheese
25g/1oz/ ⅓ cup freshly grated Parmesan cheese
25g/1oz/ ½ cup fresh white breadcrumbs
salt and freshly ground black pepper
flat leaf parsley, to garnish

1 Put the onion, garlic, carrots, celery and half the stock into a saucepan, cover and cook for 10 minutes, until tender. Add the lentils, tomatoes, tomato purée, ginger, thyme and rosemary. Stir in the remaining stock. Bring to the boil, lower the heat, cover and simmer for 20 minutes. Remove the lid and cook for about 10 minutes, until thick. Leave to cool.

2 Put the low-fat spread, flour, milk and bay leaf into a pan, and whisk over a medium heat until thick and smooth. Season with salt, pepper and nutmeg. Discard the bay leaf.

3 Preheat the oven to 180°C/350°F/Gas 4. Spoon the lentil filling into the cannelloni. Spoon half the white sauce into the base of an ovenproof dish. Arrange the cannelloni in a single layer on top and spoon over the remaining sauce to cover.

4 Mix the cheeses and breadcrumbs, then scatter over the cannelloni. Bake for 30–40 minutes. Garnish and serve.

Spinach & Hazelnut Lasagne

Lasagne is one of those dishes that almost everyone seems to like, and there will be plenty of takers for this low-fat vegetarian version.

Serves 4

900g/2lb fresh spinach leaves, stalks removed
300ml/ ½ pint/1 ¼ cups Vegetable Stock
1 medium onion, finely chopped
1 garlic clove, crushed
75g/3oz/ ¾ cup hazelnuts
30ml/2 tbsp chopped fresh basil
6 fresh lasagne sheets, precooked if necessary
400g/14oz can chopped tomatoes
200g/7oz/scant 1 cup low-fat fromage frais
salt and freshly ground black pepper
flaked hazelnuts and chopped fresh parsley, to garnish

1 Preheat the oven to 200°C/400°F/Gas 6. Wash the spinach and place it in a pan with just the water that clings to the leaves. Cover the pan and cook the spinach over a fairly high heat for 2 minutes, shaking the pan frequently, until it has wilted. Drain well.

2 Heat 30ml/2 tbsp of the stock in a large pan, add the chopped onion and garlic, and simmer until soft. Stir in the spinach, hazelnuts and basil.

3 In a large ovenproof dish, layer the spinach, lasagne sheets and tomatoes, seasoning each layer well. Pour over the remaining stock. Spread the fromage frais over the top.

4 Bake the lasagne for about 45 minutes, or until the topping is golden brown. Serve hot, sprinkled with lines of flaked hazelnuts and chopped parsley.

Cook's Tip
The hazelnuts will taste even better if they are toasted. Spread them in a grill pan and grill them until golden. Tip them into a clean dish towel and rub off the skins.

Aubergine & Mixed Vegetable Lasagne

Rather like a combination of lasagne and moussaka, this low-fat supper dish is quite filling, so it needs no accompaniment other than a small side salad.

Serves 6–8

1 large onion, finely chopped
2 garlic cloves, crushed
150ml/ ¼ pint/ ⅔ cup Vegetable Stock
1 small aubergine, cubed
225g/8oz/3 cups mushrooms, sliced
400g/14oz can chopped tomatoes
30ml/2 tbsp tomato purée
150ml/ ¼ pint/ ½ cup red wine
1.5ml/ ¼ tsp ground ginger
5ml/1 tsp mixed dried herbs
25g/1oz/2 tbsp low-fat spread
25g/1oz/ ¼ cup plain flour
300ml/ ½ pint/1 ¼ cups skimmed milk
a large pinch of freshly grated nutmeg
10–12 fresh lasagne sheets, precooked if necessary
200g/7oz/scant 1 cup low-fat cottage cheese
1 egg, beaten
25g/1oz/ ¼ cup grated reduced-fat Cheddar cheese
30ml/2 tbsp freshly grated Parmesan cheese
salt and freshly ground black pepper

1 Put the onion and garlic into a heavy-based saucepan with the stock. Cover and cook over a medium heat for about 10 minutes, or until tender.

2 Add the aubergine cubes, sliced mushrooms, tomatoes, tomato purée, wine, ginger and herbs. Bring to the boil, cover and cook for 15–20 minutes. Remove the lid and cook over a high heat to evaporate the liquid by half. Season to taste with salt and pepper.

3 Put the low-fat spread, flour, skimmed milk and nutmeg into a pan. Whisk together over a medium heat until thickened and smooth. Season with salt and pepper to taste.

4 Preheat the oven to 200°C/400°F/Gas 6. Spoon about one-third of the vegetable mixture into the base of an ovenproof dish. Cover with a layer of lasagne and one-quarter of the sauce.

5 Make two more layers in the same way, then cover with the cottage cheese. Beat the egg into the remaining sauce and pour it over the top.

6 Sprinkle with the Cheddar and Parmesan, and bake for 25–30 minutes, or until the top is golden brown. Leave to stand for about 10 minutes before serving.

Variation
Add some soaked porcini mushrooms to intensify the flavour, or cheat with a splash of good-quality mushroom ketchup.

Sweet & Sour Prawns with Noodles

Chinese dried noodles need very little cooking. Use one skein per person.

Serves 4–6

15g/ ½oz/ ¼ cup Chinese dried mushrooms
300ml/ ½ pint/1¼ cups hot water
1 bunch of spring onions, cut into thick diagonal slices
2.5cm/1in piece of fresh root ginger, grated
1 red pepper, seeded and diced
225g/8oz can water chestnuts, sliced
45ml/3 tbsp light soy sauce
30ml/2 tbsp sherry
350g/12oz large cooked peeled prawns
225g/8oz dried egg noodles

1 Put the Chinese dried mushrooms into a bowl. Pour over the measured hot water and set aside to soak for 15 minutes.

2 Strain the soaking liquid through a fine sieve into a pan. Chop the mushrooms and add them to the pan, with the spring onions, ginger and diced red pepper. Bring to the boil, lower the heat, cover and cook for about 5 minutes, until the vegetables are tender.

3 Add the water chestnuts, soy sauce, sherry and prawns to the vegetable mixture. Cover and cook gently for 2 minutes.

4 Meanwhile, bring a large pan of lightly salted water to the boil. Add the noodles and cook them until just tender, checking the packet for information on timing. Drain thoroughly and tip into a warmed serving dish. Spoon the sweet and sour prawns on top and toss to mix. Serve at once.

Cook's Tip

The Chinese vegetable water chestnuts (ma taai) are small corms with crisp white flesh and dark brown skins. They are sometimes available fresh and should be carefully peeled before use. Confusingly, there is a Chinese nut also known as the water chestnut (ling gok), but this is quite different.

Spicy Singapore Noodles

A delicious supper dish with a stunning mix of flavours and textures, as well as a hint of spiciness.

Serves 4

225g/8oz dried egg noodles
15ml/1 tbsp groundnut oil
1 onion, chopped
2.5cm/1in piece of fresh root ginger, finely chopped
1 garlic clove, finely chopped
15ml/1 tbsp Madras curry powder
115g/4oz cooked chicken or pork, finely shredded
115g/4oz cooked peeled prawns
115g/4oz Chinese cabbage leaves, shredded
115g/4oz/2 cups beansprouts
60ml/4 tbsp defatted chicken stock
15–30ml/1–2 tbsp dark soy sauce
salt
1–2 fresh red chillies, seeded and finely shredded and 4 spring onions, finely shredded, to garnish

1 Bring a large pan of lightly salted water to the boil and cook the noodles until they are just tender, checking the packet for information on timing.

2 Rinse the noodles thoroughly under cold water and drain well. Add 5ml/1 tsp of the oil, toss lightly and set aside.

3 Preheat a wok and swirl in the remaining oil. When it is hot, add the onion, ginger and garlic, and stir-fry over a medium heat for about 2 minutes.

4 Stir in the curry powder and 2.5ml/½ tsp salt, stir-fry for 30 seconds, then add the drained noodles, chicken or pork and prawns. Stir-fry for 3–4 minutes.

5 Add the shredded Chinese cabbage and beansprouts, and stir-fry for 1–2 minutes more. Sprinkle in the stock and soy sauce to taste, and toss well until evenly mixed and heated through. Divide among warmed individual serving bowls or plates, garnish with the shredded red chillies and spring onions, and serve immediately.

Egg Fried Noodles

Yellow bean sauce gives these seafood noodles a savoury flavour.

Serves 4–6

350g/12oz medium-thick dried egg noodles
30ml/2 tbsp vegetable oil
4 spring onions, cut into 1cm/½ in rounds
juice of 1 lime
15ml/1 tbsp soy sauce
2 garlic cloves, finely chopped
175g/6oz skinless, boneless chicken breast, sliced
175g/6oz raw prawns, peeled and deveined
175g/6oz squid, cleaned and cut into rings
15ml/1 tbsp yellow bean sauce
15ml/1 tbsp Thai fish sauce
15ml/1 tbsp soft light brown sugar
1 egg
fresh coriander leaves, to garnish

1 Bring a large pan of lightly salted water to the boil and cook the noodles until they are just tender, checking the packet for information on timing. Drain well.

2 Preheat a wok and swirl in half the oil. When it is hot, stir-fry the spring onions over a medium heat for 2 minutes, then add the drained noodles, with the lime juice and soy sauce. Stir-fry for a further 2–3 minutes. Transfer the mixture to a bowl and keep it hot.

3 Heat the remaining oil in the wok. Add the garlic, chicken, prawns and squid. Stir-fry over a high heat until the chicken and seafood are cooked.

4 Stir in the yellow bean sauce, fish sauce and sugar, then break the egg into the mixture, stirring gently until it sets in threads.

5 Add the noodles, toss lightly to mix, and heat through. Transfer to warmed bowls, garnish with coriander leaves and serve immediately.

Udon Pot

Fast food Japanese-style – it's a simple formula, but a winning one. First-class ingredients simmered in a good stock make a marvellous dish.

Serves 4

1 large carrot, cut into bite-size chunks
350g/12oz dried udon noodles
225g/8oz skinless, boneless chicken breasts, cut into bite-size pieces
8 raw king prawns, peeled and deveined
4–6 Chinese cabbage leaves, cut into short strips
8 fresh shiitake mushrooms, stems removed
50g/2oz/½ cup mangetouts, topped and tailed
1.5 litres/2½ pints/6 cups defatted home-made chicken stock or instant bonito stock
30ml/2 tbsp mirin
soy sauce, to taste
finely chopped spring onions, grated fresh root ginger, lemon wedges and extra soy sauce, to serve

1 Bring a large pan of lightly salted water to the boil and add the carrot chunks. Blanch for 1 minute, then lift out with a slotted spoon and set aside.

2 Add the noodles to the boiling water and cook until just tender, checking the packet for information on timing. Drain, rinse under cold water and drain again.

3 Spoon the carrot chunks and noodles into a large shallow pan or wok and arrange the chicken, prawns, Chinese cabbage leaves, mushrooms and mangetouts on top.

4 Bring the stock to the boil in a separate saucepan. Add the mirin and soy sauce to taste. Pour the stock over the noodle mixture and bring to the boil. Lower the heat, cover, then simmer over a medium heat for 5–6 minutes, until all the ingredients are cooked and tender.

5 Spoon the noodle mixture into a warmed dish and serve at once with side dishes of chopped spring onions, grated ginger, lemon wedges and a little soy sauce.

Special Chow Mein

This famous dish can be as simple or as elaborate as you like. This is a particularly luxurious version.

Serves 6

450g/1lb dried egg noodles
20ml/4 tsp vegetable oil
2 garlic cloves, sliced
5ml/1 tsp chopped fresh root ginger
2 fresh red chillies, chopped
2 lap cheong sausages, rinsed and sliced
1 skinless, boneless chicken breast, thinly sliced
16 raw tiger prawns, peeled, tails left intact, and deveined
115g/4oz green beans
225g/8oz/4 cups beansprouts
50g/2oz/1 cup garlic chives
30ml/2 tbsp soy sauce
15ml/1 tbsp oyster sauce
salt and freshly ground black pepper
shredded spring onions and fresh coriander leaves, to garnish

1 Bring a large pan of lightly salted water to the boil and cook the noodles until they are just tender, checking the packet for information on timing. Drain, rinse under cold water and drain thoroughly again.

2 Preheat a wok and swirl in half the oil. When it is hot, add the garlic, ginger and chillies, and stir-fry over a medium heat for 1 minute.

3 Add the lap cheong slices, chicken, prawns and beans. Stir-fry for about 2 minutes, or until the chicken is cooked and the prawns have changed colour. Transfer the mixture to a bowl and set aside.

4 Heat the rest of the oil in the wok, add the beansprouts and garlic chives, and stir-fry for 1–2 minutes. Add the noodles, and toss and stir to mix. Stir in the soy sauce and oyster sauce, and season to taste with salt and pepper.

5 Return the prawn mixture to the wok and toss over the heat until well mixed and heated through. Transfer the noodle mixture to warmed bowls, garnish with spring onions and coriander leaves, and serve immediately.

Singapore Rice Vermicelli

A lighter version of Singapore Noodles, this time made with ham.

Serves 4

10ml/2 tsp vegetable oil
1 egg, lightly beaten
2 garlic cloves, finely chopped
1 large fresh red or green chilli, seeded and finely chopped
15ml/1 tbsp medium curry powder
1 red pepper, seeded and thinly sliced
1 green pepper, seeded and thinly sliced
1 carrot, cut into matchsticks
1.5ml/¼ tsp salt
60ml/4 tbsp Vegetable Stock
225g/8oz diced rice vermicelli, soaked in warm water until soft
115g/4oz cooked peeled prawns, thawed if frozen
75g/3oz lean cooked ham, cut into 1cm/½ in cubes
15ml/1 tbsp light soy sauce

1 Preheat a wok and swirl in 5ml/1 tsp of the oil. When it is hot, add the egg and scramble until just set. Remove with a slotted spoon and set aside.

2 Heat the remaining oil in the clean wok, add the garlic and chilli, and stir-fry for a few seconds. Add the curry powder. Cook for 1 minute, stirring constantly, then stir in the peppers, carrot sticks, salt and stock.

3 Drain the rice vermicelli thoroughly. Heat the contents of the wok until the stock boils. Add the prawns, ham, scrambled egg, rice vermicelli and soy sauce. Mix thoroughly. Cook, stirring constantly, until all the liquid has been absorbed and the mixture is hot. Serve at once.

Cook's Tip

Curry powder varies in flavour, content and degree of heat from brand to brand. Most contain varying proportions of ground cardamom, chilli, cloves, coriander, cumin, ginger, nutmeg, pepper, tamarind and turmeric. They may also contain ajowan, caraway, fennel and mustard seeds.

Pork & Noodle Stir-fry

This tasty Chinese dish is both very easy to prepare and healthy.

Serves 4

225g/8oz dried egg noodles
15ml/1 tbsp vegetable oil
1 onion, chopped
1.5cm/½in piece of fresh root ginger, chopped
2 garlic cloves, crushed
30ml/2 tbsp soy sauce
60ml/4 tbsp dry white wine
10ml/2 tsp Chinese five-spice powder
450g/1lb lean minced pork
4 spring onions, sliced
50g/2oz/¾ cup oyster mushrooms
75g/3oz/½ cup drained canned sliced bamboo shoots
sesame oil, to serve

1 Bring a large pan of lightly salted water to the boil and cook the noodles until they are just tender, checking the packet for timing. Drain, rinse under cold water and drain well again.

2 Preheat a wok and swirl in the oil. When it is hot, add the onion, ginger, garlic, soy sauce and wine. Cook for 1 minute. Stir in the Chinese five-spice powder.

3 Add the pork and cook for 10 minutes, stirring continuously. Add the spring onions, mushrooms and bamboo shoots, and cook for 5 minutes more.

4 Stir in the drained noodles, and toss over the heat until they are heated through and have mixed with the other ingredients. Drizzle over a little sesame oil and serve immediately.

Indonesian Pork & Noodles

This spicy noodle dish couldn't be easier.

Serves 4

225g/8oz broccoli, divided into florets
225g/8oz egg noodles
15ml/1 tbsp groundnut oil
225g/8oz boneless loin of pork, cut into thin strips
1 carrot, cut into matchsticks
1 onion, finely chopped
2 garlic cloves, crushed
5ml/1tsp grated fresh root ginger
2.5ml/½ tsp dried shrimp paste
2.5ml/½ tsp sambal oelek
4 Chinese cabbage leaves, shredded
30ml/2 tbsp light soy sauce, plus extra to serve
10ml/2 tsp palm sugar
salt

1 Bring a large pan of lightly salted water to the boil and blanch the broccoli for 1 minute. Remove with a slotted spoon.
2 Bring the water back to the boil and cook the noodles until they are just tender, checking the packet for information on timing. Drain, rinse under cold water and drain well again.
3 Preheat a wok and swirl in the oil. Add the pork, carrot, onion, garlic, ginger, shrimp paste and sambal oelek, and stir-fry over a medium to high heat for 3–4 minutes.
4 Add the broccoli and Chinese cabbage leaves, and stir-fry for 1 minute more.
5 Add the noodles, soy sauce and sugar, and stir-fry for 3–4 minutes, until heated through. Transfer to a warmed serving dish and serve immediately with extra soy sauce.

Lemon Grass Pork

Chillies and lemon grass flavour this simple stir-fry, while peanuts add crunch.

Serves 4

450g/1lb boneless loin of pork
2 lemon grass stalks, trimmed and finely chopped
4 spring onions, thinly sliced
5ml/1 tsp salt
12 black peppercorns, coarsely crushed
15ml/1 tbsp groundnut oil
2 garlic cloves, chopped
2 fresh red chillies, seeded and chopped
225g/8oz dried rice vermicelli, soaked in warm water until soft
5ml/1 tsp light brown soft sugar
30ml/2 tbsp fish sauce
25g/1oz/¼ cup roasted unsalted peanuts, chopped
salt and freshly ground black pepper
roughly torn coriander leaves, to garnish

1 Trim any fat from the pork. Cut the meat across into 5mm/¼in thick slices, then into 5mm/¼in strips. Put them in a bowl with the lemon grass, spring onions, salt and peppercorns. Mix well, cover and leave to marinate for 30 minutes.

2 Heat a wok and swirl in the oil. When it is hot, stir-fry the pork for 3 minutes. Add the garlic and chillies, and stir-fry for 5–8 minutes more, until the pork no longer looks pink.

3 Meanwhile, bring a large pan of lightly salted water to the boil. Drain the rice vermicelli, add it to the water and cook briefly until just tender. Drain thoroughly and pile on to a warmed serving dish.

4 Add the sugar, fish sauce and peanuts to the pork mixture and toss to mix. Taste and adjust the seasoning, if necessary. Spoon on to the dish, alongside the noodles, garnish with the coriander leaves and serve.

Variation
Use skinless, boneless chicken breast if you prefer it to pork.

Stir-fried Noodles with Beansprouts

A classic Chinese noodle dish that makes a marvellous accompaniment.

Serves 4

175g/6oz dried egg noodles
15ml/1 tbsp vegetable oil
1 garlic clove, finely chopped
1 small onion, halved and sliced
225g/8oz/4 cups beansprouts
1 small red pepper, seeded and cut into strips
1 small green pepper, seeded and cut into strips
2.5ml/ ½ tsp salt
1.5ml/ ¼ tsp freshly ground white pepper
30ml/2 tbsp light soy sauce

1 Bring a pan of lightly salted water to the boil and cook the noodles until they are just tender, checking the packet for information on timing. Drain, rinse under cold water and drain well again.

2 Preheat a wok and swirl in the oil. When it is hot, add the garlic, stir briefly, then add the onion slices. Stir-fry for 1 minute over a medium heat, then add the beansprouts and peppers, and stir-fry for 2–3 minutes.

3 Stir in the drained noodles and toss over the heat, using two spatulas or wooden spoons, for 2–3 minutes or until the ingredients are well mixed and have heated through.

4 Add the salt, pepper and soy sauce, and stir thoroughly before serving the noodle mixture in warmed bowls.

Cook's Tip

White pepper comes from peppercorns that have ripened fully, unlike green or black peppercorns. The skin and outer flesh have been removed. White pepper is hot but not so aromatic as black pepper.

Chow Mein Combo

Every mouthful of this dish tells a different tale, so varied are the ingredients. Pork, liver and seafood are all included.

Serves 6

450g/1lb thick dried egg noodles
20ml/4 tsp vegetable oil
2 garlic cloves, chopped
2 spring onions, cut into short lengths
50g/2oz lean pork fillet, sliced
50g/2oz pig's liver, sliced
75g/3oz raw prawns, peeled and deveined
50g/2oz prepared squid, sliced
100g/4oz cockles or mussels, in their shells
115g/4oz watercress, leaves stripped from the stems
2 fresh red chillies, seeded and thinly sliced
30–45ml/2–3 tbsp soy sauce
a drizzle of sesame oil
salt and freshly ground black pepper

1 Scrape the cockles or mussels clean under cold running water and discard any open ones that do not close when tapped sharply.

2 Bring a large pan of lightly salted water to the boil and cook the noodles briefly until they are just tender, checking the packet for information on timing. Drain, rinse under cold water and drain again.

3 Preheat a wok and swirl in the oil. When it is hot, stir-fry the garlic and spring onions for about 30 seconds. Add the pork fillet, liver, prawns, squid and cockles or mussels. Stir-fry for 2 minutes over a high heat. Discard any shellfish that have not opened.

4 Add the watercress and chillies to the wok, and stir-fry for 3–4 minutes more, until the meat is cooked.

5 Add the drained noodles and soy sauce, with salt and pepper to taste. Toss over a high heat until the noodles are thoroughly heated through. Drizzle over the sesame oil, mix well and serve.

Five-spice Vegetable Noodles

Spicy, with delicious warmth from the chilli, ginger, cinnamon and other spices, this is exactly the right dish to serve for supper on a cold winter's evening.

Serves 2–3

225g/8oz dried egg noodles
2 carrots
1 celery stick
1 small fennel bulb
15ml/1 tbsp vegetable oil
2 courgettes, halved and sliced
1 fresh red chilli, seeded and chopped, plus sliced red chilli to garnish (optional)
2.5cm/1in piece of fresh root ginger, grated
1 garlic clove, crushed
7.5ml/1 ½ tsp Chinese five-spice powder
2.5ml/ ½ tsp ground cinnamon
4 spring onions, sliced
60ml/4 tbsp warm water

1 Bring a large pan of lightly salted water to the boil and cook the noodles briefly until they are just tender, checking the packet for information on timing. Drain, rinse under cold water and drain again.

2 Cut the carrots and celery stick into julienne. Cut the fennel bulb in half and cut out the hard core. Cut the flesh into slices, then into julienne.

3 Preheat a wok and swirl in the oil. When it is hot, add the carrots, celery, fennel, courgettes and chilli, and stir-fry over a medium heat for 7–8 minutes.

4 Add the ginger and garlic, and stir-fry for 2 minutes, then stir in the Chinese five-spice powder and cinnamon, and stir-fry for 1 minute more.

5 Add the spring onions and stir-fry for 1 minute. Moisten with the warm water and cook for 1 minute more.

6 Add the noodles, and toss and stir over the heat until well mixed and heated through. Divide the noodles among warmed individual bowls, garnish with sliced fresh red chilli, if liked, and serve immediately.

Beancurd Stir-fry with Egg Noodles

The sauce for this stir-fry is absolutely delicious, and the marinated beancurd adds both substance and an interesting contrast in texture.

Serves 4

225g/8oz firm smoked beancurd (tofu)
45ml/3 tbsp dark soy sauce
30ml/2 tbsp red vermouth
225g/8oz medium dried egg noodles
10ml/2 tsp clear honey
10ml/2 tsp cornflour
3 leeks, thinly sliced
2.5cm/1in piece of root ginger, finely grated
1–2 fresh red chillies, seeded and sliced into rings
1 small red pepper, seeded and thinly sliced
150ml/ ¼ pint/ ⅔ cup Vegetable Stock
salt and freshly ground black pepper

1 Cut the beancurd into 2cm/ ¾in cubes. Put it into a bowl with the soy sauce and vermouth. Toss well to coat, then set aside to marinate for 30 minutes.

2 Bring a large pan of lightly salted water to the boil and cook the noodles briefly until they are just tender. Drain, rinse under cold water and drain again.

3 Lift the beancurd from the marinade. Reserve the marinade and fry the beancurd quickly in a non-stick frying pan until lightly golden brown on all sides. Remove from the heat. Mix the honey and cornflour into the marinade and set it aside.

4 Put the leeks, ginger, chilli, pepper and stock into a large pan. Bring to the boil and cook over a high heat for 2–3 minutes, until the vegetables are crisp-tender.

5 Add the reserved marinade to the vegetable mixture and cook over a high heat, stirring constantly, until it thickens. Add the noodles and beancurd, and toss over the heat until both have heated through. Season to taste with salt and pepper.

6 Divide the stir-fry and noodles among warmed individual plates and serve immediately.

Tuna Pasta Salad

This easy pasta salad uses canned beans and tuna for a quick main dish.

Serves 6–8

450g/1lb/4 cups dried short pasta such as ruote, macaroni or farfalle
60ml/4 tbsp olive oil
2 x 200g/7oz cans tuna in oil, drained
2 x 400g/14oz cans cannellini or borlotti beans, rinsed and drained
1 small red onion
2 celery sticks
juice of 1 lemon
30ml/2 tbsp chopped fresh parsley
salt and freshly ground black pepper
fresh parsley, to garnish

1 Bring a large pan of lightly salted water to the boil and cook the pasta until it is *al dente*. Drain, rinse under cold water, drain again and tip into a bowl. Add the oil and toss well. Set aside until cold.

2 Flake the tuna and add it to the cooked pasta with the beans. Toss lightly. Slice the onion and celery very thinly, add them to the pasta mixture and toss again.

3 Mix the lemon juice and parsley in a bowl, then add the mixture to the salad. Season with salt and pepper to taste. Mix thoroughly. Allow the salad to stand for at least 1 hour before serving at room temperature, garnished with parsley.

Variations

- *Use smoked fish, such as mackerel or trout, instead of the canned tuna.*
- *Substitute canned or fresh crab meat for the tuna and 15ml/1 tbsp chopped fresh dill for the parsley.*
- *Replace one can of beans with 275g/10oz lightly steamed mangetouts or sugar snap peas.*

Mediterranean Salad with Basil

A type of Salade Niçoise with pasta, this conjures up all the sunny flavours of the Mediterranean.

Serves 4

175g/6oz fine green beans, trimmed
225g/8oz/2 cups chunky dried pasta shapes
2 large ripe tomatoes
50g/2oz/2 cups fresh basil leaves
200g/7oz can tuna in oil, drained
2 hard-boiled eggs, sliced or quartered
50g/2oz can anchovy fillets, drained
drained capers and stoned black olives, to garnish

For the dressing

90ml/6 tbsp extra virgin olive oil
30ml/2 tbsp white wine vinegar or lemon juice
2 garlic cloves, crushed
2.5ml/ ½ tsp Dijon mustard
30ml/2 tbsp chopped fresh basil
salt and freshly ground black pepper

1 Whisk all the ingredients for the dressing together and leave to infuse while you make the salad.

2 Bring a large pan of water to the boil. Add the beans and blanch for 2–3 minutes. Using a slotted spoon, transfer them to a colander. Refresh under cold water, drain well and set aside.

3 Bring the pan of water back to the boil and cook the pasta until it is *al dente*. Drain, rinse under cold water and drain again. Put in a bowl and toss with a little of the dressing.

4 Slice or quarter the tomatoes and arrange them on the base of a bowl. Moisten them with a little dressing and cover with one-quarter of the basil leaves. Then cover with the beans. Moisten with a little more dressing and cover with one-third of the remaining basil.

5 Cover with the dressed pasta and half the remaining basil. Roughly flake the tuna and add it to the salad. Arrange the eggs on top, then finally scatter over the anchovy fillets, capers and black olives. Pour over the remaining dressing and garnish with the remaining basil. Serve immediately.

Warm Scallop & Conchiglie Salad

This is a very special modern dish, a warm salad composed of scallops, pasta and fresh rocket flavoured with roasted pepper, chilli and balsamic vinegar.

Serves 4

8 large fresh scallops
300g/11oz/2¾ cups dried conchiglie
15ml/1 tbsp olive oil
15g/½oz/1 tbsp butter
120ml/4fl oz/ ½ cup dry white wine
90g/3½ oz rocket leaves, stalks trimmed
salt and freshly ground black pepper

For the vinaigrette

60ml/4 tbsp extra virgin olive oil
15ml/1 tbsp balsamic vinegar
1 piece bottled roasted pepper, drained and finely chopped
1–2 fresh red chillies, seeded and chopped
1 garlic clove, crushed
5–10ml/1–2 tbsp clear honey, to taste

1 Cut each scallop into 2–3 pieces. If the corals are attached, pull them off and cut each piece in half. Season the scallops and corals with salt and pepper.

2 Make the vinaigrette. Put the oil, vinegar, chopped pepper and chillies in a jug. Add the garlic and honey, and whisk well.

3 Bring a large pan of lightly salted water to the boil and cook the pasta until it is *al dente*.

4 Meanwhile, heat the oil and butter in a non-stick frying pan until sizzling. Add half the scallops and toss over a high heat for 2 minutes. Remove with a slotted spoon and keep warm. Cook the remaining scallops in the same way.

5 Add the wine to the liquid remaining in the pan and stir over a high heat until the mixture has reduced to a few tablespoons. Remove from the heat and keep warm.

6 Drain the pasta and tip it into a warmed bowl. Add the rocket, scallops, the reduced cooking juices and the vinaigrette, and toss well to combine. Serve immediately.

Smoked Salmon & Dill Pasta Salad

This dish makes a main course for two or starter for four.

Serves 2–4

350g/12oz/3 cups dried fusilli
6 large fresh dill sprigs, chopped, plus extra sprigs to garnish
30ml/2 tbsp extra virgin olive oil
15ml/1 tbsp white wine vinegar
300ml/½ pint/1¼ cups double cream
175g/6oz smoked salmon
salt and freshly ground black pepper

1 Bring a large pan of lightly salted water to the boil and cook the pasta until it is *al dente*. Drain, rinse under cold water, drain again and tip into a bowl. Set aside until cold.

2 Make the dressing. Place the chopped dill, olive oil, vinegar and cream in a food processor and process until smooth. Season to taste with salt and pepper.

3 Slice the salmon into small strips. Place the cooled pasta and the smoked salmon in a large mixing bowl. Pour on the dressing and toss carefully. Transfer to a serving bowl, garnish with the extra dill sprigs and serve immediately.

Warm Smoked Salmon & Pasta Salad

This is an elegant salad.

Serves 4

350g/12oz dried spaghetti
15ml/1 tbsp extra virgin olive oil
1 garlic clove, crushed
75g/3oz smoked salmon, cut into thin strips
1 bunch of watercress, leaves removed and stems discarded
salt and freshly ground black pepper

1 Bring a large pan of lightly salted water to the boil and cook the pasta until it is *al dente*. Drain and toss in half the oil.
2 Heat the remaining oil in a heavy-based frying pan and stir-fry the garlic for 30 seconds. Add the salmon and watercress, season with pepper and stir-fry for 30 seconds.
3 Spoon the mixture on to the pasta, toss and serve warm.

Pink & Green Salad

Spiked with a little fresh chilli, this pretty salad makes a delicious light lunch when served with hot fresh ciabatta rolls.

Serves 4

225g/8oz/2 cups dried farfalle
juice of ½ lemon
1 small fresh red chilli, seeded and very finely chopped
60ml/4 tbsp chopped fresh basil
30ml/2 tbsp chopped fresh coriander
60ml/4 tbsp extra virgin olive oil
15ml/1 tbsp mayonnaise
250g/9oz cooked peeled prawns
1 avocado
salt and freshly ground black pepper

1 Bring a large saucepan of lightly salted water to the boil and cook the pasta until it is *al dente*. Drain, rinse under cold water and drain again. Leave until cold.

2 Put the lemon juice and chilli in a bowl with half the basil and coriander, and season with salt and pepper to taste. Whisk well to mix, then gradually add the oil and mayonnaise, whisking until the dressing is thick.

3 Add the prawns to the dressing and stir gently until they are evenly coated.

4 Cut the avocado in half, lift out the stone and remove the peel. Cut the flesh into neat dice. Add the avocado to the prawns and dressing with the pasta, toss well to mix and taste for seasoning. Serve immediately, sprinkled with the remaining basil and coriander.

Cook's Tip

This pasta salad can be made several hours ahead of time, but without adding the avocado. Cover the bowl with clear film and chill it in the fridge until required. Prepare the avocado and add it to the salad just before serving or it will discolour, turning brown, and spoil the effect.

Seafood Salad

This is a very special salad which would look quite spectacular with one of the new and unusual "designer" shapes of pasta.

Serves 4–6

450g/1lb live mussels, scrubbed and bearded
250ml/8fl oz/1 cup dry white wine
2 garlic cloves, roughly chopped
a handful of fresh flat leaf parsley
175g/6oz prepared squid rings
175g/6oz/1½ cups small dried pasta shapes
175g/6oz/1 cup cooked peeled prawns

For the dressing

90ml/6 tbsp extra virgin olive oil
juice of 1 lemon
5–10ml/1–2 tsp drained capers, roughly chopped
1 garlic clove, crushed
a small handful of fresh flat leaf parsley, finely chopped
salt and freshly ground black pepper

1 Check over the mussels and discard any that are damaged, open or that do not close when sharply tapped against the work surface.

2 Pour half the wine into a large pan and add the garlic, parsley and mussels. Cover the pan tightly and bring to the boil over a high heat. Cook for about 5 minutes, shaking the pan frequently, until the mussels have opened.

3 Tip the mussels and their liquid into a colander set over a bowl. Reserve a few mussels in their shells for garnishing, then remove the remainder from their shells, tipping the liquid from the mussels into the bowl of cooking liquid. Discard any mussels that remain closed.

4 Strain the mussel cooking liquid through a muslin-lined sieve and return it to the pan. Add the remaining wine and the squid rings. Bring to the boil, cover and simmer gently, stirring occasionally, for 30 minutes or until the squid is tender. Leave the squid to cool in the cooking liquid.

5 Meanwhile, bring a large pan of lightly salted water to the boil and cook the pasta until it is *al dente*.

6 Make the dressing. Put the oil, lemon juice, capers, garlic and parsley into a large bowl and whisk to combine. Season to taste with salt and pepper.

7 Drain the cooked pasta well, add it to the bowl of dressing and toss well to mix. Leave to cool.

8 Tip the cooled squid into a sieve and drain well, then rinse it lightly under cold water. Add the squid, shelled mussels and prawns to the dressed pasta and toss well to mix.

9 Cover the bowl tightly with clear film and chill in the fridge for about 4 hours. Toss well before serving, then garnish with the reserved mussels in their shells.

Pasta, Melon & Prawn Salad

Orange-fleshed cantaloupe or Charentais melon looks spectacular in this salad.

Serves 4–6

175g/6oz/1½ cups dried pasta shapes
1 large melon
225g/8oz cooked peeled prawns
30ml/2 tbsp olive oil
15ml/1 tbsp tarragon vinegar
30ml/2 tbsp snipped fresh chives or chopped parsley
shredded Chinese leaves
fresh herb sprigs, to garnish

1 Bring a large pan of lightly salted water to the boil and cook the pasta until it is *al dente*. Drain, rinse under cold water and drain again. Put it into a bowl and leave until cold.

2 Cut the melon in half and remove the seeds with a teaspoon. Carefully scoop the flesh into balls with a melon baller and add to the pasta, with the prawns.

3 Whisk the oil, vinegar and chopped herbs in a bowl. Pour on to the prawn mixture and turn to coat. Cover and chill for at least 30 minutes.

4 Line a shallow serving bowl with the shredded Chinese leaves, pile the prawn mixture on top and garnish with the herb sprigs. Serve at once.

Cook's Tip

For an attractive presentation, serve the salad in the melon shells, lined with the Chinese leaves.

Variation

- *For a really special treat, substitute chopped cooked lobster meat for the prawns.*
- *For a different flavour and texture, use a mixture of Ogen, cantaloupe and watermelon.*

Crab Pasta Salad with Spicy Cocktail Dressing

A variation on a very popular starter, this salad is certain to go down well.

Serves 6

350g/12oz/3 cups dried fusilli
1 small red pepper, seeded and finely chopped
2 x 175g/6oz cans white crab meat, drained
115g/4oz cherry tomatoes, halved
¼ cucumber, halved, seeded and sliced into crescents
15ml/1 tbsp lemon juice
salt and freshly ground black pepper
fresh basil, to garnish

For the dressing

300ml/½ pint/1¼ cups natural yogurt
2 celery sticks, finely chopped
10ml/2 tsp horseradish cream
2.5ml/½ tsp ground paprika
2.5ml/½ tsp Dijon mustard
30ml/2 tbsp sweet tomato pickle or chutney

1 Bring a large pan of lightly salted water to the boil and cook the pasta until it is *al dente*. Drain, rinse under cold water, and drain again.

2 Put the chopped red pepper in a heatproof bowl and pour over boiling water to cover. Leave to stand for 1 minute, then drain, rinse under cold water and drain again. Pat dry on kitchen paper.

3 Drain the crab meat and pick it over carefully, removing any stray pieces of shell. Put the crab meat into a bowl, and add the tomatoes and cucumber. Season with salt and pepper to taste, then sprinkle with the lemon juice.

4 Make the dressing. Put the yogurt, celery, horseradish cream, paprika, mustard and pickle or chutney into a bowl and mix well. Season with salt, if necessary.

5 Stir in the diced red pepper and the pasta. Transfer the mixture to a serving dish. Spoon the crab mixture on top and mix well. Garnish with fresh basil and serve.

Chicken & Broccoli Salad

Gorgonzola makes a wonderful tangy salad dressing that goes well with both chicken and broccoli.

Serves 4

175g/6oz/generous 1 cup broccoli florets, divided into small sprigs
225g/8oz/2 cups dried farfalle
2 large cooked chicken breasts

For the dressing

90g/3½oz Gorgonzola cheese
15ml/1 tbsp white wine vinegar
60ml/4 tbsp extra virgin olive oil
2.5–5ml/ ½–1 tsp finely chopped fresh sage, plus extra sage sprigs to garnish
salt and freshly ground black pepper

1 Bring a large pan of lightly salted water to the boil and cook the broccoli florets for 3 minutes. Using a slotted spoon, transfer them to a colander. Rinse under cold water, then spread out on dish towels to drain and dry.

2 Bring the water in the pan back to the boil and cook the pasta until it is *al dente*. Drain, rinse under cold water and drain again. Leave until cold.

3 Remove the skin from the cooked chicken breasts and cut the meat into bite-size pieces.

4 Make the dressing. Put the cheese in a large bowl and mash with a fork, then whisk in the wine vinegar followed by the oil and sage. Season with salt and pepper to taste.

5 Add the pasta, chicken and broccoli. Toss well, then season to taste and serve, garnished with extra sage.

Variations

- *If you find the flavour of Gorgonzola too strong, try a milder variety, such as dolcelatte.*
- *This salad also works well with cooked turkey breast.*
- *Add 4 halved cherry tomatoes for additional colour.*
- *Use equal quantities of broccoli and cauliflower florets.*

Chicken Pasta Salad

This is a delicious and easy way of using up leftover cooked chicken.

Serves 4

225g/8oz/2 cups fusilli, preferably mixed colours
30ml/2 tbsp bottled pesto
15ml/1 tbsp olive oil
1 beefsteak tomato, peeled and diced
12 stoned black olives
225g/8oz cooked French beans, cut in short lengths
350g/12oz cooked chicken, diced
salt and freshly ground black pepper
fresh basil, to garnish

1 Bring a large pan of lightly salted water to the boil and cook the pasta until *al dente*. Drain, rinse under cold water and drain again. Put it into a bowl and stir in the pesto and olive oil.

2 Add the tomato, olives, beans and chicken. Season to taste. Toss to mix and transfer to a serving platter. Garnish and serve.

Chicken & Pepper Pasta Salad

A variation on the versatile chicken salad theme.

Serves 4

350g/12oz/3 cups dried short pasta, such as mezze rigatoni, fusilli or penne
45ml/3 tbsp olive oil
225g/8oz cooked chicken, cubed
4 spring onions, chopped
2 small red and yellow peppers, diced
50g/2oz/ ½ cup stoned green olives
45ml/3 tbsp mayonnaise
5ml/1 tsp Worcestershire sauce
15ml/1 tbsp wine vinegar
salt and freshly ground black pepper
a few fresh basil leaves, to garnish

1 Bring a large pan of lightly salted water to the boil and cook the pasta until it is *al dente*. Drain, tip into a bowl and add the olive oil. Toss well to mix, then leave until cold.
2 Add the chicken, spring onions, peppers and olives. Mix the mayonnaise, Worcestershire sauce, vinegar and seasoning, add to the salad and toss. Chill for 1 hour, then garnish and serve.

Curried Chicken Salad with Penne

There are several versions of this popular salad. This one has a dressing based on low-fat yogurt, so it is a relatively healthy option.

Serves 4

2 cooked boneless, skinless chicken breasts
175g/6oz French beans, trimmed and cut in short lengths
350g/12oz/3 cups dried penne, preferably mixed colours
150ml/ ¼ pint/ ⅔ cup low-fat yogurt
5ml/1 tsp mild curry powder
1 garlic clove, crushed
1 fresh green chilli, seeded and finely chopped
30ml/2 tbsp chopped fresh coriander
4 firm ripe tomatoes, peeled, seeded and cut in strips
salt and freshly ground black pepper
fresh coriander leaves, to garnish

1 Cut the chicken breasts into bite-size pieces. Bring a large pan of lightly salted water to the boil and cook the French beans for 2–3 minutes. Lift them into a colander, using a slotted spoon, and drain under cold water. Drain again.

2 Bring the water back to the boil and cook the pasta until it is *al dente*. Drain, rinse under cold water and drain again.

3 Mix the yogurt, curry powder, garlic, chilli and chopped coriander together in a bowl. Stir in the chicken pieces and leave to stand for 30 minutes.

4 Put the pasta in a glass bowl, and toss with the beans and tomatoes. Spoon over the chicken and sauce. Garnish with coriander leaves and serve.

Variation
For an alternative dressing, mix together 150ml/¼ pint/⅔ cup mayonnaise, 10ml/2 tsp concentrated curry sauce, 2.5ml/½ tsp lemon juice and 10ml/2 tsp sieved apricot jam. Add the chicken to the dressing and chill in the fridge for 30 minutes before mixing with the pasta and serving.

Marinated Chicken & Pasta Salad

This tastes good when the chicken is served warm, but it can be served cold, if that is more convenient.

Serves 6

5ml/1 tsp ground cumin seeds
5ml/1 tsp ground paprika
5ml/1 tsp ground turmeric
1–2 garlic cloves, crushed
45–60ml/3–4 tbsp fresh lime juice
4 skinless, boneless chicken breasts
225g/8oz/2 cups dried rigatoni
1 red pepper, seeded and chopped
2 celery sticks, thinly sliced
1 small onion, finely chopped
6 stuffed green olives, halved
30ml/2 tbsp clear honey
15ml/1 tbsp wholegrain mustard
salt and freshly ground black pepper
mixed salad leaves, to serve

1 Mix the cumin, paprika, turmeric, garlic and 30ml/2 tbsp of the lime juice in a bowl. Season to taste with a little salt and pepper. Rub this mixture over the chicken breasts. Lay them in a shallow dish, cover with clear film and leave in a cool place for about 3 hours or overnight.

2 Preheat the oven to 200°C/400°F/Gas 6. Place the chicken breasts in a single layer on a rack set over a roasting tin. Bake for 20 minutes.

3 Meanwhile, bring a large pan of lightly salted water to the boil and cook the rigatoni until *al dente*. Drain, rinse under cold water and drain again. Leave until cold.

4 Put the red pepper, celery, onion and olives into a large bowl. Add the pasta and mix carefully.

5 Mix the honey, mustard and the remaining lime juice to taste in a jug. Pour the mixture over the pasta. Toss to coat.

6 Cut the chicken into bite-size pieces. Arrange the mixed salad leaves on a serving dish, spoon the pasta mixture into the centre, top with the spicy chicken pieces and serve.

Duck & Rigatoni Salad

This sophisticated salad has a delicious sweet-sour dressing which goes wonderfully well with the richness of duck.

Serves 6

2 duck breasts, boned
5ml/1 tsp coriander seeds, crushed
350g/12oz/3 cups rigatoni
150ml/ ¼ pint/ ⅔ cup fresh orange juice
15ml/1 tbsp lemon juice
10ml/2 tsp clear honey
1 shallot, finely chopped
1 garlic clove, crushed
1 celery stick, chopped
75g/3oz dried cherries
45ml/3 tbsp port
15ml/1 tbsp chopped fresh mint, plus extra to garnish
30ml/2 tbsp chopped fresh coriander, plus extra to garnish
1 eating apple, diced
2 oranges, segmented
salt and freshly ground black pepper

1 Preheat the grill. Remove the skin and fat from the duck breasts, and season them with salt and pepper. Rub them with the crushed coriander seeds. Place them on a grill rack and grill for 7–10 minutes. Wrap them in foil and leave for 20 minutes.

2 Bring a large pan of lightly salted water to the boil and cook the pasta until it is *al dente*. Drain, rinse under cold water and drain again. Leave to cool.

3 Put the orange juice, lemon juice, honey, shallot, garlic, celery, cherries, port, mint and fresh coriander into a bowl, whisk together and leave the dressing to stand for 30 minutes.

4 Slice the duck very thinly. (It should be pink in the centre.) Put the pasta into a bowl, add the dressing, apple and oranges. Toss well. Transfer the salad to a serving plate. Add the duck slices, and garnish with the extra coriander and mint.

Cook's Tip
If you do not like your duck pink in the middle, then grill it for a little longer.

Devilled Ham & Pineapple Penne Salad

Ham and pineapple are often paired. In this salad, the combination works particularly well, thanks to the fruity dressing.

Serves 4

225g/8oz/2 cups wholewheat penne
150ml/ ¼ pint/ ⅔ cup natural yogurt
15ml/1 tbsp cider vinegar
5ml/1 tsp wholegrain mustard
a large pinch of caster sugar
30ml/2 tbsp hot mango chutney
115g/4oz cooked ham, diced
200g/7oz can pineapple chunks, drained
2 celery sticks, chopped
½ green pepper, seeded and diced
15ml/1 tbsp flaked toasted almonds, roughly chopped
salt and freshly ground black pepper

1 Bring a large pan of lightly salted water to the boil and cook the pasta until it is *al dente*. Drain, rinse under cold water and drain again. Leave to cool.

2 Mix the yogurt, vinegar, mustard, sugar and mango chutney in a large bowl. Add the pasta, and season with salt and pepper to taste. Toss lightly together.

3 Pile the dressed pasta on to a serving dish. Scatter over the ham, pineapple, celery and green pepper.

4 Sprinkle the toasted almonds on top. Serve at once.

Variations
• *Substitute garlic croûtons for the toasted almonds to garnish the salad.*
• *Instead of pineapple chunks, you could use chopped fresh or canned mangoes.*
• *Add a diced green eating apple with the celery and green pepper in step 3.*

Pasta Salad with Salami & Olives

Garlic and herb dressing gives a Mediterranean flavour to a handful of ingredients from the store cupboard and fridge, making this an excellent salad for serving in winter.

Serves 4

225g/8oz/2 cups dried gnocchi or conchiglie
50g/2oz/ ½ cup stoned black olives, quartered lengthways
75g/3oz thinly sliced salami, any skin removed, diced
½ small red onion, finely chopped
a large handful of fresh basil leaves

For the dressing

60ml/4 tbsp extra virgin olive oil
good pinch of granulated sugar
juice of ½ lemon
5ml/1 tsp Dijon mustard
10ml/2 tsp dried oregano
1 garlic clove, crushed
salt and freshly ground black pepper

1 Bring a large pan of lightly salted water to the boil and cook the pasta until it is *al dente*.

2 Meanwhile, make the dressing. Put the oil, sugar, lemon juice, mustard, oregano and garlic in a large bowl, season with a little salt and pepper to taste, and whisk well to mix.

3 Drain the pasta thoroughly, add it to the bowl of dressing and toss thoroughly to mix. Leave the dressed pasta to cool, stirring occasionally.

4 When the pasta is cold, add the olives, salami, onion and basil, and toss well to mix again. Taste and adjust the seasoning, if necessary, then serve.

Cook's Tip

There are many different types of Italian salami that can be used. Salame napoletano is coarse cut and peppery, salame milanese is fine cut and mild in flavour, and salame di Felino is said to be the best in Italy.

Warm Pasta Salad with Ham

An unusual asparagus dressing tops the tagliatelle in this tasty salad.

Serves 4

450g/1lb asparagus
1 small potato
60ml/4 tbsp olive oil
15ml/1 tbsp lemon juice
10ml/2 tsp Dijon mustard
120ml/4fl oz/ ½ cup Vegetable Stock
450g/1lb dried tagliatelle
225g/8oz sliced cooked ham, 5mm/ ¼in thick, cut into fingers
2 eggs, hard-boiled and sliced
50g/2oz Parmesan cheese, shaved
salt and freshly ground black pepper

1 Bring a saucepan of lightly salted water to the boil. Snap off the tough woody part of each asparagus spear, then cut each spear in half. Add the thicker halves to the boiling water and cook for 6 minutes, then throw in the tips and cook for 6 minutes more. Drain, refresh under cold water, then drain again.

2 Meanwhile, put the potato into a small saucepan of lightly salted cold water, bring to the boil and cook for 10 minutes, until just tender. Drain and set aside.

3 Set aside about 8 asparagus tips, for garnishing. Put the rest of the asparagus in a food processor and chop it roughly. Add the potato, olive oil, lemon juice, mustard and stock.

4 Bring a large pan of lightly salted water to the boil and cook the pasta until it is *al dente*. Drain, rinse under cold water and drain again. Return to the clean pan, add the asparagus dressing and toss well.

5 Divide the dressed pasta among four warmed plates. Top with the ham, hard-boiled eggs and asparagus tips. Serve with the Parmesan.

Bacon & Bean Pasta Salad

This tasty pasta salad is subtly flavoured with smoked bacon in a light, flavoursome dressing.

Serves 4

225g/8oz green beans
350g/12oz/3 cups dried wholewheat fusilli or spirali
8 rindless lean smoked back bacon rashers
350g/12oz cherry tomatoes, halved
2 bunches of spring onions, chopped
400g/14oz can chick-peas, rinsed and drained
90ml/6 tbsp tomato juice
30ml/2 tbsp balsamic vinegar
5ml/1 tsp ground cumin
5ml/1 tsp ground coriander
30ml/2 tbsp chopped fresh coriander
salt and freshly ground black pepper

1 Bring a large pan of lightly salted water to the boil and cook the beans for 3–4 minutes, until crisp-tender. Lift them out with a slotted spoon and place in a colander. Refresh under cold water and drain.

2 Bring the water back to the boil, add the pasta and cook until *al dente*.

3 Meanwhile, grill the bacon until crisp. Dice or crumble it and add it to the beans.

4 Mix the tomatoes, spring onions and chick-peas in a large bowl. In a jug, mix together the tomato juice, vinegar, cumin, ground coriander and fresh coriander, and season to taste with salt and pepper. Pour the dressing over the tomato mixture.

5 Drain the pasta thoroughly and add it to the tomato mixture with the beans and bacon. Toss well. Serve warm or cold.

Variation
You could substitute canned haricot beans or flageolets for the chick-peas.

Herbed Beef & Pasta Salad

Fillet of beef is such a luxury cut that it makes sense to stretch it if you can. Serving it as part of a pasta salad is an excellent way of doing this.

Serves 6

450g/1lb beef fillet
450g/1lb fresh tagliatelle with sun-dried tomatoes and herbs
½ cucumber
115g/4oz cherry tomatoes, halved

For the marinade
15ml/1 tbsp soy sauce
15ml/1 tbsp sherry
5ml/1 tsp fresh root ginger, grated
1 garlic clove, crushed

For the herb dressing
30–45ml/2–3 tbsp horseradish sauce
150ml/¼ pint/⅔ cup natural yogurt
1 garlic clove, crushed
30–45ml/2–3 tbsp chopped fresh herbs
salt and freshly ground black pepper

1 Mix all the marinade ingredients in a shallow dish, add the beef and turn it over to coat it. Cover with clear film and leave for 30 minutes to allow the flavours to penetrate the meat.

2 Preheat the grill. Lift the fillet out of the marinade and pat it dry with kitchen paper. Place it on a grill rack and grill for 8 minutes on each side, basting with the marinade during cooking, then put it on a plate, cover with foil and leave to stand for 20 minutes.

3 Bring a pan of lightly salted water to the boil, add the pasta and cook until it is *al dente*. Drain, rinse under cold water and drain again.

4 Cut the cucumber in half lengthways, scoop out the seeds with a teaspoon and slice the flesh thinly into crescents.

5 Mix all the dressing ingredients in a large bowl. Add the pasta, cucumber and cherry tomatoes, and toss to coat. Divide among six plates. Slice the beef thinly and fan out the slices alongside the salad. Serve immediately.

Avocado & Pasta Salad with Coriander

Served solo or as part of a selection of salads, this tasty combination is sure to please. The dressing is quite sharp, but very refreshing.

Serves 4

900ml/1 ½ pints/3¾ cups Vegetable Stock
115g/4oz/1 cup dried farfalle or conchiglie
4 celery sticks, finely chopped
2 avocados, peeled, stoned and chopped
1 garlic clove, chopped
15ml/1 tbsp finely chopped fresh coriander, plus some whole leaves to garnish
115g/4oz/1 cup grated mature Cheddar cheese

For the dressing

150ml/ ¼ pint/ ⅔ cup extra virgin olive oil
15ml/1 tbsp cider vinegar
30ml/2 tbsp lemon juice
grated rind of 1 lemon
5ml/1 tsp Dijon mustard
15ml/1 tbsp roughly chopped fresh coriander
salt and freshly ground black pepper

1 Pour the stock into a large pan. Bring to the boil and cook the pasta until *al dente*. Drain, rinse under cold water and drain again. Leave to cool.

2 Mix the celery, avocados, garlic and chopped coriander in a bowl, and add the cooled pasta. Sprinkle with the grated Cheddar cheese.

3 To make the dressing, put the oil, vinegar, lemon juice and rind, mustard and fresh coriander in a food processor and process until the coriander is finely chopped. Season to taste with salt and pepper. Serve the dressing separately or toss it with the salad. Serve, garnished with the coriander leaves.

Avocado, Tomato & Mozzarella Pasta Salad

Dressed farfalle and sliced avocados make wonderful additions to a classic salad.

Serves 4

175g/6oz/1 ½ cups dried farfalle
6 ripe red tomatoes
225g/8oz mozzarella cheese
1 large ripe avocado
30ml/2 tbsp pine nuts, toasted
1 fresh basil sprig, to garnish

For the dressing

90ml/6 tbsp extra virgin olive oil
30ml/2 tbsp wine vinegar
5ml/1 tsp balsamic vinegar
5ml/1 tsp wholegrain mustard
pinch of sugar
30ml/2 tbsp chopped fresh basil
salt and freshly ground black pepper

1 Bring a large pan of lightly salted water to the boil and cook the pasta until it is *al dente*. Drain, rinse under cold water, then drain again. Tip into a bowl and set aside to cool.

2 Slice the tomatoes and mozzarella cheese into thin rounds. Cut the avocado in half, lift out the stone and peel off the skin. Slice the flesh lengthways.

3 Arrange the tomato, mozzarella and avocado in overlapping slices around the edge of a flat serving plate.

4 For the dressing, put the oil, wine vinegar, balsamic vinegar, mustard, sugar and basil into a small bowl and whisk until combined. Season to taste with salt and pepper.

5 Add half the dressing to the pasta. Toss to coat, then pile into the centre of the plate. Pour over the remaining dressing, scatter over the pine nuts and garnish with the basil sprig. Serve immediately.

Cook's Tip
Choose tomatoes that are uniform in size.

Chargrilled Pepper Salad

This is a good side salad to serve with plain grilled or barbecued chicken or fish.

Serves 4

I large red pepper
I large green pepper
250g/9oz/2¼ cups dried fusilli, preferably mixed colours
a handful of fresh basil leaves
a handful of fresh coriander leaves
I garlic clove
salt and freshly ground black pepper

For the dressing

30ml/2 tbsp bottled pesto
juice of ½ lemon
60ml/4 tbsp extra virgin olive oil

1 Preheat the grill. Cut the peppers in half, and remove the cores and seeds. Place the peppers cut side down in a grill pan and grill for about 10 minutes, until the skin has blistered and charred. Put the hot peppers in a bowl, cover with several layers of kitchen paper and set aside until cool.

2 Bring a large pan of lightly salted water to the boil and cook the pasta until it is *al dente*.

3 Meanwhile, put the pesto, lemon juice and oil in a large bowl and whisk well to mix. Season to taste with salt and pepper.

4 Drain the cooked pasta well and tip it into the bowl of dressing. Toss well to mix, then set aside to cool.

5 When the peppers are cool enough to handle, peel them then chop the flesh and add it to the pasta.

6 Put the basil, coriander and garlic on a chopping board and chop them all together. Add to the pasta and toss to mix, then season to taste with salt and pepper, and serve.

Cook's Tip

You can serve the salad at room temperature or chilled, whichever you prefer.

Roasted Cherry Tomato & Rocket Salad

This is a good side salad to accompany barbecued chicken, steaks or chops. Roasted tomatoes are very juicy, with an intense, smoky-sweet flavour.

Serves 4

450g/1lb ripe baby Italian plum tomatoes, halved lengthways
75ml/5 tbsp extra virgin olive oil
2 garlic cloves, cut into thin slivers
225g/8oz/2 cups dried pipe
30ml/2 tbsp balsamic vinegar
2 pieces of sun-dried tomato in olive oil, drained and chopped
a large pinch of granulated sugar
I handful of rocket, about 65g/2½oz
salt and freshly ground black pepper

1 Preheat the oven to 190°C/375°F/Gas 5. Arrange the halved tomatoes cut side up in a roasting tin, drizzle 30ml/2 tbsp of the olive oil over them and sprinkle with the slivers of garlic. Season with salt and pepper to taste. Roast in the oven for 20 minutes, turning once.

2 Meanwhile, bring a large pan of lightly salted water to the boil and cook the pasta until it is *al dente*.

3 Put the remaining oil in a large bowl and add the vinegar, sun-dried tomatoes and sugar, and season with a little salt and pepper to taste. Stir well to mix.

4 Drain the pasta, add it to the bowl of dressing and toss to mix. Add the roasted tomatoes and mix gently.

5 Just before serving, add the chopped rocket, toss lightly and adjust the seasoning, if necessary.

Variation

If you like, add 150g/5oz diced mozzarella with the rocket.

Pasta Salad with Olives

This delicious salad combines the sunny flavours of the Mediterranean. Serve it with a radicchio and green leaf salad.

Serves 6

450g/1lb/4 cups dried, short pasta, such as conchiglie, farfalle or penne
60ml/4 tbsp extra virgin olive oil
10 sun-dried tomatoes, thinly sliced
30ml/2 tbsp bottled capers, drained
115g/4oz/1 cup stoned black olives
2 garlic cloves, finely chopped
45ml/3 tbsp balsamic vinegar
45ml/3 tbsp chopped fresh parsley
salt and freshly ground black pepper

1 Bring a large pan of lightly salted water to the boil and cook the pasta until it is *al dente*. Drain, rinse under cold water and drain again. Tip it into a large bowl. Toss with the olive oil, then set aside.

2 Soak the sun-dried tomatoes in a bowl of hot water for 10 minutes. Rinse the capers well. Drain the sun-dried tomatoes, reserving the soaking water.

3 Combine the olives, tomatoes, capers, garlic and vinegar in a small bowl. Season to taste with salt and pepper.

4 Stir this mixture into the pasta and toss well. Add 30–45ml/2–3 tbsp of the tomato soaking water if the salad seems too dry. Toss with the parsley, and allow to stand for about 15 minutes before serving.

Cook's Tip
Use capers preserved in salt, if you prefer, but soak them in hot water for 10 minutes first. Even better, use capers preserved in olive oil, if you can find them, and use some of the oil from the jar instead of the plain olive oil.

Artichoke Pasta Salad

Marinated artichoke hearts make a delicious ingredient in a pasta salad, especially when peppers and broccoli add extra colour.

Serves 4

105ml/7 tbsp olive oil
1 red pepper, quartered, seeded and thinly sliced
1 onion, halved and thinly sliced
5ml/1 tsp dried thyme
45ml/3 tbsp sherry vinegar
450g/1lb dried penne or fusilli
2 x 175g/6oz jars marinated artichoke hearts, drained and thinly sliced
150g/5oz/1 cup cooked broccoli, chopped
20–25 salt-cured black olives, stoned and chopped
30ml/2 tbsp chopped fresh parsley
salt and freshly ground black pepper

1 Heat 30ml/2 tbsp of the oil in a large, shallow pan. Add the red pepper and onion, and cook over a low heat, stirring occasionally, for 8–10 minutes, until just soft.

2 Stir in the thyme, vinegar and 1.5ml/¼ tsp salt. Cook, stirring, for 30 seconds more, then set aside.

3 Bring a large pan of lightly salted water to the boil and cook the pasta until it is *al dente*. Drain, rinse under cold water, then drain again and put in a large bowl. Add 30ml/2 tbsp of the remaining oil and toss well to coat.

4 Add the onion mixture to the pasta, with the artichokes, broccoli, olives, parsley and remaining oil. Season with salt and pepper to taste. Stir to blend. Cover and leave to stand for at least 1 hour before serving, or place in the fridge overnight. Serve at room temperature.

Variation
Use whole baby artichokes in oil rather than artichoke hearts.

Summer Salad with Pasta

Ripe red tomatoes, mozzarella and olives make a good base for a fresh and tangy salad that is perfect for a light summer lunch.

Serves 4

350g/12oz/3 cups dried penne
3 ripe tomatoes, diced
150g/5oz packet mozzarella di bufala, drained and diced
10 stoned black olives, sliced
10 stoned green olives, sliced
1 spring onion, thinly sliced diagonally
a handful of fresh basil leaves

For the dressing

90ml/6 tbsp extra virgin olive oil
15ml/1 tbsp balsamic vinegar or lemon juice
salt and freshly ground black pepper

1 Bring a large pan of lightly salted water to the boil and cook the pasta until it is *al dente*. Drain, rinse under cold water and drain again.

2 Make the dressing. Whisk the olive oil and balsamic vinegar or lemon juice in a large bowl, and season with a little salt and pepper to taste.

3 Add the pasta, tomatoes, mozzarella, olives and spring onion to the dressing and toss together well. Taste for seasoning before serving, sprinkled with the basil leaves.

Cook's Tip

Mozzarella di bufala, made from buffalo milk, has more flavour than the type made with cow's milk. It is available from most delicatessens and supermarkets.

Variations

Make the salad more substantial by adding other ingredients, such as sliced peppers, flaked tuna, canned anchovy fillets or diced ham.

Country Pasta Salad

Colourful, tasty and nutritious, this is the ideal pasta salad for a picnic.

Serves 6

300g/11oz/2¾ cups dried fusilli
150g/5oz French beans, cut into 5cm/2in lengths
1 potato, about 150g/5oz, diced
200g/7oz cherry tomatoes, halved
2 spring onions, finely chopped
90g/3½ oz Parmesan cheese, diced or coarsely shaved
6–8 stoned black olives, cut into rings
15–30ml/1–2 tbsp drained bottled capers

For the dressing

90ml/6 tbsp extra virgin olive oil
15ml/1 tbsp balsamic vinegar
15ml/1 tbsp chopped fresh flat leaf parsley
salt and freshly ground black pepper

1 Bring a large pan of lightly salted water to the boil and cook the pasta until it is *al dente*. Drain, rinse under cold water, then drain again. Leave to cool.

2 Heat a small pan of lightly salted water and cook the beans and diced potato for 5–6 minutes, or until tender. Drain and leave to cool.

3 Make the dressing. Put all the ingredients in a large bowl with salt and pepper to taste, and whisk well to mix.

4 Add the tomatoes, spring onions, Parmesan, olive rings and capers to the bowl, then the pasta, beans and potato. Toss well. Cover and leave to stand for about 30 minutes before serving.

Cook's Tips

- *Buy a piece of fresh Parmesan from the delicatessen. This is the less mature, softer type, which is sold as a table cheese, rather than the hard, mature Parmesan used for grating.*
- *Pasta for a salad should be as dry as possible when it is mixed with the dressing and other ingredients, so drain it very well and shake the colander several times while it is cooling.*